FROM THE
GAS HOUSE
GANG

TO THE
GO-GO SOX

MY 50-PLUS YEARS IN BIG LEAGUE BASEBALL

DON GUTTERIDGE

WITH **RONNIE JOYNER** AND **BILL BOZMAN**

Don Gutteridge

© 2007 Pepperpot Productions, Inc.
and Donald Joseph Gutteridge

Published by Pepperpot Productions, Inc.
P.O. Box 1016
Dunkirk, MD 20754

Written and designed by Ronnie Joyner and Bill Bozman.

On October 16th, 1933, I accomplished my number
one goal in life — I married my childhood sweetheart,
Helen McGlothlin. I'd grown up with her on the corner of
15th and Grand in Pittsburg, Kansas, since my family
moved there when I was eight years old. Helen and I were
the best of friends. We did everything together — including
playing baseball. I eventually came to see her as more
than just one of the boys, however, and now, 73 years
later, we're still happily married. Shortly after we wed,
I accomplished my number two goal in life — I became a
professional baseball player. I would spend over 50 years in
the game, and that meant many weeks of separation from
Helen. Each day of every road-trip I was on, Helen and I
would write a letter to each other. I think it was a real key
to our marriage being a strong and happy one. We were
truly meant to be together. My career in baseball was a
total team effort between me and Helen — I couldn't have
done it without her support. With that said, it seems only
fitting that we do a joint dedication for this book. Helen
and I would like to dedicate this book to our wonderful
family — Don Jr. and his wife, Sonja; their sons, Lance,
Sean, and Joshua; and their ever-growing families. Helen
and I take great pride and joy in each and every one of you.

TABLE OF CONTENTS

FOREWORD

On April 11th, 2006, the Boston Red Sox played their home opener against the Toronto Blue Jays at Fenway Park. I was there along with five other fellows, teammates from an earlier vintage Red Sox club — the 1946 American League pennant winners. That's us in the picture above. Working from left to right is Charlie Wagner, me (Bobby Doerr), Eddie Pellagrini, a couple of Red Sox employees holding the 1946 trophy, Don Gutteridge, Johnny Pesky and Boo Ferriss. Red Sox promoters had brought us in to mark the 60th anniversary of our '46 flag, and every one of us was very happy to be there. In fact, we all joked that we were just happy to be alive! At the time of the event there were only seven surviving members from our 1946 ballclub, a sobering fact to say the least. Since then we've sadly lost two more, but it was great to see each other again — the only disappointment being that Dom DiMaggio, the only other living member of our team not in attendance, was too ill to be with us.

We piled into a pair of 1946 Ford convertibles and were paraded around the Fenway Park warning track to the cheers of the fans. One of the guys wisecracked that the cars were just the type that we COULDN'T afford back in '46. Following our tour around the ballpark, we got out and headed to the mound where we all threw out ceremonial first pitches. Then it was off to our seats where we enjoyed the game together. In spite of the fact that we were all 60 years older, the warmth and affection that we'd felt for each other during our playing days came right back. It was like we'd never parted. That's how close we were as a ball-club in 1946, and that's the feeling we always rekindle whenever we have the opportunity to regroup at events such as this. By my side at this reunion was Dave "Boo" Ferriss, Johnny Pesky, Eddie Pellagrini, "Broadway" Charlie Wagner, and Don Gutteridge. Don, it turns out, was in the midst of working on an auto-biography at that time. When he asked if I would write an introduction to his book, I gladly accepted the honor.

Don's name sometimes gets lost in the shuffle when people discuss the 1946 Red Sox, but it shouldn't. His role on the club was much less visible than that of the everyday players, but his role was no less important. Don joined our team during the '46 All-Star break. I had broken a finger and it was uncertain as to how long, if at all, I would be out. We needed someone who could step right in and fill in for me, and Don more than filled the bill. Don was an experienced veteran who had broke in with the Gas House Gang back in 1936. He'd remained with the Cardinals through 1940, then moved over to the St. Louis Browns from 1942 through 1945. Don was 33 years old and managing the Toledo Mud Hens when the 1946 season began, but the temptation to rejoin the player ranks of the big leagues proved too much for him to resist, so he accept-ed the Red Sox's offer to join our club when they called him in July.

I was already well acquainted with Don from years of playing against him while he was with the Browns. Don had been a third baseman during his years with the Cardinals, but he switched to second base when he joined the Browns in '42. Whenever he'd get the opportunity, Don would ask me for advice about how to play second base — a position I'd played for my entire career. Don was such a friendly fellow that I was always more than happy to help him out. He turned into a fine second baseman, too, and I have to admit that after having counseled him I took some pride in seeing him succeed. Little did I know that by helping Don in 1942 I'd be helping myself in 1946, but that's exacty what happened because by the time he joined our ballclub he was a polished second baseman and a real asset to our team.

Being teammates with Don allowed me to see up close the things that I had previously admired in him from afar. As a person, I can't say enough good about him. Don came to Boston with a well-known reputation as an upstanding Christian man. His faith was visible in the way he conducted himself, always displaying high morals. Watching Don over time led a lot of guys on our ballclub to be better people. They could see that Don was a good Christian, and they admired that. In those days the baseball lifestyle could easily lead fellows in the wrong direction. It's a little better nowadays with the baseball chapel because they have services right at the ballpark, but it was not yet like that when Don and I played together. Don was smart about his faith, though, and he never pushed his ways on anybody to try and change them. He would simply lead by example, and that would have a positive effect on guys.

As a player, Don was a wonderful fellow to have on your ballclub. He always had a positive outlook on things. He was serious about his job and the business of it, but he was still fun. I can't tell you how enjoyable it was to listen to Don tell stories about Pepper Martin, Dizzy Dean, Joe Medwick, and the rest of his Gas House Gang teammates. We were already well on our way to running away with the A.L. pennant when Don joined us, but he brought with him something we could really use — World Series experience. He'd been a sparkplug on the 1944 American League champion Browns, and what he shared with us about his experience helped us enter what was uncharted territory for many of us. On the field, Don was the type of player who could play just about any position — he was that versatile. He was a good baseball-minded guy who could do a lot of things. He could still run well despite his age, so he could steal a base if you needed him to. He was solid in the field and a good little hitter, too. In our case with the 1946 Red Sox, he was what you would call the perfect utility player. He would do a good job whether he was filling in or playing regular — but either way you never got the feeling he was doing anything to try and get your job.

Believe me, it's not an easy job being a utility player. You have to be ready to play every day in spite of the fact that, more often than not, you do not get in the game. Don worked tirelessly to always be ready, and it was for that reason that he always seemed to do well when called upon — like in Game Five of the 1946 World Series. A recurrence of my migraine headache condition forced me out of the game that day, so Don was called on to fill in for me. Batting lead-off, Don went 2-for-5 with an RBI in our crucial 6 to 3 victory. I was back in the line-up for Game Six, so Don stepped back into his reserve role without complaint. Once on the bench he cheered on his teammates and always offered energetic encouragement. Don Gutteridge exemplified class and was a true team player in every sense of the phrase.

We went our separate ways when Don moved on to the Pittsburgh Pirates in 1948. Pulled in different directions, we didn't stay very close anymore, but we've always kept in touch through Christmas cards and such. Plus, we've always enjoyed seeing each other at various old-timers games, reunions, and other events of that sort. We were reunited in Boston in 1996 for the 50th anniversary of the '46 Red Sox, and it was at that function that I was assured that Don was the same spunky fellow he'd always been. He was 84 at the time, and while he may not have gotten around as good as he once had, he was still sharp and pretty active. A group of us were sitting around reminiscing when Don and his wife, Helen, joined us. He told us of an altercation he'd just had in the hotel elevator. He and Helen were descending to the lobby, surrounded by three large men. As soon as Don stepped out of the elevator he realized that his wallet had been stolen by one of the men. Before the elevator could leave the lobby, Don quickly pushed the button, which re-opened the doors. There stood the three thugs, towering over Don. He confronted them on the spot, frisking them and telling them that they'd BETTER return his wallet — which they did. Once we acknowledged how happy we were that he and Helen had emerged from the incident WITH Don's wallet and WITHOUT being hurt, we had a big laugh over it. That typified Don's spirit, whether it be 1946 or 2007.

Don was the perfect role player for our 1946 Red Sox team, and he's the perfect role player for the game of baseball right now. He's no longer serving the game with his bat or his glove, but the role he's now playing is just as valuable. With this book Don is serving in the role of baseball historian, preserving precious recollections for future generations to enjoy. The memories recounted here are epic in scope. Don takes you from his Gas House Gang days of the 1930's to his seasons with the Browns in the '40's. The story then goes from his '46 and '47 seasons in Boston to his brief stint with the 1948 Pirates. Finally, Don's memoir takes you through through his many years as White Sox coach in the 1950's and '60's, culminating in his two years White Sox manager in 1969 and 1970. Once you've read Don's book you'll feel privileged to have shared his experiences — just as I feel privileged to have been his teammate and friend.

Bobby Doerr
Boston Red Sox, 1937-1951

INTRODUCTION

Incredibly, it's already been been five years since I published my first auto-biography, *Don Gutteridge in Words and Pictures,* back in 2002. Good Lord will-ing, I will turn 95 years old on June 12th, 2007 — just a short time from the publication of this book. I feel great and still get around very well. My wife, Helen, and I still live in our house here in Pittsburg, Kansas. Helen has had some difficulty with her health over the last couple of years, but she's very strong and deals with it with class and grace.

I recently learned that I am now the oldest living St. Louis Cardinals play-er. It's a bittersweet title, though. You accept the achievement with pride because you know it means you've lived a long, healthy life. At the same time, however, you know it means that someone else had to pass away in order for you to inherit the crown. Either way, I'll wear it proudly until my time comes to go and be with the Lord.

Going back to the late-1990s, I had originally planned to write no more than a pamphlet-sized account of my baseball career. It was supposed to be just a little something I could give to my family and friends as a way of sharing the wonderful baseball experiences I was blessed to have lived firsthand. However, through the encouragement of those same friends and family members, my little biographical pamphlet quickly escalated into an all-out autobiography. A genuine hardback book — all about my life in the game. It's truly something I never in a million years imagined I'd do — write an autobiography. But I did it, and, believe it or not, I sold every one of them.

I was very happy when I sold the last copy of my first book — but I soon found that there was a downside. There were still folks out there who wanted my old book, but they could no longer get it. It upset me to no end having to tell people that they could no longer get my book because it was sold out. Simple enough — I decided to do a reprint. But, after much consideration, I decided against doing a reprint, instead opting to write a completely different new book. My approach when I wrote my first book was very informal. I wanted it to read as if you and I were sitting on my front porch, drinking an ice cold lemonade, and reminiscing about the "good old days." I didn't want to bog you down with lots of dates, stats, and game details, so the book was mostly written from memory. What was most important to me at that time was to convey the fun and camaraderie that I experienced while I was in baseball. And I wanted to discuss the colorful characters that I played with and against.

Having accomplished that in my first book, I decided to take a different approach in my new book. This one focuses mainly on recounting specific games from my 12-year big league career as a player. I've also included a few recollections from my 1959 season as a coach with the pennant winning Chicago White Sox, as well as a handful of memories of my stint as White Sox manager from 1969-70. While there are countless interesting incidents from my days playing, coaching, and managing in the minors, as well as many more great moments from my other years coaching with the White Sox, I decided to exclude those as to prevent my new book from rivaling *War and Peace* in length. So I dusted off my old scrapbooks and flipped through them to come up with some games that I thought you might enjoy reading about. In addition to just retelling incidents directly involving me, I've also included moments of particular interest involving my teammates or opponents. I've written them up in a timeline fashion that I hope makes it easy to read and follow.

Let me take this last opportunity to thank you for taking an interest in my baseball career and buying my new book — I hope you enjoy reading it. I know I enjoyed reliving those old ballgames as I re-read my old scrapbooks. As a matter of fact, I almost thought I could smell the peanuts and hot dogs, hear the crowd and vendors, and even see the smiling faces of my old teammates — quite a few who have long since departed this wonderful life. They may be gone, but they'll never be forgotten.

1 9 3 6

SEPTEMBER 7, 1936: I played in my first big league ballgame on this day —
and it's day I'll never forget even WITHOUT the help of my old scrapbooks. I
was having a good year down at Columbus, hitting .298 with 11 home runs and
99 RBIs, when I got the call from the St. Louis Cardinals. They wanted me to
join them on the road in Pittsburgh — A.S.A.P. That's a call every minor leaguer dreams about, but let me tell you — I was as happy as can be, but scared to
death! I caught the first train to Pittsburgh and arrived on this day, just in time
for a doubleheader against the Pirates at Forbes Field. Frankie Frisch, the
Cardinals' legendary player-manager, knew me pretty well because I had been up

with the club on a couple of other occasions — but I'd never made it into a game. Well, just before we were set to leave the clubhouse for pre-game warm-ups, Frankie came up to me and said, "Put on them damn GOOD shoes because you're playing third base today." I had two pairs of spikes, one beat-up old pair for practice and one spiffy pair for games, and Frankie was pointing at the spiffy pair. Boy, that scared the hell out of me.

I had butterflies the size of vampire bats as I sat on the bench in the top of the 1st inning of the opener. Centerfielder Terry Moore led off for us and walloped Waite Hoyt's first pitch for a home run. But batting out of the number six slot, I did not get to the plate before Hoyt, righting himself and surrendering just the one run, retired the side. As I trotted out to my position for the bottom of the 1st, I remember thinking, "I sure hope nobody hits the ball to me!" Dizzy Dean was pitching and he did Hoyt one better, getting roughed up for two tallies — but my wish came true and no one hit the ball my way. I wasn't so lucky in the 2nd inning, however. For my first-ever defensive chance in the big leagues, Bill Brubaker, the Pirates' big catcher, smashed a hard ground ball to me. I fumbled it, hurriedly picked it up with my bare hand, and then compounded my mistake by sailing my throw about ten feet over Johnny Mize's head at first base. Pepper Martin chased the ball down along the rightfield line and fired it back to me as Brubaker barreled into third. It was a great throw and I got it in plenty of time to nail him. I thought to myself, "This time I got you!" I put the tag down, but Brubaker slid in hard and kicked the hell out of the ball, my glove, my arm — everything! The ball went one way and my glove went the other — and I had spike marks all over my arms. Just like that, two errors.

No one had ever slid into me like that in the minors. It was a quick lesson in just how hard the game was played at the big league level. It was the depression and jobs were scarce — especially jobs in major league baseball. Guys were tough and would go to any length to keep those precious jobs. Meanwhile, I wasn't having any better luck at the plate. I simply couldn't do anything against Hoyt — but neither could anyone else. After dishing up the lead-off homer to Terry, Hoyt settled down, allowing just three more hits and winning the game, 4-1.

Despite my ineffectiveness in the opener, Frankie still wrote my name in at third base for the nightcap. I was relieved because it offered me a quick opportunity to try again to prove that they had not made a mistake in bringing me up. As a team we were again totally anemic on offense, dropping the game, 14-1. I was disappointed at being swept in the twin bill because we were still in the thick of the pennant race, just three games in back of the league-leading Giants at the start of the day. But I did enjoy some personal satisfaction by playing errorless ball in the second game, as well as picking up my first two big league hits. Both hits came off the Pirates' big right-hander Mace Brown. Getting my first hit out of the way and getting comfortable in the field went a long way to helping me get loose and play my best for the rest of the 1936 season. It's funny, though, but my hustle in that game seemed to impress Frankie more than my two singles. I ran all-out and went hard into second on a force-play to break up a double-play. I really sent Pirates second baseman, Pep Young, flying. Later I read in *The Sporting News* where Frankie had said, "Did you see that kid? He belongs on this team. He's really a Gas Houser." That put me on top of the world.

Frankie Frisch was a great player in his prime, and he was unquestionably the heart and soul of the Gas House Gang. I listened intently to his instruction in this photo from spring training of 1936. I really looked up to Frankie, and that's why I was so thrilled when he officially added me to the Gas House Gang by telling *The Sporting News,* "Did you see that kid? He belongs on this team. He's really a Gas Houser."

SEPTEMBER 11, 1936: This was, without a doubt, the greatest offensive day I ever had in the big leagues. It included a lot of "firsts" for me. We were still in second place, hoping to stay alive in the pennant race when we opened a series against Brooklyn at Ebbets Field with a Friday doubleheader. Here's my line in the opening game: 3-for-5 with two home runs, four runs scored, five RBIs, and a stolen base. I still can't believe it happened to me. The timing was funny, too, because I unintentionally ended up stealing the limelight that day from Jack Winsett, a slugging leftfielder who Brooklyn was pushing heavily that weekend as a future star. Jack was a fine player and just so happened to have been my teammate at Columbus, and he had recently joined the Dodgers to much hype. At any rate, here's how *The Sporting News* recapped my big game...

"It was a doubleheader with the Dodgers at Brooklyn, September 11, that Gutteridge flashed his full batting and base-running brilliance. The Dodgers were introducing Jack Winsett, hard-hitting graduate from the Columbus club. Winsett was playing leftfield and the Brooklyn scribes were very happy about it. The Dodgers had found a real hitter. But before the day was over, Gutteridge had stolen the show and Winsett was in a secondary position. On his first trip to the plate [against Dodgers starting pitcher Max Butcher], Gutteridge, who has strong arms and a modified Pepper Martin barrel chest, whacked a drive against the leftfield fence. The speedster set sail on his tour of the bases and was almost to second as Winsett tried to take the rebound off the fence. The ball took a crazy hop off the wall and when Winsett finally retrieved it and threw it toward the infield, it was too late. Gutteridge had turned the drive into a home run inside the park."

Continuing its recap of my big game, *The Sporting News* article said, "In the 7th inning, Winsett held Gutteridge to a triple, but before [Dodgers relief pitcher] Tom Baker could throw another pitch, Gutteridge set sail for the plate and made a clean steal of home. That was already a large afternoon, but Donald Joseph wasn't through by any means. In the 9th inning he went to bat again, with a runner on base, and whacked another drive [off Baker] against the leftfield fence and again turned it into a homer while Winsett chased the ball to the fence and then back toward third base."

It was quite a thrill, to say the least. We ended up winning the game, 12-8. I picked up another hit, a double off Dodgers flamethrower Van Lingle Mungo, in the second game of the doubleheader, but we lost that one, 5-4. My steal of home in the opener was pretty funny. Mike Gonzales, who was Cuban and spoke in a very heavy accent, was our third base coach. He used to jabber at you when you were on third in an effort to distract the other team's third baseman. Mike knew I could run and he kept yammering, "You steala me home? You steala me home?" I said, "What?" Again, he said, "You steala me home?" So I guessed he wanted me to steal home. Baker wasn't paying much attention to me, so I took a big lead. I timed his wind-up pretty good and took off, sliding home safely, well in front of catcher Babe Phelps' tag. Had the ball been hit, it probably would have gone right down my throat. Stealing home put a real charge in me because it was classic Gas House Gang activity, scrappy and hustling — and it was ME doing it!

There was one other item from this day that bears remembering. For the first time in my career I witnessed Pepper Martin's bat-throwing acumen. His penchant for letting the lumber fly was well known, but I had yet to see it first-hand. I would see it many more times over the next five years, but this was my first — and you never forget your first. You see, Pepper was always swinging at bad pitches. He'd over-reach for them, lose his grip on the bat, then send it flying 30 or 40 feet down the third base line, or into the stands. Sometimes the opposing pitcher was the victim, which was the case on this day, and the *New York Times* summed it up this way — "Pepper Martin swung violently at a fast one in the 5th inning of the nightcap and his bat flew directly at Mungo's shins.

The latter landed flat on his face avoiding the willow and after dusting himself off proceeded to fan Pepper with a sharp curve."

SEPTEMBER 12, 1936: I was still on cloud nine as we got set to play the Dodgers in another doubleheader at Ebbets Field on this day. It would be impossible to top my activities of the day before, but I still had a few of moments worth remembering. Amazingly enough, I hit ANOTHER home run in the opener. It was another inside the parker, again in Jack Winsett's territory — a 2-run job off Dodgers starter Fred Frankhouse. Art Garibaldi, our second baseman, repeated my feat in the next inning. The crowd was really giving it to Winsett for allowing all those inside the park homers over the course of those three games, but before you feel too sorry for him, read this blurb from the *New York Times* — "The fans blamed Winsett for the two Cardinal homers inside the grounds, but the jeers changed to cheers when big Jack hit [a homer] onto Bedford Avenue and went mad when his single won the ball game." That's right, we lost, 9-8, and Winsett was the hero. Goat to hero in a matter of minutes — that's baseball for you.

I picked up two more hits and an RBI in the second game of that day's doubleheader as we won, 10-3. I also stole a couple of bases, one of which was home. It was quite a series for me, probably the best I ever had in the big leagues. One paper quoted Dodger manager Casey Stengel saying, "Anytime you catch that Gutteridge guy it's a moral victory. Yes, he runs like a deer — only twice as fast!"

SEPTEMBER 13, 1936: We split a doubleheader with the Giants in front of a huge Polo Grounds crowd of nearly 65,000 on this day. It was, by far, the biggest crowd I had ever seen. I banged out a triple on our opening game loss, and my three-bagger was described this way in the *New York Times* — "The fleshy but stout-hearted Freddy Fitzsimmons pitched this one for the Giants. He stumbled a bit near the finish when the Cards rushed three tallies across the plate in the 9th, two of these riding home on a triple by their latest sensation from their far-flung farming system, Don Gutteridge, but in the end our famed knuckleball veteran had just enough to finish on his own power." Fitzsimmons got the 8-4 win in the first game, but it was a different story in the nightcap thanks, in part, to Roy Parmelee.

Roy pitched us to a 4-3 victory in the nightcap, and I chipped in a single in four at-bats in support of his effort. Watching Roy pitch reminded me why I was happy that he was on MY team. He threw as hard as anyone, but you never really knew where the pitch was going. The Giants batters were well aware of that, and they just couldn't get comfortable at the plate against Roy. In fact, the Giants were particularly knowledgeable about Roy's wildness because he had pitched for them from 1929 through '35 before joining our club prior to the '36 season. While with New York his control problems had prevented him from fully achieving the success that his rifle-arm warranted, and he ended up leading the

National League in hit batsmen on four occasions. That meant that a lot of guys were in a lot of pain thanks to Roy. His wildness kept him from ever getting in a full season in his first four years with the Giants, but he'd pulled it together enough from '32 through '35 so that he was able to win 13, 10, and 14 games in each respective season. The Cardinals front office guys were hoping that maybe Roy would finally reach his true potential under their watch in 1936, but it didn't happen, and he struggled to an 11-and-11 mark. So they gave up on him and let him go after the season.

Roy landed with the Cubs for the 1937 season, and that meant that I had to face him on many occasions. I had a rough time with him, too, because I just wasn't sure where he was going to throw the ball. I was shaky when I was up there against him. It was a fear that years later I had long since forgot about — until I saw Ryne Duren pitch in the 1950s. I was coaching with the White Sox at that time, and when I got my first look at Duren bringing it at around 100 miles per hour, I had a flashback of Roy Parmelee. Incidentally, Roy had a funny nickname, the origin of which is very amusing. *New York Daily News* sportswriter Jimmy Powers had taken to calling Roy "Tarzan" during his years with the Giants. Parmelee was a tall, well-built fellow, so he naturally thought that Powers was praising his Tarzan-like physique. But when Roy asked Powers about it, Powers said no, it had nothing to do with his musculature. Powers told Roy that he called him Tarzan because Roy, due to his wildness, always seemed to be out on a limb when he pitched.

SEPTEMBER 14, 1936: We lost a very tough game to the Giants on this day, 7-5, at the Polo Grounds. It was the Giants whom we were chasing for the pennant, and the loss dropped us 4-1/2 games behind them with only 13 left to play. Here's some proof of the importance of that game: Dizzy Dean and Carl Hubbell were on the mound when it ended — both in relief! The situation was obviously a little more desperate for us, so much so that Dizzy was making his fourth mound appearance in our last five games — over just a three day span. Here's another piece of evidence of the tension that we were feeling — there was a fight. That's not usually a big deal between two teams battling it out for a pennant, but here's the catch — the fight was between two of our own players! I knew all about the Gas House Gang's well-earned reputation for scrapping with opposition ballclubs, but at this point in my young career I was unaware that Frankie Frisch's boys quite often went at it with each other, too. So, on this day our big righthanded reliever Ed Heusser and Joe "Ducky" Medwick threw down in our own dugout, giving me my first close-up look at some real live in-house brawling.

The trouble started out in the field on defense. It was a close contest, and Big Ed was scratching and clawing to keep us in the game. Then a drive was hit out to Medwick in leftfield where Joe, as he was sometimes known to do, didn't make much of an effort to catch the ball. He nonchalantly took it on one bounce, allowing a run to score in the process. I had a short trip to the dugout from third base when the inning ended, so I was already sitting on the bench when Joe came trotting into the dugout. "Why the hell didn't you catch that ball, Medwick?" scowled Ed. "None of your damn business!" Joe blasted back. In a flash they were swinging at each other in a full-out knockdown-dragout fight. Luckily I was sitting close to Frisch and away from the action, so I didn't get hurt, but I was scared to death when they started flailing away. Meanwhile, Frisch sat there as cool as can be, not moving a muscle. Looking straight ahead, he deadpanned, "Well, I guess the old Gas House Gang is at it again." After letting each guy get in a few licks, a couple of guys stepped in and separated Ed and Joe. It was a funny thing to see those two scuffling with each other in our own dugout, but it shook me up. As a matter of fact, I was shaking like a young kid from the country.

Our dugout brawl had not escaped the watchful eyes of *New York Times* sportswriter John Drebinger, and here's how he described what he saw — "It was at the close of this inning, as the Cards came stumbling off the field into their dugout, that Ed Heusser and Joe Medwick, firebrand leftfielder of the Gas House Gang, were seen to flare up suddenly and indulge in a swift exchange of punches. The others, however, quickly pried the two belligerents apart while the four umpires on the field apparently took no cognizance of the incident at all. They seemingly were of a mind that those bellicose Cards could fight all they wanted to so long as they kept their state of civil war within the confines of their dugout. In other words, it was just another day at the office with the Gas House Gang."

Drebinger was right — the Heusser-Medwick fight was, in fact, just another day at the office with the Gas House Gang. Drebinger had been around a while, so to him this was old hat. It was new to me, however, but I quickly became accustomed to this type of behavior. They were simply the roughest and toughest guys I'd ever seen. When they chose to fight amongst themselves, you didn't dare interfere. You just let them go at it because it was their business. A number of fights took place right in the showers. Guys would be in there, lathering up and discussing the events of the game, when someone would say something that someone else didn't like. The next thing you knew a brawl would bust loose. Can you imagine that — naked men fighting, slipping, and sliding in the showers? I usually quickly grabbed a towel and ran to my locker to avoid the fracas. But it was a different story altogether if we fought with somebody from another ballclub. Then we'd all fight together. If you got on one of us, you'd have to whip the whole club.

For the record, I was 2-for-4 in the Heusser-Medwick game, and that extended my modest hitting streak to eight games. I was disappointed about losing to the Giants — and quite shaken over the fight between Ed and Ducky, but I was happy that the hits were falling in for me because I knew that I was auditioning for a job in 1937.

SEPTEMBER 16, 1936: I went 1-for-3 with an RBI in the opener of a doubleheader against the Phillies at Shibe Park on this day, but we lost the game, 7-3. I picked up two more hits in the nightcap, and this time we came out on top, 5-2. The score was tied at 2-2 as we opened the 8th inning of the second game, then we scored two runs to go on top, 4-2. Si Johnson had pitched admirably for seven innings, but Frankie Frisch was desperate to get us a win. So, with us now leading by two runs, he went back to his meal ticket — Dizzy Dean. Ol' Diz came in from the bullpen and pitched a scoreless 8th and 9th to nail down the victory for us.

While in Philadelphia we always stayed at the big, old, very nice and very elegant Bellevue-Stratford Hotel on South Broad and Walnut Streets. Our trip to Philadelphia for this day's twin bill was our only visit to the city of brotherly love during my call-up in September of 1936, so by the process of elimination I will attribute the story I'm about to recount to this stop in Philly. There's a chance that it occurred in 1934 or 1935 during one of my previous two call-ups — recalls in which I failed to get into any games — but I'll go with 1936 because it's as good a guess as any. One thing I can say for sure is that it did NOT occur AFTER 1936 because the incident involved our first baseman, Rip Collins — and he was gone from the Cardinals after the '36 season. Okay, with that said, let me begin by saying that this is a famous story that has been told many times before by many people, but I can verify the tale because I was there in the flesh. We had a day off the day before our doubleheader against the Phillies on September 16th, so a few of us were sitting around in the lobby of the Bellevue-Stratford, just killing time. The group was Pepper Martin, Dizzy, Rip and me. The whole time we were hanging out, there was a group of painters working across the hall. Meanwhile, there were a bunch of well-dressed executives thoroughly engaged in a big business meeting in a nearby conference room.

Sharply at noon, the painters stepped out of their white overalls, hung them in a closet, and headed off for lunch. You could almost see the light bulb go off over Rip's head as he took in this scene. Rip loved to encourage Dizzy and Pepper to do crazy stuff, and they always obliged him. Rip, with a sly smile, said, "Hey, why don't you guys put on them painters overalls, grab them paint buckets and ladders, and bust into that business meeting like you're going to paint the room. I mean really raise a ruckus to see what those businessmen will do." It was brilliant. That was all Dizzy and Pepper needed to hear. They hustled into the overalls, grabbed the ladders and buckets, and stormed into the room. Peeking in the door, Rip and I saw Dizzy and Pepper put on one of their finest shows. They were spinning around with these ladders on their shoulders, pointing this way and that way, banging into each other, and looking confused while they discussed where to start painting. Meanwhile, the executives had stunned looks on their faces while they ducked and dodged Dizzy and Pepper's ladders. Finally, Pepper set his ladder up and said, "I think this needs painting up here," and started climbing. That's when all hell broke loose. Seconds later the hotel manager came running in, screaming and hollering at Dizzy and Pepper about disrupting the meeting. Within moments, everyone found out that these crazy painters were actually Dizzy Dean and Pepper Martin of the Gas House Gang. From that point on, everything was lovely. All the executives — and the hotel manager — laughed out loud.

Dizzy and Pepper's stature as heroes allowed them to get away with murder, and Rip Collins was right up there with them in that category. He was great at cutting up, but he was also great at playing ball. Rip started with the Cardinals as an undersized first baseman in 1931, but his lively bat quickly earned him respect around the league. He was the first switch-hitter I really knew — and he was a good one, too. He could hit about the same from both sides of the plate. There was never any question that the Cardinals always wanted Rip's bat in the line-up, but where to play him on defense was a constant issue. In 1932 he split his time between first base and the outfield, but he was so slow that the experiment was abandoned and Rip played first base exclusively from 1933 through 1935. In the meantime, his bat only got better, his best season coming in 1934 when he hit 35 home runs. By spring training of 1936, however, Frisch was ready to revisit the idea of moving Rip somewhere else on the ballfield. Frankie wanted to keep Rip's potent bat in the line-up, but he wanted to open up first base for his promising young rookie, Johnny Mize. That's when Frankie decided to try and make a catcher out of Rip.

It sounded good — a catcher didn't need to be fast, and the club was always looking to improve behind the plate. The problem was that Rip didn't want to be a catcher. He detested the position. Every time Frankie tried to put him back there to get some work that spring, Rip would squawk. The worse incident occurred in an exhibition game. Our catcher, Bill DeLancey, took a foul ball off a finger on his throwing hand, so Frankie went out there to take a look at it. Frisch decided that Bill should leave the game, so he looked out to rightfield as to call Rip in to take over for DeLancey. But Rip knew what was coming as soon as he saw Frankie walk out of the dugout, so he'd turned his back on the field and appeared to be looking intently out to the bleachers. Frankie called to Rip, but Collins just kept looking out to the stands as if he couldn't hear Frisch. Eventually, everybody was calling out to Rip, but Collins continued to act as if he couldn't hear, refusing to turn around. When the calls to Rip reached a loud roar, he finally turned around and came in to catch — but he was really teed off. He caught the rest of the game, but he sure hated catching. When the '36 season opened, Frankie gave up on his plan to convert Rip to a catcher, instead returning him to his spot at first base. But Rip had to split time with Mize, and Johnny ended up turning in a good rookie year, making Collins expendable. When the season ended, Rip was quickly dealt off the the Chicago Cubs. I was sad to see him go — partly because I knew we'd miss his bat, but also because I was going to miss seeing the creative antics that he would put Dizzy and Pepper up to.

SEPTEMBER 20, 1936: Double-whammy at Wrigley Field on this day! We lost to the Cubs, 4-3, and my hitting streak was stopped. The Giants were pulling away a bit in the pennant race, and we were now battling Chicago for second place. Our loss that day dropped us to third. Dizzy pitched seven shutout innings, but a big 4-run 8th for the Cubs did us in. The key blows were a solo home run by Frank Demaree to tie the game at 1-1, then a clutch 3-run shot by Johnny Gill into the rightfield stands. Dizzy was probably a bit fatigued from all the appearances he had made over the last couple weeks. Gill had come in to pinch-hit for Ethan Allen earlier in the game and Diz struck him out with the bags full. Gill won the battle the next time, though, so he really redeemed himself. As for my hitting streak, which was at 12 games before this day's game — Cubs pitcher Bill Lee was just too good as he held me to 0-for-2. By the way, fatigued or not, Ol' Diz was back in our game the next day. He came in with one out in the 9th to get the last two outs and a save as we beat the Cubs, 5-4.

Dizzy was one heck of a competitor. He was already an American folk legend by the time I joined the Cardinals. He was a true original. His genius at pitching was rivaled only by his genius at captivating the imaginations of salt-of-the-earth Americans. Volumes have been written on Diz, yet they've still failed to do complete justice to the that character he was — on and off the pitching mound. Now, playing behind him on a regular basis, I was getting a front row view of the spectacle that was Dizzy Dean — and I was loving every minute of it. I'd been around Diz on a number of occasions over the previous few years, but never on this close a basis. I'd gone to spring training with the Cardinals for three straight years from 1934-36, so that got me a good look at Diz in his prime. In 1934 and '35 I was sent down to the minors when camp broke, but in 1936 I stayed with the Cardinals until the June 15th roster cut-down. While I never appeared in a game during those two months with the Cards at the beginning of the '36 season, it gave me an even closer look at Ol' Diz — and I, like the rest of the country, was captivated.

One of my earliest recollections of Dizzy involves our visit to the Chicago World's Fair, which ran from 1933 through 1934. Diz, along with his brother, Paul, and Pepper Martin, asked me and Pat Ankenman, another wet-behind-the-ears rookie, to go along with them to see the World's Fair when we were in town to play the Cubs. Pat and I were elated to be traveling in the esteemed company of Dizzy, Paul, and Pepper, but we were also very excited at the prospect of seeing the amazing exhibits that the Fair featured. When we got there, however, Pat and I soon discovered that Dizzy, Paul, and Pepper were not really interested in the fancy exhibits — they just wanted to throw lumpy old baseballs at milk bottles. So, that's what they did. They threw so many balls and knocked over so many milk bottles that they collected armloads of kewpie dolls and other prizes. The guy running the stand begged them to stop. "You're breaking me!" he futilely cried, but they were having too much fun to stop. The fellow finally had to close down his stand to get rid of us.

That's when Dizzy, Paul, and Pepper decided to have some REAL fun — at the expense of Pat and me. Pepper, looking toward the rides, saw a big wheel with little cars on it that spun crazily upside-down and around. Now, we'd all had a big supper before embarking on our World's Fair adventure, but that didn't stop Pepper from saying, "Don, why don't you and Pat ride that?" When Pepper Martin tells you something, you don't say no, so Pat and I agreed to go on the ride. So they bought the tickets, and Pat and I took our seats. The thing went around a few times and the next thing you know I lost my supper. Then Pat lost his. The ride seemed to be going on interminably, so Pat and I finally started hollering at the top of our lungs for the ride operator to let us off. But every time we zipped by we saw Dizzy, Paul, and Pepper feeding the operator more money — and laughing it up. We just kept going round and round. It seemed like hours before he let us stagger off. That was my first real introduction to the wit of Dizzy Dean — and when mixed with a dash of Pepper Martin, it was truly something to behold.

Little Pat Ankenman, second from the left here, was a good friend of mine from my days with Columbus. He was a good little infielder and, at 5-foot-4 and 125-lbs, he actually made me look big. He was a great player with the University of Texas before joining the St. Louis Cardinals minor league farm chain, and he, like me, got called up in 1936 but appeared in just one game. Before that, however, Pat was my sidekick as the butt of a funny prank pulled on us by Pepper Martin at the World's Fair in Chicago. This photo, incidentally, was from a promotion between our Columbus team and a local bowling alley. From left to right is Mike Ryba, Pat, Joe Sims, and me.

SEPTEMBER 22, 1936: I was one hit short of the cycle as we beat Cincinnati at Sportsman's Park on this day. The *New York Times* headline said it all — *Gutteridge Bats Across Five Runs as Cards Overcome Reds by 6-3*. The subhead added, *Rookie Smashes Triple with the Bases Filled, Double and Single*. As you can see, it was the home run I was missing to complete the cycle. They say that the triple is the hardest component of the cycle, but that wasn't really the case with me. My speed was a much greater asset to my career than my power, and my speed enabled me to hit 64 career triples while my limited power allowed me to hit only 39 career round-trippers. Still, my triple that day was NEARLY a home run. It was a rocket off the leftfield wall that scored Joe Medwick, Johnny Mize, and Leo Durocher.

Somebody had to get pushed aside in order for a raw-boned kid like me to get an opportunity to play and succeed like I did in 1936. It's always been that way in baseball — in with the rookie and out with the old veteran. I would be on the other end of the deal on 1948. But in '36, I was the kid, and the fading veteran was Charley Gelbert. At 31 years of age, he was far from old by normal standards, but he was getting up there in baseball age. Plus, Charley's body was an old 31 because of an off the field incident back in 1932. He was an outstanding young shortstop when he joined the Cardinals in 1929. He was excellent defensively, and also swung the bat very well. He fielded brilliantly in the 1931 World Series, recording 29 assists, six double-plays, and a perfect 1.000 fielding percentage in 42 chances — all records for a shortstop in a 7-game Series. Charley was a mainstay at short for the Cards through the 1932 season, but his bright future ended when he was involved in a hunting accident prior to the 1933 campaign. He shot out most of the muscles from his knee to his ankle and nearly lost the leg. It was a grisly wound, but the doctors were able to patch him up. Still, he had to sit out two years and endure some painful rehabilitation before even considering a comeback attempt.

In a testament to Charley's toughness, he made it back to the Cardinals in 1935, bucking incredible odds. He still swung the bat very well that season, but the injury severely hampered his speed and quickness. Because of that, he played in only 62 games, over half of them at third base instead of his old spot short. He appeared in 93 ballgames in 1936, upping his games at third base to 60. But the problems with his leg had now taken a toll on his hitting, too, and he was only batting about .220 when I joined the ballclub. As soon as I arrived from Columbus, Charley was sent to the bench while I took over his spot at third. When I got hot with the bat right away and stayed hot, Charley knew his days with the Cards were numbered. He never let it sully his attitude, though. He was always good to me despite the fact that he knew I was taking his job away from him. Sometime around this day with the season drawing to an end, Charley looked at my glove and said, "Here, Don — you're gonna need a good glove." Then he handed me his mitt. A few day later when the season was over, they kept me and they let Charley go.

SEPTEMBER 27, 1936: Lon Warneke, who would soon become one of my best friends after joining our ballclub in 1937, collared me with an 0-for-4 in our last game of 1936 as the Cubs beat us on this day, 6-3. Despite going hitless, I felt good about where I was. I was actually sad to see the season end because I was, as they say, on my game during my stint with St. Louis. I was disappointed that we did not win the pennant, but I had high hopes for 1937.

On a side note, this is the game where Walter Alston made his ONLY big league appearance as a player. Johnny Mize had been ejected from the game for arguing balls and strikes with umpire Ziggy Sears. Mize wasn't the only one tossed. Cubs manager Charlie Grimm and Clyde Wares, one of his coaches, were also thumbed. If it sounds like there was an extraordinary amount of tension in the air for a last game of the season with no bearing on first place, you're right. Why, you ask — because of money. We were fighting hard for the win to ensure that we would end the season with sole possession of second place. The Cubs were fighting equally hard to beat us so that they could move up in the standings and share second place with us. Their victory that day accomplished that for them, and it cost us about $10,000 because we were then forced to split the second and third place World Series money with them.

At any rate, back to Alston. When Mize got ejected, Frankie Frisch inserted himself to finish John's at-bat. When the inning ended and we took the field, Walt took Mize's place at first base. In his only at-bat later in the game, Walt struck out. I'm sure there were times when Walt felt like an injustice was done to him because he never got another chance to play, but, as the saying goes, some people, when given lemons, make lemonade. And that's exactly what Walt did when he took his misfortune as a player and used it to turn himself into a Hall of Fame manager.

1937

APRIL 20, 1937: I was thrilled to be a real live member of the St. Louis Cardinals as we opened the 1937 season in Cincinnati on this day. The torrid pace at which I had played for the last month of the 1936 season left many sportswriters speculating that I was a shoo-in to be the the Cards' regular third baseman in '37, but it didn't quite work out that way. Simply put, I got off to a slow start in spring training, so Frankie Frisch, back for his fifth year as the Cardinals' player-manager, gave veteran Frenchy Bordagaray the nod as our starter at third base. I was disappointed at not winning the job, but I didn't get down about it. I knew at sometime I would get a chance to prove that 1936 was not an aberration for me. So, for the time being, I resigned myself to enjoying the spectacle of opening day from my place on the pine.

The game turned out to be a barnburner — a real explosive way to kick off the season. There were 34,374 screaming Reds fans packed into Crosley Field to witness the first game of the new campaign — and they really got their money's worth. As our ace, Dizzy Dean received the starting assignment, and his counterpart was Reds right-hander Peaches Davis. Both men fought like the dickens, allowing no runs for the first nine innings. Davis was the sharper of the two, allowing just six hits through regulation. Dizzy was a little off, allowing a hit or two in every inning, but he was great at weaseling out of each jam. We finally broke through in the top of the 10th. Back-to-back doubles by Joe Medwick and Johnny Mize got us on the board with one run. Then Leo Durocher singled, moving Johnny to third. We scored again when our catcher, Bruce Ogrodowski, pushed Johnny across with a long fly out. The Reds failed to answer in the bottom of the inning, giving us our first win of the season, 2-0. I couldn't help but hope that this game was a sign that we were going to have a great year.

I had a slow spring training in 1937 down in Daytona Beach, but I refused to let it get me down. Terry Moore, the Cardinals great centerfielder, and I posed here with M.J. Collins, a wealthy businessman who was a huge Cardinals fan. He always came to spring training. The ballclub had just given him his own uniform, and M.J. was as excited as a kid on Christmas morning.

We traveled down to Cuba for part of spring training where we played some exhibition games against the Dodgers.

MAY 4, 1937: Overall we'd played pretty well since opening day, winning six of our next 10 games, but we'd dropped our last two at Chicago as we arrived in Boston for a series against the Bees at Braves Field. We were hoping that Lon Warneke's presence on the mound in the series-opener would help us get back on the winning track, but Lon got knocked out of the box in the 5th inning after allowing eight runs. Lon would practically have had to pitch a no-hitter to keep us in that game, however, because our bats were silent against the offerings of Boston right-hander Lou Fette. We only touched Fette for three hits on this day, finally scoring our lone run in the 8th inning when Pepper Martin tripled and then scored on a fly ball by Leo Durocher. We lost, 8-1. I wasn't much of a help to our club. I was still firmly planted on the bench, only appearing as a pinch-hitter for Bill McGee in the 8th inning — but I'd failed to hit. I had, in fact, made only two appearances prior to our game on this day, both pinch-hitting assignments — and I'd failed to hit in both of those at-bats, too. Pinch-hitting was always tough duty, and I always had the utmost respect for the guys who did it well.

Frankie Frisch read us the riot act after our loss. He really gave us hell, telling us all the things we should and shouldn't do as ballplayers. Frankie was still in the midst of his ranting and raving when Pepper raised his hand like a little schoolboy. "Yes, Johnny," said Frankie, "what do you want?" Frankie always called Pepper "Johnny" — he never called him Pepper. "Frankie," Pepper said with all seriousness, "you can't win the Kentucky Derby with mules, and we have a lot of asses in the room here." Everybody howled with laughter, and that pretty much broke up the meeting. Even Frankie had to laugh at that one. Frankie loved Pepper's go-for-broke style of play, but Pepper's frequent horseplay often exasperated Frankie. As for Pepper, he never really liked Frankie. Pepper obeyed Frankie, so they got along well enough, but the truth of the matter is that Pepper was simply not fond of our manager.

Following our lecture from Frankie, we showered, dressed, and returned to our hotel — The Kenmore. That's where we stayed when we were in Boston. Pepper was about the only player who could brag that he'd had a good day at the plate in our loss to the Bees. He'd singled, tripled, and scored our only run. Fueled by that, as well as Frankie's post-game pep talk, Pepper was still a bundle of energy when we got back to The Kenmore. He and I were up on the fourth floor balcony, just chatting and looking at the people below when Pepper realized that Frankie was on the ground floor veranda directly below us, sitting and talking with someone. Pepper bolted over to the elevator and told the operator, "Stay right here and don't you leave until I come back. Regardless of what happens, STAY RIGHT HERE." Pepper then grabbed a big laundry bag, ran over to the water faucet and began filling the bag with water. When completely filled, the bag was as big as a large medicine ball — and five times as heavy. Pepper then dragged it back to the balcony, wrestled it up onto the edge of the railing, and let it fall right in the direction of Frankie! I was horrified as I watched the giant water-bag plummet. I was afraid it would break Frankie's neck if it hit him.

Images of the great Frankie Frisch, paralyzed from the neck down by a foolish prank, flashed through my head. But the giant water-bag missed his head by inches, exploding on the veranda with a loud boom and a colossal splash. Pepper immediately grabbed me and said, "Let's go!"

The elevator operator was waiting for us, just like Pepper had instructed him. We hurried in and Pepper said, "Take me down! Take me down! Take me down!" When we got to the ground floor, the elevator doors opened to let us out — and there was Frankie, mad as hell, waiting for the elevator to take him up so he could see who'd done it. Just as clamly and innocent as he could be, Pepper walked out of the elevator and said, "Hi, Frankie," as he passed our skipper. I could tell from the look on Frankie's face that he knew damn good and well that Pepper was responsible, but he let us pass without a word because he knew he couldn't prove it.

I idolized Pepper Martin's style of play years before we became teammates with the St. Louis Cardinals. Once I got to know him I discovered what many others already knew — he was a true prankster. Here we hammed it up in a mock argument during a spring intrasquad game.

MAY 5, 1937: By the grace of God — and a poorly-aimed giant water-bag — Frankie Frisch was safely and soundly back in the dugout to lead us in game two of our series against the Bees in Boston on this day. I was surprised when I saw that I was in the starting line-up. After failing to hit in the only three games I'd played in so far this season — all three appearances as a pinch-hitter — I was anxious to make good in my first start. Frankie had me batting lead-off and playing third base. I really wanted to get on base in my first at-bat, so I bunted Jim Turner's first pitch and beat it out for a hit. Then I stole second. It was a great way for me to get it going. I ended up getting two more singles and my first home run of the season. A perfect day — 4-for-4 with three RBIs. Dizzy Dean pitched and was excellent, striking out 11 while walking none. He won his 4th straight as we romped, 13-1.

MAY 9, 1937: Still batting lead-off, I came up a homer short of the cycle as we beat the Dodgers, 7-1, at Ebbets Field on this day. I was 3-for-4 on the day, my triple coming in the 9th inning off Watty Clark with Dizzy Dean on first base. Diz got the complete game win and helped himself with two hits and an RBI.

MAY 19, 1937: Dizzy Dean again. Believe it or not, we did have other pitchers, but it seems Ol' Diz had a way of getting himself into a lot of fellows' scrapbooks. With that said, let it be known that on this day we partook in one of the biggest and most famous brawls in St. Louis Cardinals history as we engaged in a 15-minute free-for-all against the New York Giants at Sportsman's Park. It involved nearly every player on both ballclubs, and required a squad of law enforcement officers to restore order. And it all started because Dizzy didn't like the way umpires had taken to calling balks on him.

A little history on the way Dizzy pitched is in order here. Ol' Diz liked to work fast, and he'd often be throwing the next pitch before the catcher even had time to give him a signal. This habit of Dizzy's nearly got me killed one time when we were in Chicago with Diz on the mound. If the bases were empty after we recorded an out, we'd fire the ball around the infield before before returning it to the pitcher. The third baseman was always the player to toss it back to the pitcher following this ritual, so it was me who gave the ball back to Dizzy on the day in Chicago when he nearly sent me to an early death. One of the Cubs had made an out, so we fired the ball around the infield. I went up to the mound and flipped it to Dizzy, then jogged back to my position while Frank Demaree was getting ready to hit. Just as I got back to third base and turned around — whoom! — a line drive whistled right by my ear, barely missing me. When I came in after the inning, Frankie Frisch yelled at me, "Goddammit, get in the game! You know you almost got your head knocked off out there!" Before I could speak, Leo Durocher, taking the heat for me, jumped in and said, "Hey, Dutchman, wait a minute here — blame that big ox out there on the mound. He pitches the ball before we're ever ready!" So it was Dizzy's quick-pitch style that nearly got me killed that day in Chicago, and it was that same quick-pitch tendency that caused our melee with the Giants on this day.

Dizzy's quick-pitches were not only getting him into trouble with his nearly-decapitated teammates, they were also getting him into trouble with umpires for an entirely different reason. If there was a man on base, Diz would step on the rubber, cast a lightning-quick glance at the runner, and then — whoom! — he'd let the pitch fly. He'd deliver the pitch so fast that the guy on base never had time to take a lead. Teams began to complain about it, so the umpires started calling balks on Dizzy. The league knew they needed to do something, so they changed the rulebook on account of Ol' Diz. The new rule stated that the pitcher had to stop his stretch wind-up at his belt buckle — and hesitate there for one second — before completing the delivery of the pitch. Sounds simple enough, right? Well, Dizzy didn't like it and thought the new rule was unfairly singling him out. The situation came to a head on this day in our game against New York as Dizzy, fed up with the umpires, blew a gasket.

Nearly 30,000 fans packed Sportsman's Park on this day to witness our showdown with the New York Giants. The Giants were in third place and greatly coveted the hold we currently had on second place, so the stage was already set for a monumental struggle even without the subplot of Dizzy's trouble with the umpires. We had our hands full with Diz's pitching counterpart, the great Carl Hubbell. He'd won 21 consecutive games going back to the 1936 season, and he looked typically sharp as he warmed up on the side before the game started. Dizzy and Carl delivered on the pre-game expectations of a great pitcher's duel, allowing very few hits through five innings. On the strength of a 2nd-inning solo homer by Joe Medwick, we clung to a razor-thin, 1-0, lead as we took the field for the top of the 6th inning — and that's where the trouble began.

Whitey Whitehead opened the inning with a single, and was then sacrificed to second by Hubbell. Dick Bartell stepped to the plate and Dizzy stepped on the rubber. Very quickly, Dizzy half turned to second, then delivered the pitch to Bartell without hesitating at the belt. Surprised by the quick-pitch, Bartell defensively lifted a harmless pop fly to leftfield for the second out — or so it appeared. Just then we saw home plate umpire George Barr step out from behind the plate, waving off the play and hollering, "Balk!" Barr declared that Diz had failed to pause his stretch wind-up for the full second as prescribed by the rules. Barr then wiped the out off the scoreboard, awarded Whitehead third base, and recalled Bartell to the batter's box.

Dizzy was, of course, in a rage over this turn of events. Despite the fact that we all knew good and well that Diz had, in fact, balked, our whole ballclub backed our teammate by wholeheartedly supporting him in his protest. After sufficient kicking, we all returned to our positions to resume the game. Bartell promptly lined Dizzy's next pitch to Pepper Martin in rightfield, but Pepper couldn't handle the shot. He dropped the ball, allowing Whitehead to score, tying the ballgame at 1-1. This, as you'd expect, only increased Dizzy's ire. Then

Lou Chiozza singled. Then Jo-Jo Moore singled. By the time the inning finally ended, we were trailing, 3-1, and Dizzy was steamed.

A balk call by plate umpire George Barr against Dizzy Dean unleashed the wrath of the Gas House Gang upon his head. Cards seen here (from left to right) arguing are Mickey Owen, me, Diz, Leo Durocher, and Frankie Frisch.

The fact that we failed to answer with any runs in the bottom of the 6th probably helped Diz in his decision to take matters into his own hands as we took the field for the top of the 7th inning. He was fuming, and he started throwing at the Giants hitters. I tell you, he knocked every one of them down through the 7th and 8th innings. One by one they went sprawling as Dizzy fired his high hard one at their heads. "Hit that, you so-and-so," Diz would mutter as the Giants hitters got up and were dusting themselves off. This went on right into the 9th inning when New York outfielder Jimmy Ripple was sent tumbling into the Sportsman's Park dirt by one of Dizzy's dusters. Ripple picked himself up and looked over to his dugout, then nodded in a very deliberate motion to his teammates. We all knew what that nod meant — it meant that the Giants had had enough, and they were about to retaliate on Ol' Diz. Durocher, worried that a young greenhorn like myself might not have picked up on the significance of what was about to happen, came over to me and said, "Hey, kid," — Leo always called me kid — "get ready to go. There's gonna be trouble."

Anyone who was not yet aware of what was about to take place suddenly BECAME aware when Ripple bunted Dizzy's next pitch down the first base line. It was an old trick. About the only way a batter could get back at a headhunting pitcher was to bunt down the first base line, then bowl over the hurler as he came over to field the bunt. That's exactly what Ripple had in mind, but he was thwarted in his effort when his bunt rolled foul. Leo looked over at me with a look of affirmation. "Get ready, kid," he repeated. Leo and I conferred before Dizzy threw the next pitch, deciding that we'd try and get over there before Diz got knocked down should Ripple try and bunt again. Ripple bunted again, but his fear of hitting another foul made him push it too far inside the line and it bounded to Jimmy Brown, our second baseman. Jimmy scooped up the bunt and prepared to toss it to Johnny Mize at first, but when he looked up things were not as they should be. A bunt that far inside the line — one fielded by the second baseman — meant that the pitcher had absolutely no business being near the play, but as Ripple approached the first base bag, there was Dizzy — determinedly blocking Ripple from the base. Diz was apparently disappointed at Ripple's inability to lay down a bunt that would successfully result in a collision. Dizzy appeared to want this confrontation as badly as Ripple wanted it — so he took matters into his own hands, seeking a preemptive strike against Ripple by positioning himself in the baseline.

New York Times reporter John Drebinger had quite a knack for description, and here's how he described what happened next — "The two barely missed a head-on collision, but locked horns immediately. This was the spark that touched off the gas tank, and there was no helium in that tank, either. With one bound, all the Giants tore out of their dugout." Leo and I failed in our plan to get to Dizzy before Ripple. I don't know if Superman could have got there in time. But Leo and I did get to Diz in time to shield him from the mass of Giants coming at him from the dugout. Leo and I locked our arms togther in front of Dizzy, blocking the Giants' assault. We were bound and determined to keep him from getting hurt. Meanwhile, the Cardinals were supposed to be the fastest guys in baseball, but they were the slowest damned guys I'd ever seen as I waited for what seemed like an eternity for them to come to our rescue!

Continuing his description of the brawl, Drebinger wrote, "Fists flew in all directions, and for a time it was difficult to tell which players were doing the actual fighting and which were attempting to act as peacemakers. Off to one side, catchers Gus Mancuso and Mickey Owen became embroiled, apparently in belief that inasmuch as there were enough already mixed up in the main Dean-Ripple battle, another fight would do no harm. Others joined them, and umpires Barr, Dolly Stark, and Bill Stewart now had their hands full. Meanwhile, the crowd, which, curiously enough, took no part in the melee at all, roared encouragement as the belligerents swung with no holds barred as the three umpires and a special squad of policeman struggled desperately to restore order. Eventually they separated all the contestants and after long deliberation decided to evict only Mancuso and Owen, perhaps on the theory that they should not have attempted to start a battle of their own. Dean, considerably ruffled but otherwise unhurt, and the chunky Ripple were allowed to continue."

Peeved over a balk call against him, Dizzy Dean took out his frustration by knocking down every man in the New York Giants line-up, one by one. Giants outfielder Jimmy Ripple finally took exception, bunting down the first base line to get a retaliatory crack at Dizzy. Needless to say, a brawl ensued — and I got sucker-punched.

Dizzy Dean — ruffled but otherwise unhurt. That was a repeating theme in my time with Dizzy and the Cards. We'd succeeded in our mission to keep him safe, but I wasn't so lucky. As a matter of fact, I was pretty much the only one significantly hurt in the free-for-all. While surrounded by the mass of bodies and flying fists, somebody had sucker-punched me right in the eye. I think I was in five fights for Dizzy. He NEVER got hurt, yet I got hit in every damn one of them — but none as severely as I was hit in our brawl on this day. Dizzy was our number one pitcher, so if he got hurt it would hurt the team. That's why we would protect him in spite of the fact that it was usually he who started the trouble. Imagine a little 5-foot 10-inch 165-pound runt like me trying to protect Dizzy Dean! Leo and I did that many times. Protecting Diz and — whop! — I'd get punched in the nose.

With order restored and Mancuso and Owen trudging off the their respective clubhouses, the umpires were ready to have us resume the game. But they dealt Diz one more indignity when they informed us that no one had tagged out Ripple prior to the fisticuffs. Despite our protests, Ripple was awarded first base, thereby raising Dizzy's level of irritation even higher — if that was possible. Despite the fact that Diz had thrown dusters at every Giant player for the last three innings, he had, amazingly, not hit anyone. That was probably by design. I'm sure Dizzy could have beaned anyone at anytime had he wanted to. His control was that good. But he didn't want to hurt anyone. He was mad at the umps, and the Giants just happened to be the ones who paid the price. He didn't want to hurt anyone, he just wanted to send a loud message to the umps, the league, and any players who cared to listen. But when Barr ruled that Ripple was safe at first, that was too much for Dizzy to take. The next Giant batter, 1st baseman Jack McCarthy, was in the wrong place at the wrong time, and Dizzy drilled him in the middle of his back with the first pitch. There was a moment of trepidation as everyone wondered if a new brawl would break out, but the peace was maintained as McCarthy trotted down to first base. Harry Danning, subbing for the ejected Mancuso, then stepped up and hit Diz with one final slap in the face, doubling to left-center to score Ripple. Mercifully, that was the end of the scoring, but we were facing a 4-1 deficit as we jogged off the field for our final at-bat.

My wounded eye looked terrible by the time we got into the dugout. It had swelled up so much you could have hung your hat on it. When Pepper got a look at me he said, "Wow — who hit you?" I actually had no idea who did it, so I said, "I don't know, Pepper, some goon sucker-punched me." That's all Pepper needed to hear. He tore out of our dugout and ran over to the Giants' dugout. He stood there looking in at their players and hollered, "Whoever hit that kid over there — be man enough to come out here and fight me! You're a damn bunch of cowards to hit a kid like that!" Not a Giant came out of that dugout, either. No one even moved in their seats. Pepper was really teed-off because someone had hit HIS "kid." On one hand I was feeling miserable because my eye was throbbing fiercely, but on the other hand I felt great because I loved hav-

The Giants' Cuban-born pitching coach, Dolf Luque, turned out to be the guy who laid the sucker-punch on me. Paul Dean offered some comfort, but it did little to ease the pain.

ing a guy like Pepper Martin watching my back. Lou Chiozza later told me that it was the Giants' Cuban-born pitching coach, Dolf Luque, who had hit me. Luque was a fine player during his 20 years as a big league pitcher, but he had a well-deserved reputation as a tough, mean guy — even going so far as to carry brass knuckles and a knife. Not knowing then what I eventually came to learn about Luque, I feel lucky to have gotten away with just a punch in the eye!

For a few more details on Dolf Luque's punch to my eye, here's a quote the *New York Times* reported that National League President Ford Fricke said about me. "I talked to [Giants manager] Bill Terry and he said the only innocent victim of the entire disturbance was Don Gutteridge of the Cardinals, who got a black eye." For his part, Terry said, "We all feel sorry for the little third baseman." Everybody but Dolf Luque! We played the Giants again the next day and lost again, 7-4. I was only 1-for-5, but maybe it was because I was still feeling the ill effects from the brawl the day before. Maybe the *Times* thought so, too, as they wrote, "A casualty from the day before was Don Gutteridge, who emerged from the great struggle wearing a beautifully colored 'shiner' and a cut over his right eye. Both sides seemed to concede the 'wrong guy' had caught this stray shot." I can't help but wondering what Dolf Luque was thinking as he read about me in the papers, knowing that he was the one who'd dealt me the cheap shot. The book on our brawl with the Giants was finally closed shortly thereafter when Frick fined Dean and Ripple $50 each for "actions on the ballfield tending to precipitate a riot." That about summed it up!

MAY 23, 1937: I hit my second home run of the season in our 6-2 win over Philadelphia at St. Louis on this day. I also had a double. This started a brief period where I was really seeing the ball really well and I ended up hitting four homers over an 8-game period. Not a big deal for the power-hitters, but keep in mind that I only hit a total of seven long balls in all of 1937! Dizzy Dean pitched a complete game for his sixth win of the season. He was still angry about the way the umpires had, in his opinion, taken a win away from him with that balk business in his previous start. Here's how the *New York Times* reported it. "Dizzy, who hasn't been the same since he was irked by an umpire's decision last Wednesday, staged a sit-down strike on the mound in the second inning. Becoming peeved at Umpire Beans Reardon, Dizzy made sure he wouldn't make an error on the balk rule — source of last week's war — by taking 11 minutes to throw three pitches to Jimmy Wilson. While captain Leo Durocher argued with Reardon, Dizzy sat it out on the mound. Players and officials converged on him, but it was nearly three minutes before he tossed the next ball. Dizzy finally fanned the catcher-manager." Diz sure gave the paying customers their money's worth.

MAY 27, 1937: I had a 3-for-5 performance in a losing cause as we dropped one to the Bees at Sportsman's Park on this day. In my first at-bat of the game I connected with a Jim Turner pitch for my third home run of the young season. I was not, as my record shows, a home run hitter, but I was new enough on the scene that the press didn't really know that yet. This snippet from *The Sporting News* is proof. "Gutteridge, with his excellent driving power, is always dangerous." It sounds more like they were talking about Johnny Mize, but who am I to complain about good press?

MAY 29, 1937: Two days later I did my best to continue to fool the sportswriters into thinking I was a long ball hitter as I again homered. The headline in the *New York Times* read, *CARDS SCORE, 2-1, AFTER DEAN BOWS; GUTTERIDGE GETS HOMER.* It was always nice to see your name in the headlines — except on those occasions where it was because you did something to help LOSE a ballgame. But that wasn't the case on this day against the Pirates at Sportsman's Park. My home run came in the second game of a doubleheader — Dizzy Dean had lost in the opener. The paper described it this way — "The Cardinal runs came in the 1st when Don Gutteridge blasted one of Ed Brandt's offerings into the leftfield bleachers, and in the 5th when Pepper Martin scored on Mickey Owen's single." Bob Weiland pitched a wonderful complete game for the win. I was glad to see Mickey have a hand in our win. He and I played together at Columbus, and we were now reunited since he'd made the Cards this season. He was a real wild and wooly young kid. He would do anything, but he was a very good catcher. Mickey enjoyed success with St. Louis through the 1940 season, then joined the Dodgers where he stayed through the 1945 season.

Mickey Owen was a wild and wooly young fellow. In other words, you never knew what he would do. But don't let that fool you — he was a very good catcher. This photo shows me and Mickey (far right) in the spring of 1936 in Bradenton, Florida, doing an interview with Cardinals broadcaster Ray Schmidt of KWK radio and coach Buzzy Wares.

It was as a Dodger that Mickey will be eternally remembered, but, sadly, for unfortunate circumstances. Losing and down to their last strike in Game Four of the 1941 World Series, Mickey let a Hugh Casey pitch get by him. The Yankee batter, Tommy Henrich, reached safely on the play, then New York rallied to win the game. The Series turned on that play, and the Yanks went on to win it in seven games. Many people wrongly blamed Mickey for losing the Series. He told me one time, "Don, I caught thousands and thousands of balls that nobody remembers. I missed one ball and I'm known forever." Mickey died back in 2005, and once again the whole topic of the passed ball was at the forefront. It's too bad that that's how he'll be remembered by the masses, but I'll always remember Mickey as a great teammate and a fine catcher.

MAY 31, 1937: I guess good things sometime come in bunches because I hit another home run on this day, just two days after my last one. This was my fifth of the season, all of them coming in the month of May, with four of the five coming in the last eight days. I was really feeling great at the plate. Unfortunately, this day's home run came in a losing effort as we dropped the game, 4-2, to the Cubs at Sportsman's Park in the opener of a double-header. It was a 2-out bases-empty shot in the 6th inning off Chicago's tall right-hander, Bill Lee.

JUNE 19, 1937: I turned 25 years of age on this day as we beat the Bees, 7-5, at Sportsman's Park. I had a hit in the game, but it was Joe Medwick who made my birthday a happy one by leading us to victory. He continued to hit the ball inhumanly hard, collecting three hits and five RBIs. Two of his hits were scorching home runs, the second coming when we needed it most. We were tied, 5-5, with two out and a man aboard when Joe smashed the game-winning homer off the scoreboard in leftfield. It was a birthday to remember.

JUNE 20, 1937: There were numerous times when we didn't support Dizzy Dean with the kind of offense he deserved, but that couldn't be said on this day. Ol' Diz pitched a complete game 5-hitter and we backed him up with a 9-run assault on the Boston Bees in the second game of a twin bill at St. Louis. We won the ballgame, 9-2, after dropping the opener, 6-2. I was 2-for-4 in both games and was able to hit my sixth home run in the nightcap, a 2-run knock with Don Padgett aboard in the 7th inning.

JULY 5, 1937: In one of my more difficult days at the plate, I went 1-for-8 in the opening game of a double-header at Wrigley Field, a game that we lost to the Cubs, 13-12. It was an excruciatingly long game — 14 innings taking four hours and nine minutes — made even longer by my one-game mini-slump. I did manage to hit a double, which kept me from being the only guy in the game to go 0-for-8. Things got a bit better for me in the nightcap as I picked up two hits, but we dropped another tough one, 9-7. In a bizarre incident, home plate umpire

Dolly Stark was knocked unconscious by a foul ball off the bat of Stuart Martin in the opening game. It hit him on the top of the mask, but he still went out like a light. They had to carry him off the field.

JULY 12, 1937: I was out of the line-up as we took on the Pirates at Forbes Field on this day. The game was a back and forth affair, but we were leading, 4-3, when trouble erupted in the bottom of the 7th inning. An umpire's call got our guys all worked up, and by the time the smoke had cleared, Leo Durocher and Johnny Mize were ejected. Frankie Frisch barked at me to get out to shortstop to replace Leo, so I reached under the bench, grabbed my glove, and took off up the dugout steps. I got about two steps out of the dugout when I stuck my hand in my glove and — good Lord! — I stopped dead in my tracks. The inside of my glove was loaded with something cold, wet, and gooey. It was thoroughly disgusting. I knocked that glove off my hand so fast it'd have made your head spin. As the glove flew off my hand, I saw what seemed like a quart of brown tobacco juice spray out of it. I looked in the dugout and saw a look of anger on Frankie's face — but I also saw Pepper Martin with a big, wide grin. Pepper, like me, was out of the line-up that day, so to entertain himself he had snuck my glove from below the bench, then spent 6-1/2 innings filling every finger with tobacco juice. Pepper's smile only widened as he saw me pick my glove up and then stick my hand back in it. It was terrible. Frankie gave it to me good when the inning was over and I got back to the dugout, hollering, "What the hell are you trying to do, showing off by throwing tobacco juice out of your glove like that?!" I cut my eyes at Pepper, but didn't dare tell on him, so I just meekly replied, "I don't know."

Simply put, Pepper was a real cut-up. He got me — and many others — with his pranks over the years we played together. They are too numerous to remember them all, but a few stick out. Once, while I was napping on the train, Pepper loaded my fingertips with black grease, then proceeded to tickle my nose with a piece of paper. Every time I would scratch my nose, I'd smudge my face with black fingerprints. You can imagine my embarrassment when I later woke up and went to the restroom — and looked at my face in the mirror. Once, at spring training, I saw Pepper sprinkle sneezing powder on a distinguished retired group stationed below the mezzanine from which we looked down. He was in stitches when they all started sneezing. And, of course, Pepper executed many doses of the old hot-foot as we sat in the dugout during games. You'd feel that burning and want to holler, but you didn't dare because Frankie was sitting right there and he'd give YOU hell. I think Pepper burned up the shoes on half the guys on the team! Pepper was a funny guy and he enjoyed every moment we all had together with the Cardinals. Nobody ever got mad at him, they just accepted him. Anybody else and they would have gone after them with a shotgun, but not good old Pepper Martin.

JULY 27, 1937: A rare thing happened on this day at Sportsman's Park — we routed the great Carl Hubbell for a 9-8 victory. Hubbell was his usual dominant self for three innings, leading by a score 1-0 when we finally got to him in the bottom of the 4th. I started the rally by opening the inning with a single, then Johnny Mize blasted a long home run over the rightfield pavilion to put us in front. Five more hits followed in the inning and, by the time the screwball maestro strolled off the mound with only one out, we were leading, 8-1. It was a different story, however, when we came up to hit in the bottom of the 9th. The Giants had slowly chipped away at our lead, finally tying the game in the 8th. In the meantime, I'd picked up another hit and two RBIs, but it took a game-ending solo homer by Joe Medwick to put us in the win column.

My hit against Hubbell was not the norm for me. He was probably the toughest guy for me to hit. A year earlier, before I'd ever faced Hubbell, Terry Moore, our great centerfielder, had warned me how difficult it was to hit Carl. Terry was like that — he really liked to help guys out. It was September 13th, 1936, and we were in New York to open a 3-game series with the Giants at the Polo Grounds when Terry said, "Don, you haven't hit against Hubbell yet. Take a step up in the batter's box when you face him because that screwball of his looks like it's going to be waist-high, but it ends up below your knees. If you step up a little bit, you can get to it before it drops." Well, Hubbell didn't pitch that day, but, sure enough, we saw him the next day. When I went up to face him the first time, I gave Terry a knowing nod and took my place in the batter's box — a full step closer to the mound than usual.

Hubbell delivered his first pitch to me, and it looked good — just about waist-high. I swung at it, but, much to my shock, the pitch bounced in the dirt. I must have missed that ball by a foot. I couldn't believe it. I stepped out of the box and looked over at Terry. He yelled, "Get up further! Get up further!" So I did. I got back in that box, a full step closer to Hubbell than I was on his first pitch. He threw another pitch to me, and this one looked even better than the first one. It was belt-high when I swung, but I again missed as the ball bounced in the dirt. Giants catcher Gus Mancuso must have had a good laugh when he saw the astonishment on my face. I stepped out and again looked over at Terry. He broke out in laughter and hollered, "Get up in the box — further!" So I did. I think I was in front of the box by then. Hubbell's next pitch came in and I chopped down on it. The pitch again bounced — but I luckily hit it for a single. As I ran to first base I could see Terry laughing the whole time out of the corner of my eye.

AUGUST 1, 1937: This wasn't a day to remember for me as far as my production with the bat. I was 0-for-8 in a double-header split against the Dodgers at Sportsman's Park, but I always kept hustling even when things weren't going well for me at the plate. And when you hustle, good things happen, like this little moment as recorded by the *New York Times*. "Third baseman Don Gutteridge pulled an unusual play by taking Babe Phelps' bounder towards second base and beating Heine Manush to that station for an unassisted force-out. It happened in the third frame of the opener." I had great speed, but this play wasn't as amazing as it may sound. Phelps' ball carried me in the direction of second base to begin with, plus Manush, at 34 years of age and in his 15th season, wasn't exactly fleet of foot anymore. So I just did the easy thing and kept running to second base and stepped on the bag. I have to admit that it did look peculiar in the scorebook to see an unassisted putout made by the third baseman at second base.

AUGUST 19, 1937: This was a good day as we swept a double-header from the Reds at Cincinnati. It was made even better for me when I hit a solo home run in the second game. It was my seventh and last homer of the season. Reds manager Charley Dressen filed a protest in the game, and it was kind of funny. Joe Medwick was on first base when a pitch got away from Cincinnati catcher Gilly Campbell. Here's how the *New York Times* described the rest of the wacky play. "It caromed to the screen and rolled down again behind home plate. Medwick went to second, then to third. Umpire Sears threw in a new ball and Medwick was safe when Campbell apparently made no effort to tag him with third baseman Lew Riggs' return." Only in baseball!

SEPTEMBER 8, 1937: We didn't know it at the time, but this was a sad day in the history of the St. Louis Cardinals. I was 1-for-4 with a stolen base, but that was meaningless in the grand scheme of things. It turned out that this was the last game Dizzy Dean would ever pitch for the St. Louis Cardinals. As everyone now knows, Dizzy took an Earl Averill line drive off off his left foot resulting in a broken big toe in the 1937 All-Star Game on July 7th. Dizzy had been his usual dominant self in the first half of the season piling up 12 wins before heading off to the All-Star Game. He missed a few starts at the beginning of the second half while he tried to heal the toe, but then he decided to come back and pitch on July 21st despite the fact that it was still not healed. Diz pitched great that day, going the distance, but we couldn't rustle up enough runs off Boston pitcher Johnny Lanning and we lost, 2-1.

What we didn't yet know was that Dizzy had hurt his arm in that July 21st game. He then kept taking his starts even though his shoulder was killing him. Instead of "foggin' 'em through" like he'd always done in the past, Dizzy was now throwing nothing but slow stuff in his remaining appearances of 1937. As a result, he managed to pick up only one win in the entire second half of the season. It was a sad thing to see. It all culminated on this day, September 8th, when Dizzy turned in another painful, gutsy performance. He went the full nine, but the Cubs' Larry French shut us out, 4-0. Dizzy was traded to the Cubs after the season ended, but his bad shoulder allowed him to eek out just another 16 wins in his career. Dizzy summed up what went wrong in a *New York Times* article after our game on this day. "The old arm just isn't right," he said. "When I pitched in Boston 10 days [after I hurt my toe in the All-Star Game], I was unable to pivot on my left foot. The result was that I was pitching entirely with my arm. During the game I noticed a soreness in the old flipper and it has been sore ever since." Believe me, we missed Ol' Diz after he moved on to Chicago — both his talent on the mound and his one-of-a-kind personality.

SEPTEMBER 16, 1937: We took two games from the Philadelphia Phillies in a Thursday twin bill at Sportsman's Park on this day. We got great pitching from Bob Weiland in the opener as he went the distance allowing only two runs, then we got an even better performance from Howie Krist in the second game as he, too, threw a complete game allowing only one run. I was a perfect 4-for-4 with two doubles off Harold Kelleher in the nightcap.

As the ACME wirephoto caption-writer put it back on March 19th, 1937, when this photo was taken, here's "Don Gutteridge, infielder, during a bit of action in the training camp at Daytona, Florida."

SEPTEMBER 21, 1937: My last big moment of 1937 came on this day in the first game of a double-header against the Dodgers at Sportsman's Park. We were trailing by one run when I came up in the bottom of the 7th with the bases loaded. I tripled off Brooklyn reliever Roy Henshaw, driving in all three runs, and that turned out to be the margin of victory as we won, 7-5.

OCTOBER 3, 1937: An injury knocked me out of the line-up during a game on September 25th, so I spent the last eight games of the season mending on the bench. It was from that vantage point that I watched our 1937 season — my first full campaign as a big leaguer — come to a close on this day at Wrigley Field as we lost to the Cubs, 6-4. The loss put us at 81 wins, 73 losses, and three ties — and a disappointing 4th-place finish in the National League. After coming up short while competing to the bitter end for the 1936 pennant, we really thought we had a great shot to win it in 1937. We had great cohesiveness as a group, but we just never jelled as a team on the field.

One guy who jelled in 1937 was Joe Medwick. He put it all together at the plate and won the triple crown, batting .374 with 31 homers and 154 RBIs. He also led the league in slugging percentage, runs scored, hits, doubles, total bases, and at-bats. It was an amazing thing to see. It was, by far, the best season I have ever seen anyone have. It seemed like every ball he hit was a hard line drive. He would never get any cheap hits. He hit frozen ropes that would just keep carrying, and he would leg them out for doubles and triples. Joe hit his share of round-trippers, but it was his bullet-like line drives that really stick with my memory. Defensively, Joe was merely adequate. His arm wasn't very strong, and he wasn't very fast. He wasn't really a very good base-runner, either, but he sure could swing the bat. Joe was helped greatly by hitting after Johnny Mize in the line-up — and Johnny was a better hitter over a longer period, but for a couple of years, NOBODY was better than Ducky Medwick.

General Mills paid me, Lon Warneke (center), and Mickey Owen $100 each to appear in an ad promoting Wheaties. They also promised a free case of cereal for each home run we hit. We, of course, could not do the photo shoot without a little bit of monkeying around.

1938

APRIL 19, 1938: Opening day 1938 against Pittsburgh at Sportsman's Park. It felt wonderful to start a new season in front of a big home crowd in St. Louis on this day. This was my third season with the Cardinals and I was now firmly entrenched as a regular player — and it was a great feeling. Our feisty shortstop, Leo Durocher, had been traded to Brooklyn immediately at the conclusion of the '37 season, so Frankie Frisch moved me to shortstop to take Leo's place for '38. I hit lead-off in the game and went 1-for-4 with a triple and a run scored, but we lost in heartbreaking style. Here's how the *New York Times* described the finish — "As the opening day crowd was moving toward the exits feeling the

Cardinals had come from behind to win, Arky Vaughan stepped up in the 9th and hit the roof of the rightfield pavilion for a home run with one on to give the Pirates a 4-to-3 victory today." Bob Weiland had pitched a beautiful 8-2/3 innings for us. He was one out away from the finish line, but Arky came through for the Pirates when it counted. It was a tough way to open the season.

I didn't really care whether I played third base or shortstop — I just wanted to play ball. While I was now playing shortstop because of Leo being traded to Brooklyn, I have to admit that I wasn't happy at seeing "The Lip" dealt away. I'd always liked Leo as a player. I liked him even more after he joined the Cardinals in 1934 when he was traded to St. Louis from Cincinnati. When I first joined the Cardinals late in the 1934 season, Leo was one of the most impressive guys to me. I'll never forget the feeling of awe I had when I first walked into the Cardinal fieldhouse and saw Leo, Dizzy Dean, Joe Medwick, Terry Moore, Johnny Mize — and my favorite player, Pepper Martin. It was really something. Despite his reputation as a tough guy, Leo was really nice to me. He took care of me and spent a lot of time helping me develop into a pretty good third baseman. I'm sure he never imagined that his goodwill would one day serve to help me replace him, but that's how it worked out. On the field, Leo was the typical Gas House Gang player — tough, hard-nosed, scrappy, hustling, brash, and abrasive. He didn't hit much, but he was as slick a fielder as you'd ever see, and he was a heads-up player. Like most of the Gas House Gang, Leo would do anything necessary to win.

Quite often all you hear about Leo Durocher are the negative things, but he had a good side, too. Aside from helping me with my fielding, Leo would occassionally help me out of trouble when I would get mixed up in the hijinks of Pepper Martin. One incident from 1937 stands out in particular. We were playing the Reds at Crosley Field at a time when the headlines were dominated by the rise of Hitler and Mussolini. Somewhere in our travels, Doc Weaver, our trainer, had picked up rubber masks of both of the dictators. I guess he thought they might come in handy at some point. As soon as Pepper saw those masks he told Doc to always have them at the ready so he could use them when the proper situation presented itself. Well, Pepper decided that proper situation had presented itself in our game with the Reds that day when home plate umpire George Barr made a call that caused a big dispute. While everyone was yelling and arguing, Pepper told me to go get the Hitler mask from Doc. I hurriedly got the mask from Doc and returned to Pepper, at which point he said, "Now put that thing on and go give that dictator Barr a salute!" I hesitated, so Pepper exclaimed, "Go ahead — do it!" I've said it before and I'll say it again, when Pepper tells you to do something — you do it.

So I pulled on that mask and stepped out of the dugout. In that moment I stood rigid, threw up my right arm in the perfect Nazi salute and hollered, "George Barr — heil Hitler! Heil Hitler!" That brought him over in a hurry, and he demanded to know who was under that damned mask. I quickly sat down on the bench with Lon Warneke on my left and someone else on my right. Barr was enraged and wanted me to turn around so he could see my number — he wanted to know who it was that he was able to thumb from the game. Well, I was able to slink out of there without Barr finding out it was me. The ballgame finally resumed, but when it was over we learned that Barr was still teed off over the Hitler joke. He sent word to our clubhouse that he was determined to find out who the culprit was, and when he did he was going to see to it that the player responsible was going to be fined and possibly suspended. That made me very nervous. I was young and impressionable — I had no idea that following Pepper's orders could get me in this much trouble. When Leo saw how afraid I was, he said he'd take care of it for me. So Leo, along with Doc, went in to see Barr. Leo told Barr that it was me that did it, but he smooth-talked George into forgetting the whole thing. I really appreciated Leo doing that for me.

Leo's ability to smooth-talk Barr was really not all that suprising. Durocher was a very slick character on and off the ballfield. He was a great dresser and would change his clothes two or three times a day. That's where he differed from

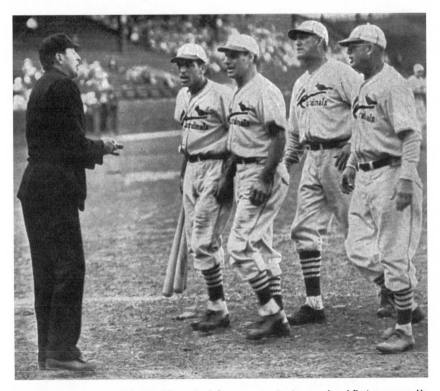

Leo Durocher, the second Cardinal from the left, was a mentor to me when I first came up. He took care of me and helped me develop into a pretty good third baseman. Here he showed me the finer points of hounding the umpire. I'm on the far left, and the other Cards are Mike Gonzales and Buzzy Wares (far right).

the rest of the Gas House Gang. The rest of the gang would only change their clothes about once a week! It was that difference in style that made Leo unpopular with the rest of the team. They put up with him, but they didn't really like him off the field — except Medwick, that is. He really idolized Leo. Joe looked up to Durocher and tried to follow in Leo's footsteps. For that reason, Joe, too, wasn't very well-liked by the rest of the team. As with Leo, the team overlooked their feelings of dislike for Medwick and put up with him because he was such a great player.

APRIL 20, 1938: Thank goodness we didn't have to think about the opening day loss for very long because we were back at it the next day, once again against Pittsburgh. But the Pirates quickly gave us a new batch of worries when they hung four runs on us in the first inning, and eventually drubbed us by a 9-4 score. Still in the lead-off slot, I picked up two hits in five at-bats on this day. One of them was a solo home run off Bucs right-hander Jim Tobin. There was only one other long ball hit that day, but it was a notable one. Enos Slaughter, our highly-touted rookie rightfielder, hit his first big league homer, also off Tobin. Enos went on to have very solid season for us that year. He got even better with time and eventually ended up in the Hall of Fame.

APRIL 24, 1938: Our first trip into Chicago, and this day in particular, was much anticipated because it featured us against our old teammate, Dizzy Dean, now pitching for the Cubs. Ol' Diz had done more than his share to build up the rivalry, on more than one occasion publicly stating his desire to whip us. His contempt wasn't really with his former teammates, his ire was really directed at Cardinals management. He felt they pressured him to pitch with his broken toe, resulting in him injuring his arm. At one point he even threatened to sue the club for $200,000.

Dizzy had already won his first start a few days earlier, but he had done it without many fastballs. He had said that "the old flipper" was as good as new, but he wasn't throwing his hard one, and that made you wonder. Well, apparently it didn't matter whether Ol' Diz had his hard one or not — he shut us out on four hits and won the ballgame, 5-0. Try as I did to make something happen from my lead-off slot, Dizzy got the best of me and I went 0-for-4. After winning his first start, Dizzy boldly told reporters that he would win 30. As he walked victoriously off the field through the crowd of autograph seekers after getting the last out, Dizzy said, "Just 28 more to go!" Dizzy's arm troubles soon resurfaced and he missed a good portion of the season, but under pressure from Cubs management he returned later in the season and, pitching in great pain, helped the Cubs win the 1938 pennant.

MAY 1, 1938: The bright lights of playing shortstop can be very hot as I found out just a week-and-a-half into my stint at the position in 1938. We opened the month of May with a loss to the Cubs at Sportsman's Park on this day. Here's the *New York Times* headline — *Chicago Halts Cards, Home Run by Tony Lazzeri with Two On Coming After Error by Gutteridge.* The text went on to say, "Don Gutteridge's fumble of a grounder was a major factor in the Cardinals' 6-to-5 defeat by the Cubs today. After Frank Demaree singled to start the Cubs second inning, the St. Louis shortstop muffed Joe Marty's blow on what appeared to observers to be an easy double-play chance. Then the former Yank, Tony Lazzeri, hit into the leftfield seats for a home run. The error was the fourth in two days for Gutteridge." The season was full of ups and downs, and this was about as down as it could get.

MAY 3, 1938: Down but not out, thanks to a key homer I hit in our game on this day. *Cards' Two Homer Subdue Bees, 3 to 2,* the headline blared. The subhead said, *Bremer and Gutteridge Connect to Give McGee Triumph.* The McGee was our rookie right-hander "Fiddler" Bill McGee. After the rough time I'd had in the field over the last few days, I was overjoyed to help Bill and our ballclub get a win that day. In describing my home run off Boston pitcher Lou Fette, the paper wrote, "Gutteridge won the game in the 6th with a mighty blow into the leftfield seats after two were out." Redemption — at least for the moment.

The story of Fiddler Bill McGee and the St. Louis Cardinals is a funny one. While Bill was right-handed when pitching, he was left-handed when he played the fiddle. He was a solid pitcher for us from 1938-40, but it was his talent as a fiddle player that truly made him irreplaceable on our club. You see, Pepper Martin had a little hillbilly band he operated on the side, an outfit he called Pepper Martin's Mudcat Band. Pepper was an entertainer at heart, so he formed the band so he'd have an outlet for his desire to perform. He'd play the banjo, guitar, or accordion, while the rest of the band was filled out by other fellows on our ballclub. At various times he had Lon Warneke playing guitar, Bob Weiland blowing the jug, Frenchy Bordagaray working the washboard, and Bill McGee sawing on the fiddle. Before McGee finally stuck with our club for good in 1938, he'd been been shuttled back and forth between the Cardinals and our minor league affiliates from 1935-37. Pepper was always very distraught when he learned that McGee was being sent back down to the minors. He was upset not because we were losing a quality pitcher — he was upset at losing his fiddler! When Bill rejoined the club for good in 1938, a season that saw him struggle to a 7-12 record, Pepper said, "McGee's better than ever — but only on the fiddle!"

Pepper's Martin's Mudcat Band was really something. When the Cardinals would arrive in town we'd all have our duffel bags and suitcases packed with clothes — just as one would expect, but Pepper and his boys would also be lugging their instruments. The hotel managers would know right away that when Pepper came down he was going to want to play. Those hotel managers would stick the Mudcat Band in a back room or in some out-of-the-way ballroom so the boys wouldn't disturb anybody. Someone said, "Why do you practice those songs? They're all the same, anyway!" It drove Frankie Frisch nuts. They played out of tune, plunking away and singing whatever words came out of their mouths. But they'd actually get gigs, and I enjoyed going along with them. Pepper would instruct me, "Get underneath that microphone and holler and clap like hell!" So I'd do it — I was the yeller and clapper for them. It was a lot of fun.

MAY 4, 1938: In an effort to help me out of my error trouble, Frankie switched me with Jimmy Brown in the field for our game on May 3rd, and he left us in that arrangement for our game against Boston on this day — me at third and Jimmy at short. The game ended in a 5-5 tie, which was unusual, but Jimmy and I both continued to field our new positions without incident. Jimmy was, however, involved in an interesting scorer's decision on this day — he was charged with a fly-out without ever hitting the ball. Jimmy, still playing shortstop, was batting in the 5th inning when he got into an argument with homeplate umpire Larry Goetz. Jimmy claimed that he had been hit by a pitch from Boston right-hander Danny MacFayden. Goetz said that Jimmy had fouled the pitch. Goetz thumbed Jimmy from the game, and Frenchy Bordagaray came in to replace Jimmy with the count no balls and two strikes. Frenchy flied out to right on the next pitch, but the official scorer decided to charge the at-bat to Jimmy because Frenchy was at a "disadvantage" in the count when he entered.

Jimmy Brown (center) was a very solid switch-hitting infielder that came up to the Cardinals in 1937. I liked him a lot and we had many fun times together. I spent much less time with Al Cuccinello (right), however, because the Cardinals never called him up from the minors. This photo was taken in spring training. Al's brother Tony, on the other hand, became one of my best friends when we coached many years together with the White Sox in the 1950's and 60's.

MAY 9, 1938: We beat the Dodgers, 9-7, at Sportsman's Park on this day. I hit a home run for our cause, described by the *New York Times* this way — "Freddy Fitzsimmons stuck to his pitching task until the end of the 7th, in which frame a home run by Don Gutteridge with one on put the Redbirds two up." This was my third homer of the season. I didn't know it yet, but I was in the early stages of one of my little home run spurts. I hit nine home runs in 1938 — eight of them coming in the first two months of the season. I only hit one long ball in the last three months of the campaign, and that was an inside-the-parker.

MAY 18, 1938: I hit my fourth home run of the season in our 12-4 win over the Dodgers at Ebbets Field. "The closest the Dodgers managed to get to the Cardinals was 4-5 in the 6th inning," wrote Louis Effrat of the *New York Times*. "Thereafter it was 'no contest' as lefty Bob Weiland limited them to six hits, while the Gas House Gang romped all over the lot, banging out 13 safeties, including homers by Joe Medwick, Mickey Owen and Don Gutteridge." Despite our win that day, Gas House Gang references were getting fewer an far-ther between as we failed to win ballgames as regularly as the Cardinals had done in the past. By the way — Frankie had now shifted me back to shortstop, moved Jimmy Brown to second base, and inserted Joe Stripp at third.

MAY 23, 1938: I hit a bases-empty home run off Phillies right-hander Hugh Mulcahy on this day, but we still lost our fourth straight ballgame, 7-6, at Shibe Park. The way it ended did a lot to undo any of the good feelings I had about my homer. We were tied, 6-6, in the bottom of the 8th. The Phils had Del Young on second and Mulcahy on third when Morrie Arnovich hit a smash to me at third base. They don't call it the "hot corner" for nothing. I couldn't han-dle it and Mulcahy scored the go-ahead. It didn't go as an error because it would have taken a tremendous play to field the ball, but that didn't make me feel any better — I wanted to make that play.

MAY 25, 1938: Another homer, another loss. On this day I belted my sixth of the season, a 5th-inning solo wallop into the Polo Grounds lower right tier off Giants right-hander Hal Schumacher, but we still lost, 3-1. It was our sixth con-secutive defeat, wasting a very solid pitching performance from our southpaw Clyde Shoun.

JUNE 6, 1938: *Cards' 14 Safeties Overcome Bees, 11-2; Padgett, Gutteridge, Medwick Get Home Run Drives.* That was the headline to the Associated Press article recounting our game at Sportsman's Park on this day. My round-tripper was a 5th-inning 3-run shot off Bees right-hander Ira Hutchinson. As mentioned in the headline, our own "Muscles" Medwick also homered that day. That put both of us at seven homers apiece — a real fluke that far into the season. With the power Medwick possessed, you know it'd be a cold day in hell before I'd ever compete with him in a home run competition. He hit a career-high 31 homers in 1937, and while his power numbers did tail off in 1938, he was still out of my league in that department. He proved it, too, as the season progressed, hitting 14 more home runs before the season was over — compared to my two.

Incidentally, over in the Bees dugout, wearing number 10, there was a pretty good little back-up catcher named Ray Coleman Mueller. He had the misfortune of playing behind a future Hall of Famer by the name of Al Lopez, so Ray hadn't seen a whole lot of playing time since he'd come up with Boston in 1935. But on this day he doubled when called upon to pinch-hit for Bees reliever Bobby Reis in the 9th inning. Since we were way out in front at the time of Ray's two-bagger, I couldn't help but be happy for him. Why, you ask? Because Ray Mueller was my cousin, born back home in Pittsburg, Kansas, just three months before me. His mother, Augusta, and my mother, Mary, were sisters. I greeted Ray with a big smile after the game and congratulated him on his pinch-double. He returned the smile and offered congratulations to me on my home run. We were genuinely happy for each other — happy that we both were living out our childhood dreams of playing big league baseball.

Ray and I were inseparable as kids growing up. We played baseball together every spring, summer, and fall day from the time we were little boys to our days as teenagers playing on the same Shop Team in Pittsburg's old City League. We didn't want to play any football — it was baseball that we always wanted to play. We'd have played in the winter, too, but the snow always prevented that. So we'd play basketball in the winter to keep us occupied, but as soon as the snow melted, we got out the bats, balls, and gloves. That Shop Team really helped us get a good start to our careers in baseball. We didn't have a high school baseball team, so the City League was very valuable in getting us the game experience that we needed to make the jump to the minor leagues. Ray went over to the Pirates in 1939 and 1940, but he was back in the minors until he returned to the majors with the 1943 Reds. He was Cincinnati's regular catcher in '43 and '44, and he played very well. In fact, he set an endurance record for catchers by playing in 233 consecutive games at that position over that span, earning him the nickname "Iron Man." Let me tell you, that's a lot of games at such a grueling position! Ray went into the service in 1945, but returned as the Reds' regular catcher in 1946. He put together a nice career, staying in the big leagues until 1951. It's hard for me to believe, but it's now been 12 years since Ray passed away. I don't get down about it, though. I have happy memories of my childhood with Ray, and it always brings a smile to my face when I remember our days as rough and tumble little guys, playing baseball — the only game we truly loved.

JUNE 8, 1938: The rollercoaster ride of highs and lows continued on this day. Two days after I'd made the papers homering in a winning effort, I made the papers again — *Dodgers Tally Four Runs in the 9th and Vanquish the Cardinals, 7-6; Babe Phelps Scores Deciding Marker on Wild Toss by Gutteridge.* Not good. The

Dodgers had rallied for three runs in the 9th to tie the score at 6-6. Then, as Roscoe McGowen of the *New York Times* recorded it, "Cookie Lavagetto hit what should have been a double-play ball to Jimmy Brown, but Gutteridge was slow to cover second, and, although he forced Buddy Hassett, his ensuing wild heave over first let Phelps tally, crashing into Mickey Owen with the winning run a trifle ahead of Johnny Mize's throw." We had one last crack to get that run back in the bottom of the 9th, but Max Butcher came on in relief and set us down in order. It was a tough one for me to swallow.

JUNE 19, 1938: I turned 26 years of age on this day, receiving as a gift a doubleheader sweep of the New York Giants at the Polo Grounds. There was nearly 40,000 folks on hand to watch, but they were sent home unhappy, their misery particularly intense after coming so close to winning the opener. The score was tied in the 10th, 6-6, with one out and Jo-Jo Moore on second base. Jimmy Ripple then hit a bullet to me at third, but it got through me for a single and rolled out to leftfield. It looked like a sure thing that Ripple would score the winning run on the play, but he stumbled as he rounded third, and was lucky to crawl back to the bag safely. The rally went nowhere after that, but we took the lead in the 12th, 8-6, when Joe Stripp hit a 2-run 2-out single. Harry Danning made things interesting when he hit a solo homer in the home half of the inning, but that's as close as Max Macon let them get, eventually nailing down the 8-7 victory. The nightcap was not nearly as dramatic, thanks to Roy Henshaw's fine pitching. He handcuffed the Giant hitters, limiting them to just seven hits as we won, 4-2. Sweeping the twin bill was about as great a birthday present as I could have asked for, but it was made even better because I helped us to the wins by knocking out a hit in each contest.

JUNE 25, 1938: I went 1-for-4 in a 3-1 victory over the Dodgers at Sportsman's Park on this day. My double off Brooklyn righty Bill Posedel extended my small-sized hitting streak to 11 games, but it was snapped the next day when I failed to hit against Brooklyn's Vito Tamulis. Also of note in the game was my attempted steal of home, of which Roscoe McGowen wrote, "Gutteridge tried to steal home in the 8th and was tagged out, but umpire George Magerkurth ruled a third strike on Curt Davis for the third out." Curt was the pitcher of record that day, going the distance on a beautifully-pitched game. He was a fine pitcher — a 22-game winner in 1939 — but he wasn't usually going to beat you with his bat. That's why we tried for the steal of home with two outs in the inning.

JULY 12, 1938: We slipped to seventh place as we dropped a 6-5 contest to the Cincinnati Reds in St. Louis on this day. I had a 4-for-5 day at the plate, coming up one homer short of a cycle as I hit two singles, a double and a triple. With the tying run on third base, Joe Medwick grounded out to Reds shortstop Billy Myers to end the game. Sitting in our dugout was none other than Lynn Myers,

Billy's younger brother. He had been recently brought up with the notion that he would replace me at short, allowing me to return to third base.

JULY 13, 1938: The Big Jawn Show. Somehow we managed to lose our seventh game in a row on this day in spite of the fact that Johnny Mize hit three consecutive home runs. The Bees beat us, 10-5, at Sportsman's Park. Back at third base with Lynn Myers now at shortstop, I chipped in a single in five at-bats — nothing to brag about. But big Johnny had something to brag about. He had been taking a lot of criticism up to that time for not living up to expectations, but he showed them what he could do with his three long round-trippers. He repeated the amazing feat a week later when again he poled three more circuit jobs in a 7-1 win over the Giants in the second game of a twin bill at Sportsman's Park on July 20th.

In hindsight, it's amazing to think that the sportswriters were complaining about Johnny not living up to expectations considering the numbers he had put up in the brief time he'd been with the Cards. He played in 126 games as a rookie in 1936, batting .329 while hitting 19 homers. But they expected more power out of him than that, so Johnny responded by upping his home run total to 25 in 1937. When his power numbers were slow to take off in 1938, the writers started in on him again. His two 3-homer games in July helped temporarily quiet his critics, but Johnny seemed to have a hard time pleasing them for very long. He had 27 long balls by the time the '38 season ended. He improved that by one in 1939, then finally realized his full potential in 1940 when he blasted 43 home runs. After falling off to 16 round-trippers in 1941, Cardinals general manager Branch Rickey traded Johnny to the Giants. I know that Rickey hoped Mize was through, but Johnny turned in some of his best years with the Giants. When the Giants made the same mistake by thinking Mize was finished during the 1949 season, they sent him across town to the Yankees. Once again, Mize proved to have a lot left in the tank, helping the Yankees to reach five consecutive World Series.

When he was with the Cardinals, Johnny Mize, without a doubt, hit the longest home runs of anyone on our ballclub. Joe Medwick also possessed the ability to really drive the ball, but Johnny was definitely the king of the tape measure homer on our team. He had a picture-perfect swing. If I was going to tell a young player to pick someone to emulate when hitting, I'd tell them to look at old films of Mize. He was tough at the plate, too, refusing to be intimidated. I NEVER once saw Johnny Mize get knocked down. They'd throw at his head, but he was so coordinated that he'd move just enough so that the ball would whistle by his ear, missing his bean by inches. If they threw lower, he'd just turn his body and take it in the back. But he'd make them pay the next time they had to pitch to him. When it came to swinging a bat, Johnny simply did everything perfectly — and that's why we'd nicknamed him "The Spaulding Guy." Spaulding perfectly manufactured the equipment we used while playing baseball, and Johnny's swing was so perfect that it looked like it, too, must have come out of the Spaulding factory.

Johnny's defense, on the other hand, was not perfect. I had a tendency to be a little wild on occasion with my throws to first, and I was often charged with errors because Johnny was unable to dig them out of the dirt. I swear, if you threw it below his knees, he just wasn't going to go down and get it. This was something you expected out of your first baseman, and most guys could do it — but not Johnny — so I sometimes would complain about that. But that was a small price to pay in return for his prolific bat. Johnny was a great player, most definitely worthy of his 1981 induction into the Hall of Fame.

Big Johnny Mize (second from right), one of the Cardinals' all-time greatest players, towered over everyone attending this spring training fishing trip. Johnny's on-field ability towered over most of the players, too. This outing was organized by the folks at General Mills cereal, makers of Wheaties. That's their account represenrative, fourth from the left. Others pictured are Cardinals traveling secretary Leo Ward (far right), Cardinals manager Frankie Frisch (third from right), me (center), and my wife Helen (far left). The rest of the ladies pictured are other wives, but their names have unfortunately escaped my memory.

JULY 20, 1938: As I mentioned, Johnny Mize clouted three homers in the night-cap of our doubleheader on this day. Well, I had a pretty nice day at the plate, too, in the opening game. The only thing again stopping me from hitting for the cycle was a home run. We won the game, 7-1, behind a 4-hitter by Clyde Shoun.

JULY 24, 1938: I picked up three hits in seven at-bats as we split a doubleheader with the Dodgers at Sportsman's Park on this day. That gave me three opportunities to see, up close, a real living legend — Babe Ruth. He'd joined the Dodgers as a coach about a month earlier. I was too much in awe of him to say anything other than hello as I reached first base. One of the real treats that day was watching a pre-game home run hitting exhibition that The Babe participated in. Here's how the *New York Times'* Roscoe McGowen described it. "The great George Herman Ruth proved that he still is the 'Sultan of Swat.' In the long-distance hitting contest before the first game, Babe topped all competitors with a drive of 430 feet, the ball landing in the second car tracks on Grand Avenue. Medwick was second with a clout of 425 feet over the leftfield barrier into Sullivan Avenue. Ruth got $50 and Medwick $25."

While the sight of The Babe in the first base coaching box and pre-game home run hitting contests thrilled fans and players alike, it didn't thrill the Dodgers' cantankerous manager, Burleigh Grimes. He hated it, in fact. Grimes, a great pitcher for 19 years in the big leagues, was in his second year as Brooklyn manager, trying desperately to turn around the Dodgers' long-time losing tendencies. But Larry McPhail had joined the Dodger fold in 1938, and he could see right away that Grimes was not going to turn around Brooklyn's losing ways any time soon. So, in lieu of wins, McPhail brought Ruth in as a gate attraction despite Grimes' objections, and Burleigh would fume as he watched The Babe's attention wander when he was supposed to be coaching up base-runners.

Grimes was the last of the legal spitballers to still be in the big leagues when he played his final season in 1934. He was just a 23-year old kid when the spitball was outlawed in 1920, but baseball grandfathered in a list of guys who relied the pitch — and Grimes was one of them. That meant he could continue to legally throw the spitter for as long as he was in the majors. Fortunately for me, Grimes was with the Cardinals when he began his final season in '34, and that gave me an opportunity to watch him pitch during spring training before I was sent down to the minors when camp broke. As I watched him work in exhibition games, I was gald that I didn't have to hit off him. When on the mound, Grimes looked every bit as mean as I'd heard he was. I could tell that he was really tough. If a fellow got a hit off him, he'd better be on his toes in his next at-bat. I saw him throw his famous spitter many times that spring, but he also often faked like he was going to throw it, thereby keeping the hitters guessing. Mean as he was, in my opinion Grimes' 270 wins made him well deserving of his 1965 election to the Hall of Fame, and I'm glad I was lucky enough to watch him pitch and close out the spitball era.

AUGUST 2, 1938: We were swept by the Dodgers, 6-2 and 9-3, in a doubleheader at Ebbets Field on this day. I managed three hits in eight at-bats that day, but what is truly memorable is the fact that we played the first-ever game with yellow baseballs. Larry McPhail got the idea from some professor that yellow baseballs would be an improvement over white baseballs because they were easier to see. In recording the historic occasion, Roscoe McGowen wrote, "Round Freddy Fitzsimmons gained his long delayed fifth victory in the opener, shutting out the Cards until the 7th when Johnny Mize hit the first yellow-ball home run of the majors into Bedford Avenue for his 15th of the season. Jimmy Brown's triple and

Don Gutteridge's single gave the Gas Houser's their other tally in the 8th."

AUGUST 3, 1938: A huge crowd of 36,129 turned out at Ebbets Field on this date to watch us pull off a 10th-inning, 3-2, win over the Dodgers in a rare night game. The game was an exciting one with Pepper Martin scoring the deciding run on a Terry Moore single in the 10th. Unfortunately, my bat was not a part of the game's excitement as I was shut down by Brooklyn's pitching tandem of Bill Posedel and Vito Tamulis. I did, however, enjoy some pre-game excitement as I participated in a race to determine the fastest man in the National League.

You see, at this time in the history of baseball night games were a rarity, and each club played just one night game at home and one night game on the road per year. Baseball executives were just starting to discover the drawing power of night games, so games under the lights had become big affairs. To add to the festive atmosphere of the night games, many clubs scheduled pre-game carnival-like activities. That was the case on this evening with the first activity being another long ball hitting contest between Babe Ruth and a host of challengers. Babe was off his game on this night, however, losing to Johnny Mize and Joe Medwick. Next there were some throwing exhibitions, and then the focus turned to the race to determine the N.L.'s fastest man.

Earlier in the season there had been a series of elimination races leading up to the final race held in Brooklyn on this night. I'd won my elimination race, so here I was in the finals set to run against Ernie Koy of the Dodgers, Herschel Martin of the Phillies, and Phil Cavaretta of the Cubs. Koy and I were lucky because we were already in town for our game, but Cavaretta and Martin had to come in by train just for the race. I was excited about the race and the prospect of winning the cash prize being offered. I was a little disconcerted, however, about something I'd learned just a few minutes earlier — guys were betting on the race. Our trainer, Doc Weaver, had come up to me during the home run hitting contest and said, "Let me rub your feet down, Don." I thought that was a little excessive for a simple exhibition race, so I said, "No thanks, Doc, you relax — I'm okay." Then Doc said, "No, really, Don, it's no problem. Plus, I bet $10 on you to win this race." I knew Doc wasn't making a lot of money, so $10 was a big risk for him. I wondered who else might have bet on me to win. It was at that point that the simple exhibition race started to take on a little pressure for me.

The pressure increased significantly when Lon Warneke approached me right before the race was set to begin as I was loosening up. When Lon joined the ballclub prior to the 1938 season, he informed Frankie Frisch in no uncertain terms that he wanted me and only me to be his roommate on the road. Lon and I ended up getting along real well, and I always enjoyed his company. Lon bent his long, rangy body down to me as I was stretching and said, "You'd better run like as hell because I just bet BOTH our meal monies — and then some — on you to win this race!" I snapped my head up at him and said, "You did WHAT?" He said I was gone when the traveling secretary stopped by our room to give us our meal money, so he accepted for the both of us — and then proceeded to lay it all on me to win. "Don't worry — I've got confidence in you," Lon added, "but you'd better run like hell."

They'd marked off a makeshift track about 80 yards long, starting in right-field and ending in left. As we lined up and took our "ready" stances, I could see Lon near the finish line. I guess he positioned himself there for incentive purposes. Here's how *New York Times* sportswriter Louis Effrat described the race — "Don Gutteridge won the 80-yard dash to determine the National League sprint champion. Gutteridge closed with a tremendous burst of speed to win going away from Ernie Koy of the Dodgers, Herschel Martin of the Phils, and Phil Cavaretta of the Cubs in 0:08.2. A $200 prize went with the title. Arky Vaughan of the Pirates and Tuck Stainback, who had qualified earlier in the season, withdrew from the final. The judges were Joe McCluskey and Archie San Romani." That burst of speed that Effrat described came from my 6-foot 2-inch 185-pound incentive at the finish line. I was lagging at the halfway point when I looked up and saw a slight look of concern on Lon's face. I then thought about starving because of no meal money, and I also thought about Doc Weaver losing his ten bucks. So I turned on the jets, and was very relieved when I came out the winner. It was quite an honor to be named the National League's fastest man. I don't think I fully appreciated it until later in life, though. What was most impressive to me at the time was the $200 cash prize. That was a lot of money in the depression-racked United States of 1938. In fact, it was more money than I was making in an entire month with the Cardinals!

Frankie Frisch offered me congratulations — and a towel — after I won a foot race that declared me the National League's fastest man of 1938.

AUGUST 26, 1938: *Gutteridge's Triple Beats Giants, 7 to 6; Blow Gives Cardinals Game in the Ninth; Was His Second.* That was the Associated Press headline after our win at Sportsman's Park this day. And a great day it was. The AP also wrote, "Don Gutteridge's second triple of the day, with two out and a mate on first in the 9th inning, broke a deadlock and gave the Cardinals a 7-to-6 victory over the New York Giants today. Gutteridge also had a double in addition to his pair of three-baggers, and drove in a total of four runs." I wish that could have been the storyline in every game!

SEPTEMBER 2, 1938: At 59 wins and 65 losses on this day, we had long ago been knocked out of the pennant picture. But we did still have plenty to say about what other ballclub might win the '38 flag, and on this day the Pirates were leading the race with the Reds and the Cubs fast approaching from behind. Then we won an 11-10 slugfest, cutting the Pirate lead to 6-1/2 games. I had a field day in this one as described by the Associated Press. "Paced by Don Gutteridge, whose home run, triple, and single drove in five runs, the Cardinals landed on Cy Blanton and Joe Bowman in the 4th, 5th, and 6th innings to score all their runs. Gutteridge enjoyed himself. An error, Gutteridge's single, Jim Brown's triple, and Mickey Owen's hit scored three in the 4th. Singles by Stu Martin, Don Padgett, Joe Medwick, Johnny Mize, and Brown, and Gutteridge's triple brought five home in the 5th. And, in the 6th, after Medwick and Mize had singled, Gutteridge hit his homer inside the park." That was my ninth, and final, home run of 1938, and it truly was a game worth remembering for me.

SEPTEMBER 14, 1938: Slowed by an injury, I didn't see much action in the month of September and was completely out of the line-up from September 5th through September 21st. This was a sad day for another reason, though — our skipper, Frankie Frisch, had been fired the day before. It's a fact of life as a big league manager — no matter how great you are, you WILL be fired. Still, it was particularly sad for me because Frankie was the one who had welcomed me to the majors so enthusiastically just a few years earlier. Mike Gonzales was named manager on an interim basis, and I was happy for Mike, but it was tough to see Frankie go. From my vantage point on the bench I watched the ballclub ease the pain of the transition by sweeping a doubleheader for Mike's managerial debut — 12-9 and 3-2 wins over the Phillies at Shibe Park. The second game was particularly interesting because it marked the first time that our rookie pitcher, Mort Cooper, won a big league game. We were happy to have Mort with us for the end of the season. He was quite a talent and had turned in a great year in the Texas League before joining us, leading that league in strikeouts. Our game this day was his first start in the majors and he came up big, giving a glimpse of his future greatness by pitching a beautiful 3-hit gem. He even picked up his first career hit.

As for Frankie, it really was tough to see him go. He was already a baseball legend by the time I first started having contact with him in the mid-1930s. He'd had an incredible run with the New York Giants from 1919 through 1926. He'd joined the Giants right out of Fordham University where he was a multi-sport star. His adventures in collegiate athletics at Fordham had earned him the nickname "The Fordham Flash" because of his great speed. In the big leagues, Frankie learned his rollicking style of play from his Giants manager, John McGraw —perhaps the most famous of all time when it came to embodying the "rough-and-tumble" style. Frankie was dealt to the St. Louis Cardinals in 1927 where he starred for the Cardinals as their regular second baseman through 1935. He led the Cards by example, playing his hard-nosed style day in and day out. The Frisch-led Cardinals made it to the 1928 World Series where they lost to his former team, the New York Giants. The Cardinals returned to the Series in 1930, but this time lost to the Philadelphia Athletics. Frankie and the Cardinals were back in the World Series in 1931, coming out on top this time as they knocked off the A's in a rematch of the 1930 Series.

The 1931 World Series was my first real close-up exposure to the Cardinals, and their style completely captivated me. After seeing the '31 Series in person, I officially wanted to be a big league ballplayer with the St. Louis Cardinals. As a kid my favorite team was the New York Yankees. Even in my far away hometown of Pittsburg, Kansas, it was the New York Yankees that you heard about more than any other ballclub. For that reason, I learned all about them and I became a big admirer of Lou Gehrig. To me, he was the best player in baseball because he was great in all facets of the game — not to mention his reputation as a wonderful person. But the 1931 World Series brought an end to my relationship with the Yankees — converting me, instead, to a Cardinals fan. As soon as it was determined that the Cards were going to play the A's in the '31 World Series, my good friend, John Rottenberry, said, "Don, let's go to the World Series when it comes to St. Louis. I'll buy the gas if you drive there."

My dad gave us the go-ahead, so John and I piled into my father's Model-A Ford and drove all the way from Pittsburg to St. Louis in one night. We arrived at 6:00 in the morning, without any tickets, but we got in line and ended up getting seats in the bleachers. It was amazing to see the Cardinals in person, especially Pepper Martin who really had an incredible Series, but it was Frankie Frisch who was the heart and soul of the Cardinals. The image of Pepper Martin executing one of his famous head-first dives has really come to symbolize the Gas House Gang, but it was actually Frankie who taught Pepper how to do it. In a final acknowledgement of Frankie's importance to the Gas Housers, he was finally handed the managerial reins midway through the 1933 season. He continued to lead by example, and got the Cards back into the Series in 1934. That was a great year for the club, culminating in a legendary Series win over the Detroit Tigers — and it was that season that saw the team begin to be referred to as "The Gas House Gang." The Gas House district was a very rough section of the lower East Side of Manhattan, an area once known for its several large gas tanks — and its notorious Gas House Gangs. In applying the "Gas House Gang" nickname to the Cardinals, it was meant to symbolize the ballclub's rowdy, go-for-broke style of play — a style that Frankie instilled in the team.

Still in awe of the St. Louis Cardinals as we drove back to Pittsburg following our World Series adventure of 1931, I looked at my pal and let him in on the epiphany I'd had, saying, "John, one of these day I'm gonna play major league baseball." Being a true friend, John supported my dream by saying, "I hope you do, Don," adding, "I think you can do it!" Just three short years later I was amazed to find myself face to face with the seminal figure of the Gas House Gang — Frankie Frisch. It was the spring of 1934 and the Cardinals had invited me to attend spring training with them following a good season I'd had with Lincoln in 1933. In the brief time since John and I had made our trek to the 1931 World Series, things had broke well for me as far as my dream of playing big league ball was concerned. I had been playing in the Old City League back home in Pittsburg when a scout named Joe Becker signed me to play for the Lincoln Links of the Nebraska State League. I joined them in August of 1932 and returned there for the 1933 season. The depression was hard on the Nebraska State League, however, and it was about to go belly-up when a few folks stepped in with some money to keep it afloat. One of those folks was Branch Rickey, the general manager of the St. Louis Cardinals. He never did anything without getting something in return, and what he got for his investment was eight Nebraska State League players. I was one of them, so that's how I became property of the St. Louis Cardinals in August of 1933.

Here I am in two of my minor league stops prior to joining the Cardinals on the big league stage in 1936 — the Lincoln Links of the Nebraska State League and the Houston Buffs of the Texas League.

So, in what seemed like the blink of an eye, I went from wide-eyed kid admirer of the St. Louis Cardinals in 1931 to wide-eyed rookie rubbing elbows with my heroes at Cards spring training of 1934. I learned a lot from Frankie during that spring, and he offered encouragement when informing me that I was being sent back down to the minors for more seasoning when camp broke. They dispatched me to Houston of the Texas League and I turned in another good season, so I was rewarded with a September call-up to the Cardinals. That brought me back under the wing of Frankie. The Cardinals were in a dogfight with the New York Giants for the National League pennant, so Frankie told me, "Don, I want you to sit and observe. When the pennant is settled, I'm gonna let you play." So I did what Frankie said — I sat and watched, sat and watched, sat and watched. As luck would have it, the Cards didn't lock up the pennant until the last day of the season, so I never got in a game. I didn't even get to see the club play in the World Series because I was added to the roster after the September 1st cut-off, so I was just sent home. It was frustrating, but Frankie kept my spirits up by telling me that one day my chance would come.

1935 was pretty much the same story for me as 1934. I went to spring training with the Cardinals, watched and learned from Frankie, but was then sent back down to the minors when camp broke. Frankie again offered encouragement, saying, "You'll sit on the bench too much up here with the Cardinals, Don. You're talented, but you need to go back down to Triple-A to get more work in. Go down there and continue to work hard — we'll call you when we need you." So I again did what Frankie told me. This time I went down to Columbus of the American Association where I continued to improve, batting

Opening day of the 1935 season with the Columbus Redbirds, my third and final minor league stop before joining the Cardinals in the big leagues at the end of the 1936 season. My big old grin gives me away — not even a little snow could dampen my enthusiasm for opening a new baseball season.

.291 with 63 RBIs and six home runs on the season. Just as Frankie had promised, they called me back up at the end of the season. But, just as in 1934, the Cards were fighting to win another N.L. pennant, this time against the Cubs. On the surface I waited patiently for my opportunity to play, but inside I was chomping at the bit to get in there and help the club win a pennant. But, again, I would fail to get into a game as the season went down to the wire with the Cubs taking the flag. Frankie seemed genuinely sorry that he had not gotten a chance to play me, but he explained the difficulties involved with trying to balance the effort to win the pennant with the need do get experience for the call-ups — the pennant was THE priority. But he again offered words of encouragement and told me to keep plugging away, saying, "Your time is coming, Don."

I again went to spring training with St. Louis in 1936, but this time things were a little different — I was not sent down when camp broke. Frankie told me that I had made the club, and I was thrilled. I worked tirelessly at practice, always hustling, but by late-May I had still yet to get into a game. Soon thereafter, roster cut-down day arrived, and Frankie told me they were sending me back down to Columbus so I could get work until they needed me. I could have been disappointed because it sounded like the same old song and dance, but I wasn't upset. I believed Frankie when he said my time was coming. I felt myself getting closer and closer, so I took him at his word. I went back down to Columbus and gave it everything I had. My 1936 season at Columbus turned out to be the best season I ever had in the minors. I worked hard on defense, stole bases, and hit the ball very well, ending the campaign at .298 with 11 homers and 99 driven in. The Cardinals brought me up again in September, and they were, once again — as you now know from reading my account of September of 1936 — still alive in the race for the 1936 pennant. Where things truly differed this season, however, was that Frankie now viewed me as someone who could HELP him win the pennant instead of seeing me as a kid whom he needed to get some experience. And, as you also know from reading about September of 1936, Frankie let me play — and I turned in one of the best months of my entire big league career.

So I will always have fond recollections of Frankie Frisch because he eased me into the majors in a way that ensured I was ready to succeed. That's why I was sad to see him fired as this 1938 season neared its end. Frankie forever sealed himself a place close to my heart when, after seeing me have my first big day with the Cards back in 1936, he told a reporter, "Did you see that kid? He belongs on this team. He's really a Gas Houser!" Nicer words could never be spoken about me. Frankie built his Gas House Gang with rough and tumble players like himself because those were the types of players he needed to be a successful manager. I was honored that he saw me as one of those types. He wanted me — and all of his players — to play hard for him. And I wanted to play hard for him, so we were a good match. It was a great thrill to play for Frankie Frisch.

OCTOBER 1, 1938: *CUBS WIN; NOW FOR YANKEES!* That was the giant-sized headline in the *Chicago Tribune* following our doubleheader split with the Cubs at Sportsman's Park on this day. We had been mathematically eliminated from the pennant race quite some time ago, so all we were playing for on this day was our pride. We were simply hoping to win both ends of the twin bill to prevent the Cubs from clinching the pennant on our time and on our home turf. We took care of business in the opener, winning, 4-3, behind Bob Weiland, and I was happy to have tallied a couple hits in support of Lefty. The nightcap didn't work out so well, however. 40-year old Charley Root, the longtime Cubs right-hand pitcher, was not to be denied. Root, still stinging from the stigma hung on him since he'd served up Babe Ruth's "called shot" back in the 1932 World Series, pitched like a man on a mission. His mission was to get his ballclub back into the Series, and he accomplished that by going the distance against us in this game. He got the win, a 10-3 romp, and his victory clinched the National League flag for the Cubs.

I singled in one at-bat against Root in our loss, but that was the last thing I was thinking about as I saw the Cubs take to a joyous celebration following the last out of the game — a pop-up to Billy Jurges at shortstop. As soon as the ball was secured in Jurges' glove, all the Cubs players took off for the mound. Once there, Jurges handed Root the ball, and then the players lifted Charley on their shoulders for the victorious trip to their clubhouse. No, I wasn't thinking about my 1-for-4 — I was, instead, thinking about how discouraging it felt to again have played below our expectations as a team. After challenging for the pennant and finishing 2nd in 1936, we'd slipped to 4th in 1937, and were destined to finish a distant 6th in 1938. As individuals, we were all having good years, but our good individual seasons weren't translating to good years for the TEAM. Instead of winning an N.L. championship — something we were sure we'd do following our close call in 1936 — we were definitely going in the wrong direction, and it made for a great deal of uncertainty about the future.

OCTOBER 2, 1938: We shut the door on the 1938 season with a 7-5 win over the Cubs in St. Louis. I was 0-for-4, unable to do anything against Chicago pitchers Larry French and Al Epperly. It was somewhat of a hollow victory for us because there was nothing on the line, but I still ALWAYS wanted to win. It's easy to point at ourselves as the sole reason why we failed to win a pennant in 1936, '37 and '38, but let me give credit where credit is due — there were some great teams in baseball at that time. The Giants were an excellent team and really earned their pennants in 1936 and '37. The Cubs, on the other hand, weren't as talented as the '36 and '37 Giants, but they were real fighters in 1938. They came on very strong at the end of the season, taking over Pittsburgh and fending off a challenge by Cincinnati. Still, they were no match for the mighty New York Yankees who swept them in the World Series.

1939

APRIL 18, 1939: On this day, for the first time in my big league career, we opened a new campaign WITHOUT Frankie Frisch as our leader. Frankie, after being fired on September 13th of 1938, had been replaced by Mike Gonzales for the last 16 games of the season. But instead of keeping Mike as manager for 1939, management opted to go with Ray Blades. Ray had been a player with the Cardinals for 10 years from 1922-32, with three really fine seasons as a regular from 1924-26. Most recently he had managed the Rochester Red Wings in 1938. We made Ray's managerial debut a happy one when we played well and beat the Pirates, 6-2, at Forbes Field. I hit out of the number two spot that day and played third base. It's always good to start the season on the right foot as a team as well as on an individual basis. Our victory assured that the team did, in fact, get off on the right foot. I was 2-for-5 with a stolen base and a run scored — not a bad way to kick off the new campaign.

APRIL 23, 1939: We returned to St. Louis following our opening day win in Pittsburgh. Once back home, the Cubs came to town for a 3-game series at Sportsman's Park. We'd split the first two games of the set and were hoping to take the rubber match on this day, but to do so we were relying heavily on the troubled right arm of Dizzy Dean's younger brother, Paul. I'd first met Paul at Cardinals spring training back in 1934, but I got to know him a little better when I was recalled in September of that season. Paul was a rookie sensation with the Cards that year, on his way to a 19-win season at the tender young age of 20. When Paul first joined the team, Dizzy, confident in their ability, bragged, "Me and Paul will win 45 games." As usual, people thought Diz was crazy, but the two of them went on to win a combined 49 games that season. Being with the team that September, I was fortunate to witness Paul pitch a no-hitter against the Dodgers at Ebbets Field on September 21st — right in the midst of a heated pennant race. It came in the nightcap of a doubleheader. The funny thing is that Dizzy had pitched a 3-hit shutout in the opener. After the game he told reporters, "I wished I'd have known Paul was gonna pitch a no-hitter — in that case I'd have pitched one, too!" Diz and Paul each won two games in the '34 World Series.

Paul had another fine season in 1935, again winning 19 games, but his career took a turn for the worse in 1936. His trouble started when he decided to hold out for more money — just like his big brother was doing. With spring training almost over, Paul finally signed. He then tried to rush himself into shape and hurt his shoulder by going too hard too fast. His '36 season was a disaster, his win total dropping to just five. He had surgery in 1937 — a move of total desperation in that archaic era of orthopedic surgery — and missed the entire season except for one lone appearance. He made an ill-fated comeback attempt in 1938, but his shoulder was still not right and he appeared in just five games. Now he was trying another comeback, hoping beyond all hope that the offseason of rest may have healed his bad shoulder. We were all hoping Paul's trouble was behind him, too — for his sake and the sake of the ballclub.

It wasn't easy being the brother of Dizzy Dean, a guy with as much charisma as anyone who ever played the game, but Paul loved Diz and really looked up to him. Paul was almost the polar opposite of Dizzy. He was somewhat shy and serious, and didn't have much to say. He stayed in Diz's shadow, just nodding and smiling at everything. The sportswriters nicknamed him "Daffy," partly because it sounded good with "Dizzy," but also because of his way of just smiling and nodding. Paul wasn't daffy, though — I just think he was self-conscious. He was not very well educated, and I think that's why he hung in the background. He didn't want to say something that might make him look ignorant. I liked him, and he was a real gentleman. While Paul liked to see all the crazy things that his big brother would do, he, himself, didn't indulge in that behavior.

Unfortunately, Paul's comeback bid took a quick hit in our game on this day. He was knocked out of the box in the 4th inning when the Cubs got to him for five hits and four runs. I chipped in one single in five at-bats as we clawed our way back into the game, but our 2-run 8th-inning rally came up one run short as we lost, 6-5. Paul started just one more game for us in 1939, but the shoulder just wouldn't respond. He was sent to the bullpen to try and work it out, but it never came around. He was gone from the Cardinals after the season, off to try equally futile comeback attempts with the 1940-41 New York Giants and the 1943 St. Louis Browns.

MAY 2, 1939: Our rookie right-hander, Bob Bowman, turned in 8-2/3 innings of tremendous pitching. Lon Warneke got the last out for Bob as we defeated the first-place Bees, 2-1, in Boston. It was Bob's first career win. He would turn in a fine rookie season for us, winning 13 games with an ERA well under 3.00. I'm proud to have helped in getting him that first victory by scoring the game-winning run in the 9th inning. It wasn't a big home run or anything dramatic like that, just baseball the way it was meant to be played. Here's how the Associated Press recorded it. *Cards Halt Bees as Bowman Stars,* was the headline. The sub-head added, *Triumph by 2-1 with Rookie Hurler Displaying Unusual Ability in Pinches; Winning Run In 9th; Gutteridge Reaches Home On Moore's Sacrifice Fly.* The text summed up our go-ahead run this way, "The winning tally was built on Don Gutteridge's safety, a fielder's choice, Ducky Medwick's bunt, and Terry Moore's sacrifice fly." Nowadays that style of play is sometimes referred to as "small ball," but back then it was just good, fundamental baseball.

MAY 4, 1939: We opened a 3-game series against the New York Giants at the Polo Grounds on this day. The series-opener was a forgettable one as my room-mate made the *New York Times* sportspage with this dubious headline — *LON WARNEKE SHELLED BY GIANT BATS, 6-3.* I wasn't much help to him, either, as I was held to 1-for-5 on the day by Giants right-hander Manny Salvo. As I said, this game is, for the most part, forgettable — unless you're Manny Salvo. For Lon and me, however, the game was worth remembering only because of the events of the day BEFORE.

Prior to our game against the Bees in Boston two days earlier, Lon and I were walking around downtown, just killing time. We stopped off at a second-hand bookstore to thumb through some books, and Lon ended up buying an old book from 1932 entitled *Twenty Thousand Years in Sing Sing* by a fellow named Lewis E. Lawes. Later that night, after the ballgame, we were sitting in our hotel room, silently reading. Lon, steadily chewing his tobacco as he flipped through page after page of his prison tome, finally stopped reading long enough to tell me that this fellow, Lawes, was the Warden at Sing Sing Correctional Facility, the notorious maximum security prison in Ossining, New York. Then Lon said, "We ought to go to Sing Sing, Don. I'd like to see the place that this book is about."

I wasn't crazy about the idea of going to visit a prison, especially one with the hardened reputation of Sing Sing, but I said, "Well, hell, Lon, just call the guy up and find out what we need to do." I thought the work involved in set-

Lon Warneke had been an outstanding pitcher with the Chicago Cubs for many years before he joined the Cardinals in 1937. We became the best of friends soon after his arrival in St. Louis, and I quickly found out that he was not only an outstanding pitcher — he was an outstanding prankster, too.

ting it up might be just enough to make Lon forget the whole thing, but much to my surprise he picked up the telephone and started making calls. Moments later he was speaking to Warden Lewis E. Lawes himself! "Hey, I'm Lon Warneke of the St. Louis Cardinals," Lon told Lawes, "and I've been reading your book. We have an off day tomorrow before we begin a series in New York on Thursday, and I would like to come by and visit you." Lawes was, of course, thrilled at the prospect of meeting a big league ballplayer — especially one of Lon's stature, so he set the whole thing up. Lon rounded up Stu Martin and Jimmy Brown to accompany us on our trip to Sing Sing. The next morning the four of us boarded a train for New York. A special stop was made for us in Ossining where an old rickety bus was waiting to pick us up. We piled into the bus, which then pulled away for our drive to the prison. The old bus stopped in front of the main entrance as we waited for the guards to open the gates to let us in. The place was an ominous sight, gray and massive as it sat there on the banks of the Hudson River. I have to admit that I had second thoughts about our visit after we pulled through the entrance and I heard those heavy gates slam shut behind us.

I soon felt different, however, after meeting Warden Lawes. He was a very genial man, and he really made us feel at ease. Still, I felt some uncertainty when he declared "all open cells," at which point the prisoners were let into the playgrounds. There were plenty of armed guards everywhere, but I couldn't help but think that a lot of bodily harm could be done if these prisoners should pick THIS moment to whip up a disturbance. But, again, I was put at ease when the prisoners swarmed around us with only the best of behavior. They followed us around and talked to us. Some would say, "Come here, I wanna show you my cell." It turned out that many of the prisoners had decorated their cells for us in anticipation of our visit. We had lunch with them, walked the grounds with them, played catch with them, and just chatted. It was a very positive experience for everyone involved.

Before we left, one of the guards asked Lon if he wanted to see death row. When that guard mentioned "death row" — snap — all the prisoners within earshot stopped dead, if you'll pardon the expression, in their tracks. That's where the fun ended for them, so we went off with the guard to see the place where many a story about condemned men were, in fact, a reality. We went to the death cell where "Old Sparky" sat — Sing Sing's infamous electric chair. It was very depressing to see that chair and think about what went on there. Lon, not being one to get caught up in a heavy moment like that, said, "Hey, Don — why don't you sit in that chair and see how it feels?" He was just trying to agitate me, so being the big shot that I wanted to appear to be — I went up and sat in the chair. The minute my backside hit the seat of that chair — CLICK — the lights in the room went off! I jumped out of that chair so fast that I nearly hit the ceiling! I hadn't noticed it, but while I was cooly strolling up to the chair, Lon had sneaked over to the light switch and snapped it OFF as soon as I sat down. Everyone laughed, including me as soon as my heart returned to normal. That's the type of funny thing Lon would always do. I have to admit, he was truly a funny guy — even when the laughs came at my expense. After that we headed back to our bus for our return trip to the train station. It was a little scary going in there, but it turned out to be a real good day. They thanked us for coming, and we said our goodbyes. Then we boarded the train for Harlem, leaving Sing Sing behind forever.

MAY 9, 1939: Brooklyn was looking much improved early in the 1939 campaign, and they would, in fact, continue to improve throughout the season, right into the decades of the 1940s and 1950s. Leo Durocher had been elevated to the role of player/manager, and he deserved some of the credit for their turnaround. But on this day we probably added a few gray hairs to Leo's balding head as we romped over his ballclub, 13-1, at Ebbets Field. I did my share of romping, too, collecting three hits in five at-bats — two doubles, a triple and two RBIs. Leo, who had mentored me when I first came up, might have been proud of me — had my success not come at the expense of his Dodgers!

MAY 20, 1939: I touched Brooklyn's Ira Hutchinson for my first home run of the season, a 2-run 5th-inning blow in a 9-1 win at Sportsman's Park on this day. I already had two RBIs after I'd pushed a couple across in the 1st inning when I looped one just out of the reach of Dodgers second baseman Pete Coscarart. Lon Warneke got the win for us, continuing the great pitching he'd been regularly turning in. It was Lon's third straight win, and his fifth of the young season.

MAY 23, 1939: Fiddler Bill McGee, making his first start of the season, scattered six hits while pitching us to our fifth consecutive win — a 6-1 victory over the Phillies in St. Louis on this day. We were leading, 4-2, when we put the game out of reach with two runs in the 8th. I was on first and Joe Medwick was on second when Enos Slaughter singled to Phils leftfielder Morrie Arnovich. Despite the fact that he wasn't the speediest of base-runners, Medwick was an easy bet to score on the drive. It was doubtful that I would be able to score all the way from first on the play, but when Arnovich fumbled the ball I just kept on going right around third base. I was running so fast that I nearly caught Medwick, but we both slid home safely in a cloud of Sportsman's Park dust.

MAY 25, 1939: Already leading the game by a slim 2-1 margin, we sealed the deal with a 5-run 7th and downed the Bees, 7-1, in St. Louis on this day. It was our seventh consecutive victory. The win allowed us to maintain our slim 1st-place lead over the only other team in the league that was hotter than us — the Cincinnati Reds. They owned a 10-game winning streak. They would come to Sportsman's Park the next day, so someone's streak was going to have to give. Unfortunately, it was ours. But we enjoyed ourselves in the meantime on this day, having our way with Boston pitchers Jim Turner, Johnny Lanning, and Bill

Posedel. I got in on the 7th-inning barrage with a double off Turner, and then scored on a single by Mickey Owen.

This action is from our game against the Phillies on May 23rd, 1939. I was on second base and Joe Medwick was on third when Enos Slaughter singled, driving in both of us. Ducky had to stay at third until he was sure Enos' drive would fall in safely, so I was right behind him by the time he slid across the plate. I still remember him redirecting my feet with his hands so he wouldn't get spiked. This photo has always been a favorite of mine because to me it captures the energy, hustle, and action of the Gas House Gang. Incidentally, the on-deck batter signaling us to slide is Mickey Owen; the Phils catcher is Virgil Davis; the bat boy is Pete Peters; and the umpire is George Barr.

MAY 29, 1939: Not a good day for us as we lost to the Pirates, 7-0, at Sportsman's Park. About all the Cardinals fans had to cheer was rare play that unfolded in the first inning. Unfortunately, it happened so fast that a great deal of them had yet to find their seats before it was over. The Associated Press wrote, "The Cardinals executed the first triple play in the majors this season in the 1st inning. With runners on first and second, Johnny Rizzo smashed a hard grounder to Don Gutteridge, who touched third, then threw to Stu Martin, forcing the man at second, and Martin's throw to first caught Rizzo."

MAY 30, 1939: Hitting into a triple play can weigh heavily on one's mind. Pittsburgh leftfielder Johnny Rizzo came up with the perfect way to put it behind him, though. We played a doubleheader against the Pirates the day after Rizzo hit into his triple play. We won the opener, but Rizzo went on a rampage in the second game that ensured that his ballclub would not lose again. It also ensured that the memory of his triple play would be erased. Here's how the papers described his heroics. "The Pirates came from behind to conquer St. Louis, 14 to 8, in the second game of today's doubleheader. Johnny Rizzo took a quick glance at the scoreboard and saw the Pirates were trailing, 7 to 1, in the 5th. He went to work and single-handedly drove in nine runs. He hit two homers, one coming with two mates on and the other with one aboard. In all, he connected safely five of the six times he stepped to the plate in the nightcap." As far as I know, Rizzo's nine RBIs in one game is still a Pirate franchise record.

JUNE 2, 1939: The newspapers seemed to spend the bulk of their reporting recounting hitting and pitching, but occasionally they would turn their attention to the efforts of the fielders. There was lots of good pitching and hitting to write about in our 8-2 loss to the Giants at the Polo Grounds, but on this day there was some fine glovework, too. Here's what the *New York Times'* Arthur J. Daley wrote — *FIELDING GEMS BRIGHTEN GAME.* "There were some gorgeous fielding plays in this engagement. Among the more sensational ones were two catches by Pepper Martin, one near the bullpen in right and the other back of shortstop, on successive batters. Don Gutteridge made two dazzling stops, also in succession, and, wonder of wonders, there was a gaudy stop and throw by none other than Bonura." See, sometimes even the writers' compliments were seasoned with a dash of sarcasm, this time directed at poor old Zeke Bonura, the Giants' big first baseman.

JUNE 14, 1939: Suffering from a little bit of a hitting slump for the previous couple of weeks, Ray Blades sat me out of the starting line-up for this day's game against the Dodgers at Sportsman's Park. I got in the game late as a defensive substitute, but had no official at-bats as we won, 9-2. It's tough to keep your spirits up when you're slumping, but, then again, with the cast of characters I played with on the Cardinals, it was hard to be down spirited. Here's a good example of why we had so much fun, this particular activity taking place before our game with Brooklyn. Roscoe McGowen of the *New York Times* reported it this way — "Don Gutteridge, Mickey Owen, Bob Bowman and Pepper Martin gave the crowd its biggest laugh when they appropriated an old-fashioned four-seated bicycle from its costumed riders and pedaled furiously around the field. Lon Warneke and Mort Cooper followed them on a more modern-looking tandem machine." The "costumed riders" from whom we took the bike were part of pre-game Flag Day festivities, and if they'd have known that Pepper Martin would be up to his usual tricks they might have opted NOT to come to the ballpark that day!

Pepper Martin couldn't resist the urge to insert himself into the pre-game Flag Day festivities that took place at Sportsman's Park on June 14th, 1939. After confiscating an old-fashioned bicycle from some costumed performers, Pepper (far right) enlisted the help of me, Mickey Owen, and Bob Bowman (left to right) to help him drive it.

JUNE 18, 1939: We broke the Giants' 9-game winning streak by beating them, 8-4, at Sportsman's Park. I contributed modestly to our win by going 1-for-4 with a double and an RBI, as well as scoring once run myself. This day was particularly interesting, however, because it was "Pepper Martin Day." Pepper was out of action due to a fractured wrist suffered a few days earlier in one of his patented head-first slides, but that didn't stop him from enjoying the festivities commemorating his great career. Here's how John Drebinger of the *New York Times* described the spectacle — "In honoring Martin, the home folks had decided to forget the customary luggage, fountain pens and wrist watches and give Pepper something useful. Pepper's friends from Oklahoma City and other points moved to home plate a marvelous assortment of farming implements and livestock. Among other gifts there were two brood mares, a sow with her litter, a heifer, two milch cows, a beagle hound, rabbits, chickens, a huge tractor, a plow, cultivator, hay rake, electric grindstone and churn, and a double set of harness.

Lon Warneke, Farmer Martin's teammate, had something to say presenting the hogs, while Carl Hubbell acted as official bearer of a 2,500-word telegram from Oklahoma City admirers of the Wild Horse of the Osage. Martin, highly elated, made a speech of acceptance and finally showed the fans how much he appreciated everything by driving the tractor out of the arena as if it were a Roman chariot." It was great, a true sign of the times as they were nearly 70 years ago. It's impossible to imagine a scene like that happening nowadays.

As is evident to anyone who reads this book, Pepper was a world class prankster, but I hope my stories about his crazy antics do not detract from the fact that he was a very good baseball player. While he does not have Hall of Fame numbers, Pepper's legend is, nonetheless, as well-known as many of the men enshrined at Cooperstown. He was my baseball hero from the time I was 19 years old in 1931 when I diligently followed all of his on-field exploits in his first big season with the Cardinals. He topped off that great season by running amok against the Athletics as the Cards won the '31 World Series, beating Philadelphia in seven games. Pepper collected 12 hits in that series, setting a new Series record. He ran and dove everywhere, swiping bases and really taking the A's out of their game. He simply dominated Philadelphia. That's why I HAD to go see him in person when the Cardinals made it back to the Series in 1934. As I stood in a long line waiting to enter Sportsman's Park, a man came by selling a very unique pin. It was a ribbon with a little red pepper on it, custom-made to celebrate the greatness of Pepper Martin. They cost 50¢ each, and that was a lot of money to me back then, but Pepper was my favorite player so I bought one and proudly pinned it on. Pepper did not disappoint once the game began. In fact, he was great. He was again the sparkplug to victory for the Gas House Gang, collecting 11 hits as he led the Cards to another World Series title, this time beating the Detroit Tigers in seven games.

Pepper was a very good all-around ballplayer. He was reliable on defense and had a good arm. He was an above average centerfielder for his first few years with the Cardinals, then made a successful conversion to third base to make room for Joe Medwick in 1932. Pepper was very fast, his speed and daring on the basepaths helping him to three N.L. stolen base titles. He was a good hitter, too, and always seemed to be near .300 in hitting. He played heads-up baseball and kept you on your toes whether you were an opponent or a teammate. Pepper was the personification of hustle and enthusiasm on the ballfield. I witnessed many examples of this, but none better than an incident often told by Andy High, one of Pepper's teammates before I came along. High used to tell of a play where Pepper stole second, sliding in so hard that he took out the second baseman and knocked the ball into centerfield. Pepper then got up and took off for third where he again hit the dirt. The play caused the ball to roll away from the third baseman, so Pepper scrambled to his feet and bolted for home where he crashed into the catcher, knocking the ball loose and scoring. Entering the dugout covered in dirt, mud, sweat, and a wide grin, Pepper said, "This is real fun!" That was Pepper Martin all the way. His rough and tumble style was fun to watch, but it was not conducive to a long career and it often got him injured.

Pepper was only about 5-foot 8-inches tall and about 170 pounds, but he was a strapping guy. He had a broad chest and shoulders that tapered perfectly down to about a 30-inch waist — and he was strong. He often used that strength in one of his favorite on-field activities — fighting. If Pepper was fighting, then he was having a good time. He'd moved back to the outfield by the time I joined the Cards, so he'd come sprinting in from his spot in rightfield whenever a brawl broke out. He'd grab someone by the nape of the neck, give him a quick pop and say, "Now stay back there!" Then he'd grab another guy and do the same thing. When the melee was over, Pepper would have about five guys standing in a single-file line, afraid to get back into the fight. Pepper was truly one of a kind.

JUNE 21, 1939: An 8-run explosion off Hugh Mulcahy in the 4th inning helped us cruise to an easy 14-2 win over the Phillies at Sportsman's Park on this day. In that inning I hit my second home run of the season and ended up with three RBIs on the day. Curt Davis continued to pitch great for us, going the distance and getting the win. He even chipped in three hits at the plate to help his own cause.

JULY 5, 1939: The Reds were leading the National League by five games when we opened a 2-game series with them at Crosley Field on this day. We were back a ways in third place, but hoping to make up some ground by winning at least one of the two games. Our hopes were dashed, however, when we dropped the series-opener, 6-2. Reds right-hander Bucky Walters kept us in check for the most part, although I was able to reach him for my third home run of the season. Of the home run the Associated Press wrote, "In the 5th, with two away, Don Gutteridge whaled the ball over the leftfield wall for a homer — his team's second hit." There was a scary moment in the game. It was one of those things you carried in the back of your mind, but you just accepted the risk as part of the game. Here's how the paper described it — "With one away in the 5th, right-fielder Ival Goodman beat out a tap in front of the plate and Mickey Owen's throw struck him in the back of the head just as he crossed first base. Dazed, he ran about 100 feet — into the Cards' bullpen — then collapsed. Teammates helped him from the field and he was taken to a hospital." He ended up being fine — just a mild concussion, but it was a frightening thing to see.

JULY 17, 1939: Okay, while I'm on the subject of the frightening aspects of the game, let me touch on this one — collisions. I've seen a lot of bad ones, and been involved in a few, too, but none were worse than the one I saw on this day. We were at New York to play the 2nd-place Giants in an important 3-game series. We ended up winning all three games, but they were all closely contested, hard-fought battles. But the thing everyone took away from that series was the memory of the violent collision between Giants infielder Lou Chiozza and out-fielder Joe Moore. Here's how sportswriter John Drebinger saw it — "Chiozza, crack utility player, who had been understudying the last two days for Billy Jurges at shortstop, crashed into Joe Moore while catching a short pop fly and suffered a compound fracture of the left leg below the knee. The mishap occurred on the first play of the 9th inning when Clyde Shoun, Cardinal pitcher, who had replaced Curt Davis in the 7th, lifted a fly in short left. Both Chiozza and Moore dashed for it, and though the play did not look exceptionally difficult, the two must have been mixed up on their signals. Chiozza caught the ball and held it just as Moore collided with him with terrific force. Both were knocked sprawling, and as they writhed on the grass the players of both sides rushed to their assistance. Moore, recovering in a few minutes, was able to get up and walk around, seemingly none the worse. But Chiozza remained on the ground, badly hurt, and after a brief examination by Willie Schaeffer, trainer of the Giants, a stretcher was brought out and the player carried to the clubhouse. He was taken to Polyclinic Hospital, where it was reported that Lou had broken his leg in two places. A piece of bone was sticking through the flesh as Chiozza was carried off the field." Lou was only 29 years old at the time of that collision, and he never played another big league game. He sat out the entire 1940 season before making an attempt at a comeback with the Memphis Chicks in 1941, but he never played professionally again after that. It was very unfortunate.

JULY 21, 1939: We were in Philadelphia for a doubleheader against the struggling Phillies on this day. We were hoping to better our position in the 1939 pennant race with a sweep against the last-place Phils, but that plan was abandoned when they surprised us by whipping us, 16-2, in the opener. We just weren't able to get anything going against Philadelphia right-hander Kirby Higbe. He held me to 0-for-4, although I was able to cross for one of our two meager runs. By the time we took the field for the nightcap we were just hoping to salvage a split. It was quickly apparent that young Mort Cooper would provide just the tonic we needed for a win. He looked very good, but when he got into trouble he pitched out of it like a veteran — and his reward was a complete game, 7-0 victory. After getting shut down at the plate in the opener, I felt good to contribute some offense to Mort's effort in the second game. With Joe Medwick on first base in the 2nd inning, I unloaded on one of Ike Pearson's pitches for a home run to get us on the board, 2-0. I added another hit later in the game. Our victory was Mort's sixth win of the season.

Mort was a strapping fellow, 6-foot-2 and 210 pounds. After his successful end-of-season trial with us in 1938, he was up for good in 1939. After playing with him in Columbus, I knew he was destined to do well in the majors. He had a great fastball, and, when he wasn't battling elbow problems, he would win with great regularity. His career record shows how good he was — 128 wins and only 75 losses with an ERA of 2.97. He was a 20-game winner for three straight years from 1942 through '44, and he won the National League MVP award in '42. All-Star appearances, World Series appearances — Mort did it all. It's funny, but as much as I remember all that great stuff Mort did on the pitcher's mound, there's something else that I remember just as much — the way Mort sweated. On hot days he would sweat down only one side of his body. Right down the middle of his forehead, down his nose, and continuing down to his feet. He'd be wringing wet on one side, but the other side would be completely dry. He'd be red as hell on the dry side, but there wouldn't be a drop of sweat. I always thought that was the most peculiar thing I'd ever seen. I've since come to learn that it's a condition called anhidrosis, and it can be serious because it can lead to heat stroke. Sweating is the body's way of cooling down, so lack of sweat slows the cool-down process. Nobody seemed to know anything about that back in 1939, however — we just thought it was a strange quirk of nature. Fortunately, it never seemed to adversely affect Mort during his playing days.

JULY 22, 1939: We pulled into Brooklyn for a 3-game series with the Dodgers on this day. I picked up where I had left off in Philly from the day before — continuing to hit the ball hard — although all I had to show for it at the end of the day was 1-for-4. My lone hit was a near homer off Brooklyn right-hander Luke "Hot Potato" Hamlin — a 9th-inning bullet off the Ebbets Field left-centerfield wall. It drove in a run, but it was too little too late as we lost, 7-2. I've mentioned how great it was to hear Pepper and his Mudcat Band play their music, and they were at it again before this game. *New York Times* writer Roscoe McGowen must have been spying nearby, because here's what he had to say about it in the paper after the game — "Pepper Martin, Lon Warneke, and a couple of other Mudcats were harmonizing lustily on *The Old Pine Tree* in the clubhouse fifteen minutes before game time. After the game they probably were singing *St. Louis Blues* — if anything."

JULY 23, 1939: Roscoe McGowen made no mention of any clubhouse singing after we swept the Dodgers, 12-0 and 8-2, to take the series on this day. He did make mention, however, of the fact that Larry McPhail's yellow ball made a return in the opener of the twin bill. "They played one game with the yellow ball and another with the regular white one at Ebbets Field yesterday," wrote McGowen, "but both contests might as well have been waged with a black ball as far as the Dodgers were concerned." I went 3-for-5 with two doubles and three RBIs in the yellow ball opener. Who knows — maybe McPhail was on to something with his yellow baseballs.

JULY 30, 1939: The end of the yellow ball experiment — for us, at least. The Dodgers exported Larry McPhail's yellow baseballs to St. Louis for the first game of a Sunday doubleheader at Sportsman's Park. Our home fans got to watch us knock the newfangled yellow ball around for 10 hits and a 5-2 win. I had a double in the game, adding to my new theory that maybe I did, in fact, see the darned thing better than the old white ball. We'll never know for sure, though, because the yellow ball was only used once more in a September game between the Dodgers and the Cubs. It's been nothing but white balls in the majors ever since, and, as a traditionalist, I think I kind of like it better that way.

AUGUST 3, 1939: There always seemed to be a subplot working where members of the Gas House Gang were concerned. That was definitely the case on this day when we played a doubleheader against the Boston Bees at Sportsman's Park. I guess it wasn't enough that we were fighting for our lives in the pennant race — we just had to liven things up even more with a little something extra. You may remember the story I told you about Ed Huesser and Joe Medwick's dugout fight back in 1937. As you may recall, the brawl broke out when Ed accused Joe of not giving maximum effort in the outfield. Well, that was again the theme of the issue at hand here, only this time it was our manager, Ray Blades, who was questioning Joe's effort on the field. Joe was very temperamental, and when things weren't going his way he would sometimes get disgruntled and appear to slack off. That was the situation at this time, and the issue reached a boiling point in our previous game when Ray replaced Joe in favor of Lynn King in left-field in the 9th inning of a 1-run ballgame. Ray said it was just a defensive move, but Medwick had heard the rumors that Blades was questioning his effort, and Joe blew his stack right on the spot creating a big scene. Both guys later tried to play it down, backing off somewhat from their earlier positions. "The removal of Medwick was just a tactical change for a moment which I thought might be beneficial on defense," Ray told reporters. "I think Medwick is a great player and have never thought anything else. He'll be in there every day." In his own defense, Joe said, "I have done my very best, and if I have missed a few more flies than ordinary it was not for lack of heart. I have no sore arm or sore leg excuses and I'm giving everything I have and will continue to do so. Blades is trying to manage the club as he sees it, I know."

I believe that Ray was sending a message to Joe, and Ducky got the point. He homered in his first at-bat of the doubleheader, and continued to swing the bat ferociously as we swept the twin bill that day. I chipped in three hits of my own in our winning effort. Joe continued to surge at the plate the next day, going 4-for-7 with three doubles and three RBIs as we again beat the Bees, 9-8. I think Ray Blades deserved an assist for those three wins. He was telling Medwick that we needed him to be at his best in order for our ballclub to make a run at the pennant, and Joe responded. Those three victories ran our winning streak to six and pulled us to within 9-1/2 games of 1st-place Cincinnati.

AUGUST 9, 1939: Muscles Medwick stayed hot, hitting for the circuit in our 5-3 win over the Pirates at Sportsman's Park. The victory ran our winning streak to ten straight. I got in on the long ball action, too, hitting my own round-tripper off Bucs tall right-hander Russ Bauers. The 6th-inning 2-run clout was my fifth home run of the season.

That's me touching them all on August 9th, 1939, after clubbing a 2-run home run off Pittsburgh's Russ Bauers at Sportsman's Park. The on-deck batter is our catcher, Mickey Owen. Terry Moore was on first base when I hit the homer, and he can be seen just beyond the Pirates' catcher. The bat boy is Pete Peters and the umpire is George Barr. By the way — that Pirates catcher I mentioned is my cousin, Ray Mueller, also from Pittsburg, Kansas. Our mothers were sisters. We were best buddies growing up and always played ball together, so we were really thrilled for one another when each of us made it to the big leagues. But we kept it professional here, not acknowledging each other until after the game when we would get together and catch up.

AUGUST 14, 1939: To shore up our defense in our push to catch the 1st-place Reds, the Cardinals front office bought 33-year old back-up shortstop Lyn Lary from the Dodgers. Lary was a slick fielder, but his best days were behind him. Unfortunately for me, I was the odd man out as they inserted Lary into the line-up at short and moved Pepper back to his old spot at third — and I moved to the bench. From August 18th through September 2nd, I was used almost exclusively as a pinch-hitter or pinch-runner. After being an everyday player from September of 1936 through August of 1939, it was very frustrating for me. Lary failed to hit for us and the experiment was shelved for the rest of September as I was reinserted into my starting role at third base, but the whole deal was a real eye-opener for me, foreshadowing events that would play out in 1940.

SEPTEMBER 2, 1939: There's a baseball movie that recently came out in which one of the main characters has to have a baseball bat taped to his hands to keep him from letting go of it every time he swings. I wish we had thought of that back in 1939! I've mentioned Pepper Martin's penchant for letting go of the bat — well, he was back at it on this day. The headline told the sad tale — *CARDINALS BEATEN BY PIRATES, 11 TO 3; MIZE OUT WITH INJURY; STRUCK IN SHOULDER BY FLYING BAT BEFORE CONTEST.* The text of the article explained, "Bad luck hit the Cardinals before the game started when a bat slipped from the hands of Pepper Martin and struck Johnny Mize on his already injured left shoulder. Stuart Martin had to substitute for Mize at first base." Incidentally, I was 0-for-1 as a late-game substitute for Lyn Lary at short-stop.

SEPTEMBER 3, 1939: On this day Ray Blades reinserted me into the starting line-up for what turned out to be the majority of the remainder of the season. I didn't know that yet — all I knew at the time was that it was a game-to-game, day-to-day situation. We were in Pittsburgh for a doubleheader, so I knew I would get ample opportunity to do something good to try and ensure that I'd be in the line-up again the next day. Back then you really felt like you were fighting for your job every day. We swept the Pirates, cutting the Reds' lead to just five games. I helped both causes at hand — my fight to stay in the line-up and our club's fight to stay in the pennant race — with a great game at the plate in the opener. "Joe Medwick set the pace with four hits," the Associated Press wrote, "but Don Gutteridge tripled with the bases loaded in the 1st and homered in the 3rd." I added another hit in the nightcap, so altogether it was a good effort to show Ray that I belonged in the line-up every day.

SEPTEMBER 8, 1939: *CARDINALS CRUSH THE CUBS, 10 TO 3; CONTINUE TO PRESS THE REDS AS SLAUGHTER AND GUTTERIDGE EXCEL AT BAT.* That was the headline after our game on this day at Wrigley Field. The text of the Associated Press article went on to say, "Enos Slaughter and Don Gutteridge batted St. Louis to a 10-to-3 victory over Chicago today, enabling the Cards to stay four and a half games behind the league-leading Reds. Gutteridge sent four runs home on two triples and Slaughter drove in one run and scored three himself on a double and three singles." My first triple was darn near a home run as I drove a Claude Passeau pitch off the left-centerfield wall in the 4th inning. My second triple came off Cubs right-handed reliever Gene Lillard in the 7th inning. Gene had actually broken in a few years earlier as an infielder, but was later converted to a full-time pitcher. He came over and played very briefly with us on the Cardinals in 1940.

SEPTEMBER 19, 1939: Our ballclub was really playing well lately in our pursuit of the 1st-place Reds. On this day we knocked off Leo's Bums at St. Louis. It was our 13th win in our last 16 games, and the victory cut Cincinnati's lead to just 2-1/2 games with 12 still left to play. I was held hitless on this day, but our pitcher didn't seem to need much help, anyway. The kid would be a future star with the Cardinals, but prior to that day he had yet to win in the big leagues. He showed just how bright his future was in that game, however, and Roscoe McGowen of the *New York Times* wrote about it. "Hubert Max Lanier, whose left arm is a rifle, shot down the high-flying Dodgers with five hits at Sportsman's Park today, while the Gas House Gang collected fourteen off three Brooklyn hurlers and romped away with the ballgame, 6-1. Lanier had been a victim of major league frustration for almost two seasons. Last year he lost three contests without winning one and he had dropped one this year when Bucky Walters beat him in ten innings. But the youngster now owns his first big-time triumph, with the Dodgers the victims of frustration."

SEPTEMBER 20, 1939: "Don Gutteridge hit No. 7, a long drive into the left-field seats off Hugh Casey in the 4th that tied the score at 1-1." That was Roscoe McGowen's description of my home run in the *New York Times* following our 10-4 win over the Dodgers at Sportsman's Park on this day. I had another hit, too, as well as scoring twice, but my homer turned out to be my last round-tripper of the 1939 season — and the 26th of my career.

SEPTEMBER 26, 1939: We opened up a 4-game series against the Reds with a twin bill at Crosley Field on this day. We were trailing them by 3-1/2 games, but time was running out for us. Our pennant hopes were dealt a severe blow when we failed to sweep the doubleheader, instead settling for a split in front of a huge, rowdy crowd of nearly 35,000. I was 3-for-9 in the double-feature with an RBI in the second game — I just wish I could have done more to help us win them both. We got good-enough pitching to win in the opener, but a big 3-run homer by Billy Myers off Curt Davis provided all the runs Cincinnati needed as they won, 3-1. Mort Cooper started the nightcap and really had his back against the wall. If we lost the game, that was it — the Reds would have clinched. But Mort came through with an incredible clutch outing, hurling a 4-hit shutout and getting the 6-0 win.

SEPTEMBER 27, 1939: Not to be outdone by Mort Cooper's season-saving win of the day before, Fiddler Bill McGee turned in his own 4-hit complete-game gem, again staving off elimination as we won, 4-0. Bill was great, using his blazing fastball to really dominate the Reds batters. Of the four hits they got, two were infield scratch singles — so Bill was really in control. It was an especially impressive win because it came against Bucky Walters, the Reds' ace who already had 27 wins on the season. Walters was very good himself that day, limiting our club to just seven hits. I was one of four who failed to hit him that day. But fortunately for us, Terry Moore seemed to have Bucky's number that day. Terry's two hits — one of which was his 16th home run of the season — provided all the offense we needed considering the fact that McGee was completely shutting down the Cincinnati hitters. The win bought us 24 more hours of hope, but we'd have to beat the Reds again the next day or our World Series hopes would end.

It wasn't a shocker that Terry Moore was our hero on this day. He'd been a great player with the Gas House Gang since his rookie season of 1935 when he took over for Ernie Orsatti. In that time Terry had made his name mainly because of his incredible defensive ability in centerfield, but this season he was making noise with his bat. He was having a career year, hitting near .300 and on his way to a career-high 17 homers. He was usually good for only five or six long balls a year, but he was really muscling up this year. Terry would again hit 17 homers the next season before settling back down to his normal power output, but all the while he continued to display great play in center. I think Terry was one of the best centerfielders ever — probably as good as Joe DiMaggio. Terry had no peer, however, when it came to the jump he would get on the ball. Nobody was quicker. He was so quick that it was almost detrimental to his career early on. He'd often take that first step so quick that his plant foot would slip out from under him, but once he got that issue under control he was amazing.

Aside from being able to go get 'em, Terry had a strong throwing arm and was very accurate. If a hit went out to him and a runner was coming around to third, I rarely ever had to move to take the throw. Terry had great hands, too, and he cultivated that asset in an unusual way — he'd catch balls bare-handed. Lon Warneke was a good fungo hitter, and it was his job to hit to the outfielders in practice. Lon would hit line drives out there and Terry would catch them bare-handed. He thought it made him a better ballplayer. His hands were also very strong and peculiar looking. It seemed like his thumb was set unusually far down on the base of his hand — like a gorilla's thumb! Because of that I used to accuse him of being part gorilla. It was fun to kid him about that, but you didn't want to let him get those gorilla hands on you because he'd grab you and squeeze you painfully tight.

As I mentioned, Ernie Orsatti stepped into a part-time role in 1935 to make room for Terry to take over. That turned out to be Orsatti's last year in the big leagues. He'd been a fine player for the Cardinals for his entire 9-year major league career. He, like Terry, was an excellent centerfielder, but not quite in the class of Moore. I didn't know Ernie very well because I only saw him briefly at spring training and on those occasions when I was called up late in 1934 and '35, but I think he was better defensively than he was offensively — and he could hit. Ernie was equally as interesting for his exploits outside of baseball as for his exploits on the ballfield. He'd had one foot firmly planted in Hollywood ever since the 1920s when he was a friend of Buster Keaton. Apparently, Keaton was a huge baseball fan and he loved having Ernie around the lots when he was filming his movies. They would always play baseball games during breaks from shooting. Ernie had even worked as a stuntman for Keaton on a few films. He stayed in the film industry after he left baseball, eventually passing the

Hollywood bug along to his sons, Ernie and Frank, both of whom had long careers as stuntmen and stunt coordinators.

SEPTEMBER 28, 1939: *CINCY CLINCHES PENNANT BY DOWNING CARDINALS, 5-3.* That was the headline in the *Los Angeles Times* after our heart-wrenching loss to the Reds on this day. It was a game we really should have won. I was again held hitless, this time by Cincinnati's big and tall right-hander, Paul Derringer. Derringer had 24 wins going into that ballgame, but my team-mates had no trouble with him, knocking Paul around for 14 hits while our pitchers held the Reds to just eight hits. But we just couldn't overcome the three runs we spotted Cincy in the first two innings. Max Lanier started the high-pressure game, but he was wild and departed in the 2nd inning with the score 2-0 and the bases loaded. Curt Davis came in and walked in another run before he put a stop to the scoring, but we were in a quick 3-0 hole. We scratched our way back to a tie in the 5th inning, but Derringer fittingly drove in the winning run in the 6th.

Failing to hit with runners in scoring position was one of the things that led to our defeat that day. Poor defense was partly to blame, too. I must admit to one error, and Johnny Mize also committed one. But one of our classic strengths, base-running, may have been the thing that really sunk us. We erred on that front a few times. *Los Angeles Times* writer Gayle Talbot described one of our key base-path mistakes this way — "Joe Medwick sent the spectators' hearts into their throats when, as the second Card up in the 7th, he hit a terrific smash to center. The ball hit the balustrade above Harry Craft's head and bounded back as Medwick tore around second. But Ival Goodman, Reds rightfielder, took the pill on first bounce and whipped a perfect peg to Bill Werber at third. Werber dived like a fullback to make the putout as Medwick came up cussing his impetuosity." Joe, to his credit, was hustling hard. But with just one out he probably should have stayed at second base UNLESS there was no doubt that he could make it to third base safely. Had Joe played it safe, he would have represented the tying run, in scoring position at second with just one out. As I've mentioned, Ducky wasn't very fast nor was he a very good base-runner, but it still took a great play to put him out at third — but big leaguers make great plays all the time. To add insult to the scenario, our guys strung together three consecutive singles after Joe made his out, but the inning was ended when Stu Martin flied out to right.

Despite not being at his best, Derringer went the full nine. He finished strongly, striking out Medwick and Mize to end the game. He was joyously swarmed by his teammates and fans. Factory whistles could be heard blowing in the distance, celebrating the victory. It was a mighty low feeling for me to watch that celebration from our dugout because I had always dreamed of participating in a moment like that. To come so close but come up short — it was a bitter pill to swallow. You just never knew if you'd get another opportunity.

SEPTEMBER 30, 1939: We still had three games to play at Wrigley following our elimination game in Cincinnati. We split a doubleheader on this day, and I had a nice 3-for-5 day at the plate in our opening game win — but it was hard to take any solace in that. We were still feeling the pain of losing out on the pennant. The season ended for us the next day when we lost, 2-1. We'd had a good year, winning 92 games and finishing in 2nd place, but I couldn't help feeling disappointed at our inability to win the pennant. We'd make great strides forward following our 6th place finish in 1938, but we still came up empty in our quest for the N.L. flag.

1940

APRIL 16, 1940: The new season did not get off to a good start for me on this day, and it was bad on two fronts. First, we lost, 6-4, to the Pirates at Sportsman's Park. Second, I was not in the starting line-up. I did get in the ballgame as a pinch-hitter for Jack Russell, one of our relief pitchers, but I failed to get a hit off Pirates left-handed reliever, Dick Lanahan. However, at only 27 years of age I was a little concerned at the prospect of no longer being an everyday player. I was not yet sure that this was to be the case, but there were signs in spring training that they might be transitioning me into a utility role in favor of Jimmy Brown at third base. All I could do was wait and see how it unfolded, then try to be ready when called upon to play. Incidentally, there was a new fellow over there in the Pittsburgh dugout managing their ballclub — it was none other than Frankie Frisch. I was happy to see Frankie get another shot at managing — he certainly deserved it. But it sure was strange to see him — Onkel Franz, The Fordham Flash — over there wearing the yellow and black of the Pittsburgh Pirates.

APRIL 21, 1940: My premature opening-day fear that I had been relegated to utility player now seemed to be legitimate. I was again used as a pinch-hitter in our second game of the season, and again I came up empty. The next day I did not play at all. That brings me to this day, and again I did not play as we won against the Cubs at Wrigley Field. But from my vantage point on the bench I got to watch Dizzy Dean make another attempt at a comeback, but it wasn't pretty for Ol' Diz. Here's how the Associated Press described it — "The Cubs unveiled the once-great Dizzy Dean for the benefit of 22,338 spectators today and nothing could have suited the Cardinals better. Dizzy had the fans buzzing with his "nothing ball" in the first three frames when he yielded only one hit, but his former teammates hopped on his slow curves for six hits and five runs in the 4th and 5th innings." You can't say the Cubs didn't try to make it work with Dizzy. Despite the clear-cut evidence that Diz just didn't have it anymore, the Cubs kept running him out there. By June, however, they sent him down to the minors. They brought him back late in the season, and tried once more in early 1941, before finally giving up for good.

APRIL 22, 1940: Following the Dizzy Dean game in Chicago, we traveled to Cincinnati for a 2-game series with the Reds. I played only briefly, entering the game late as a defensive substitute. I did not get an at-bat. Cincy looked like they were going to be strong again as they beat us, 6-1, behind Bucky Walters. Of particular interest in this game was the fact that we were in a race with Mother Nature to get the game in. There was a huge flood in progress as the Ohio River overflowed its banks. There was a foot of water in the Crosley Field dugouts when the game began. We had to sit on benches placed in front of the dugouts. The field itself was in pretty good shape when the game began, but by the time it ended the field was pretty soggy from the water rising and creeping in from the edges. Our game the next day was postponed because by that time the field was under water. It was amazing. It was the only time a National League game has ever been washed out by a flood! It wasn't the first time Crosley had been flooded, however. One of the worse floods in Ohio history happened just a few years earlier in 1937. That flood happened in January, though, too early in the year to affect any baseball games, but it put Crosley Field under 21 feet of water! There's a famous photo of Reds pitchers Gene Schott and Lee Grissom, along with groundskeeper Marty Schwab, in a rowboat in the middle of the field. If you've never seen it you should look it up.

APRIL 26, 1940: Jimmy Brown got injured, so I got my first chance to play regularly. Including the game on this day, I started eight straight games at third base while Jimmy recovered. My hope was to play myself back in the line-up permanently, and my plan got off to a good start as I went 3-for-4 with a stolen base as we beat Pittsburgh, 10-4, at Forbes Field. I must have used up all my good luck in this game because I went 0-for-4 the next day as we lost to the Cubs at home. It wasn't just me, though. Chicago pitcher Larry French was extremely sharp that day as he shut us out, 4-0.

APRIL 28, 1940: *CARDINALS HOMERS TURN BACK CUBS, 7-5; MED-WICK DRIVES 4-BAGGER AND 2 DOUBLES — MIZE AND GUT-TERIDGE ALSO CONNECT.* That was the Associated Press headline recapping our game at Sportsman's Park on this day. The text went on to say, "Held without a home run in its first eight games, St. Louis hammered three off big Bill Lee. Joe Medwick and Johnny Mize hit homers in succession in the 4th inning and Don Gutteridge parked the ball out of the lot with two on in the 5th. Maybe I was fueled by Helen's good home cooking!

MAY 6, 1940: With Jimmy Brown's return to the line-up on this day, I found myself back on the bench as we lost to the Dodgers, 6-2, at Sportsman's Park. I had struggled at the plate in the four games I started after my home run game against the Cubs, getting just one hit in 15 at-bats. Slumping like that built the pressure on me to perform, but on May 5th I came out of it with a 3-hit game against the Dodgers. Inside I knew that despite my 3-hit game I would probably be back on the bench when Jimmy returned, but it was still a little disappointing when I saw the May 6th line-up card WITHOUT my on it. I did get in the game as a late-inning sub, but I did not get an at-bat.

MAY 7, 1940: I sat this one out as we wrapped up the Dodgers series with a lopsided 18-2 victory, so there's no personal highlight here. But there was a funny side-story going on that I thought was worth recounting here. In a precursor of things to come, the Dodgers had decided to start chartering team flights to some of their games. Larry McPhail was no longer interested in the futuristic yellow ball. Now he had turned his attention to blazing the trail of air travel for his ballclub. To McPhail, trains were passé and airplanes were the coming trend. He had booked two 21-passenger American Airlines planes to carry the Dodgers from St. Louis to their next stop in Chicago. It was a short flight, more or less a practice session for the longer flight McPhail had booked to take the Dodgers from Chicago back to Brooklyn following their series with the Cubs. The Dodgers had a character on their club named Babe Phelps. He was a very good hitter, but his round shape had seen him nicknamed "Blimp." Well, it turned out that Babe was afraid of flying, and he had no intention of boarding that plane to Chicago after our game with them was completed. Babe's teammates Tot Pressnell, Pete Coscarart, and Ernie Koy were leery of flying, too, but Leo Durocher talked them into it. Babe held his ground, though, telling the papers he wouldn't fly. Dodgers traveling secretary John McDonald gave a great quote in the papers when he heard about Babe balking at the flight to Chicago. "He's the only blimp that won't fly!" Hy Turkin of the *Daily News* wrote, "All the Dodgers except scairdy cat Phelps will fly to Chicago following the game with the Cardinals." Eventually Babe was talked into getting on the plane, and the flight to Chicago went off without a hitch. Despite arriving safely, however, Babe was still uncomfortable about flying. "If I'd had a pint I'd have broken training," he said. "I still think the Wright Brothers were crazy." He wasn't kidding, either. Babe did NOT fly with the team from Chicago back to Brooklyn. Instead, he took a train — and thanks to an extra-inning game against the Cubs on getaway day, he got back too late for their next game.

MAY 13, 1940: We played to a 14-inning, 8-8 tie with the Reds at Crosley Field. I did not play and, in fact, had played in just one of our previous seven games. The game was a make-up for the postponed flood game, and it was eventually called on account of darkness after we had played for three hours and 35 minutes. We started the game about an hour late, and that didn't help the situation. It wasn't weather that held us up, however, it was the umpires — or lack thereof, I should say. Everybody was out getting loose before somebody finally noticed that there were no umpires. A phone call was made to National League president Ford Frick, and he was embarrassed when he realized that they did not assign any umps for the game. He later admitted to reporters that his office had "kicked one," adding, "It was an oversight on our part, for which I must assume full responsibility." Frick came through, though. He got hold of umpire Larry Goetz who lived nearby and was enjoying a day off at home. Goetz sped to the ballpark and took his place behind the plate. Reds coach Jimmy Wilson assumed the first base umping duties, and our own Lon Warneke umped third. Who knows — maybe it was that game that made Lon decide on his future career — umpire. He became a National League umpire when his playing days were over. I wasn't in the National League at that time — I was in the American League — but I heard he was a really good umpire.

I mentioned that Reds coach Jimmie Wilson also pitched in as an ump in our game on this day. Unfortunately, I can't mention the name Jimmie Wilson without telling of the lesson he taught me when I was a rookie and he was a catcher with the Philadelphia Phillies. Jimmie's lesson to me begins with my youthful admiration of Pepper Martin and his go-for-broke style of play. Despite Pepper's ability to hit, it was his aggressiveness on the basepaths for which he become so well known. Pepper was the first guy I ever saw slide head-first, and it became a real trademark for him. It became symbolic of his hard play. He didn't play to hurt anybody — he just played hard. In those days, the canvas bases were anchored to the ground by two straps that were tied to two spikes that were hammered into the dirt. Pepper used to slide head-first, hitting the bag so hard with his chest that he would break the spikes loose and knock the base right out of the ground. It was crazy. When discussion of his head-first slides would arise, Pepper would simply say, "Sliding head-first gets you there quicker." That's definitely debatable, but not when you're a rookie talking to Pepper Martin. So, being young and eager to impress Pepper, I decided to try and slide head-first — just like my hero — as soon as the first opportunity presented itself.

My chance came soon thereafter in a game against the Phillies. I was on second base when someone singled. The ball wasn't hit very deep, but I decided to try and score nonetheless. As I rounded third base and dug for home, I could see that the play was going to be close. In my head I heard Pepper saying, "Sliding head-first gets you there quicker," and I decided that this was it — I was going to impress him with my Pepper-like head-first slide. As I left my feet and began my dive, I saw 6-foot-2-inch 200-pound Jimmie Wilson, parked in front of the plate waiting for me. I hit the dirt, Wilson caught the ball and dropped to his knees, and I slammed into his shin guards with my face. Good Lord that hurt! Then, to add insult to injury, he whacked me right on the top of my head with the ball. I was out, and Jimmie calmly looked down at me and said, "Now, son, that should teach you NOT to slide head-first into a catcher." Pepper was laughing at me when I got back to the dugout. With my head still ringing, I said, "The heck with you, Pepper, I'm gonna slide like I want to — FEET first." I continued to play pro ball for over a decade after that — and I never ever again slid head-first. Now that's a lesson learned, thanks to Jimmie Wilson.

MAY 15, 1940: We lost our second consecutive game to the Phillies on this day, going down 6-3 at Shibe Park. The Phils buried us with a 6-run 2nd inning, and we just couldn't dig ourselves out. I made a 6th-inning pinch-hit appearance, but failed to hit safely off Phillies starter Kirby Higbe who went the distance. We almost knocked Higbe out in the 5th when we got to him for three runs, but he righted himself and pitched four scoreless frames after that. Our shortstop, Joe Orengo, was the sparkplug in our 5th-inning rally off Higbe, getting things going by clouting his second career homer. Joe had a hot hand at the time, having hit his first big league round-tripper a couple of days earlier in our 8-8 tie against Cincinnati. He was one of the reasons I wasn't playing very much in 1940. There simply were too many good guys vying for playing time in the Cardinal infield, and Joe was one of them. He was really a shortstop, but he also played a lot at third and second in 1940. Being versatile, he was able to get into 129 games for us in '40, and he made the most of it by hitting .287 with seven home runs.

Joe got his first taste of the big leagues in 1939 when he got into a handful of games for us in April. He was from San Francisco, and he came to the big leagues via the Pacific Coast League. Joe once told me about his meeting with

Branch Rickey in May of 1939 when he was called in to be informed that he was being sent back out west. "Joe, we're going to send you back out to the coast," said Mr. Rickey. "We want you to fly out there and be ready to play tomorrow." Joe, showing a lot more courage than I would have had, said, "Mr. Rickey, I'll fly IN to the major leagues, but I'll be damned if I'm gonna fly OUT of them." And he didn't. I thought that was great, and I never forgot it..

MAY 26, 1940: This was a painful day for all of us on the Cardinals who were there in 1939 when we were eliminated from the pennant race by the Reds. On this day Paul Derringer shut us out, 4-0, at Crosley Field, and to compound the misery we had to watch the Reds hoist their 1939 pennant in a pre-game ceremony attended by Judge Landis. As for the game itself, I was merely a spectator, out of the line-up once again.

JUNE 7, 1940: Going into our game against the Giants on this day, our club had a very disappointing record of 14 wins and 24 losses. There had been rumors for weeks that Ray Blades was going to be fired because of our poor start, and the rumor became fact when Ray was let go just before we took the field. Mike Gonzales was again named interim manager until our new manager, Billy Southworth, could make the journey from Rochester to join us. Southworth was currently the manager of the Red Wings, just as Blades was when he was hired to replace Frankie Frisch back in '38. Ray was supposedly fired because of his tendency to remove starting pitchers too quickly, in addition to his constantly shifting line-up. Those may have been legitimate points, but they were the same tendencies that had Ray heralded as a good manager the previous season when we won 92 games. In any case, that was — and still is — life as a big league manager. Gonzales' line-up card that day, much like Blades' line-up cards of late, did not include me. I watched from the dugout as we won the game, 3-2. I was really hoping that I'd get an opportunity to play more when Southworth joined us in a few days, and I had reason to believe it might happen. Southworth had been quoted in the papers as saying, "I intend, first of all, to install a fighting spirit in the team. I believe in a few days you'll be looking at a different ballclub." If it's one thing I've always had, it's a fighting spirit, so I was hoping beyond hope that I might fit into Southworth's plans.

JUNE 12, 1940: We did not play on this day, and that gave the front office plenty of time to think up more ways to shake-up the ballclub. What they came up with was a blockbuster — they traded Joe Medwick to the Dodgers. It was a shocker, to say the least. Just 2-1/2 years earlier Muscles had been National League MVP. But despite being very good since then, with occasional down periods, he'd never again reached that level of play. Joe's constant dickering over salary, his bouts of moodiness, his occasional failure to give 100 percent, and his increasing inconsistency had seen him fall out of favor with management —

and, believe it or not, Cardinals fans. *New York Times* writer John Drebinger, after watching us play a doubleheader against the Giants at Sportsman's Park on June 9th, summed up Joe's situation perfectly when he wrote, "Heroes may come and go, but none seems to ever have fallen harder than Joe Medwick, who, roundly booed for his dismal efforts in the first game, finally heard his name cheered when the announcer revealed that Ducky Wucky had been benched for the nightcap." Joe could be a difficult personality at times, but it was still tough to witness his downfall. For the record, here are the specifics of the trade: the Cards sent Medwick and Curt Davis to Brooklyn in exchange for outfielder Ernie Koy, right-handed pitcher Carl Doyle, and minor leaguers Sam Nahem and Bert Haas.

JUNE 14, 1940: Billy Southworth managed his first game on this day as we beat the Phillies, 6-2, at Shibe Park. It was the first of a 4-game series. I was happy that we got the win for him in his debut, but I was disappointed not to be in our line-up. But there was always tomorrow, so I just tried to be ready. By the end of the series, however, after appearing in just one game as a defensive sub and another as a pinch-hitter, I began to believe that my new role as a utility player was going to be permanent. It didn't sit well with me because I believed that I had proven myself to be a better player than one relegated to occasional use as a pinch-hitter, pinch-runner, and defensive substitute. Also, the fact that all three of our 1940 managers (Blades, Gonzales and Southworth) had used me strictly in this manner, with the exception of my short stint as a starter while Jimmy Brown was injured, led me to believe that this was a decision that came down from the top. And that was more than a little disconcerting. Still, I was not the type to pout or gripe, so I put on a brave face and tried to make the best of the situation.

JUNE 18, 1940: We'd opened up a 3-game series with the Dodgers at Ebbets Field the day before on June 17th. I was not in the line-up that day, but I watched the action attentively from the dugout. It was our first time facing Brooklyn since Joe Medwick was traded to them, so all the focus was on how Joe would do against his former team. We won the game, 3-1, with Clyde Shoun going the distance and, seemingly more importantly to the sportswriters, holding "the celebrated Joe Medwick" to 0-for-4 at the plate. That built the tension for the second game of the series on this day, June 18th. It didn't take long for the tension to explode. Here's how the beginning of the game was described by Louis Effrat of the *New York Times* — "A fast ball, thrown high and on the inside by Bob Bowman, hit Joe Medwick on the left side of his head in the opening inning of the Dodger-Cardinal game at Ebbets Field and knocked the new Brooklyn outfielder unconscious. Medwick was carried off the field on a stretcher and removed to the Caledonian Hospital where it was said he was suffering from concussion and would have to remain under observation for at least five or six days."

Needless to say, it was a pretty frightening moment, hearing the sickening sound as the ball made solid contact with Joe's head, then watching him crumple to the ground. He was laying there on his back, spread-eagle and motionless, ball cap a few feet from his head and his bat a few feet from his right hand. Players from both clubs rushed to home plate to check on him. For a moment it looked as if there might be a brawl as a few Dodgers players rushed at Bowman and accused him of throwing an intentional bean ball, but they were restrained by the umpires. I think everyone knew that this was serious and that the focus should be solely on Joe. A bunch of fights would just further complicate an already dangerous situation. While Joe was being removed from the field, a very angry Larry McPhail came over to our dugout and really let us have a piece of his mind. Billy Southworth removed Bowman from the game when it was resumed. He did it for Bob's own safety, fearing possible reprisals from the irate Brooklyn fans. Two plain-clothed detectives sat in the dugout with Bob for a time, but eventually McPhail had them removed, assuring everybody that he would make sure we were all protected.

Joe was apparently conscious and rational in the dressing room while he awaited an ambulance to take him to the hospital. According to the papers, Joe even joked, saying, "It's funny, that makes two bad days in a row. Yesterday I couldn't get a base hit and today this thing happens." I read that and thought, "That sounds just like Joe." The game itself was anything but anticlimactic. It was hard-fought with the Dodgers hell-bent to defeat us in support for their stricken teammate. I got in as a 7th-inning pinch-runner for Johnny Mize, but I did not come around to score. We were down, 3-5, in the 9th when Enos Slaughter hit a dramatic 2-run homer to tie things up. We finally prevailed in the 11th, scoring twice to win, 7-5.

JUNE 19, 1940: There was no reduction in tension as we closed out our set against the Dodgers on this day — a day that also just happened to by my 28th birthday. It was believed that Ducky Medwick would be alright, so that was comforting to all, but Joe would remain hospitalized for a while as doctors kept a close eye on him, watching for any number of possible serious complications such as brain swelling or blood clots. Ebbets Field was sold out, with thousands of blood-thirsty fans being turned away out of fear that an overcrowded ballpark could possibly lead to an eruption of hostilities. The 100 policeman on hand were evidence of the possibility for trouble. Billy Southworth was well aware of the mood in the air, so he made Bob Bowman stay back at the hotel while we played the game. Following the conclusion of the game the day before, there had been a new piece of information making the papers that added to the ill-feelings surrounding the whole incident. It was now being reported that prior to the game in which Medwick was beaned, Leo Durocher and Medwick were in an elevator with Bowman, and words were exchanged. When Bob subsequently hit Medwick with the first pitch he threw him in the game that followed their elevator altercation, it looked as if it was an intentional beaning.

So that was festering when the game began. Unlike the previous game, however, this game was not much of a contest. Brooklyn jumped on us for two quick runs in the bottom of the 1st, and went on to win easily, 8-3. I didn't get into the game. But what the game lacked in competitiveness, it made up for in extracurricular activities. As if the situation with Medwick wasn't enough, our catcher, Mickey Owen, and Leo Durocher had been engaging in a personal feud that was threatening to come to a head. It did, in fact, come to a head that day, and here's how *New York Times* writer Roscoe McGowen recorded the events — "The Durocher-Owen threatened battle came in the 3rd inning when Mickey slid high and wide into Pete Coscarart at second base to break up a possible double-play. As Owen started for the bench, Durocher said something to him and Owen wheeled angrily. Durocher moved promptly to meet him, but umpire Bick Campbell rushed between the belligerents, while at the same time players from both dugouts swarmed onto the field. Owen took one solid swing at Durocher and in a moment the two were lost in a melee of players and umpires. But order was restored quickly, and the game was resumed with Owen banished and Durocher still playing."

There turned out to be a criminal investigation of Bob, but he was never charged with anything. With all that happened in that series, I can't think of any other time that I was ever happier to leave Brooklyn for Boston, the next stop in our road trip.

JUNE 23, 1940: I hadn't started a game in nearly three months when I was written into the line-up for the nightcap of a doubleheader against the Bees this day in Boston. I played third base and led off, contributing a single in four at-bats against 6-foot 4-inch 210-pound Bees right-hander Manny Salvo, but we were swept. With the Joe Medwick incident still in the papers, the reporters enjoyed relating a relatively ordinary occurrence from the first game of that day's twin bill to the Ducky situation. "Bob Bowman," wrote the Associated Press, "the Cardinals' pitcher whose 'beaning' of Joe Medwick caused a furor in Brooklyn a few days ago, was a victim of the accident jinx himself today. He was spiked by Seb Sisti, Bees' third baseman, in the first inning of the opening game while attempting to cover first base on a slow roller to Johnny Mize. Suffering a gash in his right ankle, Bowman was carried from the field and four stitches were needed to close the wound."

JULY 4, 1940: Normally, delivering a non-game-winning pinch-hit single would not warrant mention in a timeline like the one I've written here, but there were extenuating circumstances. With the 1940 decision from high that I was now a role-player, pinch-hitter was one of my new specialties. From 1936 through 1939, I had just 12 big league pinch-hit at-bats, and I wasn't particularly successful at them, either, getting just two hits. Pinch-hitting is a very difficult task, and not everyone was suited for it. A good pinch-hitter is rare, and a valuable asset to any team. Well, despite our managers' efforts to make me a pinch-hitter in 1940, it didn't go so well for me. Prior to the game on this day, I had pinch-hit 12 times in 1940 — and I had exactly zero hits in those 12 at-bats. There had been occasions where I had entered the game to bat for someone — and delivered a hit, but in those cases I had stayed in the game on defense, so technically those weren't pinch-hit appearances. At any rate, on this day I entered our game against Chicago in the 7th inning as a pinch-hitter for our relief pitcher, Jack Russell. We were trailing, 4-2, with a runner in scoring position. Cubs pitcher, Larry French, gave me one I liked and I connected for a run-scoring pinch-single to tie the game up. Although we failed to score again and ended up losing the game, 4-3, it still felt great to FINALLY deliver in this capacity and get the monkey off my back. Wouldn't you know it — I got two more pinch-hit singles over the course of the next nine days, but that was it for the year. I made five more pinch-hit appearances after that and was 0-for-5. All told, I was 3-for-20 in pinch-hit at-bats in 1940. It's tough duty!

JULY 20, 1940: The Brooklyn Dodgers came to St. Louis for a 3-game series on this day. I played in none of the games, but did my best to enjoy all three of the hard-fought contests from my place in the dugout. This was our first time facing the Dodgers since the series back in Brooklyn where Joe Medwick got beaned and Leo Durocher fought Mickey Owen. Joe had returned to the Dodger line-up and was swinging the bat well for them as we kicked off the series on this day. He had just three home runs at the time of his sale to Brooklyn about six weeks earlier, but since his return from the beaning he'd hit four round-trippers for the Dodgers. I'm sure the fans in St. Louis were glad that Joe was not killed when he was drilled by Bob Bowman, but that didn't stop a lot of them from booing Muscles when he stepped up for his first at-bat as a Dodger in St. Louis. Don't get me wrong — there were some cheers from those who remembered all the great baseball that Joe had played in St. Louis, but there was also a lot of undeserved boos. In any case, Joe shut up the boo-birds when he launched a tremendous 430-foot 2-run homer off Lon Warneke — a shot that bounded off the Sportsman's Park scoreboard. We rallied to win the game, 3-2, but it was nice to see that the beaning seemed to have had no ill-effect on Medwick.

In looking back now at Joe's career, it's true that he was never quite the same feared power hitter AFTER the beaning that he was before it. He was just 28 years old at the time that he was hit by Bowman, so he still should have had many productive years ahead of him. But the numbers show that he hit 148 home runs before he was beaned and just 57 afterwards. Many have tried to say that his drop-off was a result of the beaning, but I don't think so. I think that the problem many have when analyzing Joe Medwick is that they compare everything he did to his triple-crown season of 1937. But that year wasn't really indicative of Joe — it was a career year when everything fell in place for him. Ducky had, in fact, seen a steady drop-off in production after that season — well BEFORE the beaning in Brooklyn. Joe's 1941 season with the Dodgers is more indicative of his typical year — .318 with 18 home runs and 86 RBIs. Why he dropped off so drastically in 1942 is hard to say. He was 30 years old and maybe he was an "old" 30 by then, but I doubt that it was a delayed reaction his beaning two years earlier.

JULY 31, 1940: I was 2-for-6 at the plate with an RBI as we trounced the Bees, 17-8, in the second game of a doubleheader in Boston. It was my second start in two days after going nearly four weeks since my previous start. In fact, I started four of our next 10 games, too, and I hit in each one of them. I collected 8 hits in 18 at-bats in those six starts, and that made me happy because I knew I needed to hit well when given the opportunity because chances were few and far between for me at that time.

AUGUST 26, 1940: "Don Gutteridge saved the Cards from a shutout with a home run, his second of the season, in the 9th." That was from the Associated Press article recapping our 3-1 loss to the Bees at Sportsman's Park on this day. It was a bottom-of-the-9th solo shot off Boston right-hander Nick Strincevich who I'd reached for a single earlier in the game, but overall he was great that day, holding us to just five hits. My start on this day was my first start in 20 days, and I had played very little in the interim.

AUGUST 27, 1940: I started at third base again on this day, but Boston right-hander, Jim Tobin, held me hitless. We won the game, however, 4-3, through the heroics of one of my rookie teammates — a young kid who was partly responsible for edging me on to the Cardinals bench in 1940 — Marty Marion. Slats, as he was nicknamed, was a great shortstop. Burt Shotton, one of Marty's minor league managers, came up with the name because Marty was about 6-foot-2 and only 170 pounds. The sportswriters hung another nickname on Marty, too — The Octopus. They said that his long and rangy arms made him look like an octopus whenever he reached down to field ground balls — and they were right. In my opinion, Marty was probably one of the best fielding shortstops there ever was. Plus, he had a great arm to go with his great glove. Before Marty, everyone thought that a shortstop had to be a little guy who could move very quickly, but he changed that thinking. While not usually known for his power, Marty was a decent hitter. On this day, however, it was his power that got him in the papers as he hit the game-winning home run. The round-tripper was the first if his career. One more thing on Marty — he'll always hold a special place in my heart because he helped me by giving me a coaching job when I really needed one in 1955, the year he took over as manager of the Chicago White Sox.

AUGUST 28, 1940: For the third day in a row, I started at third base. And for the second time in three days, I hit a 9th-inning home run. This one was a bases-empty knock off 6-foot 4-inch 295-pound right-hander, Jumbo Brown. My homer didn't help us win the ballgame, though, as the Giants beat us, 5-2, at Sportsman's Park. At 295 pounds, Brown was the complete antithesis of his pitching counterpart on this day — 6-foot 2-inch 185-pound right-hander Lon Warneke. Lon had come into the game seeking his ninth straight victory and his 14th overall, but he wasn't at his sharpest and we didn't offer much offensive support. He left for a pinch-hitter in the 7th, trailing 4-1, and we never caught up.

Flying high on an 8-game winning streak, Lon was feeling good the night before as we rode the train into New York from Boston, so he decided to have some fun at the expense of one our rookies. The rest of us sat there listening in the back of the pullman, trying not to laugh as Lon told the rookie, "There's a thief around here, you know. The last time I was on this train somebody stole my shoes." Lon had perfectly baited the hook, and the rookie bit. "You know what we ought to do," the rookie said excitedly, trying to help, "we ought to lay a trap for him. Take turns watching out to see who the thief is."

"That's a great idea, kid," Lon replied, "let's do it tonight." With that, the stage was set. The rookie, being unfamiliar with the procedures involved in first-class train travel at the big league level, was a sitting duck. You see, in those days we used to set our shoes on the floor outside our berths when we went to bed at night. Later, the porter would come by, pick up the shoes, shine them, and then return them — all for a little extra tip. Unaware of this ritual, the rookie was prime game for the stunt. Lon set up the look-out schedule as to guarantee that the rookie would be on guard when the porter made his usual stop for our shoes. Lon awakened the kid at midnight to take his shift. "Watch out," Lon said with convincing seriousness, "and be CAREFUL!" Right on schedule, the poor unsuspecting porter came by for our shoes. As soon as the porter picked up a pair, the rookie leapt out of his berth and pounced on the porter's back. As the stunned porter spun in circles with the rookie on his back, the kid kept hollering, "I got him! I got him! I got him!" The rookie continued to cling to the porter's back, waiting for the rest of us to come to his rescue — but the hall remained empty. The kid was hung out there alone, feeling mighty foolish, as he slowly realized that he'd been had.

It's true that Lon loved to have fun, but that should not overshadow what a fine pitcher he was. After trials with the Cubs in 1930 and '31, Lon hit it big in 1932 when he won 22 games for Chicago. He was rock-solid for the Cubs from then on, winning 76 more games for them from '33 through '36, including a 22-win season in 1934 and 20-win season in '35. When Chicago lost the 1935 World Series to the Detroit Tigers, 4 games to 2, it was Lon who won both games for the Cubs. He'd lost some of his velocity by the time he joined our ballclub in 1937, so he had to pitch with a little more finesse. He was the first guy that I ever saw throw a slider. He used to call it his knuckle-curve, or his buster, but it wasn't really a curveball at all — it was a slider. He worked and worked on that thing until he perfected it. I'd see him right back working on it the day after he pitched a ballgame.

Lon had a set routine when it came to getting his work in. He'd get some-body to catch him, then warm up by throwing 30 pitches. He'd tell the catch-er to hold the mitt over his left knee, then he'd hit it. Next, he would tell the catcher to move the mitt to his right knee, then he'd hit it again. Then inside the waistline. Then outside the waistline. It was this great work ethic that made him such a good pitcher. Although I was no longer with the Cardinals at the time, I was very happy when I heard about Lon's no-hitter against the Reds on August 30, 1941. He really deserved it. I missed rooming with Lon when my days with the Cards were through, but I made sure to stay in touch with him right until the year he passed away in 1976. Lon was just a good old time Arkansas boy, and it was a real pleasure to be pals with him.

SEPTEMBER 1, 1940: Another start for me on this day but, despite there being a whole month left to play in the campaign, it turned out to be my last start of the season. I got the nod in the second game of a doubleheader against the Pirates at Forbes Field, but despite going 2-for-3 with a double and a stolen base, I didn't stay in until the end. As the game went into extra innings I was lifted in favor of Stu Martin who was held hitless in his two at-bats. My two hits in this game turned out to be my final hits in a Cardinals uniform. The game was eventually called because of darkness after the 11th inning, with a final score of 5-5.

SEPTEMBER 29, 1940: We played our last game of 1940 on this day, and it was anything but a highlight in my career with the Cardinals. I was not in the line-up, but that was certainly nothing new. In fact, I had only appeared in four of our previous 32 ballgames — three games as a pinch-hitter and one as a pinch-runner. It was a hard thing to take. We won the game on this day, a 6-0 victory over the Cubs at Sportsman's Park, and we finished the season in 3rd place with 84 wins. As I sat there in the dugout that day I couldn't help but wonder what the future held for me with the Cardinals — if I had any future with them at all. With the way things had gone that season, I couldn't help but wonder if I was taking part in my last game as a member of the Cards. I didn't want it to end because I felt we still had unfinished business to take care of — and that was to win a pennant. We'd had all the pieces in place to win a flag during my career with the Cardinals, but I'd have to say we underachieved by not getting the job done. Many guys had great individual years, but we could never get it all to come together at one time, and the result was a lot of close finishes, but no championship. That was my only true regret as I considered the possibility that I'd never get another chance to compete again with my Cardinals teammates.

My years with the St. Louis Cardinals were more fun than you could ever imagine. We played serious baseball, but we always had a great time. How could you not have fun when you're playing alongside guys like Pepper Martin, Dizzy Dean, Lon Warneke, and a host of other crazy characters?

1942

APRIL 14, 1942: On this day I drew an 0-for-4 at the plate as my team, the St. Louis Browns, won our 1942 opening day game, 3-0, over the White Sox at Comiskey Park. 0-for-4 is not the type of day that most ballplayers would feel the need to recount in their memoir, but my 0-fer on this day was special. It was my first day back in the major leagues after spending 1941 in the Pacific Coast League, playing under rookie manager Pepper Martin.

My 1940 premonitions that the Cardinals were phasing me out of their plans turned out to be true. Branch Rickey called me in to his office at the completion of the season and informed me that they were sending me down to

Sacramento in 1941. Despite the fact that I'd seen it coming, the news stunned me. Rickey told me that Billy Southworth was returning as Cards manager in 1941, and I simply wasn't the type of player he wanted. Plus, they had a bright young up-and-coming talent in Whitey Kurowski, and they thought he would do a better job than me. That was his opinion, and that was fine, but I decided that if I could no longer play in the majors, I wouldn't play anywhere. I wasn't usually very argumentative where Rickey was concerned, but I adamantly told him no — I wouldn't go. "I have six years in the big leagues," I told him, "and I think I deserve to stay." In so many words, I was told to take the Sacramento demotion or leave it. So I left it — and I left Rickey's office.

That meeting certainly did not do anything to endear me to Rickey, a man for whom I already had less than warm feelings. Branch Rickey is known by many as the great brain of baseball. He was a Sunday school teacher and supposedly never went to a ballgame on the Sabbath. But rumor had it that Rickey would look out of one of the 5th floor windows of the YMCA building adjacent to Sportsman's Park and count the Sunday attendance. So, as you can see, he was very much about money. When I met him back in 1933 — the year he signed me out of the Nebraska State League — he impressed me very much. He impressed me so much that he talked me into signing for peanuts. There was a $500 bonus in my contract, however, should I make the club and stay with them until June 1st. I finally made the club in 1936, so I was really looking forward to getting that $500 bonus when June rolled around. I'd heard stories about how cheap Rickey was, so as June 1st approached I began to fear that Rickey would send me down just to save himself the $500. Sure enough, on the last day of May, Frankie Frisch broke the news to me — they were sending me down. I knew it wasn't Frankie's fault — I knew it was Rickey trying to save a dollar, but I had no choice but to accept the demotion and stew over the loss of my $500.

It was believed that the reason Rickey was so cheap with the players was because his frugality helped him line his pockets. Story had it that Cardinals owner Sam Breadon gave Rickey a budget from which he was to pay the players. If Rickey could somehow come in under that budget, Breadon would allow Rickey to keep the surplus for himself. With that as his incentive, Rickey really squeezed us, using his gift of smooth talk to get us to sign well below market value. He really worked you over, pointing out all the negative aspects of your game. He somehow even managed to negatively spin the things you did well. By the time you were done with your contract negotiations, you actually believed that you were not entitled to the money you were asking for. Sometimes you even wanted to give him your pocket change, he was so broke! It was ridiculous. I learned very early that it did no good to dicker with him, so I rarely ever did — it just wasn't my way. I understand the importance of some of the good things he did for baseball, but he was definitely NOT my favorite person in the world.

I wasn't the only one booted off the Cardinals following the 1940 season — Gas House Gang legend Pepper Martin was also told it was the end of the line for him as a player. With Rickey it didn't matter whether you were a little guy like me or a legend like Pepper — when Rickey was done with you, you were OUT! Possibly fearing the negative fallout from casually disposing of a Cardinals legend, Rickey decided to try and ease Pepper out by offering him a job as manager with the Sacramento Solons. If there was one thing Pepper was not cut out to be, it was a manager — and he knew it. Shortly after accepting Rickey's offer, Pepper and his wife, Ruby, came to visit Helen and me. A little while into the visit, Pepper said, "I know it's bad what they're doing to you, Don, but I'd like to ask you to do something for me. I want you to come to Sacramento and be a player-coach for me."

Because of my anger at Rickey, my first inclination was to say no, but I let Pepper continue. "Hell, Don, I've never been a manager. I don't know much about managing and I'm gonna need some help. YOU can help me if you just come out and be with me."

Helen and I though it over for a while, carefully weighing the pros and cons. We finally came to a decision to do it. We'd never been to California, so we were looking forward to the opportunity to see it — plus, it was Pepper. Even if my year with Sacramento did not result in a return to the majors, at least we'd be with Pepper and Ruby. Pepper was thrilled when I told him we'd decided to go to Sacramento with him, and he promised me that we'd have a great time. If there was one thing that I was sure of, it's that we DEFINITELY would have a great time. How could we not with Pepper in charge.

Playing under manager Pepper Martin turned out to be even more of an experience than I'd imagined. He played rightfield and managed while I played third base and coached. Being of closer proximity to the umpires than he was way out in right, Pepper had instructed ME to initiate all arguments with umpires on any questionable calls. He would, in short order, relieve me of my duty as soon as he hustled in from the outfield. It sounded good in theory, but it didn't always work out so well. For example, once there was a sinking liner hit to Buster Adams, our centerfielder. From my spot at third I could see that Buster made a very tough catch on the ball. Pepper, positioned even closer to Buster than me, HAD to have also seen that it was a catch. But the umpire ruled that Buster had trapped the ball, so I initiated the argument and waited for reinforcement from Pepper. I kept arguing, but no Pepper. I started stalling, telling the umpire all sorts of things about his family, a quick Sunday school lesson, and that sort of stuff. Still, no Pepper. It seemed like an eternity, but Pepper finally came strolling in from rightfield to save the day. He pushed me aside and asked the umpire, "Do you think Buster caught the ball?" The ump, red-faced and glowering, said, "NO! He didn't catch it." Pepper, just as polite and helpful as can be, said, "Well, sir, I didn't think he caught it either." And with that he spun on his heel and walked back out to rightfield. The ump, now madder than ever, turned to look for me — but I was gone. I left in a hurry! That's how it was with Pepper. He knew Buster had caught the ball, but he'd rather have fun messing with me than to make sure the ump got the call right.

As a player under Frankie Frisch, Pepper had struggled with signals. He never seemed to know what the signs were. He was just one of those guys — and there were a bunch of them — that could never catch on to the signs. Becoming a manager did not solve his problem. It turned out that he was no better at giving signs than he'd been at receiving them. So, in turn, it seemed like guys on our Sacramento club were always missing signs or simply getting them wrong. Pepper came up with a solution, though. He had little signs made — a piece of cardboard nailed to a wooden stake. One sign said "HIT AND RUN," one said "STEAL," and so on. We kept them in the corner of the dugout. We'd get a guy on first and Pepper would tell someone to put out the "STEAL" sign. So somebody would grab the little "STEAL" sign and stick it in the ground in front of the dugout. The opposition thought it was funny, but they could never be sure if it was the real sign or a decoy. They'd be laughing it up and looking around — then our guys on base would take off running!

Pepper's spirit had a way of rubbing off on teammates. I got caught up in it when I'd attempted my ill-fated head-first slide in 1936, and, while with Sacramento, our influential young catcher, Clyde Kluttz, also tried to emulate Pepper. We were in Oakland playing the Oaks, and it was a real tight ballgame. A ball was hit out of the park down the leftfield line. Clyde and I thought it hooked foul before it cleared the wall, but the umpire ruled it a home run. We quickly descended upon the ump to take up the fight until our fearless leader arrived from rightfield. We told him, in no uncertain terms, what we thought of the call, not to mention his immediate and extended family members. Anything you can imagine was said. During the course of the yelling I had felt some pressure on my foot, but I ignored it, instead continuing to focus on my verbal assault. Finally, I heard a SCRUNCH and felt an immediate bolt of pain. I howled and jumped back and looked down to see what had happened. I was horrified to see my shoe sliced wide open and my big toe bleeding profusely. Through for the day, I hobbled off to the clubhouse for treatment.

Later, laying on the bed of my hotel room with my big toe throbbing, Clyde came in. He was my buddy and roommate when on the road. "Hey, partner," he said, "I'm sure sorry about your foot."

"Yeah, me too," I replied, wincing from the pain.

"No, you don't realize how REALLY sorry I am," Clyde said mysteriously.

"What do you mean?" I asked, my curiosity now elevated.

"Well, why we were arguing with the ump, I thought I was stepping on HIS foot," Clyde confessed. "When I didn't get a reaction from him, I really stepped down hard on it. It wasn't until I saw your reaction that I realized it was YOUR toe I was stepping on!" All I could think of was PEPPER! In any case, poor old Pepper had to argue on his own for the next three weeks as I sat out while my BROKEN toe mended.

Aside from his personality, Pepper also imparted his playing style onto our

1941 Sacramento Solons ballclub. In a word, RUN. As a player, Pepper loved to go from first to third on a hit — every hit. It didn't matter if it was sometimes unwise, he did it anyway. And, for the most part, it served him well. Often on the occasions where he should have been out by a mile, he would knock the ball loose with one of his hard head-first dives. Well, Pepper decided that since this philosophy had worked for him in his career, he now wanted his players to do it. "If you're on first base and someone gets a hit," he told our team, "don't stop at

1941 saw my big league career take a 1-year detour back to the minors with Pepper Martin's Sacramento Solons of the Pacific Coast League.

second base. I'd rather you get thrown out at third rather than stop at second. I want you all to go from first to third on EVERY hit. Just GO — I don't care what's going on."

So that's what our guys did — they ran. Needless to say, we had a lot of guys thrown out. A few safe, but a lot thrown out. It wasn't too bad at first, but it got worse as the season progressed. You see, we had only 16 players on our roster. Other clubs in the P.C.L. carried 20 or so, but not the Cardinals organization. With only 16 players and Pepper's running philosophy, fatigue quickly set in on us. That's one of the reasons we didn't win the pennant that season — Pepper just wore us out. We literally ran ourselves right out of the pennant.

My time with Pepper and the 1941 Sacramento Solons was great fun, and I wouldn't trade that experience for anything in the world, but it was the minor leagues, and I wanted to be in the bigs. I'd played pretty darn well for the Solons, hitting .309 with 13 home runs and 88 RBIs — numbers I felt were worthy of a return trip to the major leagues. I was hoping that Branch Rickey would feel that way, too, despite the fact that he was pretty negative about my chances back when he'd sent me down. My notion that Rickey would give me a return ticket to the Cardinals turned out to be fool-hearty. He was even more negative than he'd been the year before, telling me, "You'll never play major league baseball again, or be on ANY winning ballclub." That really hurt me because I still believed that I could play big league ball. Rickey's assault on my playing ability officially ended my relationship with the St. Louis Cardinals — but I hoped it wasn't ending my playing days altogether. I really wanted to prove him wrong, but it was going to have to happen elsewhere — if at all.

News of my release from the Cardinals organization made its way around the league and into the consciousness of Luke Sewell, catcher-manager of the St. Louis Browns. He soon called me and told me that he felt that they could use me on their 1942 ballclub. The catch was that he wasn't looking for a third baseman — he was looking for a second baseman to replace the Don Heffner/Johnny Lucadello platoon he'd had in '41. Luke knew all about my service with the Cardinals, as well as my recent good season at Sacramento, so he said, "Don, I want you to be my second baseman. I know you haven't really played second base in the majors, but I want you to learn — I KNOW you can do it. I want you to learn everything. Talk to the second basemen you know — they'll help you. If anyone has any thing negative to say about it, tell them to take it up with me."

If there was ever a hint of doubt in my mind about my ability to make the switch at this point in my career, Luke's confidence in me quickly buried it. I jumped at the opportunity and told him I'd do it. I went to Browns' spring training and really worked my butt off. When we played exhibition games against the Yankees, I'd ask Joe Gordon for help — and he gladly obliged. When we'd play the Red Sox, I'd ask Bobby Doerr — and he, too, was very helpful. I picked the brains of every second baseman I could, taking their input and implementing it in a way that best suited my abilities. Luke's experiment with me worked well through spring training, so I happily found myself in the St. Louis Browns start-ing line-up when the 1942 season kicked off on this day — and I owe my good fortune to Luke.

So, with all of that said, you'll now understand why my 0-for-4 at the plate in my Browns debut on this day was just fine with me. Sure, I would have loved to have helped out with a hit or two, but we won the game, 3-0, over the White Sox at Comiskey Park, and that's all that mattered. I batted lead-off and started at second base — my new position. We got a finely-pitched 3-hit shutout from our 25-year old right-hander, Bob Muncrief, assuring us a good start to the new season. It felt good to be back in the Big Show.

Being back in the major leagues wasn't my only reason for being especially grateful that day. With the dark and uncertain turn that our country had taken just four months earlier on December 7th, 1941, I felt very lucky to be playing any ball at all considering our nation's entry into World War II. There was talk of canceling the season altogether, but President Roosevelt decided that that would be bad for the country's morale, so he "green lighted" baseball to go for-ward with the season. In 1942, at the age of 29, I registered for the draft and was prepared to serve — but at that time they were not taking guys that "old," so I got passed over. I also had a child, and at that time the military wouldn't take a family's sole provider. Later on, as the war intensified, the services had a greater need for more men, so they began taking guys regardless of their age or family situation. With that being the case, it looked like a sure bet that I would enter

I chatted with one of the sportswriters prior to our 1942 season-opening series against the White Sox at Comiskey Park. I am, no doubt, telling him how happy I was to be back in the big leagues.

the military immediately — and I was ready. But, as peculiar as it sounds, while I was perfectly capable of the tough physical demands required to play big league baseball, the military designated me physically unfit to serve — 4F — because of a trick knee and a kidney problem. It just wasn't meant to be, I guess. Still, I knew there was a chance that my 4-F status could change in the future, so I decided to play hard and enjoy baseball while I could.

APRIL 15, 1942: We played game two of our season-opening series against the White Sox on this day, and we won again, 6-5. It was an exciting win. We scored five runs in the top of the 9th to take a 6-3 lead, the big blow being a 3-run homer by our rookie shortstop, Vern Stephens. Elden Auker pitched eight great innings for us, but Sewell opted to bring in reliever George Caster to pitch the bottom of the 9th. George made it interesting by allowing two runs to score, but then he finally closed the door. I picked up my first hit and stolen base for the Browns in this game.

APRIL 16, 1942: Right-hander Denny Galehouse pitched us to our third win in a row, a 13-3 romp to close out our series with the White Sox. I had a nice day with the bat in the win, going 3-for-5 with a triple and three RBIs.

APRIL 17, 1942: For our fourth game of the season we moved home to St. Louis for a 4-game series with the Tigers at Sportsman's Park — and we won again! I was 1-for-4 in the game. The Browns were a truly miserable ballclub as recently as the late 1930's, but their fortunes had gotten a little better as we moved into the decade of the 1940's. After finishing dead last in 1939, the Browns improved to 6th in 1940 and 1941. We were hoping to move into the first division in 1942, and our 4-game winning streak to open the season gave us the confidence we needed. Our streak ended the next day, however, when we ran into Tigers rookie right-hander, Hal White, who shut us out, 4-0.

APRIL 28, 1942: We rolled into New York for our first series against the world champion Yankees on this day. It was my first time playing at Yankee Stadium, and it was quite a thrill to be in the legendary ballpark. We'd fallen on hard times since opening the season at 5-and-1, losing our next nine in a row. But we got another great pitching performance from Elden Auker, plus just enough offense against Yankee-great Red Ruffing to enable us to snap our losing streak with a 3-1 victory. I had one hit in four at-bats, but my one hit was kind of funny, at least in the eyes of *New York Times* sportswriter Arthur Daley. "Big Red had a superb 1-hitter after five frames," Daley wrote, "and was riding along nicely on the 1-0 lead handed him by Tommy Henrich's initial homer of the year into the right-field bleachers in the 4th. But disaster overtook the veteran in the 6th. Don Gutteridge added insult to injury — or maybe it was injury to insult — by caroming a single off Ruffing's shins with one out."

APRIL 29, 1942: Red Ruffing may have been nursing sore shins during our game against New York at Yankee Stadium on this day, but when the game was over I was nursing an 0-for-5. That was always frustrating, but it was always an easier fate to accept when your team won the game. And we won big, too — 11-6. Plus, my 0-fer was somewhat productive as I was able to pick up two RBIs. Leading our club's offensive attack on this day was our centerfielder Walt Judnich. Walt was a good looking left-handed hitting and throwing 25-year old who'd broken in with the Browns back in 1940. He'd originally been New York Yankee property, but they dispatched him to the Browns because the Yanks already had a pretty good centerfielder by the name of Joe DiMaggio. Walt validated the Yankee scouts' belief in him by turning in an excellent rookie season in which he hit .303 with 24 home runs. He suffered a bit of a sophomore slump in 1941 when he dipped to .284 and 14 long balls, but he rebounded for us in 1942 with a solid season in which he batted .313 with 17 homers and 82 RBIs. Two of those round trippers and three of those runs batted in came in our win over the Yankees on this day, and I know that Walt particularly loved to do well against New York since they had originally signed him. Walt's future looked bright in St. Louis, but he was lost to the U.S Army from 1943 through 1945. He was a great kid and I liked him a lot. We really missed him while he was gone. Walt did have a couple of nice years upon his return, but he, like many of the guys who'd sacrificed so many prime years to World War II, was never quite the same player that he was before the war.

I forced Yankee shortstop Phil Rizzuto at second base in this play from our game against them in the Bronx on April 29th, 1942.

MAY 16, 1942: Being new to the American League, I had yet to be a firsthand witness to any of Ted Williams' heroics — until this day. We were facing the Red Sox at Sportsman's Park, and it was a real pitcher's duel between Bob Muncrief and Sox right-hander Tex Hughson. We were trailing, 2-0, when I came up in the 5th with runners on second and third — and Hughson had yet to allow a hit. I singled to break up the no-hitter and tie the game, but we got only one more hit the rest of the way. The score was still tied when Williams came up in the 9th with a man on, and he promptly smashed a home run into the stands to win the game, 4-2.

MAY 31, 1942: *BROWNS OVERCOME INDIANS, 5-4 AND 8-3; GUT-TERIDGE SETS PACE WITH SIX HITS.* That was the headline summarizing our sweep of the Indians in a Sportsman's Park doubleheader on this day. I was 2-for-4 with a triple and an RBI in the opener, and 4-for-4 in the nightcap. It was the first REALLY big offensive day I had with the Brownies, and it was a thrill to do it in front of the home fans — although there were only about 8,000 of them there!

JUNE 5, 1942: I was 2-for-7 on this day as we played a 16-inning nail-biter against the Athletics at Shibe Park, but we finally prevailed, 1-0. Our right-handed knuckleballer, Johnny Niggeling, pitched 12 innings before giving way to George Caster. Niggeling was 39 years old and had not done much in his career up to that point. He broke in with two games for the 1938 Bees, pitched in several games with the Reds in '39, then came to the Browns in 1940 where he won just 14 games between '40 and '41. But he came on strong for us in '42 and won 15 games, and his fine work in this day's ballgame was very typical of many of the great performances he turned in for us.

JUNE 9, 1942: I stroked a single off Red Sox southpaw Oscar Judd in a 7-4 loss at Fenway Park. We had been going very well lately, winning eight of our last ten, but our loss to Boston on this day ushered in the beginning of a 7-game losing streak. That wasn't the only thing that went bad while in Boston. I had a little batting streak going, and my single off Judd that day extended it to 10 straight. But Tex Hughson held me hitless in five at-bats the next day to snap my streak and hand us a 10-3 defeat.

JUNE 19, 1942: I celebrated another birthday, my 30th, right where I was happiest — on the ballfield — as we played the Athletics at Sportsman's Park on this day. A 4-hit shutout victory by Johnny Niggeling ensured that my birthday was a happy one despite the fact that I had a long day at the plate, collecting no hits in five at-bats. Even an 0-for-5 couldn't dampen my spirits these days because everything was going so well with Luke's experiment with me at second base. Heck, it wasn't even really an experiment anymore — I was now entrenched in the line-up. A United Press sportswriter had noticed what was going on, so he came to town and wrote a very nice piece about me. Under a headline that touted our recent climb in the standings, the subhead read *CARDINAL CASTOFF DOES WELL AT SECOND FOR BOSS, LUKE SEWELL.* "He was 'washed up' when the Browns took him this spring on a 'make good or else' proposal," the article wrote. "So today, Don Gutteridge, the St. Louis Cardinal castoff is the best 'paper second baseman' in baseball, and if it wasn't for Joe Gordon and Bobby Doerr he might get some attention."

Continuing, the article said, "The little Pittsburg, Kansas, scrambler has such an amazing fielding record you have to go back over it to be sure you didn't make an error yourself. But there it is, just three miscues in 60 games and 364 chances handled. The season is more than a third gone and he is so far ahead of the all-time big league fielding record he seems a cinch to set a new one. And it is the first time in 10 years of baseball that he ever played second base! Sewell took him in hand in spring training and liked his fiery spirit and his scrambling technique of going after everything. By April 15, Gutteridge was the most valuable man on the team and Sewell said the Cards couldn't have him back for double the money." I felt great when I read that column, and I was hoping that Branch Rickey would see it, too.

JUNE 23, 1942: "Gutteridge exploded his first homer of the year into the left-field bleachers as the enemy's opening gun, but Joe DiMaggio opened his three-hit night with a single starting the 2nd, when the Yanks tied the count." That was the *New York Times'* James P. Dawson describing the early action in our game against the Yankees at Sportsman's Park on this day. My lead-off homer against Yanks right-hander Atley Donald was quite a thrill for me, and I added a single later in the game, but I was no match for the great Joe DiMaggio. Three hits for Joe usually meant a Yankee win, and that was the case on this day as we lost, 6-5. My round-tripper turned out to be my only one of the season despite the fact that I ended up getting over 600 at-bats in '42. I hit doubles and triples like I always had, but I just no longer seemed to have the home run range I had back in my days as a Cardinal.

JUNE 24, 1942: I was having another good game at the plate against the Yankees on this day, slapping out three hits in five at-bats through eight innings, but we were trailing, 5-4, in the 8th when my day came to an end. Umpire George Pipgras was already in a bad mood after getting berated by Yankee catcher Bill Dickey an inning earlier when Pipgras called Dickey out at second on an attempted steal. I should have considered that before I got into it with Pipgras for the same thing. James P. Dawson of the *New York Times* wrote it up this way — "It took umpire George Pipgras to stifle the ardor of manager Luke Sewell of the Browns and Don Gutteridge. Pipgras found it necessary to banish both in the 8th inning when exception was taken to his decision on whether Gutteridge had pilfered second." Luke and I were in the clubhouse when New York tacked on another run in the 9th to win, 6-4.

JULY 5, 1942: Here's an especially good day for a pitcher — giving up just two runs in a complete-game 6-hit win while helping your own cause by hitting a double, a triple, and a home run at the plate. That's what right-hander Steve Sundra did for us on this day as we beat the White Sox, 13-2, in the second game of a twin bill at Comiskey Park. I had a couple of hits with two RBIs in the win, but Steve obviously needed no help from me or anyone else on this day. He had just come to us a few weeks earlier in a trade with Washington, and he ended up pitching pretty well for us winning eight and losing only three in 13 starts after coming over. Steve was especially valuable to us in 1943 when he won 15 games, but we eventually lost him when he entered the service in 1944 and was gone through '45.

JULY 9, 1942: Rookie sensation Hank Borowy collared me on this day — along with a lot of my teammates — as we lost to New York, 5-2, at Yankee Stadium. Because of the war, there was a real awareness of world events every day, and this day featured a stark reminder of what was going on overseas. A fresh-faced 17-year old boy dressed in a military uniform threw out the first ball of the game to Yankee catcher, Buddy Rosar. The kid, it turned out, was King Peter of Yugoslavia. His country had recently been conquered by the Nazis, and King Peter had fled to England. His country was now occupied, and I couldn't help but think what a burden of responsibility that was for such a young boy. It was the first ballgame he'd ever seen, and I was very happy that he was able to briefly escape his troubles at the ballpark. That's what millions of Americans did — and still do — every summer.

JUNE 10, 1942: King Peter of Yugoslavia was gone, but our inability to beat the Yanks remained as they again beat us on this day, 5-2, at Yankee Stadium. Johnny Niggeling couldn't control his knuckler, walking three and hitting another in the 1st inning. He never made it out of the frame, with New York tallying all five of their runs before Luke Sewell pulled him with two outs. I racked up a couple of singles off Yankee starter Atley Donald, but he was pretty tough on us, allowing just five total hits while hurling a complete game. I was able to score following one of my hits, but I was erased on a double-play following my other single. The New York double-play combination of Phil Rizzuto and Joe Gordon was one of the best in baseball, and they were on a record pace at this early point of the season. Their twin-killing involving me in this game was their 108th of the campaign. Incidentally, I had a stolen base wiped from the record in this one. Here's how John Drebinger of the *New York Times* explained it — "There was quite a harangue in the 1st inning when Don Gutteridge, after drawing a pass, lit out for a steal of second while Harlond Clift, the batter, reached far out for a futile stab at the pitch. Umpire George Pipgras called Clift out for interfering with the catcher, but before play resumed it seemed as if George had to explain the matter to everyone on the field, including his two fellow umpires, Art Passarella and Bill Summers." To tell you the truth, I'm still confused about it!

I was out at second as the Yankees turned their 108th double-play of the season, a phenomenal pace for this point in the season. This one went Frank Crosetti-to-Joe Gordon-to-Buddy Hassett. We dropped the game, 5-2, at Yankee Stadium on July 10th, 1942.

JULY 11, 1942: Every now and then we'd get sick and tired of getting mauled by the New York Yankees — and we'd finally bite back. That's what we did on this day as we scored four 9th-inning runs to beat the Bombers, 5-1, in the Bronx. John Drebinger of the *New York Times* said it best when he wrote, "Under cover of conditions that were bleak and dismal, the Browns suddenly decided at the Yankee Stadium yesterday that they had played the role of stooges for the world champions long enough. They had lost eight games in a row to Joe McCarthy's relentless steamroller and were trailing for eight dreary innings when, with scarcely a word of warning, they cracked down on the Yankees like a clap of thunder." The big blow of our rally in the 9th was a mammoth 2-run homer off Ernie Bonham by Chet Laabs — a name that would come to repeatedly be a thorn in the side of the New York Yankees.

JULY 17, 1942: We swept a double-header from the Athletics at Shibe Park on this day, and the victories gave us an 8-game winning streak. I hit a double in each game, but the man stealing the headlines during our streak was our leftfielder, Chet Laabs. He was a short, stocky guy, no more than 5-foot-8 and 175-lbs, but he could really drive the ball. He hit a homer in both games of our twin bill on this day, and, in fact, hit a total of eight long balls during our 8-game winning streak. Plus, he had a knack for hitting them in the clutch. Chet had been around for a few years, but he'd never hit more than 15 round-trippers in one season, but he was really on his game in 1942 and ended up finishing second in the A.L. in homers with 27.

JULY 25, 1942: I had a 4-hit day against Red Sox pitchers Oscar Judd, Mace Brown, and Mike Ryba in a game at Sportsman's Park on this day. We scored four runs in the 8th and another in the 9th, but still ended up losing in the 10th, 9-8, when Bobby Doerr drove one across for the winning margin.

AUGUST 1, 1942: We opened up August with this very positive headline in the *New York Times* — *SUNDRA OF BROWNS CHECKS YANKS, 7-3; GUTTERIDGE AND BERARDINO STAR AT BAT*. After describing how the Yankees had scored a pair of 2nd-inning runs to take a lead, the text of the article went on to say, "That pair wiped out a 1-run margin the Browns had obtained in the 1st inning when Don Gutteridge singled and counted on Johnny Berardino's double. But Red Ruffing's lead vanished in the 3rd. Gutteridge again singled and Berardino this time belted one into the leftfield bleachers for his first homer of the year. Gutteridge's third straight single started the 5th-inning rush on Ruffing." Berardino started the season in the Army Air Corps, but he was honorably discharged in July because of some failed tests, so he re-joined us at that time. He was persistent, though, and eventually re-entered the Army where he served from 1943-45. The headline mentioned Johnny starring at bat for us that day. You may not know it, but he went on to star in movies and TV, too, after his baseball career ended. He was in a number of movies before enjoying a long stay as Dr. Steve Hardy on the daytime soap opera, *General Hospital*.

AUGUST 9, 1942: Here's another one of those timeline entries I put in to remind you that it wasn't always highlights in baseball. I was 3-for-5 with a double in the opening game of a doubleheader against the Tigers at Sportsman's Park on this day, but we lost the game, 9-3. I was pleased to have been good at the plate, but I committed an error, one of five our club made in the game, and I was disappointed to see us play so poor on defense. It took a turn for the worse in the nightcap as we committed six errors on our way to a 3-1 loss. Considering that I was learning to play second base while on the job in 1942, I feel I played pretty solid. But one of the six errors in the nightcap was mine, and it was a key in our loss. Here's how the Associated Press summed it up in their recap of the game — "The winning margin in the nightcap came in the third when two Detroit runners counted on two errors made on one grounder. Don Gutteridge made the original bobble and then Mike Chartak kicked the ball around."

SEPTEMBER 6, 1942: We split a doubleheader at home against the Indians on this day. I had a long day at the plate in the opener, getting just one safety in five official at-bats as we won the game, 3-2. Wouldn't you know it — I got hot in the second game and we lose! I went 4-for-5 with a double, an RBI, and a stolen base in the nightcap, but we lost, 6-5.

SEPTEMBER 14, 1942: As I mentioned earlier, the Browns had seen many years of hard times in the past, but things were officially brighter on this day. We won a hard-fought 16-inning victory over the Athletics at Sportsman's Park, and with our win we clinched 3rd place in the American League. I was 3-for-7 against Philly right-hander Lum Harris, and it was quite a thrill to make a solid contribution to our clinching of 3rd place. It may sound silly to celebrate climbing to 3rd place, but when the fans are used to a perennial 2nd-division finish, 3rd place looks mighty fine. Plus we felt like we were a team on the rise, so we viewed 3rd place as a stepping stone to even better finishes in the near future. Many of the Brownies who had never finished in the first division, like Harlond Clift for example, were also looking forward to finally receiving a check for the 3rd-place share of the World Series gate receipts. Only 1st-division clubs received World Series shares.

SEPTEMBER 20, 1942: We closed out the 1942 season on this day with a doubleheader split against the White Sox at Sportsman's Park. I sat out both games as Luke Sewell let some of the back-up guys play. Unlike the empty feeling I had as I sat out the last game of the 1940 season with the Cardinals, I felt good as we wrapped up the '42 campaign. I had just completed a full season back in the majors, and I had been an important contributor to our team's vast improvement. It was something that seemed impossible just a year earlier when Branch Rickey told me I was through as a big leaguer. I had great satisfaction in proving him wrong, and I felt confident that my future with the Brownies held even bigger and better things for me.

1943

APRIL 21, 1943: Opening day 1943 — and we made the most of it with a 3-0 win over the White Sox in front of a small home crowd at Sportsman's Park. World War II travel restrictions were blamed for the small turnout, but the fans who did make it were treated to a fine game. Al Hollingsworth, a left-handed pitcher who had done very well for us in 1942, appeared to be in mid-season form and pitched a complete game. Vern Stephens and Chet Laabs, two more players who excelled for us in '42, gave reason to believe that we could expect repeat performances from them in the new season when they delivered clutch hits to drive in all of our runs. I was 1-for-4 out of the lead-off slot with a run scored, and on defense I was back at my customary spot at second base. As always, I was very excited to begin a new season.

MAY 2, 1943: After dropping a 5-4 decision the day before, we wrapped up a series against the White Sox at Comiskey Park on this day with a doubleheader sweep. The first game was a tight affair with Johnny Niggeling going nine strong frames before giving way to Bob Muncrief with the score tied, 2-2. A key double-play erased Sox catcher Mike Tresh and pitcher Thornton Lee, allowing us to keep the game tied for Chet Laabs' 11th inning heroics, a solo shot off Gordon Maltzberger that turned out to be the game-winner. The nightcap was less of a nail-biter as we won easily, 5-1, behind another strong pitching performance, this time turned in by Steve Sundra. I contributed a hit and a run in each game. All in all, it was a good day on the job, which made for a nice dinner with my teammates back at the restaurant in the Hotel Del Prado on the corner of 53rd and Hyde Park Boulevard where we stayed whenever we were in Chicago.

A comebacker to Johnny Niggeling led to this double-play, which forced the White Sox's Mike Tresh at second base. I then threw over to George McQuinn to complete the twin killing. This play was from the opener of a doubleheader at Comiskey Park on May 2nd, 1943. We swept the double-feature, 3-2 and 5-1.

MAY 13, 1943: As a team, we were inconsistent over the next few weeks, and our record stood at 8-and-7 as we got set to play Boston at Sportsman's Park on this day. As for me personally, I had been very consistent since the start of the season — consistently in a horrible slump. After my opening day hit, I went hitless in our next four games — 0-for-15. I picked up one hit in each of our next three games after that, but then I failed to hit in our next seven games after that — 0-for-24. So I was hitting a miserable 4-for-55 — an .073-mark — when we began our game against the Red Sox on this day. Luke Sewell had been very patient, continuing to bat me lead-off and leaving me in for every inning, hoping that I would break out. He finally made a subtle change, though, dropping me down to the number eight spot in the batting order. I guess he was hoping that I would press less without the responsibility of being the lead-off man. I don't know if that's the reason, but I responded with my first 2-hit game of the season. The game turned out to be a 12-inning battle with the Sox winning, 6-4. You hate to lose an extra-inning game like that, especially at home, but, in an effort to find something positive, I was hoping that the game signaled an end to my slump.

MAY 29, 1943: My slump did not end. I had exactly zero hits in the eight games that followed my 2-hit game against the Red Sox. In some of those games Sewell finally resorted to using me as a substitute, even sitting me out completely in one game on May 21st. It hit an all-time low on this day, however, when I was benched in favor of Don Heffner — one of the players I was brought in to replace the previous year. It was tough to take, and it didn't help me feel any better when we lost the game that day, 10-2, to the Athletics at Shibe Park.

MAY 31, 1943: I sat out the next four games with the exception of one contest where I was put in as a late-game defensive substitute. Heffner had failed to hit, too, so Sewell started me in the second game of a twin bill against the Red Sox at Fenway Park on this day. I can't exactly say that I busted out of my slump, but I did get one hit in four at-bats. It wasn't anything worth writing home about, plus we lost the game by one run in the 10th inning, but I had a feeling that maybe I had hit rock-bottom and was now on my way up.

JUNE 3, 1943: We arrived in New York for our first trip to Yankee Stadium on this day — a 5-game series. We played them tough in every game except the finale, even battling into extra innings in three of the games. But when it was all said and done, the results looked all too familiar — the Yanks won four out of five. We dropped the opener on this day, 2-1, and only a 5th-inning solo homer by George McQuinn stopped us from being shut out. The game was tied, 1-1, until the bottom of the 9th when we GAVE the game away. Here's how Louis Effrat of the *New York Times* described the game-ending action. "First up in the New York 9th, Charlie Keller hoisted a high fly to rightfield. Mike Chartak dashed madly toward the low barrier, turned suddenly, reversed steps and obviously lost the ball in the sun. Chartak didn't even have time to hide his embarrassment, having to hustle to hold Keller to a lucky double. A great stop and throw by Don Gutteridge, while off balance, retired Johnny Lindell, but could not prevent Keller from reaching third, so Luke Sewell ordered intentional passes to Bill Dickey and Joe Gordon, loading the paths and setting the stage for a possible double-play. Muncrief saw Nick Etten rifle two straight fouls, though the Yankees protested the second one was fair. Then he fanned Etten with a slow curve. With the comparatively weak hitting Bill Johnson up and two down, it appeared that Muncrief might escape. However, the right-hander suddenly lost the range, threw four successive balls and forced Keller home with the winning marker. Johnson, turning to run to the clubhouse, had to be reminded by the batboy that the rules insisted that he go to first." There you have it — one gift-wrapped victory, with regards from us, to the New York Yankees. It's funny, though, how the good teams seem to get all the "gifts." Maybe their talent allows them to position themselves to be gift recipients more so than the second division clubs. And at 12-and-20, and in last place following this defeat, we were the epitome of a second division ballclub.

George "Snuffy" Stirnweiss did his best to try and turn two on this play, but my wide slide slowed him down just enough to help Milt Byrnes reach first safely in this game at Yankee Stadium on June 3rd, 1943.

JUNE 4, 1943: Instead of losing to the Yankees in the 9th inning on this day, as we'd done the previous day, we let them beat us in the 10th. It was very frustrating. Vern Stephens almost single-handedly won the game for us, however, by singling, doubling, and homering twice to drive in three runs. Vern's great day at the plate raised his already impressive average to .404, and he had so menaced the Yankees that Johnny Murphy intentionally passed him in the top of the 10th with the game tied, 4-4, two down, and me standing on second. Murphy got out of the jam, unfortunately, and that gave Joe Gordon an opportunity to win it in the 10th, which he did with a towering 2-run homer off George Caster into the deep reaches of Yankee Stadium's lower leftfield stand. Gordon, my one-time second base mentor, was an absolute nuisance to us on this day. In addition to his game-winning bomb, Joe had a single, a stolen base, three RBIs, and his usual stellar play in the field.

I received the peg from our catcher Frankie Hayes, but not in time to snap the tag down on Joe Gordon — he was safe on the steal. Gordon continued to dog us later in the game, too, delivering the final insult in the bottom of the 10th inning when he homered off George Caster. That led New York to a 6-4 victory at Yankee Stadium. The date was June 4th, 1943.

JUNE 12, 1943: After losing five of seven extra-inning games over the previous two weeks, we got a much-needed overtime win in our game on this day, beating the Indians, 7-6, at Cleveland. The Indians pitchers were having control problems all day, and it was a walk to me that finally did them in. The pitcher on the mound in relief at that time was a young rookie flame-thrower who would soon go on to greatness. Here's how the Associated Press recapped the game-winning run — "It was the seventeenth walk to St. Louis that did the business. Allie Reynolds was on the throwing end, and the free ticket went to Don Gutteridge with one down in the 11th. Milt Byrnes fouled out, but Chet Laabs popped a single behind second base and Gutteridge made it all the way home from first to give the pitching triumph to George Caster, who had relieved Al Hollingsworth in the 6th."

As for my slump, I was, in fact, gradually coming out of it. Since returning to the line-up on May 31st in Boston, we'd played 11 games in which I knocked out 10 hits. That translated to just a puny .222 average over that span, but when you're climbing your way back up from .073, .222 was clearly a trend in the right direction.

JUNE 19, 1943: On this day there was a slight hiccup in my recovery from my big slump. Detroit pitchers Tommy Bridges, Hal White, and Hal Newhouser held me to 0-for-7 as we lost, 4-3, in 12 innings. When you go 0-for-7 AND lose the ballgame, it's a tough afternoon on any day — but it's especially painful when it happens on your birthday. That was the indignity I suffered on this day as I turned 31 years of age. I didn't have to suffer for long, though. The next day we exacted a measure of revenge on Detroit by sweeping them in a doubleheader. I saw it as a belated birthday gift, sweetened by the fact that I collected four hits in eight at-bats on the day.

JUNE 26, 1943: My slump was over. The newspapers said as much when they reported on our victory at Sportsman's Park on this day. The Associated Press headline blared, *BROWNS' 3 DRIVES SUBDUE TIGERS, 6-3; TWO RUNS RESULT FROM EACH ATTACK — SIX HITS SPLIT BY GUTTERIDGE AND KREEVICH.* The text went on to announce my breakout from my slump with what could only be classified as a true backhanded compliment. "Don Gutteridge and Mike Kreevich, two of the weakest of the weak-batting Browns, came through with three hits apiece today to lead the way in a 6-3 victory over the Tigers. Gutteridge, who apparently has emerged from an extended slump, slammed out three doubles, one in each of the Browns' 2-run scoring innings."

For those of you who like statistics, here are some to mull over. I've detailed the phases of my slump up through this day, but the totality of it is this — in the 50 games in which I played prior to our win against Detroit on this day, I batted .196. From this day on I hit just over .300, which allowed me to finish with a season-ending mark of .273. It was quite an accomplishment for me considering the deep hole that I'd dug for myself through the first quarter of the season. Amazingly, my .273 average for the 1943 season turned out to be my highest big league average with the exception of my rookie season in 1936 when I only played in the month of September. It just goes to show you that you should never give up — always keep battling.

JULY 5, 1943: Games against the Yankees were always very important to us. As a perennial 2nd-division club, playing the Yankees gave us an opportunity to show the fans that we were, in fact, a big league team who could compete with New York — OCCASIONALLY. Games between us and New York had become more and more competitive as we rose in the standings in 1942, and that trend continued in 1943 as the Yankees made their run at yet another pennant. That said, it was bad enough to lose to the Yanks in the usual ways, but the way they beat us on this day was particularly hard to take. It was the first game of a doubleheader and we were trailing, 2-1, with one out in the bottom of the 9th inning when I came up to bat. I hit the ball hard to short where Frank Crosetti bobbled it for an error. Our next batter, left-handed swinging centerfielder Milt Byrnes, singled to center. I went from first to third on the hit and continued right on home to score the tying run when Yankee centerfielder Johnny Lindell's throw went into our dugout. Then umpire Bill Summers motioned Milt home, too, so he quickly crossed the plate with the winning run. Our entire team celebrated euphorically, beating a hasty exit to the clubhouse where we would rest until the time came to return to the field for the nightcap. However, within minutes Summers appeared in our clubhouse telling us to get back on the field to finish the game. He admitted that he had erred in allowing Milt to score, saying Byrnes should have remained at third. We knew Summers was right, but we griped anyway. Many games had been won or lost on bad calls by umpires, but it was rare to have one reversed. Nevertheless, we had to go back out there, and wouldn't you know it — Yankee second baseman Joe Gordon won the game for New York, 3-2, with a solo homer in the 11th. It was quite disheartening, and we went on to lose the nightcap, too, 8-5.

July 5th, 1943 — I was safe at third following a single by Milt Byrnes in the opener of a doubleheader against the Yankees at Sportsman's Park. A wild throw from the outfield went out of play, and the umpires waved me and Milt home. That gave us a 3-2 win — or so we thought.

JULY 8, 1943: *BROWNS SINK RED SOX, 5-2; GUTTERIDGE AND CHAR-TAK LEAD ATTACK.* That was the Associated Press headline for their article about our game at Sportsman's Park on this day. "Don Gutteridge led in hits with four out of five times at bat, including a triple," the text reported, "but Mike Chartak's two singles drove in three of the runs. Gutteridge had four straight, then fouled out his fifth time at the plate as he attempted to sacrifice." Mike was a big, left-handed hitting outfielder who had been buried in the Yankee farm system for years before coming to us in the middle of the '42 season. He struck out a lot, but he would occasionally chip in some very clutch hits. His career was cut short, however, when he contracted tuberculosis following the 1944 season.

JULY 9, 1943: Mike Chartak stayed hot, and I did, too, as we beat the Red Sox again, 5-4. It ended when Mike hit a dramatic game-winning 9th-inning solo homer on the Sportsman's Park rightfield roof. Earlier in the game I had homered, too, a bases-empty clout off Tex Hughson. It turned out to be my only round-tripper of the season.

JULY 17, 1943: I continued to swing the bat well as we beat Cleveland on this day, 3-1, at Sportsman's Park. I was 3-for-4 with two doubles and an RBI. Denny Galehouse, our veteran right-hander, continued to pitch very well for us, allowing just six hits while going the distance.

AUGUST 10, 1943: Galehouse won again on this day, out-pitching Yankee rookie Hank Borowy as we whipped New York, 10-2, in the first game of a 5-game series in St. Louis. I went 2-for-5 with a double in the game. This game turned out to be the first of 14 straight that I would hit in. The only negative to the game was that somebody got hurt, and I was sort of responsible. *INJURY FORCES GORDON OUT* said a headline in the *New York Times*. James P. Dawson's text went on to say, "Joe Gordon, his leg and back hurt as Gutteridge barged into him at second in the 1st inning, had to retire for the first time this year after the 4th." Dawson's use of the word "barge" might lead you to believe that my slide to take Gordon out was dirty, but it wasn't. It was clean, intended only to break up a double-play, but Gordon got hurt and had to miss a few games. It was unfortunate, but it was part of the game — something I had experienced myself on countless occasions. Still, I felt bad for Gordon because he was so helpful to me when I first started playing second base the previous season. I often sought out Gordon's advice on various aspects of playing second, and he never failed to offer valuable input.

AUGUST 11, 1943: We drubbed the Yanks again, 9-1, behind stellar pitching from Steve Sundra on this day. A subhead in James P. Dawson's *New York Times* column declared, *YANKEES YIELD SIXTEEN BLOWS TO WINNERS, GUT-*

TERIDGE LEADING THE ATTACK WITH FOUR. It didn't seem to matter to me whether it was Yanks starter Marius Russo or reliever Jim Turner on the mound that day, I was seeing the ball great no matter who was pitching. Hitting is a funny thing. If someone could figure out what makes a player "see the ball well" during a hot streak, he'd make a million dollars. I could never figure it out. Still, whether I was in a hot streak or a cold spell, I never saw a pitcher that I didn't think I could hit. Confidence like that may not always be well-founded, but it's probably necessary for any athlete who wants to make it to the top level of his particular sport. Thinking I could hit any pitcher was not to say that I thought I would get a hit EVERY time I went up to the plate, but I did honestly believe that I was capable of getting a hit off any pitcher any time I went up to bat. That was my philosophy every time I walked to the plate with a bat in my hand. I think that's why I did as well as I did — because I was positive and knew I was going to be able to hit. It didn't matter who was pitching — I proved that I could hit them all.

Most hitters, regardless of what they say, are guess hitters, but I tried NOT to guess. I tried to make myself follow that ball, follow that ball, follow that ball. I think I was a better hitter by doing that. Now they teach you what pitches to look for in certain situations. If you are ahead in the count, look for a fastball — or look for a curveball — or look high — or look low — or whatever. I always thought it best to just see the ball and follow it. That may sound like an oversimplification of the hitting process, but I believe that it is really the key to making solid contact with the baseball.

AUGUST 18, 1943: We beat the Philadelphia Athletics, 4-0, at Sportsman's Park on this day. I was continuing to swing a hot bat, this time getting three hits in four times at bat with a double and two RBIs against a 34-year old rookie named Orie Arntzen. It was the tenth straight game in which I had hit safely. Before we took the field we were informed that the front office had traded Harlond Clift and Johnny Niggeling to the Washington Senators. It was a bit of a surprise because Niggeling was pitching pretty well for us, but it was particularly surprising to see the very popular Clift be traded. Harlond had been a star for the Browns for years — and this at a time when Brownie stars were few and far between. But Clift was getting up in age and, more importantly, he represented the old guard of the Browns. I hate to say this, but Clift was a losing ballplayer. It wasn't completely his fault — it was an inevitable side effect of playing for the old-guard Browns for so long. Luke Sewell felt the old-guard Brownies had come to accept defeat as part of playing with the Browns, and he believed that Clift fell right in that category. Harlond was a great guy, but Sewell did not think he fit in with the new direction in which we were headed.

The new Browns direction was to win and not accept defeat. Sewell wanted guys who wanted to win, guys who reflected his philosophy. We'd made significant headway into instilling Sewell's new philosophy in 1942, and we were continuing to hammer home his theory in 1943. The fellow we picked up in the Clift trade definitely embodied Sewell's philosophy — infielder Ellis Clary. Ellis was 26 years old and had been a good utility player for the Senators from his rookie season in '42 right through the time of his trade. Clary continued to play well after joining us, hitting .275 in 23 games while showing solid glovework in the field. His numbers were never going to wow anybody — in fact he never played in more than 26 games over the next two seasons — but he brought an intangible spirit to the club that would prove invaluable in 1944. Clary was small, just 5-foot-8 and about 160 pounds, but his charisma was very big. He proved to be a pretty good ballplayer, but he did his best work in the street. He loved to go out at night, but he'd never over do it. He'd play four or five great games, and then he'd hit the street. He wasn't a consistent day-in and day-out 150-game player, but he was a good fielder and filled in ably at third, second — wherever. Where Clary helped the team most, however, was with his ability to keep everybody loose.

Ellis was a fun guy and very witty. He always had something to say that made everyone laugh. In the clubhouse, he was always keeping everyone on their toes. A recurring gag from spring training of 1944 stands out in my recollection. It involved Fred Hoffman, our first base coach. Everyone played tricks on Hoffman because he was so good natured and he was okay with everything. So, as you can imagine, that made him a particularly easy target for Clary. We took spring training of 1944 at Cape Girardeau in Missouri because of World War II travel restrictions. There was a big pond next to the ballfield on which we worked out, and on the pond there were always lots of ducks and geese. Where there are lots of ducks and geese, there are always lots of goose eggs. Clary used to covertly slip goose eggs into Hoffman's uniform pants pockets. Then, when we were all dressed, Ellis would walk by and whack Fred's backside with a bat leaving a real mess on his pants. As I said, Hoffman was a lovely person — very outgoing, so he never got mad at Clary.

There was another side to the fun-loving Clary — the scrapper. Ellis wasn't afraid to fight anybody, I'll tell you that, and he got into a number of scrapes over the next couple years. He was a tough little fellow, and he would never back down. And it was Clary's fighting spirit — plus his desire to win — that made Sewell want to have Ellis on his ballclub.

SEPTEMBER 11, 1943: I had another 3-hit game on this day as we beat the White Sox, 4-1, in St. Louis. This was the last of a 10-game hitting streak that I had started back on August 29th against Detroit. Ever since emerging from my bad start, I was in one of those great hitting zones. During this 10-game hitting streak I batted .419 with five multi-hit games. When you're hitting the ball that well you kind of hate to see the end of the season up on the horizon.

SEPTEMBER 12, 1943: Two great complete-game pitching performances on this day and we had a doubleheader sweep of the White Sox at Sportsman's Park. Bob Muncrief pitched a 4-hitter in the opener to get a 2-0 win, and Denny

Galehouse tossed a 7-hitter in the nightcap for a 6-2 victory. After taking an 0-for-4 in the first game, I came back with a nice day at the plate in the second game, going 3-for-4 with two RBIs. Our two wins that day moved us into 6th place, which is where we ended up when the season concluded three weeks later. It was somewhat disappointing after rising to 3rd place the previous year, but we still felt like we were a team on the rise, and no longer a doormat to the elite teams of the American League.

SPETEMBER 19, 1943: *WHITE SOX DIVIDE PAIR WITH BROWNS; WIN 6-1 AFTER LOSING 7-4.* That summed up our twin bill at Comiskey Park on this day — the last games in which I played in 1943. I made the most of it, too, going 3-for-5 in the first game and picking up another hit in the nightcap. The text of the article wrote, "Don Gutteridge and George McQuinn led the Browns' attack in the opener, connecting for three safeties apiece. Gutteridge walloped a triple and a double." The ballclub still had 13 games left to play, but as I mentioned, I did not play in any of them. Following our doubleheader at Chicago, I had to rush home and then off to Leavenworth for an Army physical. *The Sporting News* reported the results in their October 7th issue — "Infielder Don Gutteridge of the Browns was rejected for the Army in his pre-induction examinations in Kansas because of a bad knee." That simply meant that for now I could focus on the 1944 campaign, which, as it turned out, ended up being a very special season.

Jeff Eastman, a good friend of mine from back home in Pittsburg, Kansas, stopped by to see me while we both were in Chicago. I was playing for the Brownies and Jeff was playing for Uncle Sam. We were schoolmates at Kansas State Teachers College, now called Pittsburg State University.

1 9 4 4

APRIL 18, 1944: *KRAMER OF BROWNS DEFEATS TIGERS, 2-1.* That was the headline of the Associated Press article reporting on our opening day victory at Briggs Stadium on this day. Tigers right-hander Dizzy Trout was very sharp, holding us to just six hits. I singled off him to open the game, then scored later in the inning. We didn't score again until the top of the 9th when Vern Stephens hit a solo home run. Stephens' run turned out to be a big one when Pinky Higgins answered with his own bases-empty homer in the bottom half of the inning, but Kramer shut the door after that to get the 2-1 win. Jack Kramer was a 26-year old right-handed pitcher who would play an immense role in our season by posting a great campaign in which he won 17 games. He'd been up and down with the Browns over the previous five years, his baseball temporarily interrupted by a recently completed 18-month stint with the Seabees, but Jack had failed to put it all together — until 1944. He was an interesting guy, too. Most definitely the snazziest dresser on the team.

As I previously mentioned, because of wartime travel restrictions we stayed in Missouri for spring training in 1944 — Cape Girardeau to be exact. It was sort of a small port city on the banks of the Mississippi River, about 100 miles south of St. Louis. The people there were great, and they really welcomed us to their town. There was one family there that was especially warm and welcoming to me and my roommate, Vern Stephens — the Suedekum's. Dub Suedekum was a little 7-year old fellow who would show up every day, bright and early, at Capaha Park where we worked out. He would run around, shag balls — anything to be involved. His father was away in the service and I sort of took him under my wing. Before you knew it, Dub had taken me under HIS wing, and Vernon and I would have dinner at the Suedekums' house a couple times a month to escape the monotony of the food at the Idan-Ha Hotel where we stayed. Dub's mother was a wonderful cook, too, so good that once a week she would bake us a delicious pie. She and Dub would deliver it to us at the side entrance to the hotel, and I would always give him a couple of practice balls as a gesture of thanks. I think I even got a few team-signed balls for him which might fetch a handsome sum in today's hot baseball memorabilia market.

Here's a foursome for you — Vern Stephens, 7-year old Dub Suedekum, me, and Rex — the dog. Dub's wonderful family was one of the main reasons that it was so enjoyable to train at Cape Girardeau in 1944.

As we were preparing to break camp and head north to open the season, Dub showed up with a bagful of buckeyes that he had gathered from a tree in his backyard. Many folks, like Dub, believe that buckeyes are a symbol of good luck, so he gave me the bag and asked that I give one buckeye to each player on our team — which I did. Who knows, maybe it is Dub Suedekum who should get credit for the only pennant in the history of the St. Louis Browns! In any case, Dub is all grown up now — 70 years of age and still living in Cape Girardeau. He must have been paying close attention to what he was seeing as he watched our practices because he went on to play college baseball at Valparaiso University just south of Chicago. In fact, Dub came out to a White Sox game in 1956 while he was at Valpo and I was a coaching with Chicago. He caught up with me as I came out of the clubhouse, and we had a nice visit as we recalled old times in Cape Girardeau. I heard from him again by mail a couple of years ago, and once again I was transported back to the Cape and the wonderful spring of 1944.

The people of Cape Girardeau gave us a warm welcome to their town, and that made our 1944 spring training a great experience. The fire department took advantage of our presence in town and asked us to partake in this publicity photo aimed at helping them sell the firetruck pictured here — and we were more than happy to oblige. Heck, we were all still kids at heart, and what kid wouldn't want to play on a firetruck! From left to right is Al Hollingsworth, Nelson Potter, a Cape Girardeau official, Frank Demaree, Fred Hoffman, and me.

APRIL 20, 1944: We completed a sweep of our 3-game season-opening series against Detroit with an 8-5 win on this day. I was held to just 1-for-5 against a trio of Tiger pitchers — Hal Newhouser, Joe Orrell, and Chief Hogsett — but the rest of our club banged them around pretty good. Our pitcher that day was a 34-year old rookie — 6-foot-2-inch 200-pound right-hander Sig Jakucki. Our win on this day was Jakucki's first big league victory, and he'd go on to notch 12 more before the season was over. He was a key to our success in 1944 in spite of his personal demons — mainly alcohol. As a matter of fact, Jakucki stands as a testament to just how good Sewell was at handling pitchers — on and off the ballfield.

Jakucki was in the Marines for 10 or 12 years before he came to the Browns. He'd gotten into a handful of games with the 1936 Browns at the tail end of the season, but never made it back to the big leagues until 1944. He was down in Galveston pitching for a semi-pro team when one of the Browns scouts saw him and suggested that we bring him back. "Jakucki can pitch," the scout told the front office boys, "and, better yet, he's already served his military time so he won't have to go back in the service." That's how they thought about things back in 1944 with rosters ravaged by World War II. So they brought him up — and he won 13 games for us. Sewell wasn't afraid to put Jakucki into any game because he challenged the hitters. Jak not only challenged them on the mound — I mean anywhere else, too! In a barroom — wherever. He got into the hitters' heads and made them think he'd win. Then, not being afraid to throw strikes, he'd fire that ball over the plate. Jakucki threw hard with a little twist on the ball. In other words, his fast ball did something — it had movement on it. He didn't have a great curve, only a little one he'd use once in a while. His fast ball was his out pitch and he could control it. When Jakucki wanted to throw strikes, he could throw strikes.

Off the field, well, let's say Jak loved the night life — and the drink. He was a real character and there are many stories about his drinking. We all knew he was going to drink and we accepted him. Sometimes he would pitch on a Tuesday, for example, and then disappear until Thursday or Friday. "Jakucki didn't come today," we'd say. But when every fourth day rolled around and it was his turn to pitch, he was there and ready. Sewell just let him do his thing because he knew he couldn't stop it. More importantly, Luke knew that Jakucki could still do a great job on the mound despite his drinking problem. I know it's not right, but I think that helped Jakucki excel. He knew we wouldn't get mad at him for his off-field troubles if he didn't let it affect his job of pitching. That's the way Sewell worked. Each guy was an individual to him and treated in a way that best served that particular guy. I think that came into play more than once in 1944. Sewell knew some of these fellows needed help. He knew who to get after and who NOT to, and that worked very well — especially as far as Jak was concerned.

APRIL 21, 1944: We became the only undefeated team in the American League when we downed the previously unbeaten Chicago White Sox, 5-3, on this day at Sportsman's Park. The victory ran our record to 4-and-0, but our undefeated start had certainly not yet made believers out of the Brownie fans. Proof is in this fact — this game was our home opener, yet only 2,021 fans were there to witness it. Those who were there saw another great performance from our starting rotation. This time it was Nelson Potter. Nels, like Jack Kramer, Steve Sundra, and Sig Jakucki who started the previous three games, was dominant. Potter allowed just six hits while going the distance. He was very strong until he tired in the 8th, at which point he allowed successive singles to Wally Moses and Thurman Tucker before surrendering a home run to Hal Trosky. But we'd staked Potter to a 5-run lead by that point, so Nelson buckled down and got the job done from that point on.

The bulk of the heavy lifting on offense in this game had been done by our rightfielder, Mike Kreevich. Mike was by no means a power-hitter, but he could have fooled you on this day as he clouted two round-trippers and drove in four RBIs. His two homers were twice as many as he'd hit in the past three seasons combined. Kreevich was 36 years old at the beginning of the '44 season and his career had definitely turned in a decidedly downward direction over the previous few seasons, but he had been a bright star when he broke onto the scene in 1936. He'd made his debut as a September call-up with the 1931 Cubs, then disappeared back into the minors until he made another brief big league appearance with the 1935 White Sox. He was ready to stay in the majors the following season as his numbers attest — .307 with five home runs and 69 RBIs in 137 games. Only Joe DiMaggio was a better American League rookie than Mike Kreevich in 1936.

Kreevich spent the next five years as the White Sox's centerfielder, and he had some good seasons — particularly the 1937 campaign when Mike hit .302 with 12 homers, 73 RBIs, and a league-leading 16 3-baggers. After two more fine seasons with the Sox in 1938 and '39, Kreevich struggled with the bat in 1940 and '41 and was dealt to the Philadelphia Athletics prior to the 1942 season. He failed to regain his form with the '42 A's and was released at the end of the season. Word had it that Kreevich's problems had nothing to do with any loss of baseball ability — it was alcoholism. Learning of this, Luke Sewell thought he might be able to work with Kreevich, so the Browns signed Mike as a free agent prior to the 1943 season. Luke used Kreevich sparingly in 1943, trying to gradually feel out exactly how to get the most out of Mike in spite of his drinking problem. Kreevich ended up playing in 60 games for us in '43 and batting .255 in 161 at-bats. Those numbers were far below what he'd posted during his prime, but Sewell was pleased with what he saw and hoped he could get even more out of Kreevich in 1944. Plus, Sewell's experiment with Kreevich helped him greatly when it came to figuring out how best to handle his other alcoholic player of '44, Sig Jakucki.

Sewell's gamble with Kreevich would pay off not only in our win on this day, but all season long. Mike would play in 105 games for us in '44 and hit .301 with 44 RBIs. He would hit only three more long balls for us the the rest of the year, but his value to the ballclub was not based on his home run output. Kreevich was simply a solid hitter — plus he was a very good outfielder with decent range and a strong arm. But, let me tell you, it took every ounce of strength that Sewell had to get Kreevich to produce at the level that he produced in 1944. And Luke found out just how hard it would be to handle Kreevich as soon as we hit Cape Girardeau where we trained during the war. Cape Girardeau was a very small town and there wasn't too much to do there. There was only one or two movie theaters and, of course, two or three bars. Our players seemed to find those bars pretty quick — especially Kreevich. Our 1944 ball club loved to have fun, and Mike fit right in with that. Periodically, however, Sewell would decide that the boys were having a little too much fun and he'd make a sweep through the bars to see who was in there. Of course the guys would usually see Luke coming and they'd sneak out the back door right quick. One time Kreevich was sitting in the bar having a drink when Sewell quietly slipped onto the stool beside him. "Mike," Luke gently said, "let's go back to the hotel. You've had enough and it's way past curfew."

"Okay," Mike said with resignation, and they went back to the hotel. Sewell even escorted Mike to his room and shut the door for him to make sure that Mike's night was officially over. Then Luke went back out to finish his sweep. Well, you can imagine Sewell's shock when he went back in the same bar minutes later and found Kreevich sitting there at the same table where he was before. Mike's explanation was simple — "I just needed one more drink, skipper." That was it. He just couldn't help himself. Kreevich drank a lot, but like Jakucki, he was always ready to play. He could just handle it, I guess, and a great deal of credit has to go to Luke.

APRIL 26, 1944: Cleveland came to St. Louis for a 2-game series on this day. We'd swept the 3-game series from Chicago following our sweep at Detroit. That put our season-opening winning streak at six as we got set to play the Indians. It's a long season, so we didn't get carried away with our winning streak, but winning the first six games of the new season made me contemplate the idea that maybe we could legitimately compete for the '44 pennant. We ran our streak to seven in a row on this day when we beat the Indians, 5-2. That equaled the American League record for consecutive victories to open a season. The outcome of the game was in doubt through five innings with the score 0-0. I opened the 6th with a triple and started the scoring when I was driven in by a Vern Stephens double. We scored three more that inning and tacked on another in the 5th. The game also marked the fifth straight in which I had hit safely. I hit in five more before being stopped.

APRIL 27, 1944: *UNBEATEN BROWNS CRUSH INDIANS, 5-1; TAKE EIGHTH GAME IN A ROW TO SET LEAGUE RECORD FOR AN OPEN-ING-SEASON STREAK.* That was the headline to the Associated Press recap of our record-setting win on this day at Sportsman's Park. The text went on to say, "Like 'Ol' Man River,' the unbelievable Browns just keep rollin' along." That was something people just never expected to see written about the St. Louis Browns, but we were showing them that we were for real. More great pitching was again the catalyst for our win. This time it was our right-handed screwballer Nelson Potter going the distance and holding the Indians to just seven hits. Nelson had pitched great for us in 1943, and he was even better in 1944. He probably would have been a 20-game winner for us in '44 had he not been suspended later that season for 10 days. Instead, he finished with 19 wins, and his victory on this day was his second of the season. I was 1-for-3 with an RBI and two runs scored in the game, and I was very excited with our big win. Proof of my state of mind can be found in the closing paragraph of the Associated Press article. "The triumph sent the Browns shouting to their dressing room," the clipping explained. "Peppery Don Gutteridge yelled, 'Only 146 more to go!' "

I was safe at second on this steal against the Indians at Sportsman's Park on April 27th, 1944. Early on, the 1944 season was proving to be unlike any other in the history of the St. Louis Browns. We won on this day, 5-1, and the victory was our 8th win in a row to open the new campaign. For the record, the Cleveland second baseman is Lou Boudreau and the umpire is Bill McGowan.

APRIL 29, 1944: We won again on April 28th to extend our own record to nine straight wins to open a season, but our streak came to an end on this day when we lost to the White Sox, 4-3, at Comiskey Park. It looked like we might run our record to ten in a row as we led the game, 3-0, after 6-1/2 innings, but the Sox rallied for two runs in the bottom of the 7th and another in the 8th. We were tied, 3-3, when we fumbled the lead in the 9th. George Caster was pitching after having come on in relief in the 8th. The 9th opened with Jimmy Webb reaching safely when Vern Stephens bobbled his ground ball. Webb was moved to second on an infield out off the bat of Myril Hoag. Hal Trosky was walked to set up the double-play, but Guy Cartwright wrecked that strategy when he singled to right, scoring Webb with the winning run. Just like that, the streak was over. There was no hooting and hollering this time as we left the field, but we still liked where we were and the way we were playing. I had a hit in four trips, which meant that I'd hit in eight straight ballgames. I hit in two more before being stopped by Detroit's Hal Newhouser in a 4-3 loss at Sportsman's Park on May 2nd.

MAY 10, 1944: On this day I found out what a lot of other American Leaguers already knew — that Johnny Niggeling's knuckleball was very tough to hit! I went 0-for-4 against Niggeling in our first game against him since he'd been traded to the Senators back in August of 1943. I wasn't the only one on our ballclub that struggled hitting his dancing knuckler. In fact, he held us to just five hits as we lost the night game, 5-1, at Griffith Stadium in Washington. Niggeling's achievement is even more remarkable when you factor in his age — he was 41 years old. While he didn't have arm trouble per se, Niggeling's age had made him one of the guys who would need a little more time with the trainer in between starts back when he was with our ballclub the previous year. It's just a simple fact that rigorous physical activity makes older guys sorer, and they take longer to recover. A good trainer is a necessity if you have older guys on your ballclub, not to mention the value he brings if you have injury prone players or even guys who might have psychological issues. Our 1944 Browns team was packed with guys that fit those descriptions, so it's a good thing that we had a great trainer.

His name was Bob Bauman, and he is a real unsung hero of our 1944 success. Bauman joined the ballclub back in 1942 when Luke Sewell had taken over as Browns manager. Sewell knew when he took the St. Louis job that he was going to have his hands full in reversing the losing attitude of the Browns players, but he had no idea how bad things really were until he got his first look at the ballclub in spring training. What Luke saw was a complete lack of team spirit, repeated acts of insubordination, and poor physical conditioning. Sewell knew he was going to need help to get a lot of these guys to shape up, so he turned to Bauman. Bob was a well respected, no-nonsense trainer at St. Louis University, and Luke thought he would be the perfect guy to help him get our team in line and in shape. It turned out to be another of Sewell's wise decisions. Immediately upon joining the team, Bauman gathered everyone together and gave us a talk where he informed us that Sewell had put him in charge of seeing to it that we got in shape mentally and physically. He instituted a bed-check curfew, and also was in charge of enforcing it. He did a great job of helping Sewell set the right tone in 1942, and his hard work would finally bear fruit in 1944.

The fact that Bauman was in his third year with the Browns in 1944 did not stop our players from making him earn every penny of his salary. Not only did he have to be a great trainer — and he was one of the best in the business — he also had to be part psychiatrist. Bauman would talk to the players when he was taking care of them for one thing or another. He would use that time as an opportunity to teach them, thereby helping them mentally as well as physically.

Bob could tell right quick if a fellow had a sore arm or was just faking it. He'd tell those he suspected of faking, "You know, I'll just rub a little alcohol on it and you'll be okay. You'll be good enough to play." Or, "Your ankle's not damaged. I'll wrap a little tape on it and you'll be alright." He kept more players playing than any trainer that I ever knew, and that was very important to our 1944 ballclub. And Bob, of course, knew all about the serious drinking problems that we had on the team. One time he told me, "There is only one thing wrong with this ballclub — there are a FEW drinkers on the team. I have to hide my damn rubbing alcohol or they'll come in and drink it!" I think he was just kidding — but maybe not!

Bob Bauman (left), the trainer for the Browns, enjoyed a night in his honor — and he deserved it. Not only was he great at dealing with the physical maladies that plague all ballplayers, but he was also especially adept at dealing with the mental issues that many of our players faced. Bob was very instrumental in our success in 1944.

MAY 19, 1944: We came back down to earth, somewhat, following our season-opening 9-game winning streak. We won just five of our next 13 games after that, finally relinquishing 1st place when we lost to the Athletics on May 13th. Writers had been predicting that we would, like Cinderella at the ball on the stroke of midnight, eventually return to being the losers we'd always been in the past. But on this day we beat the 1st-place New York Yankees in their own stadium to re-take the top spot in the American League. I feel that our victory sent a message to those non-believers — a statement that we were not going away. I hit just 1-for-4 in the game, but thank goodness someone else stepped up big to help deliver us to victory. The man that sparked us to our win that day was our third baseman, Mark Christman. Mark, already with two singles to his credit, hit an 8th-inning solo homer to increase our lead to 6-4. It looked like just an insurance run at the time, but when the Yanks answered with their own run in the bottom of the inning, Mark's homer ended up being the game-winner. Christman did a fine job for us all season long. He'd started his career with the Tigers back in 1938, then joined the Browns in 1939 as part of a big 10-player trade. He ended up back in the minors in 1940 and remained there until 1943 when he rejoined the team and played a valuable utility role at all the infield positions. Harlond Clift's trade to Washington in August of '43 cleared the way for Christman to take over at third base, and he responded by doing a very good job. Mark was very dependable with the glove, but don't let his home run against the Yankees on this day fool you. Mark was generally NOT a power hitter, but he was steady with the bat and often delivered in the clutch for us.

We were in New York playing the Yankees on May 19th, 1944, when this photo was shot. Yanks second baseman Snuffy Stirnweiss got caught in this rundown while trying to swipe second, and Vern Stephens finally ended the action by tagging him out. Number 6 is our third baseman Mark Christman, and number 4 is me. The feet in the upper right corner belong to umpire Bill Summers.

MAY 20, 1944: Our 4-game series against New York at Yankee Stadium continued on this day, but we failed to win any of the remaining games, beginning with
a 3-2 defeat at the hands of the Yankees' 26-year old rookie right-hander Walt
Dubiel. In just the third start of his career, Dubiel went the distance, allowed just
four hits, made two great defensive plays, singled, doubled, scored, and drove in a
run. He did it all. Dubiel, a husky kid from Hartford, Connecticut, was discovered
by legendary Yankee scout Paul Krichell after he'd pitched three different semi-pro
teams to championships in Hartford. He pitched well for the '44 Yankees, too, eating up lots of innings while winning 13 games. He slid a bit in 1945, and was back
in the minors in '46 when the returning war veterans flooded the majors. But
Dubiel was tough and fought his way back into the big leagues in the late-40's and
early-50's. One of the four hits Dubiel surrendered on this day was a double by me.
I thought I'd legged out an infield hit, too, when my grounder to Yankee shortstop
Mike Milosevich resulted in a close play, but first base ump Bill Summers rang me
up. That was a key play in our loss because Brownie base-runners were at a premi-
um thanks to Dubiel's great work on the hill.

Despite running hard the whole way, I was out at first after grounding a Walt Dubiel pitch to
Yankee shortstop Mike Milosevich in our game against New York at Yankee Stadium on May
20th, 1944. Making the put-out is number 5, Yanks first baseman Nick Etten.

JUNE 11, 1944: Our 1944 Browns seemed to define the term "team." It seemed
like everyone made valuable contributions to our success that season. On this
day it was Gene Moore who was the hero. Gene had been a very good everyday

player with the Boston Bees in the late 1930's, but by now he was reduced to fulfilling the role of part-time outfielder for us. He still had some pop in his bat, though, something that the Indians found out on this day. We had dropped the first game of a Sportsman's Park twin bill to them by the lopsided score of 13-1, but we were locked up in a tight one in the nightcap. Luke Sewell sent Gene in to pinch hit for our catcher, Frank Mancuso, in the bottom of the 7th. We were trailing, 1-0, with the bases loaded and a new reliever, right-handed pitcher Joe Heving, entering the game. Gene unloaded on Heving's first pitch and sent it onto the rightfield pavilion roof for a grand slam home run. It was a great moment as we all greeted a smiling Gene in the dugout, and we went on to win the game, 4-2. It's funny, but Gene didn't even want to come to St. Louis following his trade to us from the Senators just as '44 spring training was set to begin. He refused to report, and the deal was almost cancelled, but Nats owner Clark Griffith ended up giving Gene a cash bonus to report to our club. He joined us and played a valuable role as a reserve all season long. Then, just as the 1944 World Series was set to begin, Sewell played one of his hunches — and Gene found himself a regular player throughout the Series. It was a dream-come-true for him.

JUNE 28, 1944: We opened up an important 3-game series against the Yankees in the Bronx on this day, but we set a bad tone for ourselves by committing three errors that directly led to our 7-2 defeat. There were other plays, too, that didn't go into the book as an error, but we knew we should have made, like a Mike Milosevich pop-up that Gene Moore and I let fall between us for a hit. We showed flashes of the solid defense that we were capable of — like the crisp 4-6-3 double-play that I turned with Vern Stephens and George McQuinn — but we knew that we were going to have to turn it up a notch if we truly wanted to compete for the pennant.

Yankee third baseman Oscar Grimes is about to become the first out in a 4-6-3 double-play at Yankee Stadium on June 28th, 1944. That's Vern Stephens making the throw as I watch.

JUNE 29, 1944: We were in and out of 1st place through much of May. We slipped into 1st place on June 1st and maintained our hold throughout the month, but the sportswriters still just couldn't believe that we'd be able to hang on. That was especially evident on this day after we lost our second game in a row to the Yankees, 1-0, in the Bronx. Here's what Yankee beat writer John Drebinger wrote in his *New York Times* article following the game — "The rarified atmosphere that prevails in the upper levels of the American League's sizzling pennant race is still proving entirely too much for Luke Sewell and his pace-setting Browns. For eight innings at the Stadium yesterday, the St. Louisans battled the Yankees tooth and nail while their Sig Jakucki remained locked in a blistering scoreless tie with Walt Dubiel. But in the last of the 9th the Brownies once again fell victims of that dizziness which assails so many clubs unaccustomed to the thin air that envelopes 1st place." Dizzy or not, we were still in 1st place, 2-1/2 games ahead of the Yanks, and despite our disappointment at losing, we were elated to be at the top of the A.L. heap.

JUNE 30, 1944: Apparently cured of the dizziness that John Drebinger of the *New York Times* had said afflicted our ballclub, we extended our lead by beating the Yankees on this day, 3-0, behind Al Hollingsworth. Al was really sharp, allowing just two Yankees to reach second base while going the route. Vern Stephens was the hero on offense, quickly getting us on the scoreboard by poling a 2-run homer off Joe Page in the 1st inning. I had a tough series in New York, getting no hits in 11 at-bats over the course of the three games, but I didn't let it get to me. We were leaving the Bronx in 1st place with a 3-1/2 game lead, and that was what really mattered to me. There was an interesting side story to our win on this day, and it involved what I mentioned about Al allowing just two Yankees to reach second base. His sinker was really dropping off the table, inducing lots of ground balls. On five occasions Al got Yankee players to ground into double-plays. I was involved in turning all five of the twin killings, and it was a new record for second baseman. For you details guys, here's how they went down: 1. Stephens to Gutteridge to George McQuinn; 2. Mark Christman to Gutteridge to McQuinn; 3. Gutteridge to Stephens to McQuinn; 4. Gutteridge to Stephens to McQuinn; 5. Gutteridge to Stephens to McQuinn. The record has since been surpassed, but it was quite a thrill to pull it off, especially at Yankee Stadium.

As you can see, Vern Stephens was in on four of those five double-plays, and let me tell you — he was a fine double-play partner. I think we made a very good combination. He had an above-average arm and was very accurate. When he threw that ball to first base, he hit that mitt. When he threw it to me at second, he gave me the ball right where I wanted it. He'd throw it to me a little to the right behind second base if a guy was coming, or in front of the base if I had plenty of time. He could feel when to cut the ball loose and when not to. He really could read me, and because of that he made me a better second baseman. And, everybody knows he could hit. While he was only about 5-foot-10, Stephens was powerfully built. He had a wide, slightly open stance, and stood deep in the batter's box — and he packed a heck of a wallop. He hit .294 with 14 home runs and 92 RBIs as a rookie in 1942, then followed that with another great year in '43 as he hit .289 with 22 homers and 91 runs driven in. He had MVP-type numbers for us in 1944 — .293 with 20 home runs and 109 RBIs.

Everybody knows that Vern Stephens (second from left) was a great hitter, but his fine play at shortstop is sometimes overlooked. His supporting cast of infielders weren't too bad, either. On the far left is Ellis Clary, then working from right to left is George McQuinn, me, Mark Christman, and Floyd Baker.

The Browns had signed Stephens in 1937 for a $500 bonus, and he was a real plum product at shortstop. There were some other clubs who'd wanted him — the Red Sox and the Indians to name a couple — but Vernon's father advised him to sign with the "lowly" Browns because he believed that he'd get to the major leagues faster. Mr. Stephens turned out to be right. Like me, Vernon was classified 4-F because of a bad knee, and that allowed him to stay with us throughout the war. Because of his bad knee, Sewell tinkered with the idea of permanently shifting Stephens to the outfield in 1943. He tried it in 10 or so games, but ultimately decided that Vernon was too valuable at short even with a bum knee. It was the right decision to keep him at short. He may have slowed down in his later years, but he still had good range during his years with the Browns from 1942-46.

Stephens' on-field accomplishments are even more amazing when you consider his lifestyle. Vernon, like so many others on that 1944 club, took part in a lot of extracurricular activities. He would go out on the town night after night, yet he'd still get the job done in the games. I couldn't believe it — he was like Superman. And I got a close-up look at his nocturnal activities, too, because I was his roommate on the road. I used to tell people that I roomed with his suitcase because I hardly ever saw him. We'd get off the train and Vernon would say, "Don, take my suitcase up to the room and I'll see you later." I'd take it upstairs — and then back downstairs when we left town. Sometimes he'd never unpack. He'd return in the early morning, sleep an hour or two, and then be off to the field. One time Luke Sewell went to him and said, "Vernon, you are a fine ball player, but you could be GREAT. Why don't you just lay off the nightlife, get some sleep, and see what happens." It was quite a fatherly talk. Well, the next day Stephens started being very good, eating with us, and getting to bed early. He didn't get a base hit in his next 15 times at bat! Finally, Luke said, "Forget it, Vernon — go have yourself a good time!" He knew Stephens was going to do it anyway, and this was a good opportunity to take the pressure off of Vernon and cut him loose again. The experiment had failed. Even though Vernon's nighttime activity was against the rules, Sewell knew that Stephens was going to get out of curfew one way or another. So from then on, Vernon went back to his old ways. I didn't care about any of that, though — I really liked Stephens, and he was very good to me. I have to admit, though — Sewell was right. Vernon could have been one of the greats of all time had he taken better care of himself — but that was Vernon. Still, he was a fierce competitor with a winning attitude and he wanted to beat you every time out. In spite of his weakness for the nightlife, he was still great in my opinion. In fact, I believe that he should be in the Hall of Fame.

JULY 9, 1944: We split with the Washington Senators at Griffith Stadium in D.C., but still maintained our grip on 1st place. We dropped the nightcap, 4-0, when we failed to get to Senators right-hander Dutch Leonard. I went hitless against the knuckleballer in that game, but I did manage to bang out two doubles and an RBI in the opener as we won in a blowout, 10-0. That game featured major contributions from a couple more of our important role players of 1944 — right-handed pitcher Tex Shirley and centerfielder Milt Byrnes. Tex was the winning pitcher, allowing just two hits while tossing a complete game. Milt, for his part, hit a 425-foot inside-the-park home run in support of Tex. Byrnes, 4-F because of asthma, was a very good ballplayer. Solid on defense with good speed, he was also very adept with the bat. He hit very well for us as an everyday player in 1943, and he batted even better in 1944. Milt was also a very funny guy and his impersonation of Luke Sewell kept us laughing all season. Shirley, impressive with his complete game victory that day, turned out to be more valuable to us as a quality relief pitcher and occasional spot starter as the season played itself out.

Right-handed pitcher Tex Shirley, standing with the big wad of chew in his cheek, played a valuable role for us in 1944 as a quality reliever and occasional starter. Tex was prematurely bald and very self-conscious about it, so you would rarely catch him when he was not wearing either his ballcap or a cowboy hat. Ellis Clary used to tell a story in which he claimed he'd seen a bouncer toss a rowdy Tex out of a bar. "Tex did about four or five cartwheels as he flew out the door," Ellis said, "yet the cowboy hat never came off of his head!" Also pictured in this dugout shot at Sportsman's Park is Bob Bauman (far left), then working from right to left is me, Sam Zoldak, Len Schulte, and Ellis.

JULY 16, 1944: We won two hard-fought 12-inning games in a double-header against the Indians in front of a big crowd of over 30,000 on this day. I had been held to just one hit in five at-bats in the first game, so I was hoping to make something happen when I came up in the top of the 12th with none out, George Caster on first base, and the score tied at 7-7. I failed to deliver a hit, instead forcing Caster at second, but Milt Byrnes and George McQuinn hit successive singles to push me across with what proved to be the winning run as we won, 8-7. It was deja vu in the second game when I came up to the plate to lead-off the 12th inning with the score tied, 1-1. I was again just 1-for-5 in the game as I took my place in the batter's box, but this time I was able to do something positive when I connected with a Joe Heving pitch for a 350-foot triple. Byrnes followed with a sac fly that scored me, then Jack Kramer held the Indians scoreless in the bottom half of the inning to gain the 2-1 win. Kramer pitched all 12 innings, and our sweep kept us in 1st place, two games in front of New York.

JULY 19, 1944: On July 18th the Yankees came to St. Louis for a big 4-game series. We took the series-opener, 8-0, but lost the second game on this day, 6-5. At the same time, the Cardinals were running away with the National League pennant. I don't recall exactly when the first talk of an all-St. Louis World Series began, but the *New York Times* made mention of it in their write-up following our loss to the Yanks. New Yorkers had grown accustomed to appearing in the World Series, so they weren't ready to accept the concept of an all-St. Louis match-up because it didn't include their Yankees. John Drebinger reflected that superior attitude when he wrote, "There was no rush tonight, so far as anyone could detect, to file hurried ticket applications for that long-cherished All-St. Louis World Series. For the Yankees came roaring back this evening and by twice coming from behind succeeded in overpowering Luke Sewell's Browns, 6-5, to the bitter disappointment of 16,130 onlookers."

JULY 20, 1944: We gained the edge in our series with the Yankees on this day by beating them, 7-3, but the score doesn't quite reflect the intensity of this game. Here's how the *New York Times* described the key turning point in the game — "It was a tempestuous struggle, with a crowd of 13,093 as well as the Browns being thrown into quite a heat in the 5th inning when umpire Cal Hubbard, after repeatedly warning Nelson Potter not to moisten his fingertips between each pitch, wound up ordering the Browns pitcher out of the game. Irate fans showered the field with pop bottles and play had to be interrupted while attendants cleared away the debris."

The "going to the mouth" trouble actually began because Luke Sewell kept complaining to Hubbard that Yanks starter Hank Borowy was going to his mouth to wet the ball. Art Fletcher, the Yankees' third base coach, finally got sick of hearing Sewell complain, so he decided to give Luke a taste of his own medicine. Fletcher began to repeatedly complain that Potter was going to his mouth, and eventually Hubbard went out and warned Nels about it. "You do that again and I'm gonna have to call a balk," Hubbard said. "It's an automatic fine and suspension, too." Moments later, Potter forgot himself and again went to his mouth. Hubbard walked out and said, "Your out of the ballgame and suspended for 10 days!" As you can imagine, that didn't go over well with us, so we kicked about it — and our anger inspired the Sportsman's Park crowd to rain down debris on the field.

Well, maybe Potter's ejection rattled us a bit because we gave up two runs in the 6th and were trailing, 2-1, when we came up in the 7th. Yanks starter Hank Borowy had two outs on us, but an error put Red Hayworth on second with Vern Stephens up to pinch-hit for Denny Galehouse. Borowy intentionally walked Vern to get to the man in the on-deck circle — me! I already had one hit on the day and I would have liked the opportunity to break the game open for us in that situation, but Luke Sewell decided to send the power-hitting Mike Chartak in to hit for me. At that point I became a cheerleader for Mike, and don't you know he went up there and slammed a long homer over the rightfield pavilion! That opened the floodgates, and we went on to score five runs before the inning was over. It was a great win for us, but it was tempered somewhat when we later learned that Nelson was suspended for 10 days because of the incidents of that game. We lost the final game of the series the next day, but we'd held our own, splitting the four games and maintaining our 2-game lead over the 2nd-place Yankees.

After the game when Potter learned that the suspension was for real, he said, "If I can't pitch for 10 days, then I'm going home." And he went home. Nine months later he and his wife had a baby boy. We used to kid Nels that he should have named his son "Cal" after Hubbard as a way of thanking the ump for sending him home to spend some time with his wife. The whole Nelson Potter incident just brings in to focus what a big role umpires play in baseball. It's always been said that a good umpire is the one you DON'T notice, but all too often the umpire and his personal style greatly affect the events on the field. For example, umpires definitely used to call the letter-high pitch a strike. Batters used to complain if they called it a strike, and the pitcher would complain if they called it a ball. Now I think the strike zone is really from your belt to your knees. Because of that hitters can really focus on a smaller area. They know it's going to be right there, and that gives them a little edge.

The other side of the story is that really good pitchers don't have to throw strikes all the time because the umpires will give them anything close. By the same token, a wild pitcher loses a lot of close calls. Umpires are like that. They claim they're not, but I think they are. Before the game they think, "Well, today I'm going to umpire behind the plate of a wild guy," and I believe that influences their decisions during the game.

Some umpires call different strike zones altogether. Some will give you inside or outside pitches, high or low. We were okay with that as long as they were consistent. After you are in the league a while you should know your umpires so you know what to expect. There were two or three umpires that I thought were good — Bill McGowan from the American League and Bill Klem from the National League. I felt like when I walked up to the plate I was going to get a good call and I didn't have to worry about it. I think in general we had great umpires, though. Later on in my career when I was coaching we used to call Ed Runge a pitcher's umpire because he would give a pitcher strikes that were six inches off the plate. As a batter you had to be ready because you weren't going to be able to take that pitch for a ball. Big George Magerkurth was a pretty good umpire, too. He knew he was bigger than everyone and he enjoyed that power. Along with those greats I'll always remember Cal Hubbard, too. He's a Hall of Fame ump, but it's his role in the Nelson Potter game that will always define him for me.

JULY 30, 1944: My bat heated up a bit on this day as we swept a twin bill from the Nats at Sportsman's Park. I went 2-for-5 with two doubles and two RBIs in the opener, and followed that with 3-for-5, a double, and an RBI in the nightcap. We scored four runs in the opening frame of the nightcap, so that kind of killed the suspense as we went on to win easily, 7-3. But the first game was a real nail-biter, and I was overjoyed to play a key role in our win. *GUTTERIDGE'S DOUBLE DECIDES THRILL-PACKED OPENER AFTER MUNCRIEF AND HAEFNER PITCH NINE SCORELESS FRAMES* — that was the Associated Press sub-headline describing the action. Washington broke through with a run in the top of the 10th, so our backs were against the wall when we came up to hit in the bottom of the inning. Then I came up with two men on, and here's how the text of the article described the finish — "Don Gutteridge was the Browns' hero when he slammed a double to the wall to score Frank Mancuso and Newman Shirley, a pinch-runner, with the winning tallies." It's funny that Mancuso and Shirley should both score on that play. Most of the time Tex would pinch-run for Frank. In fact, Tex ran so often for Frank that we nicknamed him "Mancuso's Legs." Frank, one of our catchers, was never the fastest guy to begin with, but an accident while training for the paratroopers had severely injured his back, slowing him even more. It ended his military career before it had much of a chance to begin, but the Army's loss was our gain as Frank contributed greatly to our success in '44. I think the fact that he'd already been in the military — and the fact that he'd nearly been killed — made him hungry to win NOW. Frank may not have acquired the "win now" attitude in the conventional way for a ballplayer, but he had it nonetheless — and that was the attitude Luke Sewell wanted to see in ALL his players. Teammates saw that "win now" attitude in Frank, and they started to pick up on it, too — and that was very good for our ballclub.

JULY 31, 1944: More late-inning drama on this day as we again treated the Sportsman's Park fans to another thriller. *BROWNS OVERCOME SENATORS, 3-2; HOMERS BY STEPHENS AND MCQUINN AND SINGLE BY GUTTERIDGE GIVE LEADERS VICTORY,* blared the Associated Press headline in the next day's newspapers. The text went on to succinctly say, "The two homers brought about ties in each inning [the 2nd and the 7th]. The Browns moved ahead in the 8th when Don Gutteridge singled to score Frank Mancuso." I can't

Me posing with great drama and the wonderful backdrop of Yankee Stadium on August 9th, 1944.

think of a better way to have ended what was a great month of July.

AUGUST 9, 1944: July ended with four consecutive wins for us, and we kept on rolling as August got under way. We won our first four games of August to run our winning streak to eight as we got set to play New York at Yankee Stadium on this day. It was the first of a 4-game series, a series that the writers were calling "crucial." Our winning streak had provided us with a little separation from the pack, and as it stood prior to this day's game we were in 1st place with the Red Sox 6-1/2 games back in 2nd and the Yankees having slipped to 3rd place, 8-1/2 games back. The paying customers got their money's worth because they saw a crisp, well-played ballgame, but Yankee fans went home disappointed as we won the game, 3-2, after a dramatic 9th-inning solo homer by our leftfielder, Al Zarilla. It didn't look good for us early as Hank Borowy was sharp, setting down all nine of us in order through the first three innings, but I led off the 4th with a triple to leftfield and then scored on a single by Mike Kreevich. The Yanks answered with two off Bob Muncrief in the bottom of the 3rd, but we came back to tie it at 2-2 in the 8th. That's where it stood in the 9th when Zarilla delivered his clutch home run into the rightfield stands. Just before Al homered he had driven one into the seats in the same area, but foul. As we watched him hit the next pitch we feared that it would again hook foul, but it stayed fair, clearing rightfielder Bud Metheny's outstretched glove by no more than a foot.

Al was a 26-year old from Los Angeles, very fast with a good bat. He'd shown his potential with our club as a rookie in 1943, but he came on very strong in 1944, particularly in July when he went on a terrific streak at the plate that saw him get 21 hits in 35 at-bats. Al was very important to our 1944 success. Here's what the *New York Times'* Louis Effrat had to say about Al after witnessing his stickwork against the Yankees — "There is quite a story in this young Zarilla, a California lad, who until about three weeks ago was riding the bench and filling in at various utility jobs. In a game against the Red Sox during the Browns' last home stand, Zarilla was sent in as a pinch-hitter and he drove home two runs with a double. Since then there has been no stopping him and his batting average for the last dozen games is over .600."

AUGUST 10, 1944: We won game two of our series against New York, 3-0. Denny Galehouse pitched an impressive complete-game 6-hitter to get the victory. The win was our 10th in a row, breaking our own 9-game season-opening win streak and setting a new 1944 American League high-mark for consecutive victories. I was 1-for-4 in the game with a stolen base, and my hit extended my own personal hitting streak to ten games. But it wasn't my hitting that got me a mention in the papers that day — it was my glove. "GOOD CATCH FOR GUTTERIDGE — Don Gutteridge, one of the most improved of the Brownies, was a big help to Galehouse in the 7th. With two aboard he raced into short rightfield to catch pinch-hitter Bud Metheny's Texas Leaguer."

Mike Kreevich grounded to Yankee shortstop Frankie Crosetti who stepped on the bag at second to force me, then he threw to first to double-up Mike as second baseman Snuffy Stirnweiss looked on. We won this game, however, 3-0, on August 10th, 1944 at Yankee Stadium. It was our 10th victory in a row.

AUGUST 12, 1944: The Yankees snapped our 10-game winning streak when they beat us, 6-1, on August 11th, but we bounced right back with an 8-3 victory on this day. That meant we'd taken three of four from New York during this series, our last appearance in the Bronx for the season. We were still scheduled to close the campaign with a 4-game set against the Yanks, but that would be on our home turf back in St. Louis. Even *New York Times* writer John Drebinger was no longer spewing prose about our inability to survive the "rarified air" of 1st place. We'd made a believer out of him as you can see from the intro to his article following our win this day — "New York got its last glimpse of the Browns for 1944 yesterday and what it saw convinced a gathering of 16,053 that, regardless of what may happen to Luke Sewell's men when they collide with the all-powerful Cardinals in next October's World Series, nothing is going to prevent them from getting into the classic." We knew that there was still a lot of baseball left to be played in 1944, so in no way were we counting our chickens, but you can't imagine how strange it was to read words like that about us — the St. Louis Browns.

This photo was snapped prior to our game on August 12th, 1944. Here's what the newspaper caption said — "Bob Muncrief (left), star pitcher for the Browns, and Don Gutteridge, second baseman, indulge in a bit of horseplay in the dugout before the game with the Yankees at Yankee Stadium, New York. Muncrief, who lives in San Antonio, Texas, has won 12 and lost 6 games this season and expects to enter the Army before World Series time."

AUGUST 21, 1944: Well, no sooner had the writers begun to consider us a shoo-in for the pennant than we began to falter. We'd lost six of nine since our win on August 12th, and four in a row as we got set to play Washington at Griffith Stadium on this day. Because of our slump, our comfortable 8-game lead had narrowed to just 4-1/2 games, so we really needed a win to get back on track. We got it, beating the Nats, 5-3, in 12 innings, and in doing so I experienced one of my most thrilling moments of the season. The Associated Press headline summed up the situation with this headline — *BROWNS OVERCOME SENATORS IN 12TH; GUTTERIDGE HOMER WITH 1 ON WINS, 5-3 — ST. LOUIS LEAD NOW 4-1/2 GAMES.* Yep — I guess you could say I picked a good time to hit my first homer of the season.

AUGUST 22, 1944: The elation we felt in pulling out our win the day before quickly dissipated when the Senators rebounded to beat us, 3-0, on this day. Johnny Niggeling had my number again, holding me hitless in four at-bats, but he also seemed to equally perplex the rest of our club, allowing just six hits while going the distance. A subplot to the ballgame was a fight that broke out in the 7th inning. There had been season-long tension between our club and the Senators, the ill-feelings emanating from the rough bench-jockeying that went on back in those days. They accused our bench jockeys, and they felt it started right at the top with Luke Sewell, of being overly nasty to the Nats' Cuban contingent — Roberto Ortiz, Gil Torrez and Mike Guerra, to name just a few. Their players retaliated, and that just heightened the tension. That tension set the stage for the fight that broke out in our game on this day. Nelson Potter's screwball was working beautifully through six innings, the Nats unable to hit it. They changed their strategy in the 7th, however, resorting to bunting — and it worked. Their bunts resulted three runs, all scoring in the 7th inning. Nelson was mad about it, and he was yelling insults to them from the mound, stuff about their inability to hit him unless they bunted. Here's how the Associated Press described the boiling point — "George Case tapped out a bunt that rolled foul as Case raced for first. Nelson Potter, St. Louis pitcher, dashed over to field the ball and, without warning, he and Case started swinging. In seconds, their teammates joined in and the fists swung for three minutes before police and military police quieted the players." Shirley Povich of the *Washington Post* added some additional details when he wrote, "It was when Potter called Case a nasty name as they met on the first base line that Case took a swing that was no bunt, and landed on Potter's chin." Needless to say, Nelson and Case were ejected, along with Nats reserve infielder Ed Butka.

SEPTEMBER 1, 1944: Our free-fall continued as we lost six of eight games following our brawl in Washington. In the meantime, the Tigers were making a charge at us from behind, having pulled to within 2-1/2 games of us prior to our game with them at Sportsman's Park on this day. Hal Newhouser held me to 1-for-4, allowing just six total hits as he pitched Detroit to victory. There's not much good here worth recalling, but there was a triple-play, and they're always worth remembering. Here's how it was described by the Associated Press — "The Browns killed a Tiger rally in the 6th with a triple-play. Eddie Mayo singled to center and Pinky Higgins walked. Rudy York hit to Mark Christman, who stepped on third and threw to Don Gutteridge at second. Gutteridge completed the relay to George McQuinn." The triple-play gave us a glimmer of hope, keeping us within reaching distance of Detroit who was leading, 6-2, but we could only scratch out one more run before it was over.

SEPTEMBER 3, 1944: *BROWNS BEAT TROUT, TIGERS' ACE, BEHIND KRAMER'S FINE HURLING, 4-1; ST. LOUIS STICKS TO LEAGUE LEAD AS*

ZARILLA AND GUTTERIDGE STAR AND YORK AND WAKEFIELD GO HITLESS. That was the Associated Press headline to our win at Sportsman's Park on this day. I was 2-for-4 with a double, an RBI, and two runs scored as we finally broke through with a win against Detroit in the last game of a 4-game series. Our win kept us in 1st place, albeit slimly, a half game ahead of the Yankees and two games in front of the Tigers.

SEPTEMBER 10, 1944: A loss to the White Sox on September 8th knocked us into 2nd place, a game behind the Yankees. A second straight defeat at the hands of Chicago on September 9th pushed us further down in the standings, now trailing the Yanks AND the Tigers. Despite being in 7th place in the American League, the Sox continued to hound us on this day, too, forcing us to settle for a doubleheader split when we really needed a sweep. Things got off to a great start when we won the opener, 6-2, behind an excellent outing from Nelson Potter. I had two hits and an RBI in the game. I added a 2-bagger and a run scored in the nightcap, and it looked like luck might break our way when Mike Kreevich hit a game-tying solo homer in the 8th, but we lost in the bottom of the 11th when relief pitcher Orval Grove slashed a game-winning run-scoring triple.

White Sox shortstop Jimmy Webb did a nice job in coming up with the ball to force me at second in this game at Comiskey Park on September 10th, 1944. It was the 4th inning of the opener of a doubleheader, a game which we won, 6-2, but we dropped the nightcap, 3-2.

SEPTEMBER 16, 1944: We regained the top slot in the A.L. after beating the White Sox at Sportsman's Park on this day. Jack Kramer pitched a 1-hitter and we provided him with nine runs. One of those runs came on my second home run of the season, a 7th-inning solo clout off Sox left-hander Jake Wade.

SEPTEMBER 17, 1944: We ended our 4-game series with the White Sox at Sportsman's Park with a twin bill on this day. We split the doubleheader, and that dropped us back into 2nd place, a half game behind the Tigers. Nelson Potter pitched beautifully in the opener, allowing just six hits as we won, 5-1. For the second straight game I hit a 7th-inning solo home run when I cleared the fence against right-hander Bill Dietrich. It turned out to be my last long-ball of the season. I singled and scored in four trips in the nightcap, but a late-game 7-run splurge by the Sox earned them the 8-2 victory. Our run at the pennant did not always net us big crowds at the turnstiles, however. It was simply a tough concept for the longtime Browns fans to accept — they REALLY had a pennant contender this year. But the fans showed up in droves for this beautiful Sunday doubleheader — 22,094 of them, to be exact, and it was always a lot more fun to play in front of a big crowd.

Both of these photos are from our doubleheader split with the White Sox at Sportsman's Park on September 17th, 1944. At left I'm seen crossing home plate following my 7th-inning bases-empty home run off Bill Dietrich in the opener, which we won, 5-1. At right I'm seen reaching first base following my single off Joe Haynes in the nightcap, which we lost, 8-2. The split dropped us out of 1st place, a half-game behind the Detroit Tigers.

SEPTEMBER 21, 1944: We concluded a heated 3-game series with the Washington Senators on this day, taking the series two games to one with a 9-4 win in the finale. They'd taken the first game of the set in an extra-inning struggle, winning the game, 6-0, when we fell apart in the 11th inning. We bounced back to take game two of the series, 5-2, behind great pitching from Jack Kramer and clutch hitting from Chet Laabs. The carping back and forth that had marked our previous series' with the Nats had continued in the first two games of this set, and things finally came to a head prior to our game on this day. Another fight broke out, this time between our reserve catcher, Tom Turner, and Senators rightfielder, Roberto Ortiz. It started during batting practice when Tom Turner was riding Washington's Cuban players as they took their swings. Little Mickey Guerra replied to Turner's taunts with a challenge to fight. Turner outweighed Guerra by 50 pounds, but Mickey didn't care. Ortiz was much bigger than Guerra, so he told Mickey HE'D fight Turner instead. Ortiz came over to our dugout carrying a bat. Turner told him to drop the bat, so he dropped it and they went at it. Here's how the *Washington Post's* Shirley Povich described the fight — "Ortiz won the fight, which was a beaut. If he hadn't broken his thumb the first time his right hand landed on Turner's head, he'd have given the catcher a fearful beating. At one point, Ortiz, his right hand useless, fought Cuban style, bringing his knee up to Turner's face. That might not have been cricket, but Ortiz didn't care, nor did any of the Washington players seem to. Even on the Nats there may be some antipathy toward the Cubans, but in this case they were solidly with Ortiz."

Turner had only been with our club since July 31st when he was purchased from the White Sox. Our catching platoon of Frank Mancuso and Red Hayworth had struggled at the plate throughout the season, so the front office had hoped that Turner could bring some occasional offense to the catcher spot. And he did, too, in the limited number of games he'd appeared in, but he was well-known throughout the league as an expert bench jockey, and that backfired on us on this day. So angry was mild-mannered Nats manager, Ossie Bluege, that a fight between him and Luke Sewell nearly broke out as they swapped line-up cards just before the game started. Sewell and Bluege had been roommates on the 1933 Senators, but this incident stomped out any good feelings that Bluege may still have had for Luke. Here's more from Povich's article — "The usually placid Bluege, red with anger, shook a warning fist in the face of Sewell and said, 'Lay off my Cubans or you and I are going to fight! You sent a third-string catcher who isn't playing out to start a fight with one of my regulars hoping they'd both get thrown out of the game. Any manager who would sit on the bench and let his ballplayers call another team the kind of names they called us tonight is as contemptible as his players. Luke, you and I are finished.' At the cost of a broken thumb, Ortiz struck a mighty blow for all of the Washington Cubans when he tied into big Turner and gave him a beating in full view of the players of both teams." I really don't know whether Luke and Bluege ever patched things up after that.

SEPTEMBER 29, 1944: It all came down to this — a 4-game season-ending series with the Yankees beginning on this day with a twin-bill at Sportsman's Park. We were tied for 1st place with the Tigers, and New York was in 2nd place, three games back. Our fans never did really believe that we could win the pennant, and the low turnout of 6,173 proved it. Here we were with a legitimate chance to win the American League championship — the first in Browns franchise history — and very few fans were there to see it. At any rate, the ones who were there witnessed some tension-soaked drama. Jack Kramer came up with a great performance in the opener, going the full nine and limiting New York to eight hits and one run — their lone score coming in the 1st inning. We took the lead, 2-1, in the 3rd inning when Kramer hit a long double over Johnny Lindell's head in center, I bunted for a hit, and we both scored on successive singles by Mike Kreevich and Chet Laabs. George McQuinn added a couple of insurance runs in the 8th when he hit a 2-run homer off right-hander Ernie Bonham, who also pitched a complete game. The nightcap just raised the level of tension as Nelson Potter and Hank Borowy got locked up in a real pitcher's duel. In his article recapping the game, John Drebinger of the *New York Times* described the only run scored in the game — "A two-base thrust by Don Gutteridge, leading off the [bottom of the] 1st inning, sent the Brownies on their way to the only tally of the nightcap. A wild pitch put Don on third and Mike Kreevich's infield out sent him over the plate." Drebinger also described the play that ended the nail-biter — "Again in the 9th the Yanks looked to have the tying run on the wing. With Nick Etten on second and two out, Paul Waner, hitting for Mike Garbark, appeared to have popped a single into short right until Gutteridge, with a desperate leap, clutched the ball in his gloved hand for the final out."

You better believe that I wasn't happy when I saw the legendary Paul Waner step out of the dugout to pinch-hit for Garbark, the Yankees' catcher. I'd seen plenty of Paul and his brother Lloyd from my days playing third base for the Cardinals back in the National League. They both played for Pittsburgh — Paul in rightfield and Lloyd in centerfield. They were little guys, but they were great ballplayers and both of them could really handle the bat. I tell you, they gave me a rough time playing at third. If I came in so they wouldn't bunt, then they'd hit it by me. If I played back a little bit, they'd bunt. They were tough to defend, and they never struck out. Definitely two of the best. So, you can understand my trepidation at seeing Paul Waner step up to hit with our season on the line. But, boy was I happy when Big Poison's little blooper settled into my mitt after I made a jumping, over-the-shoulder catch! After I caught the ball we all jumped around joyously as we ran to the clubhouse, and here's some of what the United Press wrote about the excited scene in our dressing room — "Center of the celebration was little Don Gutteridge, still clutching the ball which he caught for the last out in the thrill-packed 1-0 second game. Chatterbox of the Browns infield, Don was speechless for a few minutes. With a wide grin, he planted big smacking kisses on the ball he took off pinch-hitter Paul Waner's bat in the 9th inning. When he broke away from a knot of Browns all trying to embrace him, he screamed above the din, 'That's all right fellows, but the next time let us get a few runs!' " What a happy scene it was.

What you see here are three very happy fellows following our doubleheader sweep over the Yankees at Sportsman's Park on September 29th, 1944. From left to right are centerfielder Mike Kreevich, me, and Nelson Potter, who pitched tremendously in the second game 1-0 win. The sweep guaranteed that we would be, at the very least, tied for 1st place in the American League when the season ended. We still had two games to play and a chance to win the pennant outright. I caught the last out of the nightcap, a dangerous little blooper off the bat of Paul Waner. It was a tough grab, and my first reaction upon catching it was simply to kiss the ball.

SEPTEMBER 30, 1944: On this day, despite our happiness at sweeping the Yankees the day before, we were assured of nothing. Our sweep had officially eliminated the Yankees, but we were still in a dead-even tie with the Tigers, with both clubs still having two games left to play. Even though we had yet to clinch anything, our double-win over the Yankees had made believers out of about 11,000 more of our fans than the day before, and a total of 17,011 showed up for our game with New York on this day. As in our previous game, runs were hard to come by as Denny Galehouse and Walt Dubiel matched each other hit for hit, each allowing only five safeties. But where New York was unable to eek out any runs from their meager hit production, we managed to scratch out two for the 2-0 victory. Our first run came in the 1st when I led off with a walk, Mike Kreevich followed with a single, and Chet Laabs bunted safely. We had the bases loaded with no one out, poised to break the game open early, but the only run we got was when I scored on a sac fly off the bat of Vern Stephens. That's how it stayed until we added another run in the 6th when Gene Moore homered onto the rightfield pavilion. It was Denny's great pitching and a great game in the field that sent us to victory on this day. Here is *New York Times* writer John Drebinger's description of some of our fielding gems that day — "BROWNS FIELDING THRILL FANS: There was a note of disappointment in the crowd when the Browns, after filling the bases with none out in the 1st, exacted only one run. A full-throated roar went up at the start of the 2nd, though, when Johnny Lindell streaked what looked like a hit toward left only to see Mark Christman rocket in the air to spear the ball in his glove. Before the inning was over George McQuinn was making an equally brilliant play as he lunged to snare Frank Crosetti's sharp drive inches off the ground. These plays rocked the Yanks back on their heels and were surpassed only when Kreevich made a diving catch of Herschel Martin's smash in the 4th."

OCTOBER 1, 1944: *BROWNS WIN FLAG; HALT YANKEES, 5-2; ANNEX THEIR FIRST PENNANT IN AMERICAN LEAGUE BY FULL GAME AS TIGERS LOSE; JAKUCKI PITCHES TRIUMPH; LAABS' TWO HOMERS GOOD FOR FOUR RUNS.* Those were the unbelievable headlines in the *New York Times* after we clinched the pennant on this day. We were wide-eyed with amazement when we took the field because there was a crowd of 37,815 packed in to see if we could pull off the impossible. Three days earlier we drew just over 6,000, and now Sportsman's Park was filled to the brim. It was the largest crowd that had ever paid to see the Browns play. It was quite a sight to see. Sig Jakucki, despite still smelling of liquor, pitched the game of his life to get the complete game win. "This climactic struggle made one Sigmund Jakucki the toast of the town tonight," wrote the *New York Times'* John Drebinger. "For it was this strapping right-hander, a former minor league pitcher whom the Browns resurrected from a shipyard last spring, who hurled this decisive struggle, which now sends the Browns against their city rivals, the high and mighty Cardinals, in the World Series that opens here Wednesday." Jakucki's partner in heroics was Chet Laabs. We were trailing, 2-0, in the 4th when Chet ripped a Mel Queen pitch into the leftfield bleachers for a game-tying 2-run homer. Only moments after Chet had crossed the plate they posted the final of the Tigers-Senators game on the scoreboard — Nats 4, Tigers 1. That meant that if we could win this game, we'd win the pennant outright. Chet had been used very sparingly in 1944 because of his job at a war plant, and the homer was just his fourth of the season. I'm sure it seemed very unlikely to the Yankees that he could repeat the task when he stepped up in the next inning, again with a runner on base — but he did. Another 2-run homer off Queen in almost the same spot. It was amazing. We added a final run in the 8th when Vern Stephens hit a solo shot, then it was just a matter of waiting for Jakucki to set down the side in the 9th.

This is action from the game in which we clinched the '44 American League pennant — a 5-2 victory over the New York Yankees at Sportsman's Park on October 1st, 1944. The photo shows me turning a double-play in the top of the 4th, forcing Oscar Grimes at second. We were trailing, 2-0, at the time of this play, but moments later, in the home half of the inning, Chet Laabs would tie the game with a huge 2-run blast. Then, in the next inning, Chet iced the game with another 2-run clout to almost the exact same spot. It was unbelievable.

We got two quick outs, and that brought up Oscar Grimes as the possible last out. Whenever people ask me to recount the highlight of my career, the next play is always one of the two or three I point to. Grimes lifted a pop-up behind first base. As George McQuinn moved under it to make the grab, I moved over very close to him. "Squeeze it, George, squeeze it!" I hollered. It's a darn good thing I didn't scare him into dropping the ball, but George squeezed it and we won the pennant. That wondeful moment was etched in my mind for eternity, and I can visualize it as if it were yesterday. A split second after McQuinn caught the ball, the place went wild. We mobbed Jak, then the overflow crowd mobbed us. It took quite a long time for us to make our way into the clubhouse, but once there we had a heck of a celebration. There would have been no celebration, or it would have at least been delayed, had the Senators not defeated the Tigers on this day. If the Tigers had won we would have ended the season tied with them for 1st place. It had already been determined that there would have been a 1-game playoff had the season ended in a tie, so it was quite a relief to no longer have to worry about that. So with the weight of the pennant race off our backs, we celebrated deliriously. The once-in-a-lifetime feeling of that moment is something I'll never forget.

The fact that Jakucki could come through in a big game like that is amazing. As I mentioned, Jak took the mound that day still smelling of liquor — and here's why. Luke Sewell had done a great job all season in balancing Jakucki's drinking problem with the goal of still getting Jak to deliver on the mound. So far it had gone well, but with the importance of this game, Sewell felt he needed to head off any possible problem this may present in such a crucial game. Sewell went to Jak the night before and said, "Now, Sig, I don't want you to drink tonight. I want you to go to the hotel and behave yourself because tomorrow you're pitching in the biggest game of your lifetime." He really gave him a pep talk.

"Okay, Luke. I promise. I'll not take a drink tonight," Jakucki said, and he went back to the hotel — the Old Melbourne Hotel where we were staying.

Zack Taylor, one of our coaches, saw Jakucki that night about 10:00. "Now remember, Sig," Taylor reminded him, "you're not supposed to drink tonight."

"That's right, Zack," Jakucki replied, "I'm not going to drink tonight. I'm going to bed right now," and he went up to his room. At least that's what Taylor thought. Shortly before our game on this day Jakucki came to the stadium smelling of alcohol. He wasn't exactly drunk, but he'd obviously had a few drinks. Sewell, concerned about this development, called Jak in and said, "I thought I told you not to drink last night, Sig — you were supposed to keep sober."

"Well, I told you I wouldn't drink last NIGHT," Jakucki replied, "but you didn't say anything about drinking this MORNING." Luke just looked at him dumfounded. I know it sounds like fiction, but it's absolutely true. Jakucki's performance for us in this pennant-clinching game was incredible sheerly on its baseball level, but with the understory of Jak's alcoholism, it goes to another level.

We held a joyous clubhouse celebration following our pennant-clinching win over the Yankees on October 1st, 1944, at Sportsman's Park. Sig Jakucki (shirtless), was the pitching hero of the day, and Chet Laabs was the hitting star, but our pennant was a total team effort — and there's a good portion of our club on display in this photo. Team president Donald Barnes is shaking hands with Mike Kreevich. Directly behind Mike is Vern Stephens. Behind Vern is Al Hollingsworth, and behind Al is me. Behind Barnes is Luke Sewell, and behind Luke is bat boy Bob Scanlon. That's Babe Martin looking in behind Bob. Additional faces in the background that I can make out, working sort of left to right, are Fred Hoffman, Zack Taylor, Ellis Clary, Mike Chartak, Gene Moore (with the sunglasses), Sam Zoldak, and Bob Muncrief. My apologies to those I couldn't make out.

OCTOBER 4, 1944: World Series Game One — *BROWNS, WITH 2 HITS, BEAT CARDS IN OPENER OF WORLD SERIES, 2-1.* That was the headline in the *New York Times* after we pulled off the unlikely upset (in the minds of the "experts") of beating the heavily-favored Cardinals in Game One of the Series on this day. The stadium looked great trimmed in bunting and the stands were packed. Even the Sportsman's Park field, which usually left a lot to be desired, was beautifully manicured. There wasn't very much in the way of pre-game festivities. Ohio Governor John W. Bricker, also running for Vice President on the Republican ticket with Thomas Dewey, was on the field just before the game began. He shook hands with Luke Sewell and Cardinals manager Billy Southworth, both of whom were Ohio residents. But there was no first-pitch ceremony, so we quickly got started.

We were the visitors in Game One, so we batted first and I hit lead-off. I was well aware of what a big moment this was in my life. Baseball fans all across the country were waiting for ME to step into the batter's box so the 1944 World Series could begin. But before I dug in, however, I stood there for a few moments and engaged in some quiet reflection. The path my life was taking had become pretty

That's me awaiting the first pitch of the 1944 World Series on October 4th, 1944. The enormity of the situation was not lost on me by any stretch of the imagination — I was nearly overwhelmed.

clear by the time I turned 20 years of age back in 1932, and I remember sitting down around that time and making a list of lifetime goals that I aimed to achieve. I narrowed the many things that came to my mind down to four. Number one — marry my sweetheart Helen, which I did on October 16th, 1933. Number two — play professional baseball, which I first did in the Nebraska State League in August of 1932. Number three — play in the big leagues, which I first did with the Cardinals on September 7th, 1936. And number four — play in the World Series, which I was about to accomplish on this day, October 4th, 1944. I literally thought about all of this as I prepared myself to hit. During my moments of reflection, Mort Cooper, my old teammate with the Cardinals, stood on the mound and waited for me to step up to the plate. Mort had grown into the ace of the Cardinals staff, and his 22 wins that season guaranteed that he drew the Game One starting assignment for the Cards. So after a moment of quiet reflection, I got in there and took my stance. Mort gave me a little friendly high heat for old times sake, and eventually got me to pop out to Marty Marion out behind third base. I would have liked to have gotten on base, but, nonetheless, I was glad to have my first World Series at-bat under my belt. I felt that I would definitely be more comfortable at the plate from then on. Our next two batters, Mike Kreevich and Chet Laabs, struck out.

The photo on the left shows Cardinals pitcher (and my former teammate) Mort Cooper throwing me the first pitch of the 1944 World Series. The catcher is Mort's brother, Walker, and the second baseman is Emil Verban. The plate ump is Ziggy Sears, and the other visible umpire is Tom Dunn. The photo on the right shows the result of the pitch — high and tight. Mort was a tough competitor who wanted to win. That meant our friendship was on hold until after the game.

We took the field, and our pitcher that day, Denny Galehouse, took the mound. Sewell had surprised the writers when he'd announced that Denny would pitch Game One. "It's Galehouse," he told the writers the day before the

Series began, "and I think he'll do all right." Luke had actually told Denny that he was his Game One starter immediately after Denny had beaten the Yankees on September 30th. In the interim the writers had all speculated that Sewell would go with Nelson Potter because he had led the team in wins. But Sewell was playing a hunch, and he had the utmost confidence in Denny. When the writers questioned his decision, Luke just told them, "Don't forget, he's the man who pitched us into a tie for the lead the day before the season ended by shutting out the Yankees, 2 to 0." Denny took it in stride and appeared to be unfazed by the spotlight of being the Game One starter, telling reporters, "It's just another ballgame to me. I never even saw a World Series game before, because I resolved long ago that I wouldn't see one until I was in it. I never thought I'd make it, but here I am."

As far as being unfazed, Denny appeared to have been speaking the truth because he went out in the 1st inning and cut down the first two Cardinals batters four pitches, popping up lead-off man Johnny Hopp and then striking out Ray Sanders on three pitches. Stan Musial singled, but Denny got Walker Cooper to fly out to Kreevich in center to end the inning. Neither club scored in the 2nd or 3rd — in fact, we had yet to come close to hitting Cooper. For a moment it looked like I might have had a hit in my second at-bat when I hit a fly to Hopp in center. He stumbled while chasing it, but recovered in time to make the catch. It looked like Mort was going to cruise through the 4th, too, as he got two quick outs on a fly ball by Laabs and a pop by Vern Stephens, but then Gene Moore singled between first and second base. George McQuinn then stepped up and sent a Cooper pitch high and deep to rightfield. It looked good right away and we all rushed to the top of the dugout steps. Zack Taylor, one of our coaches, was flapping a towel up and down as if to help push the ball out of the park. Sure enough, George's clout had just enough to clear the roof of the rightfield pavilion for a 2-run homer. As you'd expect, we were overjoyed, but in no way did we think that two runs would be enough to beat a good-hitting team like the Cardinals.

We failed to add to our lead, but our 2-run cushion looked more and more like it might be enough as Denny seemed to get stronger, allowing no hits from the bottom of the 4th through the 8th. I was involved in an interesting play in the 5th inning that is worth recalling here. We were in the field and had one out with Sanders on first after a base on balls. Musial then hit a high pop-up to me, so Sanders stayed on the bag at first. As I waited for Musial's pop to come down to me, I noticed out of my peripheral vision that Musial was not running hard. So I let his pop-up drop at me feet, then quickly picked it up, whipped it to Stephens at second, and Vern fired it to McQuinn for a double-play. Governor Bricker, who I mentioned earlier was in attendance, was interviewed by reporters after the game. They wanted to know his impressions of the big event. Of all the things he could have commented on, he chose to mention my double-play. "It was the smartest play of the game," Bricker said, "it required fast thinking." I really enjoyed reading that. By the way, in the top half of that inning I was out on a come-backer to Cooper in my third at-bat of the game. My last at-bat of the game came in the 8th inning when I flied out to Augie Bergamo in leftfield.

The Cardinals made their only serious threat to our lead in the 9th inning. Shortstop Marty Marion led off with a double down the line in left. Kreevich made a great diving attempt for it — even had it in his glove, but it rolled out when he hit the ground. Bergamo was up next, and he hit a grounder to me. There was no play on Marion going to third, so I threw Bergamo out at first. Ken O'Dea pinch-hit next and flied out to Kreevich, scoring Marion. Then Denny retired Hopp on another fly ball to Kreevich for the last out of the game. We all watched Mike haul in that final out and then we moved in on Denny to celebrate. We were all smiles after pulling off the unlikely win, and we headed to the clubhouse to enjoy the moment. Milt Byrnes led the celebration with his cries of, "Just three more to go, boys, just three more to go! We'll take 'em for sure!"

I was 0-for-4 in the game. In fact, we never got another hit after Moore's single and McQuinn's home run. Just two hits total. Until then, no team had ever won a World Series game with such a scarcity of hits. No pitcher had ever lost a World Series game when tossing a 2-hitter — until tough-luck loser Mort Cooper accomplished it on this day. Denny was just too good to be beaten on this day. The reporters were knocking us a bit for winning with only two hits. Luke Sewell, relaxing in his chair amongst the commotion, took their jibes in stride. "That's all right with me," he said. "That means we have a lot of them coming to us. It isn't the hits that count in this game. It's the runs. We got them, didn't we?"

Prior to the game, the writers marveled at how our club looked to be in awe of being in the World Series. We were new to the spectacle, and amazed by our surroundings. The Cardinals, they said, were a club already experienced in World Series play, and they took the whole extravaganza in stride. It was true, too, but it didn't equate to a Cardinal win as the writers had all predicted. As we celebrated in the clubhouse the writers noticed a new sense of confidence to our team — maybe even cockiness. One of them asked Mark Christman if we were now overconfident, and he gave a great answer. "Why shouldn't we be confident?" Mark asked. "We've been playing tough games all season. We had to win each one the hard way. Today's game was another tough one, but we will go on from here." Christman reflected the thoughts of the whole ballclub. We really believed in ourselves. It was the sportswriters and baseball fans who couldn't believe it, but now they were all sitting up and taking notice. We beat St. Louis' favorite team — the Cardinals! It left them thinking maybe the Browns could really do it.

One of the happiest fellows in the clubhouse that day wasn't even a player on our team, but the saga of the 1944 Browns would not be complete without telling his story. The smiling round face of which I speak belonged to an 18 year old kid from New York named Arthur Richman. That name may not be familiar to you, but amongst baseball insiders it is now legendary. Back then, however, Arthur was just a just a Browns fan — he just happened to be absolutely our biggest rooter. The route he took to become the number-one Brownie fans was indirect, but it got him there nonetheless. Like a lot of kids of the depression, Arthur and his brother Milt didn't usually have enough money to get in to Yankee Stadium to see the ballgames, so they would hang around outside the ballpark with hopes of getting autographs from the Yankee players as they arrived at the stadium. This was the mid to late-30's. What they discovered over the years, however, was that the Yankee players weren't very nice. On the other hand, though, they found that the St. Louis Browns players were extremely friendly. Arthur always said it was because the lowly Browns weren't used to receiving much adulation in their home town, much less New York City. Over time, Arthur and Milt struck up friendships with the Browns players, sealing their fate as Browns fans forever. It seems unfathomable in this day in age, but the Browns players and Arthur eventually became so close that he was invited to go on road trips with the club. Not in an official capacity, mind you, but as a stowaway. With the blessings of his parents, Arthur went on countless trips with the Browns, hiding in the players' upper pullman berths at night and sneaking out when the conductor wasn't around in the morning.

Arthur was a fixture around the Browns clubhouse by the time I joined the club in 1942. Every time our train pulled into New York City, there was Arthur eagerly waiting for us. He would ride over to the hotel with us in our taxi cab in hopes of staying with us. He just loved to be around the Brownie players and we embraced him as one of us. Arthur would hang around the hotel and talk with the players as they came through the lobby. Usually one of the players would let Arthur sleep in his room at night — so Arthur wouldn't even have to go home while we were in town. He'd sleep in a chair or on the floor — anywhere — it didn't matter just as long as he was with the Browns players. By 1944 Arthur was a copyboy for the one of the newspapers in New York. He was elated over the success that the Browns were enjoying that season, and, despite having no money, he was determined to get to St. Louis to see his favorite team play in their first-ever World Series. One of the paper's sportswriters gave Arthur $30, so he bought a one-way bus ticket and took off on the grueling 30-hour ride to St. Louis. With no money upon his arrival for a room anywhere, not to mention the fact that the city was completely booked for the big trolley car series, Sam Zoldak, one of our pitchers, let Arthur sleep on the floor in his room. The next day I went to the manager of the Gateway Hotel where we were staying and asked him if he could fix Arthur up with a cot somewhere. He ended up sticking Arthur on a cot in the corner of one of the ballrooms as that was the only place where there was any room in the hotel. It turned out that Arthur had a roommate in his corner, too. It seems the hotel manager had also put up Army Air Corps Chaplain (Major General) Charles I. Carpenter in the same corner. Not coincidentally, Charles was a friend of mine, too, who, like Arthur, had no where to stay for the Series. So Arthur slept right next to an Army Air Corps General — he was in good company!

We took Arthur in with us when we went to Sportsman's Park for each of the games of the Series because he had no tickets. He'd go into the clubhouse with us and just walk around the stands watching the ballgame once it got under way. Arthur never had a seat in the Series, but he saw every game and was forever grateful for the opportunity. We took up a collection to get him back to New York after the Series, and we sent him on his way. As I said, Arthur's name is now legendary in baseball's inner circles. He eventually became a well-respected sportswriter for the *New York Daily Mirror,* then later became an executive for the Mets. Arthur's brother Milt Richman also made good as he became a great sportswriter and is now enshrined in the writers wing of the National Baseball Hall of Fame. At 81 years of age, Arthur is still active in baseball. He's been a senior advisor with the New York Yankees for many years now, and when he speaks, people listen — even George Steinbrenner. In fact, it was Arthur who recommended that Steinbrenner hire Joe Torre as manager back in 1996. Four World Series titles later, Arthur's recommendation still looks like a real winner.

OCTOBER 5, 1944: World Series Game Two — *CARDS BEAT BROWNS IN 11TH, 3-2, AND EVEN WORLD SERIES AT 1-ALL.* That was the headline in the *New York Times* after we dropped Game Two of the Series on this day. It was a heart-wrenching defeat with every play of the extra-inning game loaded with tension. The pitching match-up featured Nelson Potter against Max Lanier, and both guys showed up with their A-game. We were the visiting team again, so I was the first from our club to find out that Max was on his game when I struck out swinging to start the ballgame. Lanier then made short work of Mike Kreevich and Chet Laabs to get out of the first inning 3-up, 3-down.

Nelson was just as sharp, matching Lanier with a 1-2-3 first inning. Neither team did anything in the 2nd inning, either, but the 3rd inning saw the game's first scoring. We threatened in the top half of the inning when I worked a 2-out walk, but I was forced out at second when Kreevich grounded to Marty Marion. The Cardinals, however, were able to sqeeze out a run from their efforts in the bottom of the inning. Cards second baseman Emil Verban led off with a single to left. Lanier then attempted to bunt Verban to second, but he popped it up between the mound and the plate. Red Hayworth, our catcher, Mark Christman, our third baseman, and Nelson all converged on the routine pop, but no one took control and it fell in. Nels hurriedly picked it up and fired it to first base, but his throw was wild. He was charged with two errors, and now the Cards had Lanier on first and Verban on third with none out. Augie Bergamo was up next, and he grounded to me. I had no play on Lanier or Verban, so I threw Bergamo out at first, but Emil scored. Nelson did a great job of bearing down and getting Johnny Hopp to strike out next, then he got Stan Musial to ground to me and I threw Stan out at first. We were lucky to get out of the inning allowing just the one run.

Lanier held us hitless again in the top of the 4th inning, then they added another run against us in the home half of the inning. Walker Cooper had struck out to open the inning, but Nelson then walked Ray Sanders. Whitey Kurowski then executed the hit-and-run to perfection, singling to right in the hole I vacated when I left to cover second base. That put runners at first and second with one out. Marion was up next, and he smashed one to Christman at third. Mark made a great stop, but fumbled the ball when he tried to rush his throw to me at second in hopes of turning a double-play. Bases loaded and one out. Verban hit a run-scoring sac-fly to Laabs in left, but that's all they got when Lanier hit an inning-ending ground ball to Vern Stephens.

We finally notched a hit off Lanier in the top of the 5th when Gene Moore led off the inning by pushing a bunt into no-man's land past the pitcher's mound. We were unable to capitalize on Moore's lead-off hit, however, when we followed with a fielder's choice by Red and a ground-out by Nels. That brought me up, and I really wanted to do something to drive in Red who was standing on second. I got a good pitch to hit from Max and drove it to deep centerfield, but Hopp tracked it down for the third out. Just when it looked to the outsiders like we were finished, we surprised them with a 7th-inning rally. Here's how the *New York Times* described it — "The plucky Browns roared back, and the crowd had by far its liveliest session. With two down, Sewell's men tore off a trio of hits, a single by Moore, a double by Red Hayworth, and a single by Frank Mancuso, batting for Potter. The two runs that resulted from that outbreak deadlocked the score."

Bob Muncrief relieved Nelson after Mancuso had pinch-hit for Nels in the bottom of the 7th, and he looked sharp setting down the Cards in order while striking out two. We had a great chance to take the lead in the top of the 8th when Kreevich led off with a double, but things didn't go our way after that. Arthur Daley of the *New York Times* succinctly summarized the rest of the inning when he wrote, "[Cardinals relief pitcher] Blix Donnelly strode in from the bullpen with the winning run on second base, nobody out and without the benefit of warm-up. Thereupon he proceeded to strike out the side. Wonder what he would have done had he had the chance to unlimber his arm." The Cardinals made some noise of their own in the bottom of the 8th. They had Musial on second with one out when Kurowski popped one into shallow left. Vern Stephens made a great over-the-shoulder catch at full speed, then wheeled around and fired to me to double Stan up at second.

Neither team mounted any real threats in the 9th or 10th innings, but the 10th is one that I would have personally liked to forget. I was set to lead off the top half of the 10th, and I was really hoping to get on base. I was 0-for-3 with a walk up to that point, so I was very anxious to do something here to help us score, but Donnelly won the battle and struck me out. To make matters worse, I fumbled a ground ball by Musial in the bottom of the inning for an error. But, fortunately, were were able to erase my mistake when the next batter, Walker Cooper, grounded into an inning-ending double-play — Stephens to me to George McQuinn.

We had our best chance to win the game in the top of the 11th. The inning opened with a near-homer by McQuinn who instead settled for a double off the rightfield fence. Next came a play that I have always thought was not only the turning point of the game, but perhaps the entire Series. Here's how John Drebinger described it in the *New York Times* — "As Mark Christman pushed a bunt down the third-base line for an attempted sacrifice, Donnelly pounced on the white pellet and in one motion spun around to throw the ball to third base in time to nip McQuinn by an eyelash." Arthur Daley, also of the *Times,* added, "Whitey Kurowski made a phenomenal catch of the throw and an even more phenomenal stab at the sliding McQuinn." Donnelly had no business even attempting to throw out McQuinn at third base. The second that Christman's bunt went down it became plainly obvious that a play at third would be so close that it would be foolish to even try it. But Donnelly did it anyway. He quickly scooped up the ball and with no time to look at third just wheeled around and rifled a throw. Donnelly's throw was amazing — right on the bag — and McQuinn slid right into the tag. They just barely, barely did get him. Summarizing the deflating effect this play had on our club and our fans, Drebinger wrote, "For the Browns, it was a disheartening play, inasmuch as Gene Moore followed with a long outfield out that would have easily scored a man from third. As it was, it merely supplied the second out with a runner on first, and the crowd, still relishing the resolute fighting of the underdogs, appeared keenly disappointed." When Red struck out to end the inning, we were disappointed, too.

The game ended suddenly, like a punch to the face, in the bottom of the inning. Sanders led off with a single, Kurowski sacrificed him to second, and Marion was intentionally walked. Then pinch-hitter Ken O'Dea smacked Muncrief's second pitch to him into right field for the game-winning hit. 24 hours after experiencing the high of winning Game One, we walked off the field under the weight of a new low achieved by losing a Game Two heartbreaker. It was particularly tough to swallow when you thought about the great opportunity we'd had in the 11th. It looked then like we might go up two games to none, but instead we were tied at one game each. We had a resilient club, however, and once in the clubhouse we quickly tried to turn our disappointment into determination to bounce back in the next day's game, and it started with leadership from Luke Sewell. "I don't like it a bit when we lose a ballgame," he said, "but we didn't fold up in the pennant race and we won't fold in the Series. We'll get 'em tomorrow with Jack Kramer doing the pitching!"

Bob Muncrief pitched very well but took the hard-luck loss. I felt for him because he had had a tough season, starting well but struggling late in the season with a sore elbow. Nonetheless, he'd gone out there and pitched his heart out. He had a great attitude about it, however, and refused to be discouraged, and that lifted all of our spirits. "You'll never see me with my chin in my hands over a ballgame," he said. "I do the best I know how and if I lose I try harder the next time. These Cards have some good hitters, but they hit no better than Cleveland and Boston in the American League. Our hurlers took care of them all right." By this time our disappointment-turned-determination had risen to the level of a loud roar in the showers, so Luke came in and told us to pipe down. "Just get out there tomorrow and we'll take those Cardinals on the field — not in the clubhouse." That statement closed the door on the events of this day, and with that we began to focus on Game Three.

OCTOBER 6, 1944: World Series Game Three — *BROWNS WIN, 6 TO 2, FOR 2-1 SERIES LEAD.* That was the *New York Times* headline after we won Game Three of the Series on this day. Our two-games-to-one Series lead over the heavily-favored Cardinals was really shocking to the baseball community. It's been so long since that Series, and there have subsequently been so many other important Series moments, that the true magnitude of what we were accomplishing is long forgotten. In writing about the game he had just witnessed, however, *New York Times* writer John Drebinger's opening comments really go a long way to reminding today's baseball fans of what a colossal upset we were attempting to pull off. "Bounding back with the resilience of a pre-war rubber ball," Drebinger wrote, "the Browns once more tossed baseball's outstanding academic minds into complete consternation today as they thrashed the supposedly infinitely superior Cardinals in the third game of this all-St. Louis World Series and again moved into the lead."

Arthur Daley, also of the *New York Times,* was even more flabbergasted at what we were doing, writing, "This is easily the most astonishing ballclub ever to reach the Series. The Cardinals are a pre-war team of acknowledged strength and class. The Brownies are an ill-assorted collection of cast-offs. However, in the three games the mighty Redbirds have made the startling total of two earned runs. Maybe it doesn't make sense, but that's the way this dizzy Series is going."

For the third day in a row we had incredible weather for the game. It was cool and rainy for a couple days before the Series got under way, but the skies had cleared in time for Game One and it had remained sunny — unseasonably hot, in fact — and in the 90's for Games Two and Three. Jack Kramer got the start, and as he grabbed his glove to go limber up he turned to the writers and said, "Gosh, it's hot. And, brother, I don't like it when it's hot. But if the boys will just get a few hits and a few runs for me, I should do all right."

We were the home team for Game Three, so we switched dugouts and wore our home white uniforms for the game. Just prior to us taking the field, Luke Sewell tried to loosen us up by joking with the writers, saying, "Things ought to perk up for us today because now we have those guys on our own home field." Well, Luke's attempt to lighten the atmosphere didn't seem to work at first when we gave up a quick run in the top of the 1st. Vern Stephens let lead-off man Johnny Hopp's grounder get through him for a 2-base error, and Hopp went on to score, but we settled down after that, restricting the damage to just that one run. I led off our half of the 1st, but Cardinals starter Ted Wilks struck me out. Mike Kreevich and Gene Moore followed with two quick outs, and the 1st inning was in the books. The game cruised along at 1-0 until we exploded in the

3rd inning. I led off the inning with another strikeout, this time getting caught looking. Kreevich made it two outs when he then flied to center. It was very frustrating for me not to have delivered a hit yet in the World Series. My frustration evaporated quickly, though, when my teammates mounted a 2-out rally. Five consecutive singles by Moore, Stephens, George McQuinn, Al Zarilla and Mark Christman netted us three runs and sent Wilks to the showers. Right-handed reliever Fred Schmidt came in and intentionally passed Red Hayworth to load the bases, but then he uncorked a wild pitch, which allowed another run to score. Schmidt then got Kramer to ground out, but we were ahead, 4-1.

The next three innings were scoreless. I faced Schmidt in the bottom of the 5th, but I still couldn't wrangle a hit. I grounded to Whitey Kurowski at third base, and I ran like heck to try and beat it out for an infield hit, but I was out at first on a very close play. The Cardinals scratched out a run in the top of the 7th, but we came right back with two runs in the bottom of the inning to make the score 6-2. I was right in the middle of the scoring action, too — for both teams! The Cards had Ray Sanders on first with none out when Kurowski grounded to Stephens. Vern threw to me at second to force Sanders, but I threw wild to first when trying to double-up Kurowski, and he moved up to second on my error. Marty Marion continued his fine hitting, cashing in on my mistake by scoring Kurowski with a single to center. Believe me, I was not happy to see that run cross because you never knew if it would come back to bite you later. But I helped make amends for my error when I led off the bottom of the inning against new right-handed reliever Al Jurisich, driving one of his pitches off the rightfield screen for a double. I felt like I was running on air as I tore for second, the weight of notching my first Series hit now off my back. I later scored on a passed ball.

Jack got off to a rough start in the 8th. Hopp singled to open the inning and Musial followed with a long fly ball out that backed Moore up to the rightfield wall. Walker Cooper then doubled off the leftfield wall, putting men on second and third with just one out. Sewell didn't like what he was seeing, so he came out to the mound. He just wanted to check with Kramer and Hayworth to make sure that Jack wasn't tired and that he still had his control. They both reassured Luke that everything was fine, so Sewell went back to the bench. Kramer then bore down and struck out Sanders and got Kurowski to end the inning on a foul-out to Moore in right. The score was still 6-2 when the Cardinals came up for their last at-bat in the top of the 9th. Kramer gave up a lead-off single to Marion, but Jack then coolly fanned George Fallon. Pinch-hitter Ken O'Dea, hero of Game Two, grounded to me for the second out, bringing up Danny Litwhiler. Jack quickly put him in the book as his 10th strikeout victim, and the game was over. Kramer was amazing that day, and we all surrounded him with slaps on the back and congratulatory handshakes.

The mood was a little more subdued in the clubhouse after our Game Three win. No one made the mistake of yelling "only two more to go" this time. We were like kids in a candy store after our Game One win, but this time we accepted our victory as a matter of course. Sewell was full of praise for Kramer, telling the writers, "That was a great piece of pitching — a great piece of pitching. He certainly had a rough ballgame." Luke even came to the defense of Stephens and me when reporters asked him if he was concerned about the runs our errors had allowed. "Errors always come along," Luke said, writing them off as an accepted part of the game. "I hate to see them come, but you just can't help it sometimes." I wasn't dwelling on my error. In fact, once that final strike popped into Red Hayworth's mitt, simple euphoria was all that I was experiencing. Still, I couldn't help but again think back to the 11th inning of Game Two. Had Blix Donnelly not made his incredible play to nail McQuinn at third base, we very likely would now be leading three games to none — and I know good and well that we would have definitely been able to win one of four to take the Series title. But that was all wishful thinking, so I turned my focus to tomorrow's Game Four.

OCTOBER 7, 1944: World Series Game Four — *MUSIAL'S BAT WINS; THREE HITS, INCLUDING 2-RUN HOMER IN FIRST, SINK THE BROWNS.* That was the *New York Times* headline after the Cardinals evened the World Series at two games apiece by beating us, 5-1, in Game Four on this day. We were the home team again, but that just meant that the Cards could jump on us that much sooner by batting first. Sig Jakucki started for us, and deserved a better fate than he received, but he was gone by the 4th inning with us trailing, 4-0. Jak got us started on the right foot by striking out Cards lead-off man, Danny Litwhiler. He induced a ground ball from the next man up, Johnny Hopp, but the ball went in no-man's land behind second base. I ran hard for it and got my glove on the ball, but I couldn't hold it and Hopp was safe. Stan Musial then stepped in and drove the first pitch he saw over the rightfield pavilion on a line for a 2-run homer. Jak set the next two batters down easily, but we found ourselves trailing, 2-0, before we'd even broken a sweat on this warm Indian summer day.

I led off our half of the 1st, and for the third straight day I went down swinging in my first at-bat. I can't really explain why other than just to attribute it to the fine Cardinals pitchers and my unfamiliarity with them. On this day it was little right-hander Harry Brecheen who was pitching for the Redbirds, and from the looks of things in my first at-bat, he was going to be tough with his mixture of curves and screwballs. He set us down without much of a fight in the 1st inning, but we had him in some trouble in the 2nd when we had the bases loaded with only one out. But Brecheen was able to get out of hot water when he got Red Hayworth to hit into an inning-ending double-play. Jak wasn't so lucky, however, and he was touched for two more runs in the top of the 3rd, which increased the Cardinal lead to 4-0. The events of this inning back up my earlier statement that Jak deserved a better fate than he received in this game. The inning began with Jakucki striking out Brecheen, but then Litwhiler was safe when he legged out an infield hit on a ground ball to Vern Stephens. Jak followed that by striking out Hopp, but then Musial reached with another infield hit, this one in between the pitcher's box and second base. That put men at first and second despite the fact that there hadn't been a solid ball hit in the inning, but Walker Cooper changed that when he lined a run-scoring single to left, moving Musial up to second.

Ray Sanders batted next and grounded sharply to me. Despite the ball being hit very hard, I should have fielded it cleanly — but I didn't. The ball went through me for an error, allowing Musial to score. I was sick about it. I wish I could blame it on a bad hop, but I can't. It's possible that I took my eye off the ball for a split second to look at Musial, but I can't say for sure. It was just one of those inexplicable errors. I felt particularly bad for Jak because he relied on me to make plays like that, but he showed no animosity over it. Jakucki knew those things happened from time to time. He retired the next man, Whitey Kurowski, to end the inning, and walked slowly to the dugout. No one thought about it at the time, but that would be the last time Jak would pitch in the Series. Ellis Clary pinch-hit for him in the bottom of the 3rd, and Al Hollingsworth took over on the mound after that.

It was an unfortunate way for Jakucki's season to end, especially after pitching so well all season — the pennant-clinching game in particular. Jak came back and pitched well again in 1945, but that was his last hurrah in the majors. For the most part we were a very close-knit team in 1944. There were many different personalities on the team, some outgoing and some quiet, but we banded together to form a strong bond — and Jak was right in the mix. He was a great guy, but sadly fell on hard times after his playing days were over — mostly due to his continuing problems with alcohol. He lived in Galveston, not far from Frank Mancuso in Houston. Frank and Jak were always good friends, even after they'd quit baseball. Frank went on to become a long-time city councilman in Houston, and Jak would often stop by Frank's office to visit. Frank knew Jak was down and out, so he would always slip Jakucki $20 even though Jak never asked him for anything. Jakucki would take the $20 and go to the bar and spend it on beer. When Jak passed away in 1979, it was Frank who paid to have him buried. Jak didn't have anyone, and Frank couldn't stand to see him not get a proper burial. Some time later, a Houston city employee showed up at Frank's office and gave Frank a watch he said had belonged to Jak. The employee told Frank that a bartender had given it to him. He said that the bartender had gotten it from Jak one day in exchange for some drinks. Jak had apparently told the bartender to please get it to Frank Mancuso on the occasion of his death — a thank you for all that Frank had done for him. Frank still has that watch. He keeps it in his baseball room next to a photo of Jak.

The Cardinals added a run in the top of the 6th to make the score 5-0, but we failed to get anything going in our half of the inning. We finally pushed a run across in the 8th when Gene Moore scored from third while the Cards were turning a 6-4-3 double-play. The game ended when I was forced out on a ground ball by Mike Kreevich to Marty Marion who flipped to Emil Verban covering second. As I walked off the field I thought about the contrast in emotions that the game had conjured up in me. I struggled at the plate in the first three games, getting just one hit in 12 at-bats. I was happy, though, because we'd won two of those three games. On the other hand, my bat had come around in this game and I'd collected two hits and a walk in four at-bats — yet we lost, and I was upset about it. We were all upset about it, but not to the point of panic. The Series was tied at two games each, and we were confident that we'd get back to our winning ways in Game Five.

Other baseball folks, however, were not so confident in us — especially the sportswriters. The *New York Times'* Arthur Daley typified the opinion of the scribes in his column entitled *BACK TO NORMALCY,* this excerpt being particularly good at illustrating the press' feelings about us — "The World Series returned to normal today and the actors in this tense and fantastic drama began to follow the script. The Cardinals looked like the aristocratic champions of old. They hit with their old-time authority, got pitching they've come to expect, and were completely dominant. The forlorn Brownies didn't appear too bedraggled, but it was the kind of game everyone anticipated the Series would produce each day." One thing he got right — we weren't bedraggled. Despite our disappointment at losing Game Four, we were determined to bounce back, led by our leader, Luke Sewell. He was quick to reassure us, telling us as we filed into the clubhouse, "That one's gone — let's talk about tomorrow. Galehouse will be our pitcher and we'll take 'em."

St. Louis Cardinals leftfielder Danny Litwhiler was out at second when I put the tag on him as he tried to stretch his 7th-inning single to a double in Game Four of the 1944 World Series on October 7th. Mike Kreevich made the throw. The Cards won the game, 5-1, evening the Series at two games apiece.

OCTOBER 8, 1944: World Series Game Five — *CARDS, WITH COOPER, BEAT BROWNS ON HOMERS, 2-0, TO LEAD IN SERIES.* That was the *New York Times* headline after the Cardinals took a 3-2 lead in the World Series by defeating us, 2-0, in Game Five on this day. In a rematch of the Game One starters, Mort Cooper and Denny Galehouse again put on a display of amazing pitching, only this time the roles were reversed and it was Denny who was undone by the long ball and a lack of offensive support. When the game ended, both guys had gone the distance, Mort striking out a then-record 12 and Denny fanning 10. They both pitched well enough to win, but I guess it was Mort's turn after suffering the tough-luck loss in Game One.

We were the home team once more for this game. It was still bright and sunny, but the Indian summer was gone and there was a real chill in the air. Things didn't start well when Cardinals lead-off man, Danny Litwhiler, slammed Denny's second pitch of the game into left-center for a booming double. But Denny got it together and struck out Johnny Hopp, pitched around the hot-hitting Stan Musial and walked him, and then struck out Walker Cooper and Ray Sanders. I led off our half of the 1st and, for the first time since Game One, did NOT strike out in my first at-bat. I was close, though. I fouled off Mort's first five pitches before working him for a base on balls. I was left stranded, though, when Mort retired us by getting Mike Kreevich on a strikeout, Gene Moore on a fly ball, and George McQuinn on a ground ball.

Vern Stephens turned this 2nd-inning double-play by himself as I simply watched in Game Five of the 1944 World Series on October 8th. Vern had scooped up Mort Cooper's grounder near the bag at second, so he just stepped on it himself to force Emil Verban, then he fired to George McQuinn at first to retire Mort.

Mort and Denny had everybody swinging at air through five innings, and neither club scored. I fouled out to catcher Walker Cooper in my second at-bat in the 3rd inning. I tried to bunt for a hit with two out and Red Hayworth on second in the 5th, but I failed to push the ball past Mort, and he threw me out at first base. We'd recorded two quick outs in the top of the 6th when Sanders, with the count full, unloaded on a Galehouse fastball and sent it into the screen that projected above the rightfield roof for a solo home run. Denny got out of the inning by popping up Whitey Kurowski.

Redbirds hurler Mort Cooper popped me up to his brother, catcher Walker, in the 3rd inning of Game Five of the 1944 World Series on October 8th. The umpire is Ziggy Sears. Mort was really on his game in this one, avenging his Game One loss by shutting us out, 2-0, and leading his club to a three games to two Series edge.

If it's one thing we didn't do in 1944, it was give up in the face of adversity. We knew we needed to get that run back quick, and we loaded the bases in the bottom of the 6th with just one out. Billy Southworth went out to the mound, but after a short talk with Mort he returned to the dugout — and he left Cooper in the game. To his credit, Mort really rose to the occasion, getting out of the jam by striking out Al Zarilla and Mark Christman, both on called third strikes. We were disheartened, but we kept fighting. Denny singled in the 7th, which brought me up to hit, but Luke Sewell decided to play a hunch and send in Floyd Baker to pinch-hit for me. It was a tough spot for a young kid like Baker to make his World Series debut. Here's what Arthur Daley of the *New York Times* had to say about Luke's decision — "Not since Chicago's hitless wonders of 1906 had a .235 batsman as their heaviest slugger has there appeared in a World Series a pinch-hitter with the average Floyd Baker carted to the plate today. Either Luke Sewell is running out of emergency batsmen or he's running out of hunches. At any rate, he sent up Baker, who sports an awesome batting average of — hold your hats on this one — .177. The young man fanned in right smart fashion."

I was disappointed to come out of the game at that point. I wanted to go up there and have the opportunity to do something to help our club. Still, I was rooting for Floyd to deliver once I was out of the game. It wasn't my place to second guess Luke. His hunches had often worked and were a key to our success in 1944, but this one failed so the writers ridiculed him. Had Floyd singled, though, they would have hailed Luke as a genius. Danny Litwhiler hit a bases-empty homer in the 8th, and an inning later Mort closed out the game in astonishing fashion when he struck out the side. Luke, continuing to play hunches, sent up three pinch-hitters that inning — Milt Byrnes, Chet Laabs, and Mike Chartak. Cooper fanned all three.

The clubhouses were a study in contrast. I read about the understandably happy scene in the Cardinals dressing room — they were just one win away from a World Series title. Their quotes in the papers were very complimentary of us, though, nothing disrespectful. "Galehouse pitched a wonderful game," Southworth told the reporters. "He was just a victim of home run hits." Even my old pal Pepper Martin was praising us. Pepper, out of the big leagues since 1940, had returned as a utility man and played in 40 games for the 1944 Cardinals. "I

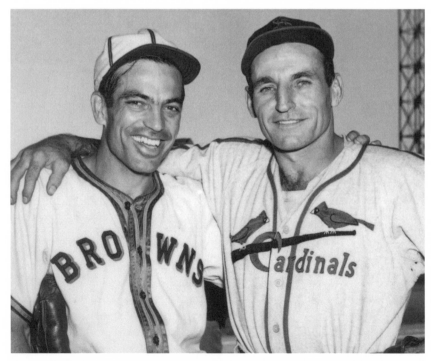

My good friend Pepper Martin and I enjoyed a reunion at the 1944 World Series. Out of the big leagues since 1940, Pepper had returned to the Cards as a utility man in '44.

can see why the Brownies won the American League pennant," he said. "Them guys don't know when they're licked." That was true, too. Our clubhouse was a bit solemn, but despite now having our backs against the wall, we never adopted a defeatist attitude. Luke Sewell, as usual, led the way, turning our attention to the positive instead of the negative. He told reporters about our ability to rebound the next day, showing the utmost confidence in our pitching as he announced, "I'll pitch Nelson Potter tomorrow. While we're speaking of pitchers, let's take a look at a real flinger — Galehouse. He's pitched 18 World Series innings, given three runs on 13 hits. That's good in any language. That guy has the guts of a bank robber."

OCTOBER 9, 1944: World Series Game Six — *CARDS TAKE SERIES BY BEATING BROWNS; TRIUMPH BY 3-1 FOR MARGIN OF 4 GAMES TO 2 AND CAPTURE THEIR FIFTH WORLD TITLE.* That was the *New York Times* headline after the Cardinals closed out the 1944 World Series by edging us in a close-fought battle in what turned out to be the decisive sixth game on this day. We certainly did not dwell on the prospect that this game could be IT as the Cardinals took the field to start the ballgame. We switched dugouts and wore our road grays as the Cards returned to the role of home team for this game. The weather, although it looked threatening in the morning, continued to be perfect for the sixth straight day — blue skies and comfortable temperatures. With Nelson Potter on the mound, we felt confident that we could extend the Series to a seventh game, but we were facing Max Lanier again and we knew we'd have to hit him better than we had back in our Game Two loss.

I led off the game but failed to get on, popping out to Ray Sanders near the field boxes in back of first base. Max then struck out Mike Kreevich swinging and got Gene Moore looking to quickly end the 1st inning. It was not the start we'd hoped for, but Nelson looked sharp in the bottom of the inning and set down the cards 1-2-3. We broke through with a run in the top of the 2nd, the score coming as a result of a triple by Chet Laabs and an ensuing RBI-single by George McQuinn. George was quietly (he did everything quietly) putting together a fine Series at the plate. He ended up the leading hitter in the Series, batting well over .400 in addition to leading the club in RBIs. As I said, George was a quiet fellow. He was one of those clichéd guys who said "hello" in the spring and "goodbye" in the fall. McQuinn was never very outgoing, but he got along with everybody and actually had a good sense of humor once you sat down and talked with him. And he was an excellent ballplayer with a pretty darn good glove down there at first base. He'd been trapped in the Yankee farm system for years — buried behind Lou Gehrig — before finally getting his first full shot in the big leagues with the 1938 Browns. Given the chance to play every day, George turned in a fine year in '38, batting .324 with 12 homers. He'd been a regular with the Brownies ever since, although a bad back had robbed him of some of his power. His back was so bad that he often needed to immediately lay down for a few hours after some of our games. But McQuinn was tough and he played through the pain, making an invaluable contribution to our pennant.

First baseman George McQuinn, far right, was a pretty quiet fellow, but there was nothing quiet about his bat — he could hit! He was a great glove man, too, and his all around contribution to our 1944 pennant was enormous. Also pictured here with George from left to right is third baseman Mark Christman, shortstop Vern Stephens, and me.

The 1-0 lead McQuinn posted us to held up until the 4th inning when the Cardinals got to us for three runs. It was frustrating, too, because we really should have gotten out of that inning without allowing them any runs. We had one out with Walker Cooper on second and Sanders on first. Whitey Kurowski then hit a bounder to Vern Stephens at short. Vern fielded it cleanly, but he rushed his throw to me at second to try and turn an inning-ending double-play. His throw pulled me off the bag, but I continued the pivot and threw to first — too late to get Kurowski. When it was all said and done, we had pulled off the perfect phantom double-play — a pretty-looking turn in which you get exactly NO outs. Cooper scored on the play to tie the game, 1-1. Nelson appeared to be on a track to minimize the damage when he got Marty Marion to pop out, but 2-out singles by Emil Verban and Lanier pushed across two more runs. Bob Muncrief relieved Potter and stopped the bleeding, but we were now in a 3-1 hole.

Cardinals third baseman Whitey Kurowski was unable to escape this 2nd-inning pickle from Game Six of the 1944 World Series on October 9th. Number 25 is Cards first base coach Mike Gonzales; number 24 is Nelson Potter; George McQuinn is in the upper left corner of the photo; that's me right behind Kurowski; and the legs in the top of the picture belong to Vern Stephens. Our 3-1 loss in this game gave the Cardinals the title, four games to two, ending our World Series dream.

There would be no more scoring by either club. Our bats had gone dead, and it's hard to mount a come-from-behind win when you get only three hits on the day. Lanier was forced out of the game in the 6th, but it was more HIM than us who did him in. Max opened the inning by retiring Stephens on a ground ball, but then he walked Laabs and McQuinn in succession. Then he wild-pitched the runners up to second and third. Cards manager Billy Southworth had seen enough, so he quickly replaced Max with Ted Wilks. We'd roughed up Wilks in our Game Three win, so this looked like a great opportunity to break the game open. Mark Christman greeted Wilks with a ground ball to Kurowski at third — but Laabs broke for home. Kurowski quickly threw a peg to catcher Walker Cooper who had planted his 200-pound frame across the plate. The much-smaller Laabs lowered his shoulder and hit Cooper hard, but then bounced off Cooper as if he'd hit a brick wall. Chet was out, and it was very dis-heartening. Our threat fizzled out completely when Red Hayworth ended the inning with a routine fly out to center.

I have to share the blame for our lack of hits in the game. After fouling out in the 1st inning, I was out in the 2nd when Stan Musial made a great running catch of a long foul ball I hit down the rightfield line. I was out again in the 5th when I flied out to Danny Litwhiler in deep left. 0-for-3, and I was very frustrated. When it was my turn to bat in the 7th inning with one out, Luke Sewell sent Floyd Baker up to pinch-hit for me. Poor Floyd struck out again, just like he'd done when he pinch-hit for me the day before. He looked right at strike three with the bat stuck on his shoulder. Sewell, still desperate to try and do something to spark our offense, kept up his pinch-hitting moves when we came to bat in the 9th. McQuinn had opened the inning with a fly ball out, but then Luke sent Milt Byrnes up to hit for Christman. Milt had a good at-bat, working the count to 3-and-2, but then he struck out swinging. We were down to our last out when Luke sent Mike Chartak up to hit for Hayworth. Mike went down swinging, and it was over.

We were a dejected bunch as we walked off that field. On the other hand, the Cardinals, of course, were gleeful. One Redbird was particularly joyous, and his story is worth retelling here. Emil Verban, the Cardinals' 28-year old rookie second baseman, was 3-for-3 in Game Six, and his RBI-single in the 4th inning turned out to be the game-winner — and, essentially, the Series-winner. I wasn't aware of it at the time, but I later learned that there was an interesting subplot to Verban's big Game Six. The Cards were the home team for Games One and Two, and that meant that their front office handled the task of providing tickets to us for our wives, family, etc. We were the home team for Game Three, and that's where our trouble with Verban began. The Browns front office had apparently assigned Emil's pregnant wife, Annetta, an obstructed-view seat directly behind one of Sportsman's Park's support posts. Emil, who was 0-for-2 in Game Three, complained to Browns owner Don Barnes after the game. Barnes, as the story goes, supposedly told Verban, "The way you're playing, YOU ought to be sitting behind a post" — then he proceeded to deny Verban a ticket upgrade for Annetta. Verban was not a big guy — just about 5-foot-10 and 165 pounds — but the old saying "never awaken a sleeping giant" still seems appropriate here. Sparked by his mistreatment by Barnes, Verban proceeded to rap out five hits in the next three games of the Series, culminating in his great Game Six performance. To cap off the story, Verban went up to Barnes after Game Six and said, "Now you can sit behind the post, you meathead."

In hindsight, the Verban story is a funny one, but humor was the last thing on our minds as we trudged off the field, defeated. We didn't view losing to the Cardinals like most everyone else did. Because we were seen as such a rag-tag inferior opponent, most folks said that we should just have been happy to get to the World Series. If we ever bought into that belief it quickly dissipated as soon as we got a good look at the Cards and realized that we could compete with them. The closeness of all the games proves that we could. The words of *New York Times* writer Arthur Daley are very indicative of the way most people viewed us. "The Series ended as it should have ended," Daley wrote, "in a Cardinal triumph. But those never-say-die Brownies made them work hard to attain it. The championship belongs to the Redbirds, but Luke Sewell deserves a brisk pat on the back for even getting his odd assortment of talent in the classic. No man ever did so much with so little."

Sewell wasn't buying into the overachieving theory, however. He'd already gone over to the Cardinal clubhouse and congratulated Southworth when he came back and gave us words we'll never forget. "The Cards got the breaks and they won," Luke told us while reporters scribbled in their pads. "That tells the whole story. But we've STILL got a better club." Milt Byrnes then chimed in on this theme by saying, "Yeah, they never could have won a pennant in our league!" Once we got over the initial shock of losing, we all came to appreciate what a great thing it was to have participated in the one and only St. Louis "Streetcar Series." It was a wonderful event, its uniqueness captured perfectly by John Drebinger when he wrote, "And another diamond classic has come and gone, and St. Louis, which this time could not lose in any event, felt reason to be pleased by the outcome on practically all counts. The victor had entered the struggle an overwhelming favorite. The Brownies, after winning their first American League pennant in history, had made a stirring fight of it when they held matters even in the first four games, and no one could ask much more."

Our 1944 American League pennant was the realization of an unbelievable concept — the St. Louis Browns were finally winners — and I credit Luke Sewell with making it all possible. It was an impossible scenario to fathom at the time he took over as manager prior to the 1941 season. Luke inherited a Browns club that had finished 20 games below .500 in 1940. In fact, the Browns hadn't even had a winning season since 1929, so not only was Sewell inheriting a poor team, he was inheriting a legacy of losing. In three short years, however, he turned all of that around. Luke, upon taking over in '42, immediately began to preach an attitude of winning, and we began to improve right away. He stuck to his mission statement in 1943, but there were still some old guard players there that didn't buy into Sewell's philosophy. They still had the old attitude of, "Hurry up and beat us so we can go home and get supper," or something like that. One by one, Sewell weeded those guys out, sending them off to other ballclubs. He simply would no longer allow the Browns to employ guys who just went through the motions.

Finally, by spring training of 1944, Sewell had assembled a group of players who, as a group, were true believers in what he'd been preaching — WE COULD WIN. Having the right attitude allowed us to be successful on the ballfield, and that's why we became a good team. Any doubt still lingering in anyone's mind it was laid to rest when we started the season by winning our first nine ballgames. From that point on we were in the first division all year long. One time we got down four or five games, yet we still never doubted that we were going to win in the long run. Sewell called me in one day and said, "Don't worry about those five games, Don. We're going to win some and lose some — but in the end we'll WIN." The "old guard" Browns would have folded because they were already mentally beaten down. They had been a doormat in the American League for so long that they expected things to go bad. When things were going well they thought, "When are things going to go wrong?" When things finally turned bad they thought, "See — we knew we'd lose." We had changed that. Sewell saw in me, and a few of the other guys, too, that we wouldn't stand for that. We were winners — not those old Browns anymore. They were losers. He got new talent with a new attitude, and that made the difference. Luke kept telling us we could win. He never said anything about losing — only winning. He always had a positive attitude.

Not only was Sewell, like all successful managers, an excellent motivator, but he was a good baseball man, too. He was very good with pitchers. He'd been a catcher to begin with, so he was very good at knowing when pitchers were starting to lose their stuff. That enabled him to be excellent at changing pitchers at just the right time. He also handled them as well off the field as he did on the field. Luke also believed that good defense was key in winning, and he built the 1944 team with that in mind. He wasn't lax about telling you when you were doing something wrong — he'd let you know. But he wouldn't say anything in front of anyone else — he would tell you in private. That made a difference, too. We didn't have the best talent of all time on that team, but we made the most of what we had — and I think that's a testament to Sewell's managerial ability. The Brownies left St. Louis prior to the 1954 season, becoming the Baltimore Orioles. The Orioles went on to build a rich tradition of winning, so much so that the St. Louis Browns are unknown to most baseball fans of today. One thing that will always keep the Browns from being completely forgotten, however, is that lone pennant of 1944 — and for that we can all thank Luke Sewell.

On a personal level, Sewell will always have a warm place in my heart because he believed in me. He showed faith in me by bringing me back the the majors in 1942 and converting me to a second baseman. I was very happy that I was able to make good on his belief in me by helping to deliver him a pennant. At the other end of the emotional spectrum for me, however, was Branch Rickey. While he will always be the man that facilitated the realization of my dream to play in the big leagues, any remaining feelings of goodwill (and there weren't many good feelings left after years of poor treatment at contract time) for him were exterminated by the mean things he said when he released me from the organization back in 1941. "You'll never play major league baseball again," he said, "or be on ANY winning ballclub." There was no excuse for saying that to any player, much less one like me who'd given 100% effort every day that I was affiliated with the Cardinals organization. I never wanted to call someone and give them a piece of my mind as badly as I wanted to call Rickey after we beat the Yankees to clinch the 1944 flag. I was finally a winner! I just wanted him to know that it takes several kinds of ballplayers to make a winning team. I never called him though. I decided that my play on the ballfield showed him that he was wrong, and that's what really counts.

This photo captures the way that I will always remember the magical season of 1944 — scoring runs on sunny days at Sportsman's Park in the company of my wonderful teammates with plenty of fans enjoying the once-in-a-lifetime occurrence of the St. Louis Browns winning the American League pennant.

1945

APRIL 17, 1945: Our ballclub was still enjoying the idea that we were the 1944 American League champions as we got the new season underway on this day. We had high hopes of repeating as A.L. champs, too, because the bulk of our '44 roster remained intact with a few minor additions and subtractions. One MAJOR addition to our ballclub was outfielder Pete Gray. His saga ended up overshadowing the story that was our attempt to win another pennant. In fact, Pete's story would come to define the ENTIRE major league baseball season of 1945. Why — because Gray had only one arm. Historians have used Gray's handicap as a way of illustrating their contention that World War II had by 1945 so depleted major league ballclubs that teams were now reduced to filling out their rosters with "cripples." It's true that big league teams were, in fact, ravaged by the war, but it's an overstatement to say that it was necessary to turn to "cripples" in order to fill rosters. There were plenty of players available who could have turned in numbers equal to or better than Gray's 1945 stats. Pete hit .218 with 43 singles, 6 doubles, 2 triples, 0 homers, 13 base on balls, 13 RBIs, 26 runs scored, and 5 stolen bases — this in 77 games and 234 at-bats. A look at those numbers leaves no doubt that Gray was overmatched with the bat even though he was supposedly facing big league talent that was at an all-time low. But those same numbers are also a testament to the fact that Gray's achievement was amazing. There were more than a few guys with two healthy arms who would have loved to put up Pete's numbers. Without question, Pete got the absolute most out of his body.

Baseball does not lend itself to being played with only one arm, yet Gray was amazingly proficient at it — not proficient enough to be a successful hitter in the major leagues, but certainly proficient enough to excel in the war-depleted minors. And excel he did in 1944 when he'd posted a great season with the Memphis Chicks, batting .335, leading the Southern Association in stolen bases, and being named MVP of the loop. The Browns front office executives then made news by spending $20,000 to acquire Gray from Memphis. The fact that Pete had only one arm led many critics to suggest that it was just a publicity stunt geared at boosting attendance. Team owner Don Barnes denied it, and Gray's minor league numbers certainly made him seem worthy of a shot in the majors, but the debate would follow us throughout the '45 season. I believe that the Browns execs honestly thought that Gray would do well up on the big league level. Why wouldn't they — Jack Fournier, the Browns' number one scout, told them, "War or no war, Gray is a big leaguer. Advise you buy at once." So they bought him. It was a no lose situation for the front office. Their perfect scenario was that Pete would succeed on the ballfield, but they were going to do well at the gate whether Gray was good or not.

Pete had lost his right arm when he was just six years old. He'd been riding on the running board of a truck when he fell off. His arm got mangled in one of the wheels requiring it to be amputated just below the shoulder, leaving nothing but a bit of a stump. Gray re-taught himself to do everything left-handed, eventually developing into a fine ballplayer as he grew. After years of kicking around with semi-pro teams and minor league clubs, Gray suddenly found himself with the big league Browns when we opened camp at Cape Girardeau. He claimed to be 27 years of age, but he was actually 30. Like a lot of guys, Pete had shaved a few years off his birth certificate. Most of our players weren't shocked by the sight of a one-armed ballplayer. In fact, we'd seen that phenomenon on a daily basis the previous year because Orville Paul, one of our batting practice pitchers, had only one arm. But, to be honest, we were shocked when we saw what Gray could do here on the big league stage.

Hitting from the left side with a full-sized 36-ounce bat, Gray stood deep in the batter's box and choked up about six inches. He whipped the bat through the zone quickly, lashing out line drives and hard grounders. He was a good bunter, too. To lay one down he would plant the knob of the bat against his side, then slide his hand about a third of the way up the handle. And he displayed very good speed when running the bases. It was on defense where Gray was particularly fascinating to watch. He'd come in fast on grounders and scoop the ball up in the air in front of him. He'd then flip his glove away while the ball was in mid-air, snag the ball with his now-bare hand, and fire it in to the infield — and I mean he'd FIRE it. He had a very good arm. He did all this in one quick, seamless, fluid motion. He was just as smooth on fly balls or throws from teammates. He'd catch the ball directly in front of him and in a split second slip the glove under his stump and remove the ball — again, all in one non-stop movement. He'd really honed these techniques down to a science. Helping Gray in his fielding was the custom-made glove he used. It was floppy with little or no padding. That helped him maneuver it easier. Gray ditched the glove altogether when he was backing up another outfielder. His fielding techniques required that every motion be executed perfectly, and that led to an occasional error that might not happen to players not operating at his disadvantage — but he was anything but a liability on defense. His technique was truly amazing to see.

As amazing as Gray was to see, however, very few can actually admit to having watched him make his major league debut on this day. In fact, just 4,167 fans were in attendance at Sportsman's Park as we opened up the '45 season with a 7-1 win over Detroit. Gray can't be blamed for the low turnout, though. It was a very cold day and that is believed to have been the reason for the small crowd. In any case, the curiosity of the fans and press was finally answered when Sewell penciled Gray in as our starter in leftfield. Pete's spring hadn't exactly won him the job outright. In fact, he'd missed a little time with a sore throwing shoulder, but he finished strong in our City Series with the Cardinals at the end of spring training. That allowed Sewell to start Gray in the opener without it appearing that he was simply bowing to front office pressure. Whatever the reason for his place in the starting line-up, Pete made a good showing of it. He played flawlessly in the field and even managed to silence some of his critics by picking up his first big league hit. He'd have had another hit, too — probably a double — had Detroit centerfielder Roger Cramer not robbed him with a shoe-top tumbling grab of a line drive. As for me, I wasn't as lucky as Gray on this day. Hal Newhouser and Tiger relievers Les Mueller and Walt Wilson shut me down, holding me to 0-for-5 from my lead-off slot. Fortunately, my bat wasn't missed as Sig Jakucki looked to be in mid-1944-season form, allowing just six hits while going the distance.

MAY 2, 1945: There was no grandiose season-opening winning streak in 1945. In fact, we'd looked more like the "old" Browns by losing five in a row after winning the opener against Detroit. We righted ourselves, however, and won three straight as we prepared to play Cleveland on this night at Sportsman's Park. Despite cold temperatures in the low 40's, it was a special night filled with warm memories — a one-of-a-kind in the history of the Browns. In a pre-game ceremony presided over by baseball commissioner-elect Happy Chandler (Judge Landis had died just five months earlier), we raised our 1944 American League pennant. It was a final nod to our great achievement — but it also closed the door on '44. It was a new year, so we now had to look forward. The game that followed ended up being a microcosm of the 1945 season — a tough-fought contest that ended in disappointment. Cleveland's big fastballer Allie Reynolds was at his best, setting us down in rapid fashion. He allowed just four hits while going the distance — and then some. He pitched every inning of a 13-inning battle, and got the 2-1 win. He was really something that night. We had the bases loaded with none out in the 12th, but Reynolds pitched his way out of the jam. I managed to get one of our four hits, but Reynolds got me out the other five times I faced him. One-for-six. Not to be overlooked was our starter, Nelson Potter. He, too, was amazing, pitching 12 innings of 5-hit ball, but Bob Muncrief relieved him in the 13th — and it just wasn't Bob's night. The first three men he faced — Mike Rocco, Myril Hoag and Ed Carnett — all singled, and that pushed across the winning run.

We received our 1944 A.L. championship rings prior to our game against the Indians under the lights at Sportsman's Park on May 2nd, 1945. That's team president Donald Barnes handing me my prize, and that's catcher Red Hayworth in line behind me.

MAY 8, 1945: *BROWNS CONQUER SENATORS, 7 TO 1.* That was the Associated Press headline after our victory over Washington on this day at Sportsman's Park. There were some great performances by my teammates in this game. Nelson Potter pitched a 3-hitter and added a hit and an RBI. 1944 American Association batting champ Boris "Babe" Martin, our leftfielder, had a single, a double, a triple and an RBI. On a more modest level of success, I was 1-for-3 with an RBI and two runs scored. All of us, however, will remember that day for a more significant reason — it was V-E Day — the day the Nazi regime surrendered. The war in Europe was finally over. It was a truly wonderful day, one never to be forgotten.

MAY 20, 1945: We wrapped up a 4-game series with New York by sweeping a twin bill on this day at Sportsman's Park. I went 2-for-3 with a double and two RBIs in the opener, and 1-for-4 in the nightcap — and I did this out of the number-eight slot in the batting order. Luke Sewell moved me out of the number-one spot in this series to make room for Pete Gray to hit lead-off. Pete had only appeared in a few games following his successful debut in our season-opener — two or three as a starter and a couple more as a substitute. The preseason hype surrounding Gray had created a great deal of intrigue amongst fans in St. Louis and on the road, so the fact that he had so far seen very little playing time started to create pressure on Sewell to play Pete. The fans in other cities would actually be angry if Gray wasn't in the line-up when we came to town. That, plus probable front office coaxing, finally persuaded Sewell to allow Gray to play for an extended period. After not playing at all in our previous eight games, Luke gave Pete seven straight starts beginning with the second game of a twin bill against the Athletics on May 13th, a game in which he singled once in our 8-2 victory.

Our 4-game set with New York was next, and Gray delivered a hit, a walk, and a stolen base in the series-opener — much to the delight of our fans. He went hitless in the second game, but flashed his amazing one-handed catch-transfer-and-throw technique on a number of occasions. He made an error in that game that cost us a run, and it showed our fans that Gray's handicap could, on occasion, be a liability on defense. But his tremendous catch of a long foul down the leftfield line by Mike Garbark demonstrated Gray's up-side and left the crowd cheering. Then Pete gave them another fine showing in the series-ending doubleheader on this day. He was 3-for-5 with two RBIs in the opener, and 1-for-3 in the nightcap. There was an interesting dynamic at play in the early part of the season when it came to Gray and the pitchers that were facing him, and Pete's at-bats against Atley Donald in the opener are a good illustration of it. I think that opposition pitchers couldn't believe that a one-armed player could hit them. They were big leaguers, and no "cripple" could get the best of them. With that in mind, they would try and blow their fast-balls by Gray. By doing that, however, they were playing right to Gray's strength. Pete could hit a fastball, but pitchers didn't believe it until they saw it with their own eyes. When Gray stepped in the box to lead off the game, Donald came in with a fastball, which Gray took. When Atley came in with another fastball, Pete promptly lined it into rightfield for a single. Donald was mad as hell out there, kicking the dirt in frustration. He challeneged Gray with another fastball in Pete's next at-bat, and the result was another single to right. Donald looked even angrier, glowering at Gray. Still in disbelief that he couldn't throw his fastball by Gray, Donald challenged Pete again in his next at-bat. Gray again singled and Atley was irate. Fortunately for Donald, he was out of the game by the time Pete hit again. Pete really got a kick out of Donald's reaction, saying, "He really couldn't handle the fact that I got a hit off him. After all, who wants to give a hit to a cripple, especially one who has the nerve to crowd the plate?"

Sportswriter James P. Dawson tried to capture the amazement of Pete Gray for his readers back in New York when he wrote, "One-armed Pete Gray was a positive menace. He led a Brownie 15-hit assault in the first game with three blows, batted in two runs, scored another, came close enough to stealing a base to have the crowd give the Bronx cheer to the decision against him, and backed to the fence in the first for Frankie Crosetti's lusty drive to end the inning. In the afterpiece Gray pulled down seven flies, including powerful drives near the fence on Johnny Lindell and Oscar Grimes in the 2nd inning, and a spectacular running knee-high clutch on Bud Metheny to end the third. His lone hit in this game nudged along the tying run, and he scampered home shortly afterward with the run that put the Browns in front." Gray's big game against the Yankees was incredible to see, and his success on this day ensured that Pete would be a hot topic of conversation for quite some time.

MAY 24, 1945: *RED SOX' 5 IN 6TH SINK BROWNS, 8 TO 6.* That was the newspaper headline recapping our loss at Sportsman's Park on this day. It was our second straight defeat after having won five in a row. I was held hitless by Boston's right-handed starter, Pinky Woods, and right-handed reliever, Mike Ryba. I was still hitting out of the number eight slot as Pete Gray was still batting lead-off. This turned out to be the last game in Gray's string of seven straight starts. His bat had cooled after the Yankees left town, and he, like me, was 0-for-4 in our game on this day. 14 games would elapse before Gray would get another start, and in the interim he would make only a handful of appearances as a substitute.

One thing about Gray that was well established by this still-early point of the season was the fact that he was a loner — and it seemed that he was intent on remaining a loner. He just didn't fit in, but that was by his choice. And it was apparent to everyone that he was going to make no effort to fit in. Gray was sullen and withdrawn. He developed no real friendships amongst our players and rejected most who reached out to him — at least as far as I saw it. Al Hollingsworth was Gray's roommate and I know he tried to be helpful to Pete. But Gray's insecurities about whether he was in the majors as a publicity stunt prevented him from opening up to anyone, including Hollingsworth. I asked Pete on a number of occasions to join me and some of the other fellows for dinner, but he always declined. I finally gave up. I think Gray went out to dinner with Vern Stephens a few times, and he played cards with us in the clubhouse on rare occasions, but for the most part he was always alone. He just didn't want to let anybody inside.

One doesn't have to be a psychiatrist to understand the probable reasons behind Gray's reluctance to embrace the guys on our team. From day one, Pete had a chip on his shoulder and acted like the world was against him. His attitude is somewhat understandable, though, when I look back at it. There's a much heightened sensitivity to handicapped people nowadays, but it wasn't like that back in the 1940's. In fact, I'd bet that Pete was persecuted about his handicap by many of the kids with whom he grew up, and that probably set the tone for his sullenness. He certainly was persecuted by opposition players around the league in 1945. As despicable as it sounds today, that was par for the course back then. The bench jockeys would look for something that bothered you — then attack it with a vengeance. They attacked Pete for his handicap, calling him all sorts of terrible names and accusing him of not belonging in the majors. When they saw that it got to him, they'd just do it more. Gray was hell-bent to prove to everyone that he belonged in the majors, and I think that was the key thing behind his solitude. He did not want to be viewed as a sideshow, and the fact that many accused him of that festered in him.

The debate as to whether Gray was with our ballclub as a sideshow or as a legitimate player was with us from the very beginning at spring training. We were all fighting for our jobs, so the last thing anyone wanted to believe was that he might find themself out of a job so the team could keep Gray even if it turned out that he was not up to big league standards. Luke Sewell told us in no uncertain terms that would not happen, and he mirrored that sentiment when he told the reporters at Cape Girardeau, "Pete Gray is just another ballplayer to me. I'll promise him every opportunity to make the grade, but he will have to stand or fall on what he shows. We can't play him if he weakens the team." With this air of tension surrounding Gray it's really no wonder that he showed up for spring training defensive and withdrawn. I remember one incident that demonstrated just how tightly he was wound up. It was near the end of camp and we were in Toledo to play an exhibition game with the Mud Hens. Guys were always playing tricks on each other for laughs, so George Caster decided to give the business to Gray. Caster slipped a dead fish into the pocket of Pete's suit jacket, and when Gray stuck his hand in the pocket he cut his fingers on the scales. He was livid and took off after Caster after finding out that George had done it. Caster was unfazed and said he'd whip Pete with one hand tied behind his back to even the fight. We stepped in and prevented the two from coming to blows, but the altercation proved that Pete was not up for our usual brand of kidding.

MAY 26, 1945: I was approaching my 33rd birthday and I was well aware of the fact that good offensive days were a bit fewer and farther between for me — so I appreciated them more than ever when they happened. I had a nice 3-for-5 game as we beat the Red Sox at Fenway Park on this day. I also had three RBIs and a stolen base, but it wasn't ALL good as I committed two errors at second base.

MAY 27, 1945: We opened a 3-game series against New York with a double-header at Yankee Stadium on this day. The Yanks turned the tables on us from the week before, sweeping the series on their home turf. I had a couple of hits in the opener, but went a combined 0-for-7 in the second and third games of the set. There were fine performances all around in the series, but it was Pete Gray that the Yankee fans really wanted to see here on our first trip to the Bronx in 1945. There was an audible sound of disappointment in the stands when we took the field in the opener because Boris Martin, a great looking kid who'd been up with us in a handful of games in 1944, trotted out to left-field INSTEAD of Gray. Boris made them pay for their groans of disappoint-ment, however, when he walloped his first career homer in the top of the 7th inning, but Luke Sewell responded by sending Gray in to replace Martin in the bottom of the inning. The Yankee fans cheered when they saw Gray take the field. Here's some of what *New York Times* writer James P. Dawson had to say about Pete's play that day. "STADIUM DEBUT OF GRAY ACCLAIMED — The fans got their first glimpse of Pete Gray, amazing one-armed outfielder. Sewell inserted Gray in left for Martin, the move a gesture to the fans' curiosity. Bud Metheny swept across the winning run in the open-er with a blow that, although officially scored a single, shot past the diving clutch of Gray to the leftfield fence as Frankie Crosetti charged over the plate. FANS' CURIOSITY GRATIFIED. Whole-heartedly the onlookers cheered Gray when he struck a pinch-single in the seventh of the nightcap. Friends from Nanticoke, PA, presented a $50 war bond to Gray between games under the stand."

Sewell took some heat from the New York writers for not starting Pete in either game of the doubleheader. They said Luke had led them to believe that Gray would play more. They complained that they'd reported Sewell's prom-ise in their papers. Their columns had helped draw a huge crowd of curious fans, only to have them disappointed when Gray played in only a few innings as a substitute. Sewell tried to set them straight, saying, "I didn't misrepresent anything. I didn't say Gray would be in our line-up today. If you had been watching the box scores, you would have known he wasn't in the line-up in the last two games at Boston. I'm not using Gray as a crowd-puller when he isn't hitting." This was a tough predicament for Sewell. The front office, press, and fans were pressuring him to play Gray, but Pete had yet to demonstrate that he was an everyday player. Sewell was truly between a rock and a hard place.

The Universal Newsreel people were at Yankee Stadium on this day to watch Gray make his New York debut. They were prepared to shoot lots of film of Pete since it was a twin bill, but they — like the fans and sportswriters — were probably disappointed when Gray played just a few innings of the opener and the nightcap as a late-game substitute. Still, those few innings, in addition to pre-game warm-ups, gave them ample opportunity to film Gray in action. I forgot all about the whole thing until a week later when I went to the movies. There in a darkened theater I saw a couple of cartoons followed by a newsreel. The newsreel started with a few stories about the war and politics, then BANG — there was a 20-foot tall image of Pete Gray right there on the silver screen. It was something to see. His segment began with the typical up-tempo newsreel music playing over a splashy title-frame that read, "Baseball's Miracle Man." Then the familiar voice of narrator Ed Herlihy began to tell Gray's story while footage of our Yankee Stadium doubleheader played in the background. "Sensation of this year's baseball season is Pete Gray," Herlihy said to open Gray's segment, which ran for only ran for a minute or two. But in those few flickering moments it showed Pete playing catch in the pre-game warmup. That gave moviegoers a good look at his catch-and-transfer technique. Then they showed him swinging a couple of bats in the on-deck circle followed by some footage of him grounding out. Finally, they showed him making a routine catch out in leftfield. Pete's segment ended with some footage of him standing near the stands with a big wide grin — a rare sight to say the least. But, in my opinion, Herlihy was right on target when he concluded Gray's segment by saying, "His pluck and determination is an inspiration to all."

JUNE 1, 1945: I had one of my best offensive games of the season on this day as we beat the Athletics, 4-0, at Shibe Park in Philadelphia. Sig Jakucki was pitching wonderfully but was being matched pitch for pitch by a 32-year old rookie just back from the war — a right-hander named Steve Gerkin. Jak finally took matters in his own hands by slamming one of Gerkin's pitches off the leftfield wall for a triple in the 6th, then I drove Jakucki in with a single. Gerkin was still in there when I batted in the 8th with Jak again on base, and this time I really laid good wood on the ball for a 2-run home run. Jakucki went the route and allowed just three hits.

JUNE 2, 1945: My bat stayed hot on this day in the second game of our series against the Athletics in Philly. I rapped out two singles, scored once, drove in one, and even stole a base in our 9-0 rout. Jack Kramer got the shutout win. Everyone got at least one hit except Kramer, but the offensive standout of the day was shortstop Len Schulte who sprayed three safeties.

The throw from Athletics catcher Buddy Rosar to third baseman George Kell was late and I was safe on this play from the 1st inning of our 9-0 victory at Shibe Park on June 2nd, 1945. The umpire is Cal Hubbard.

JUNE 3, 1945: We closed out our 4-game series in Philadelphia with a double-header against the Athletics on this day. The Associated Press wrote, "A Shibe Park crowd of 25,151 saw the Browns' lead-off hitter, Don Gutteridge, smash a home run in the 1st inning of the opener for the American League champs' only score in twenty-two innings." That's right, we lost the opener, 3-1, on a 5-hitter by A's right-hander Russ Christopher, then we played to a 13-inning, 0-0 tie in the nightcap. Tex Shirley pitched all 13 innings of the second game and walked away with nothing to show for it. The funny thing is, Tex also pitched all ten innings of a 1-1 tie we played against the Senators back on May 11th. Talk about tough luck. Incidentally, my homer on this day was my last in a Browns uniform. For some inexplicable reason, I'd found my power and hit two home runs in three days, yet I never hit another the rest of the season.

JUNE 7, 1945: I had a great time running around Comiskey Park on this day as we swept a doubleheader from the White Sox by scores of 6-0 and 6-2. It was a beautiful day, our club battered the Sox pitchers for 20 hits, and we won both games easily. Not that I needed any reminding of how lucky I was to be a big leaguer, but this was the kind of day that really emphasized my good fortune in being able to make a living playing the game that I loved. I was all over the place on defense, making putouts and slinging the ball around. I had plenty of action on the bases, too, lashing out two singles, one double, scoring twice, driving in one, and stealing three bases. I can't think of a better way to spend an afternoon.

Johnny Dickshot, White Sox leftfielder, was out in this attempted steal of second base in the 4th inning of our 6-0 win in the opener of a twin bill at Comiskey Park on June 7th, 1945. I slapped the tag on him following a great throw from catcher Red Hayworth. Ringing up Dickshot is umpire George Pipgras.

JUNE 10, 1945: A doubleheader split with the Indians in Cleveland on this day allowed us to remain one game over the .500-mark. That was good enough for 3rd place in the A.L., just four games behind the Yankees and well within striking distance. I started in my usual place at second base the opener, but found myself on the bench in the nightcap. That began a period of 14 games where I would start only three times. I appeared in a handful of other games in that span as a pinch-hitter, pinch-runner, or late-inning defensive substitute, but it was a little disconcerting to be suddenly benched for an extended period of time after having been an everyday player all season up to that point. But that was part of the game that I had dealt with before, so I just worked extra hard to stay mentally and physically ready to play when called upon.

I think there were two things at hand in landing me on the bench. One was Luke Sewell's constant struggle to find a line-up that would produce more offense. He instituted a number of changes to reach that desired effect, one being playing Len Schulte at second base to see if he would hit better than me. Schulte was 29 years old, so he was a bit younger than me, but he had very little experience having played in just one game in 1944, so Sewell wanted to get a good look at him to see what he could do. The second thing that I feel helped put me on the bench — as well as some other guys, too — was the continuing pressure on Sewell to play Pete Gray. I don't resent Sewell or Gray for this problem, it was just a tough situation for everyone. Pete hadn't started a game for about 2-1/2 weeks until he started both ends of a doubleheader at Chicago on June 6th. Gray then went on to start our next nine ballgames, and it was midway through his run as a regular that I took my turn on the bench.

JUNE 19, 1945: I got an unexpected birthday gift on this day — my first appearance back in the starting line-up after having not started in nine days. My 33rd birthday was made even better when we defeated the White Sox, 4-3, at Sportsman's Park. Despite going hitless in the game, I was a happy fellow. Strangely enough, though, my re-entry into the line-up did not come at second base. It was, of all places, in leftfield, and this was, in fact, the first time in my career that I ever played the outfield. Luke Sewell was still giving Len Schulte a shot to make good at second, so he put me in the outfield as a way of getting my bat back in the line-up without displacing Schulte. The guy who got displaced, however, was Pete Gray, and he was obviously not happy about it. Gray tended to brood when he was benched, and that was the case on this day. Pete had hit well at the beginning of his 11-game stint as a starter, but he cooled off significantly in the second half of his run. I guess Sewell felt that gave him the opportunity to make the change while still being able to say that he'd given Gray a fair chance. In any case, there I was all of a sudden out in leftfield. I'd shagged plenty of fly balls over the years, so I wasn't particularly nervous about the switch — but there was a different dynamic to playing the outfield in an actual game. It was much more involved than just catching pop flies. At any rate, I made five putouts in the game with no mishaps, so it was a good way to break into the new position. I didn't care where I played — I just wanted to play regularly for as long as I possibly could.

JUNE 20, 1945: On this day I played my second game as Brownie leftfielder. Unlike the previous game, however, this one was very eventful. We played the White Sox at Sportsman's Park again, and there was nothing out of the ordinary about my chances in left — I easily handled four fly balls — but activities in the infield were very atypical. That is if you think a near riot is atypical baseball activity. Our Al Hollingsworth was locked in a scoreless pitcher's duel with Sox left-hander Eddie Lopat through seven innings. The 8th opened with a single by Lopat, another single by Wally Moses, and then an intentional walk to Leroy Schalk to load the bases. George Caster was sent in to relieve Al. A long fly ball scored Lopat. Then the Sox scored three more runs off singles by Tony Cuccinello and Cass Michaels. We got two outs after that, but then Luke waved in Tex Shirley to relieve George. Instead of handing the ball to Tex, George fired it INTO the Sox's dugout. George was aiming at Karl Scheel, the Sox's batting practice pitcher. Scheel was an ex-marine, freshly returned from his service overseas. It was true that he was being used as a batting practice pitcher — but his primary duty with the Sox was bench-jockey. He had really given it to Sig Jakucki in our game the previous day, and he was back at it throughout our game on this day. It culminated with his heckling of George, and George snapped. White Sox beat writer Irving Vaughan did a nice job describing the events AFTER George rifled the ball into the Chicago dugout...

"Manager Dykes stepped to the plate to protest [Caster's actions] to Umpire in Chief Art Passarella, who quickly advised Dykes to return whence he came," wrote Vaughan. "Almost instantly, the Browns, as if acting under orders, burst from their dugout and started across the field. When the Browns got as far as home plate, Passarella and the other umpires endeavored to herd them back into their corral. Sig Jakucki, however, apparently enraged over what Scheel had said to him last night, plowed past the umpires, even a flying tackle by Passarella failing to halt his advance. Jakucki leaped into the Sox dugout, followed by a dozen or so Browns, among them Ellis Clary, Myron Hayworth, and manager Luke Sewell. The fans surged onto the field, gathered around the dugout, and weren't dispersed until a few policeman arrived five minutes later. Meanwhile, according to reports of what went on in the depths of the dugout, the marine veteran of South Pacific campaigns was kicked and pummeled, allegedly with Jakucki doing the heavy work."

When police got things under control, they escorted Scheel from the field for treatment. Jak and Ellis were a little banged up, too, but they were okay. Ellis was a firebrand kind of guy and he lived for that kind of stuff. Luke made a statement to reporters after the game, saying, "The whole thing is very regrettable, but you can't expect anybody to take what our boys took without doing something about it." American League President Will Harridge disagreed. He fully expected us to do nothing in the face of insulting heckling, so he fined Luke, George, Ellis and Jak to make his point. Scheel, for his part, got off scot-free except for the beating he took. It was a shame that a once fine minor league pitcher and soldier was now reduced to playing the role of bench jockey, but some guys would do anything to be in the major leagues. Scheel redeemed himself later in life, though. He eventually became a highly-decorated Chicago firefighter who risked his life to save a family of five in a hotel fire that killed eight people.

JUNE 28, 1945: The Yankees were holding down first place on this day as we played them in the final game of a 3-game series at Sportsman's Park. Despite a line-up that was far inferior to their stout pre-war roster, they were still the 1st-place Yankees, winners of seven in a row. We snapped their streak with a 9-4 victory, though, and I was happy to have a good day at the plate to help us in our win. I went 2-for-5 with 2 RBIs and two runs scored. Sig Jakucki went the full nine for his sixth win of the season. Pete Gray was again on the bench as I played in the outfield, and that was continuing to irritate him. Sportswriter Fred Lieb had spent a great deal of time writing about Gray so far this season, so he asked Pete where he felt he stood at this point in the campaign. Revealing his frustration, Gray said, "I don't think I've made good yet — especially when I have to sit on the bench while Luke Sewell plays Don Gutteridge, and infielder, in leftfield." I took no offense at Pete's comment. I knew his anger was not personal towards me. Despite achieving occasional success when he got to play, I think he was frustrated by his inability to produce numbers like he'd posted the year before in Memphis. It's always tough to replicate one's great minor league numbers on the big league level. It's especially tough to do it when you're fighting for playing time. Gray had been an everyday player in the minors, but now he was playing sporadically and that made it difficult for ANY player to get into a rhythm.

No matter how tough it was for Gray to be consistent on the field, he could do no wrong with the writers and fans. People love rooting for an underdog, and that's what Pete represented to them. John E. Wray of the *St. Louis Post-Dispatch* openly campaigned in his column for Gray to be played more often. He felt that Pete improved with more usage, and I guess there were some statistics to back up his theory. As for the fans' affection for Gray, I didn't need any additional proof that they were true blue for him — but proof is what I, nonetheless, got one day. Pete was in centerfield during one of my early games in leftfield when someone drove a ball between us in left-center. I tracked the ball but ran into Gray who was stationed under it waiting to make the catch. The collision knocked Pete over and he dropped the ball. It was my inexperience at my new position that caused this mishap. This is not an uncommon scenario — especially with the Brownies — so that's why I was so surprised at the reaction of the Sportsman's Park fans. They LOUDLY booed me. I had crossed up their boy — Pete Gray — and they didn't like it one bit. I heard Pete tell the sportswriters on many occasions that he was touched by the fans' affection for him, but at the same time he questioned what was behind their cheers. He said he sometimes thought they were motivated by sympathy — and Gray was angered by anyone who demonstrated sympathy for his handicap. It's that ongoing emotional battle that I think conflicted Gray and made him hard to get along with. Although the papers had started to carry the occasional story that speculated about disharmony between Gray and a few players on our team, those issues were still, for the most part, unknown by the general public. That's why the fans were still, without a doubt, absolutely true blue for Pete.

JULY 3, 1945: *BROWNS TURN BACK ATHLETICS BY 2-1; SINGLE BY GUT-TERIDGE DECIDES.* That was the Associated Press headline following our win at Sportsman's Park on this day. I'd still been playing pretty regularly in leftfield, but Luke Sewell had me on the bench at the start of this game. While sitting there I watched our left-hander Weldon "Lefty" West and A's right-hander Lou Knerr engage in a great pitcher's duel. We were trailing, 1-0, when Luke pinch-hit for Lefty in the bottom of the 7th, so Tex Shirley went the final two innings, shutting out the Athletics in both frames. Luke, playing one of his hunches, sent me in to replace

Len in the late innings despite the fact that Schulte had already touched Knerr for a single earlier in the game. Well, I got on base with a walk in the 8th inning and scored the tying run following a single by Vern Stephens. In the 9th I came up with Tex on base and bounced a single into centerfield off Knerr to score Shirley with the game-winning hit. It was always a big thrill to win a game with a game-ending hit, one where you touch fist base and then walk off the field in victory. I wish all of you reading this could experience that. It's really something special.

JULY 20, 1945: Three days of rain had wrecked havoc on our scheduled series with the Yankees in New York, but the skies cleared on this day and we were able to get in a doubleheader before leaving immediately for Boston. Another day of rain would have been ideal for New York, too, because we ended up sweeping the twin bill, thereby dealing a serious blow to the Bombers' pennant hopes. It was the first time that season that New York had lost both ends of a doubleheader. And, in a fashion uncharacteristic of the Yanks, we won both games with late come-from-behind rallies. Sig Jakucki was pitching for us in the opener and we were trailing, 2-0, when he stepped up to hit in the 5th with one on, two out, and two strikes. That's when the Yankees' 27-year old rookie right-hander Al Gettel made a rookie mistake — he laid a fat one in to Jak. Sig pounced on it, sending it into the lower

This play occurred on July 20th, 1945. The *Daily Mirror* photo caption described it this way — "STATUE. Foot off ground, Gutteridge of Browns looks like something carved in marble after taking throw from Mancuso in 1st inning of first tilt at Yankee Stadium." George Stirnweiss, by the way, is the baserunner, and he was safe on a steal. Vern Stephens is backing up the play, and the umpire is Bill McGowan.

leftfield stands for a game-tying 2-run homer. Two innings later with the Yanks back in front, 3-2, Gettel repeated his mistake. After walking Mark Christman, Boris Martin dug in to face Gettel. With the count at one-and-two, Gettel came in with the same pitch he'd thrown to Jakucki — and the results were the same, too. Boris blasted a 2-run shot that landed in almost the exact same spot as Jak's. Jakucki bore down from then on, making the 4-3 lead stand up for a win.

The nightcap was equally disheartening for New York. Al Hollingsworth and Floyd "Bill" Bevens were really going at it, and the score was tied at 2-all after seven innings. "Bevens, on the mound for the home side, opened the 8th with successive passes to Don Gutteridge and Mike Kreevich," wrote Louis Effrat of the *New York Times*. "Right then and there, the handwriting was on the wall. George McQuinn sacrificed both runners along, and Vern Stephens propelled a fly to Tuck Stainback in center. That was long enough to permit Gutteridge to tag up and cross the plate after the catch. That also was the ballgame." I'd had a rough day at the plate, being held hitless in eight at-bats, but that meant nothing to me when Al retired the last Yankee batter to secure the win. I'd scored the game-winner, and I was one happy fellow.

Let me quickly jump back to the characters involved in the first game — Sig Jakucki and Boris "Babe" Martin. It's funny that Jak and Boris would be linked as co-heroes in our win in the opener on this day. Not that they disliked each other or anything like that, but Boris has long told of an incident that is very insightful into each man's personality. I've already written extensively in this book about what a tough guy Jakucki was, but Boris was pretty darn tough, too. He was solid muscle, and he'd done a good deal of boxing around the St. Louis area from where he grew up. One day we were riding the train to our next stop. A bunch of guys were sitting around the club car talking, drinking, playing cards, etc. — the usual activities. Frank Mancuso, Ellis Clary, Red Hayworth, and Boris were in the middle a game of Fan-Tan when some ladies stuck their heads in the car and said that they'd heard that there were some St. Louis CARDINALS on board. The ladies then asked if these gentlemen were, in fact, Cardinals players. The Browns had always played second fiddle to the Cardinals in St. Louis, and this really bothered some of the Brownies — including Jakucki. Sitting off to the side, Jak looked up from his drink and glared at the ladies, then told them in no uncertain terms that we were the St. Louis BROWNS — NOT the Cardinals. "We're the BROWNS," he said. "Get out of here you old bags!" This was Jak, of course, so needless to say his tirade was fueled by alcohol and laced with profanity. I took the opportunity to clean it up a bit. For good reason, the ladies were completely offended and left in huff. A lot of the guys chuckled at Jak's outburst, but Ellis, a tough guy in his own right, didn't like it a bit. He said, "Hey, I don't think it's right that Jakucki should talk to those ladies that way. He's half a foot taller than me and 50-pounds heavier, but if one of you big guys don't make him go back and apologize, I'M gonna make him."

That's where Boris took over. In spite of the fact that he, too, surrendered height and weight advantages to Jak, Boris took up Ellis' cause. He got up and walked over to Jak, demanding that he go and apologize — or else. I'm sure everyone in the car thought all hell was going to break loose, but Jak knew Boris was a tough customer. At first he hesitated, saying things would be different if he wasn't drunk, but he then got up and apologized. One might think that an incident like this could cause a strain on the relationship between Boris and Jak, but it didn't. In fact, Jak showed Boris a great deal of respect the for rest of the season, making sure he was on his best behavior any time Boris was within earshot. Boris is a very bright guy and he continued to use his toughness to succeed in everything he did following his career in baseball. He spent many years as a professional wrestling referee, encountering countless numbers of half-crazed tough guys — and never backing down. He eventually moved into the real estate field where his toughness helped him achieve a great deal of success in that sometimes cut-throat business. Boris is retired now, but his toughness still comes in handy from time to time. While he endures the usual aches and pains from which all of us former-ballplayers suffer, he's still in great shape with big arms of solid muscle and fists like sledge hammers. Recently, while limping to his car with a bag of groceries in one hand and his cane in the other, he was approached by four young thugs. One stepped forward, kicked at Boris' cane, and demanded his wallet. Now, Boris is one of the nicest guys you'll ever meet — but this was a big mistake by this unsuspecting young crook. All of a sudden, the 80-year old Boris "Babe" Martin was once again the 25-year old club boxer. With a quick and devastating short right hand he dropped the thug to the pavement, where he remained, unconscious. At the same time he'd quickly loaded his left hand, preparing to deliver another quick punch to any of the other three punks that may come at him next. But as he turned to unleash the blow, all he saw were the heels of the other three thugs running away. All I could do when I heard that story was laugh and think, "That's the old Boris that I know and love!"

JULY 21, 1945: I clouted a double and a single off Red Sox rookie right-hander Jim Wilson as we downed Boston, 4-1, at Fenway Park. Wilson pitched the whole game, and we only got seven hits off him — but a rocky 1st inning did him in. He walked me to open the game, then Eddie Lake fumbled a routine grounder by Mike Kreevich. Vern Stephens was walked to fill the bases following George McQuinn's sacrifice, then subsequent blows by Milt Byrnes and Mark Christman made the score 3-0 by the time Wilson retired the side. He was very good after that, but the Red Sox bats failed to catch up against Nelson Potter. Our win that day gave us a record of 40 wins, 38 losses, and 3 ties — and that left us still in the thick of things at five games behind the league-leading Detroit Tigers. Incidentally, Jim Wilson was nearly killed by a line drive off the bat of Hank Greenberg just 18 days after our game on this day. Greenberg's liner caught Wilson square in the head, knocking him unconscious and forcing him into emergency surgery. Wilson was having a pretty good rookie year, too, but the injury really seemed to set him back. He returned to the majors for very brief, unsuccessful stints in 1946, '48 and '49, but he didn't really get back on track until 1951. Fortunately, he made a nice comeback and pitched well throughout the 50's — even hurling a no-hitter in 1954. That scenario — an indefensible line drive back at the pitcher — is one of the scariest aspects of baseball. It's a risk that no pitcher likes but all are willing to accept in order to play the game they love. When you think about it, it's amazing that no big leaguer has ever been killed considering how many pitches have been thrown since the inception of the major leagues.

AUGUST 1, 1945: We lost to the Tigers, 9-8, at Briggs Stadium on this day, and there were a number of interesting things worth noting. Luke Sewell's experiment with me in the outfield was over. He'd given it up about a month earlier, returning me to second base. I would never again play in the outfield. Our front office had recently purchased 35-year old Lou Finney from the Red Sox, and he was playing in his first game for us on this day. Lou wasn't a power hitter at all, but he must have been pumped up on adrenaline because he hit a 5th-inning grand slam to give us a 5-2 lead. In 56 more games with us that season, Lou hit only one more long ball. His clout should have earned him headlines, but he was upstaged by the great Hank Greenberg who hit a 2-run homer in the 8th. Greenberg had been back from the service for only a month, but he was already up to his old heroics again. In fact, he'd hit a game-winning home run on July 1st — the first game he'd appeared in since his return from the war.

AUGUST 6, 1945: I had one of those tough 1-for-8 doubleheaders as we dropped two to the Cleveland Indians at Sportsman's Park on this day. I wasn't concerned for myself, though — I was worried about Mark Christman. The whole ballclub was worried about him. We'd jumped on Indians starting right-hander Pete Center for three runs in the 2nd inning of the opening game, so Allie Reynolds replaced him. Reynolds threw very hard, and he was wild with one of his fast ones in the 3rd inning — up and in to Mark. Christman couldn't get out of the way, and the pitch struck him in the head. He was knocked out cold. He tried to walk off the field under his own power when he came to, but he was too wobbly. Then Luke Sewell ordered Tex Shirley and George Caster to carry Mark off on a stretcher. Seeing a scene like that conjured up horrific recollections of the deadly Ray Chapman beaning of 1920. We were all well aware that serious injury was just one pitch away for any of us, but we tried not to think about it too much. Fortunately, Mark would be all right. X-rays revealed that his skull was not broken, but he had a serious concussion and missed quite a few games while recuperating.

AUGUST 12, 1945: We opened up a 5-game series with the Washington Senators at Sportsman's Park on this day. The Nats and the Tigers were the top two contenders for the American League pennant at this time, so this was a big series for Washington who trailed 1st-place Detroit by one game. We split the twin bill, dropping the opener, 9-5, before taking the nightcap, 5-1. I was held hitless in the first game, but I managed to slap out a double and a single in our second game win. Of note here is the fellow who was the Senators offensive sparkplug this day — Mike Kreevich. The Nats had acquired Mike about a week earlier in a waiver deal. We were not happy to see him go because we still had hopes of making a run at the pennant despite the fact that we were about seven games back at this time. We were only two games below .500, and the Tigers were not exactly running away with the pennant — so there WAS still hope. But, the front office sold Mike and we missed his bat in the line-up. In question was whether Senators manager Ossie Bluege would be able to manage Kreevich's drinking problems the way Luke Sewell did. Well, from the looks of things in our series against them, it looked like the answer was YES. Kreevich had four hits and two RBIs in the opener and another hit in the nightcap.

Many guys on the team believed that Kreevich was released because team owner Don Barnes wanted to clear the way for Sewell to play Pete Gray more often. Before his departure, Kreevich had been one of the more outspoken players when it came to the Pete Gray situation. Whenever he had to sit the bench so Gray could play, Kreevich would often say, "If I'm not playing well enough to keep a one-armed man from taking my job then I should quit the big leagues." Suspicions that Kreevich was released to open centerfield for Gray were fueled by the fact that Pete, who had not started a game for nearly a month, all of a sudden got 10 straight starts following the departure of Kreevich. This situation only increased the tension between Gray and a number of our players. Perhaps the guy who took the greatest offense at the release of Kreevich was Sig Jakucki. He'd never warmed up to Gray, and his dislike for Pete only increased after Kreevich's release. It's possible that they were drawn together by their common addiction to alcohol, but either way Jak and Mike were good friends — and Jakucki held Gray responsible for Kreevich's departure.

I didn't witness it, but I've always heard that Pete once asked Jak to help him tie his shoes, to which Jakucki, still peeved over the release of Kreevich, supposedly replied, "Tie your own goddamned shoes you one-armed son-of-a-bitch!" That sounds like Jak alright, but I find it hard to believe that Gray would ever ask Jakucki for help of any kind knowing how Jak felt about him. I can tell you this, though — asking for help with getting his shoes tied was just about the ONLY thng Pete would ask of anyone. Most of the time he would ask Frank Mancuso. Frank was a good soul and he dressed right next to Gray, so it was a natural that Pete would get Frank to help him. But Gray was proud, and he would never ask Frank for help in front of anyone. Pete would always wait until everyone was gone or out of earshot before he would ask Frank for assistance. One story has it that Gray decked Jakucki with one punch because of their conflict over Kreevich — but I don't believe it for a minute. I'd have known about it had they ever fought. Plus, Jak was a big, 200-pound brawler. There's simply no way that he would have ever let ANY 170-pound guy knock him down, much less, Pete Gray.

AUGUST 13, 1945: Another doubleheader with the Nats on this day, and another split. Mike Kreevich was our friendly nemesis again, this time hitting a home run into the Sportsman's Park seats in the opener. I went hitless in the first game but finally got a hit in the second game off Washington right-hander Alex Carrasquel. There was a moment of tension in the nightcap. It was one of those incidents where you were never really sure if the fans would snap and rush the field. Here's how the scene was described by the Associated Press — "Play was held up for 15 minutes in the 8th inning of the second game when irate fans hurled pop bottles and seat cushions onto the playing field in protest of an umpire's decision. Catcher Al Evans of the Senators hit a ball which George Pipgras, head umpire, ruled hit the back screen of the pavilion roof and was a home run under Sportsman's Park ground rules. The Browns protested briefly, but the fans continued the demonstration while players of both teams and man-ager Luke Sewell of the Browns helped the groundskeepers pick up the debris."

AUGUST 15, 1945: We had a knack for winning ballgames on the same day that great wars ended. We'd trounced the Senators on V-E Day back on May 8th, and on this day we routed the Bronx Bombers, 10-4, at Sportsman's Park, a day that would be forever remembered as V-J Day — the day the Japanese empire surrendered. I went 2-for-5 with an RBI in the game — sort of a cherry-on-the-sundae that was the end of the war. What a great day it was. After nearly four solid years of war, we finally had peace.

The war against Japan wasn't the only war that ended on this day. The war in the Browns front office had apparently ended on this day, too. Team owner Don Barnes, under pressure from the rest of the ownership, sold his 31 percent of the club to Browns stockholder Richard Muckerman. I mention this only because of the impact that it was going to have on Pete Gray's situation. Barnes had been the chief person responsible for pressuring Luke Sewell to play Gray. It was rumored, however, that Muckerman, upon taking control of the club, had relieved Sewell of any further obligation to play Pete. Gray was just five games into his new run as a starter when the front office shake-up happened on this day, but Sewell let Pete start another five consecutive games before pulling the plug. Luke should be credited for giving Gray a solid chance to get hot, but Pete failed to hit in his 10-game run as an everyday player, batting just .200 in that span.

AUGUST 16, 1945: The loss of players to war service had really taken a toll on the Yankees as we played the second of four games against them at Sportsman's Park on this day. They'd lost six in a row and were struggling, like us, to stay in the pennant race. They'd received word that help in the form of a recently discharged Charlie Keller was on its way soon, but that didn't help them on this day. We got a solid outing from Bob Muncrief and our bats banged out 13 hits as we beat the Yanks, 7-2, to draw even with them for a tie for 5th place. New York may not have been the powerhouse they were prior to the war, but they were still the Yankees to me. So it was always nice to have a good game against them, and that's how I remember this day. "Vern Stephens and Don Gutteridge were the thorns in Al Gettel's side," wrote the Associated Press, referring to New York's starting right-hander. "Stephens led a 13-hit assault with three blows, two of them doubles. Gutteridge banged three, one of them a triple. Gutteridge's triple, with George McQuinn's single, sent the Browns off in front with a run in the first. A single by Gutteridge [off lefty Joe Page in the 6th] hammered home two more runs."

AUGUST 18, 1945: This entry is merely to point out a superlative performance by one of my teammates on this day. Lefty West pitched very well for us in 1945, mostly in relief. Luke Sewell did give him an occasional start, however, his first coming in our game against the Yankees on this day at Sportsman's Park. One hour and 47 minutes after he'd thrown his first pitch to New York lead-off man Snuffy Stirnweiss, Lefty owned an amazing 2-hit, 3-1 victory over the Yanks. I was thrilled to kick in a single and a run scored in support of Lefty's great game. Here's a little bit of how *New York Times* writer James P. Dawson described it — "A 30-year old rookie, named Weldon West, did all of this to the Yankees. A fork-hand flipping product of Kernesville, N.C., making his first start of the season, West celebrated with a 2-hit exhibition that thrilled 11,501 fans in a ladies' day throng. West yielded a single to George Stirnweiss as the game got under way. Then not until one was out in the ninth were the Yanks able to hit him again." Lefty's great day is an example of how fleeting success in the major leagues could be — but also how sweet it is. He'd worked long and hard for his shot at the Big Show, and he finally got it late in his "baseball life" thanks to World War II. He made the most of it and was finally rewarded with a wonderful day that any fellow who never quite made it to the big leagues would have loved to experience. Despite pitching well throughout the entire '45 season, Lefty never again returned to the majors. It just shows you how fickle the whole thing could be. But on this day Lefty was king — and over the Bronx Bombers, no less — and that's something he could hang onto forever.

AUGUST 29, 1945: We were still optimistic about our chances to catch the league-leading Tigers as we prepared to play them on this day at Sportsman's Park. We'd played very well of late, winning 19 of 25 to pull to within five games of Detroit, then we beat them on this day, 5-4, to cut their lead to four. It wasn't long ball heroics that won us this game, either, just good old sound baseball. Here's how it was described by the Associated Press — "The Browns' winning run came in the 8th inning when Don Gutteridge opened with a single over third base, moved to second on Lou Finney's sacrifice, to third on an infield out and romped home when Gene Moore singled sharply to left."

SEPTEMBER 8, 1945: Any realistic hopes we had of making a late-season charge to the pennant took a serious blow as we lost to the Senators, 4-1, on this day. It was the last of a 5-game series with the Nats at Griffith Stadium, and they beat us in four of the five games, dropping us seven games behind the 1st-place Tigers. I was 2-for-3 with a triple off 41-year old Washington right-hander Pete Appleton. Appleton had actually been with us in '45 before being released and picked up by Washington. He made us pay for this indignity, too, holding us to just five hits while going the distance. And in front of President Truman, no less! It was the first game attended by a president since 1941. President Truman, a southpaw, threw out the first ball and stayed until the last out was made.

Harry Truman threw out the first ball for our game against the Senators in Washington, DC, on September 8th, 1945, and he stayed at the ballpark until the last out was made. He was a huge baseball fan. Things had certainly changed a great deal for Truman since the last time he'd appeared at one of our games. That was nearly a year earlier at the 1944 World Series when this picture was snapped. Truman was merely a senator from Missouri at that time, but he was now the President of the United States of America, and the one who'd overseen the end of World War II, no less. That's George McQuinn to the President's right, and me to his left.

SEPTEMBER 9, 1945: Our disappointment at losing in front of President Truman seemed like a pittance compared to the frustration we faced the next day as we lost a twin bill to the Athletics at Shibe Park. The two losses ran our losing streak to six games, but the worst part was that we were no-hit in the night-cap by Philadelphia right-hander Dick Fowler. Fowler had just recently been discharged from the Canadian Army, and his start against us was his first since his

return. We just couldn't do anything against him. Even when he walked somebody, we just seemed to erase it by hitting into a double-play. We hit only five
balls to the outfield all day. It was ridiculous. On the other hand, our starter,
John "Ox" Miller, was nearly as good as Fowler. Ox held the A's to just five hits,
and it was a scoreless tie until the 9th when Philadelphia scored a run to win it.
Incidentally, Fowler wasn't through with his heroics following his no-hitter. The
next day he was called in to PINCH HIT in the 9th inning and he delivered a
triple! Talk about an impressive return from the war.

SEPTEMBER 15, 1945: We opened a 6-game series against New York with a big
Saturday twin bill at Yankee Stadium on this day. We split the doubleheader, and,
as the saying goes, it really did feel like like kissing your sister — but I enjoyed being
in the mix of both games. I was 1-for-4 with a run scored in our 7-4 loss in the
opener, then I was 2-for-3 with three runs scored and an RBI in our 8-3 victory in
the nightcap. Our split meant that we had won five of our last seven ballgames, but
despite playing well we still trailed the 1st-place Tigers by 8-1/2 games with just nine
games left to play. With our chances of catching the Tigers looking very slim, Luke
Sewell played the role of opportunist and brought Pete Gray out of storage for second game of the double-feature. Gray hadn't started a game in nearly a month, and
in that time span he'd only appeared in a handful of games as a pinch-hitter, pinch-
runner, or late-inning defensive substitute. In fact, he'd had just five at-bats over the
previous 31 games and he was hitless in all of them. It was, no doubt, a trying period for him. Pete, however, fought off the rust and rose to the occasion. Here's how
James P. Dawson of the *New York Times* described Pete's activities — "Gray distinguished himself by contributing three hits to the Browns' attack, driving in a run,
and robbing Aaron Robinson of an extra-base blow with a 6th-inning catch against
the centerfield wall. He held the ball despite a crack-up with Gene Moore."

Gray played in the remaining four games of the Yankee series. Sewell might
have thought Pete was going to get hot after he went 3-for-5 in the nightcap of
the series-opening doubleheader, but a more likely scenario is that Richard
Muckerman pulled a page from Don Barnes' book and pressured Luke to play
Gray for the additional revenue his appearances would generate in the cavernous
Yankee Stadium. Either way, it was downhill for Pete for the rest of the series. He
got a hit in game three of the set, but he was then held hitless in eight at-bats over
the course of games four and five. He hit rock bottom in the series finale — game
two of a twin bill on September 19th. We'd won the opener, 6-5, in 10 innings.
Gray had gone 0-for-5 in the game, so I'm sure his level of frustration was
approaching its peak as we started the nightcap. Here's how the *New York Times*
described what went down — "One-armed Pete Gray of the Browns got the
'heave-ho' for the first time in his major league career, and a fan was forcibly
restrained afield while remonstrating with umpire Bill McGowan. McGowan's
authoritative finger had waved Gray out of the pastime in the 1st inning of the
second game following a dispute on a close decision at first. Gray was dismissed

as he trod to his position for the [bottom of the] 1st inning, and later was almost mobbed by autograph seekers when he sought to watch the game from the stands. He had to leave in self-defense." Unfortunately for the Yankees, Moore replaced Gray, and Gene ended up winning the game for us with a 10th-inning single.

It's amazing that this was the first time Gray got ejected. As the season had progressed and Gray's frustration continued to mount, he had become increasingly more and more argumentative with the umpires. Pete's ejection from the Yankee game is a perfect illustration of the dynamic that had come to exist between the Gray, the umps, and the fans. Pete would argue what he felt was a bad call and the fans would immediately come to his defense whether he was right or wrong. The fans' unwavering support of Gray made the umpires reluctant to thumb him from a game, so Pete got away with quite a lot. I guess McGowan finally got to the point where he wasn't worried about what the fans thought, so he tossed Gray. And you see where it got him — he was nearly mugged by a crazed fan!

It took some fancy footwork for me to avoid Yankee first baseman Nick Etten in the 1st inning of our game in the Bronx on September 21st, 1945, but he was out at second following a grounder by teammate Mike Milosevich to Vern Stephens who tossed to me.

SEPTEMBER 30, 1945: For the second straight year, the fate of the American League pennant came down to the last day of the season and a game involving us. Unfortunately, this time we were in it only as possible spoilers. At five games behind the league-leading Tigers, our hopes of repeating as A.L. champs were just a memory, but the pennant hopes of Washington and Detroit were still alive. It came down to this: if Detroit could beat us in just one game of our scheduled doubleheader on this day, they'd win the pennant outright. If we could sweep the Tigers, then that would result in a 1st-place tie between the Tigers and the Senators — and they'd have to play a playoff. It was damp and misty as we ran on the Sportsman's Park field to start the opener. It would be like that all day. Nelson Potter went for us and the Tigers started Virgil "Fire" Trucks. The Tigers failed to score in the top of the 1st, so I stepped in to lead off our half of the inning. Trucks had been out of the Navy for only about a week, so there was a lot of pre-game second-guessing of Tiger manager Steve O'Neill's decision to start him. And the second-guesser's became told-you-so's when I quickly doubled to right and scored following a single by Lou Finney. But Trucks settled down after that and kept us in check, leaving in the 6th with a 2-1 lead.

We'd re-tied the game in the 7th, touching Trucks' replacement, Hal Newhouser, for a run following a double by Gene Moore and a single by Vern Stephens. That's where it stood in the top of the 8th when I was involved in a wild play. "Hank Greenberg led off with a single to right, and Roy Cullenbine was safe when he beat out a bunt to George McQuinn with none out," wrote Shirley Povich of the *Washington Post.* "Don Gutteridge then turned in the play of the ballgame. On Rudy York's slow grounder past McQuinn, Gutteridge grabbed the ball and beat York to first base for an unassisted putout as Greenberg raced to third. Gutteridge was knocked sprawling in a collision with York, and Greenberg started for home, whereupon the Browns' second baseman scrambled to his feet and threw to Len Schulte. Greenberg barged into Schulte, who held the ball, and it was a double-play." The importance of Greenberg's base-running mistake was magnified when we took the lead, 3-2, in the bottom of the 8th.

It was the daring base-running of Pete Gray that earned the lead. Luke Sewell had returned Gray to the bench following the Yankee series. He'd sat out every inning of five straight games until this day. Gray came off the bench late in the game to replace Milt Byrnes in centerfield. His only at-bat of the game came here in the bottom of the 8th, and, as it turned out, it would be the last at-bat of Pete's big league career. Facing Newhouser with Finney on first base, Gray forced Lou but reached first on the fielder's choice. That brought up McQuinn, and he doubled to right field. With the score tied and less than two outs, the safe thing would have been for Gray to pull up at third — but he decided to go for broke and tore for home plate. Pete scored with a head-first slide across the plate, just barely beating the relay throw to Tiger catcher Paul Richards.

Gray's run was all we got in the 8th, so we still held a slim 1-run lead as the Tigers came up for their last shot in the top of the 9th. I guess big Hank didn't like the idea of playing the nightcap for all the marbles because he decided to set-tle things NOW. Pinch-hitter Hub Walker led off the top of the 9th with a sin-gle. Then Skeeter Webb laid down a bunt which McQuinn fielded and threw to second — too late to get Walker. Eddie Mayo moved both runners up on a sacrifice, and then Potter intentionally passed Doc Cramer. That loaded the bases with one out and Hank Greenberg strolling to the plate. All Hank needed to do was to lift a fly ball to the outfield to tie the game. Instead, he connected solidly off Potter's curveball, sending it rocketing into the distant, hazy leftfield stands for a grand slam. "Around the muddy bases galloped the gleeful Greenberg," wrote Povich. "Hub Walker, Skeeter Webb, and Doc Cramer ahead of him on the bases, waited for him at the plate. Rushing out to greet him, too, was the entire delight-crazed gang from the Detroit bench. They mobbed him with their embraces, and two Tigers rode his back to the dugout." Although we gave it our maximum effort, we failed to score in the bottom of the 9th and the Tigers won the pennant.

We played one inning of the meaningless nightcap before it was called because of rain. Watching the Tigers celebrate, I couldn't help but recollect our own ballclub's joyous celebration just one year earlier. Certainly I would have felt much differently if our pennant destiny, like that of the Senators on that day, had been crushed by Greenberg's homer, but I was happy for the Tigers. Now that I had experienced the joy of winning a pennant, I could fully understand what the Tigers players were feeling. Seeing it first-hand again reminded me of what a great treasure our national pastime of baseball is.

As you now know, Pete Gray scored the last run of the 1945 season for us. I guess that was a fitting way to close the book on the '45 Browns. Gray's saga dominated the story of our ballclub, and all of baseball for that matter — and that's why I've recounted his season in such detail. Over the past 62 years I've been asked about Pete Gray about as much as I've been asked about anything relating to my career, so I know there's a desire out there to learn about Gray. Despite finishing strong by winning 11 of our last 16 games, we failed in our attempt to repeat as American League champions. There were more than a few guys who blamed this on Gray. The usually quiet McQuinn went on the record years later and said, "Even though Pete Gray was a miracle man in a lot of ways, he still could not do as good a job as a guy with two arms. Let's face it. He couldn't field ground balls or flies or shift his glove quickly enough to get the ball back to the infield as fast as the average man. There's no question that he cost us quite a few ballgames. I'll be frank and say we did get to resent Gray being played over a ballplayer with two arms just to draw people into the ballpark. We felt it was unfair to do that when we were trying to win a pennant."

Mark Christman echoed McQuinn's position when he told a writer, "Pete Gray cost us the pennant in 1945. There were an awful lot of ground balls hit to him when he played centerfield. When the kids who hit those balls were pretty good runners, they could keep on going and wind up at second base. I know that lost us eight or ten ballgames because it took away the double-play, or somebody would single and the runner on third would score, whereas if he had been on first it would take two hits to get him to score."

McQuinn and Christman certainly make good points, but I don't blame

Gray for our failure to win the pennant. I think we simply didn't play as well as we had the previous year. While the Pete Gray storyline was somewhat of a distraction, I definitely do not believe that it cost us the flag. I tend to agree with Sewell when it comes to remembering Gray. Luke told one interviewer, "I knew he couldn't last in the major leagues very long. Although he did a wonderful job — no, a remarkable job — with the facilities he had, the game is just too difficult for any one-armed man to play. I think, deep down, Pete realized he was being exploited. I surely thought so. That's why I didn't play him much. But as far as his personal behavior was concerned, I have nothing but fond memories of him." I think Sewell's thoughts on Gray are really on the mark, and I know that Pete always thought very highly of Luke for treating him so well. With the perfect vision of hindsight it's clear that Gray didn't belong in the majors. Thanks to the inflated egos of many pitchers, Pete had success early because he was fed a steady diet of fastballs. Pitchers let their pride get in the way and they tried to blow Gray away with heat because they didn't want to believe a one-armed guy could hit their fast one. But they slowly came to the realization that Pete COULD hit their fastballs, so they finally resorted to off-speed stuff to get Gray out. That was the undoing of Gray at the plate. Despite his failure to consistently hit the big league pitching I still think it's a good thing that he played in the majors when he did because he was a true inspiration to a lot of amputees returning from World War II. Pete often visited these guys in hospitals to offer encouragement. He was also a hero to handicapped kids all over America. Although he played minor league ball into the early 1950's, Gray never returned to the big leagues — and I never saw him again after our season-ender against Detroit. I heard he eventually returned to his hometown of Nanticoke, Pennsylvania, and lived somewhat reclusively for the rest of his life. The St. Louis Browns Fan Club tried to bring Pete back to St. Louis for many of their reunions in the 1980's and 1990's, but he never wanted to come. That seemed to lend creedence to the recluse story, and that always made me sad.

My sadness turned to happiness, ironically, on the occasion of Pete's death back in 2002. In reading his obituary I learned that Pete had, in fact, returned to Nanticoke, but he was far from a recluse. He was very private when it came to the media, but he was very outgoing when it came to kids in his town. He often watched the town's Little League team play and enjoyed sharing baseball playing tips with the youngsters. He also liked to show kids his baseball memorabilia. His obit quoted Gray as saying, "If they insulted me, I didn't pay attention. I mostly kept to myself. That's why I got the reputation of being tough to get along with." That was true to say the least, but the best news was his final comment — "But, I've mellowed." I'm glad to know that Pete Gray was at peace in the latter years of his life.

As I changed out of my Brownie uniform following our game against the Tigers, I wondered what the future held for me. The future was so uncertain that I actually wondered if I'd ever wear a Browns uniform again. I was getting up in age and I knew that 1946 would be a different situation with the huge influx of ballplayers returning from the war. My doubts about my future in St. Louis were clarified when Browns general manager Bill DeWitt told me in the offseason that my days as a player with the Browns were through. I thought about trying to latch on with another big league club, but DeWitt offered me a great opportunity as a player-manager with the Toledo Mud Hens. Getting a plum Triple-A managing post like that in your first year as a skipper was quite a break, so I accepted the job. I really thought that I would never play big league ball again, accepting my new role as manager with no regrets.

Opening day of 1946 was certainly much different for me than it had been in 1945. In a decision geared at my long term desire to coach and manage following my playing days, I accepted the Browns' offer to manage the Toledo Mud Hens, their Triple-A American Association affiliate. Just three months later, however, I'd be back in the bigs as a player — but, for the first time in my major league career, it wouldn't be in St. Louis.

1 9 4 6

JULY 9, 1946: *BOUGHT BY RED SOX.* That was the short-but-sweet United Press headline that appeared in sports pages on this day. "After a brief career as a minor league manager," wrote the U.P., "Don Gutteridge, playing-pilot of the Toledo Mud Hens in the American Association, today was sold to the Boston Red Sox for an undisclosed sum and an option on outfielder Charley Gilbert, now with the Red Sox' Louisville farm club. Gutteridge, 34-year old infielder, was named manager of the Toledo farm club last winter. The club, handicapped by a lack of pitching talent, quickly skidded into seventh place." Yep — after a brief run at managing, I was on my way back to the major leagues as a PLAYER. It's not that I was running from our problems at Toledo, it's just that when the majors come calling for you as a player, you GO. Especially at 34 years of age. And it didn't hurt that the Red Sox were running away with the American League pennant. I still felt like I had something to offer a club. The Red Sox wanted me, so my decision to leave Toledo and join the Sox was an easy one. Bobby Doerr, the great second baseman of the Red Sox, was having a career year, but he'd broken a finger on a bad-hop grounder. Boston immediately called me with the express purpose of using me to fill in for Bobby while he recovered. Even in this limited role I was thrilled to go back to the majors. It turned out that Bobby played through his injury, so they didn't really need me, but they kept me around for the rest of the season as insurance — and what a season it was.

Getting out of Toledo wasn't without its complications, however — complications that resonated all the way back home to Pittsburg, Kansas. You see, months earlier the St. Louis Browns and my hometown had planned a big celebration in my honor. "DON GUTTERIDGE DAY" had been scheduled to take place on July 17th, 1946, at the ballpark in Pittsburg. Festivities were to be held prior to an exhibition game between my Toledo Mud Hens and the Pittsburg Browns, a brand new class-D affiliate of the St. Louis Browns. They were one of six new teams playing in the debut season of the Kansas-Oklahoma-Missouri League. There was great excitement back home, but there was now one problem — I couldn't be there! In the end it didn't really matter, though. They still held the big day, but standing in for me were my mom and dad, Mary and Joe Gutteridge, and Helen's parents, Sidney and Cecile McGlothlin. I later received word that a good time was had by all, and I was very happy to hear it.

My parents and Helen's parents attending "Don Gutteridge Day" at the ballpark in Pittsburg, Kansas, on July 17th, 1946. From left to right is Joe and Mary Gutteridge; Cecile and Sidney McGlothlin.

My career with the Red Sox started off with a bang as Helen and I arrived in Boston on this afternoon — July 9th. It just so happened to be the day of the All-Star game, which just happened to be at Fenway Park. We didn't know where to go when we got to Boston, so we just decided to go to the ballpark. The place was packed to capacity with a festive crowd, but Helen and I were let in and we began making our way up the ramp. All of a sudden I heard the crowd roar, so I ran up the ramp and looked out on the field to see what was causing all the commotion. There I saw a laughing Ted Williams galloping around the bases behind my old teammates Jack Kramer and Vern Stephens. Everyone was laughing and smiling, so I asked someone what happened. It was then that I learned that Ted had slammed one of Rip Sewell's "blooper" pitches into the rightfield bleachers for a 3-run homer. It was the 8th inning when this happened, so Helen and I watched the rest of the game, which consisted of just four more outs. Sewell got Charlie Keller out on a foul pop to end the top of the 8th, then Kramer set the National Leaguers down 1-2-3 to end the game. The American League won, 12-0, and I was glad that I arrived in time to see at least part of that now-historic game.

JULY 11, 1946: I was in uniform and available for manager Joe Cronin should he have needed me on this day, our first game following the All-Star game. He didn't need me, however, but it felt great to be back in the game as a big league player. The Red Sox were 54-and-23 with two ties as we got set to play the Tigers in Boston. That was the best record in the majors, and it positioned us in 1st — 7-1/2 games ahead of the 2nd-place Yankees. In a word, this club was a powerhouse. It was loaded with great athletes and lots of talent, unlike some of the other teams that I had played on. Of the three great teams I played on, the Red Sox were by far the best. The Cardinals were a rough-and-tumble bunch who played hard and were always doing things for a laugh. The Browns were a rag-tag group that didn't have the most ability, but we worked together to achieve success. This Red Sox team, however, was talent-rich. All three were very different, yet all three were successful in their own way. Another key thing that separated these Sox from my other teams was the way in which they conducted themselves. Evident right off the bat was the fact that this ballclub was all business — very little rowdiness. All of the players on this team were real gentlemen, and they behaved as such on and off the field. The 1946 Red Sox elevated winning to a professional, business-like manner that I'd never before witnessed.

My first game with the Red Sox, albeit it as a spectator from the bench, turned out to be an edge-of-your-seat affair. Our tall right-hander Tex Hughson, number two behind Boo Ferriss in our big one-two pitching punch, hurled masterfully en route winning his 10th game. He'd win 20 on the season. He had to go 10 innings to notch this day's victory, however, because the score was tied, 2-2, when we came up to hit in the bottom of the 10th. We had two outs when Bobby Doerr singled off left-hander Fred Hutchinson, Detroit's starter who was still out there battling. That brought up our third baseman, Rip Russell, and he doubled off the leftfield wall, scoring Bobby with the winning run. Knowing about Hutchinson's legendary temper tantrums, I can only imagine what it would have been like to have to see him in the clubhouse after that game!

JULY 14, 1946: I'd been in Boston less than a week and I'd already seen enough of Ted Williams to decide, without a doubt, that he was the best hitter I'd ever seen. I'd already gotten a good look at what a fine hitter Ted was back in 1942. That was my first year in the American League and it was Ted's last season before he went into the Marines. He punished our pitchers that season just like he'd punished the rest of the pitchers in the league, so I already knew he was incredible. But to now see his method of operation firsthand, that really enlightened me to the secret of his success. It was his great work ethic that garnered his amazing results — not natural ability. He hated when people said he was a natural hitter. He insisted it was his hard work that made him successful.

It was a real thrill to play with Ted and get a close-up look at how he operated. Over the course of the season I would learn what an absolute perfectionist he was about hitting. If he got up 100 times, he wanted to get 100 base hits. If he had a bad day at the plate, he'd stay after the game and get somebody to pitch to him for extra batting practice. I'd often stay and shag balls for him in these extra hitting sessions. I enjoyed it because I knew he was trying to perfect himself as a hitter and I wanted to help. Sometimes I even pitched to him — but not much, though. At that time my arm was no longer as strong as it had once been, and Ted wanted somebody with a strong arm. There's never been anybody quite like him. He loved to hit and he loved to talk about hitting, too. Sometimes we'd be walking down the street and a stranger would say, "Ted, how did you hit that left-hander today?" Or, "Hey, Ted — what do you look for in a left-hander?" Always, Ted would stop right there and start talking.

Ted let his bat do the talking on this day, and its games like this that really leave me in amazement at just how good he was. In perhaps his best game of the season, Ted homered three times as we beat the Indians, 11-10, in the first game of a twin bill at Fenway Park. His first long-ball came on a 1-and-0 pitch from Cleveland starter Steve Gromek — with the bases loaded. It was a towering smash that bounded off the top of the wall between the bullpen and the rightfield bleachers more than 400 feet away. The second round-tripper came on the first pitch thrown to him from reliever Don Black. It was a line drive that landed on the runway between the bleachers and the grandstand in rightfield, then it bounced high into the stands. His third 4-bagger was another line drive that whistled into the stands where they curve in deep right. It was a 3-run shot, giving Ted eight RBIs on the day. All I could do is smile and shake my head in amazement.

Cleveland manager Lou Boudreau unveiled his "Williams Shift" in the nightcap. Boudreau dreamed it up to try and nullify Ted's strength — pull-hitting. Lou, the shortstop, played deep on the grass mid-way between first and second. Jimmy Wasdell, the first baseman, positioned himself in the grass near the first base foul line. Third baseman Ken Keltner posted himself deep in the grass just to the left of second base. The outfielders were shifted over to right, too, with the centerfielder and rightfielder playing very deep. In essence, the whole left side of the field was open for Ted if he wanted to hit over there. He could easily have bunted for a hit, but that wasn't his style. Ted wanted to beat Boudreau at his own game. The face-off ended in a draw on this day, however. Boudreau robbed Ted of a sure single when Williams hit a hot grounder right at Lou, but Ted later scorched a double over the outstretched glove of Wasdell. This little game-within-a-game would continue throughout the season, and it was very intriguing to see.

JULY 16, 1946: We were off on July 15th, but we wrapped up our 3-game series with the Indians with a 6-3 loss on this day. From my seat in the dugout I watched Bob Feller strike out seven as he went the route and got the victory. Lou Boudreau's "Williams Shift" storyline continued to unfold in this game. In one of his at-bats in this game Ted got the notion to take what Boudreau was giving him — meaning the whole left side. Here's how it was written up in the papers — "WILLIAMS CROSSES UP INDIANS. Ted Williams turned in a triple and a single in five times at bat, and on the latter occasion he completely crossed up the right wing defense set up by manager Lou Boudreau of the Indians. With all the Cleveland infielders on the right side of the diamond and two of the outfielders in rightfield, Williams slammed the ball down the third base line and laughingly sauntered to first base while the leftfielder was retrieving the ball." We all broke up, too, at the sight of Ted laughing his way to first base, although I have to admit that Boudreau viewed this as a victory for his shift. Getting Ted to hit to left, AWAY from his power, was exactly what Boudreau wanted to accomplish whenever he put on the shift. It was a fascinating game of cat and mouse.

JULY 19, 1946: We beat the White Sox, 9-2, at Fenway Park on this day. From my seat on the bench I witnessed a one-of-a-kind occurrence — the ejection of 14 White Sox players. We'd jumped on Chicago for two quick runs in the first, Ted Williams driving in both with a double off the leftfield wall. When Ted came up to hit again in the third, White Sox right-hander Joe Haynes threw a purpose-pitch at Ted's head. Ted hit the deck and then nonchalantly got up and dusted himself off. In the meantime, chief umpire Red Jones went out and cautioned Haynes. Well, the White Sox players took offense at that. They felt Ted was getting preferential treatment, so they voiced their disapproval by unmercifully heckling Jones. So Jones immediately chased Ralph Hodgin, Dario Lodigiani, Ed Smith and coach Bing Miller from the game. When the ruckus had settled down Ted stepped back in the box and casually lined a single. That got the heckling started up again, and by the next inning Jones had had enough. He thumbed 10 more White Sox players, leaving just three men on the bench when the team was on the field — manager Ted Lyons, coach Mule Haas and the trainer. It was really funny.

JULY 25, 1946: On this day I made my first game appearance for the Red Sox since joining the club 2-1/2 weeks earlier. Joe Cronin sent me up in the 7th inning to hit for Joe Dobson, our starting pitcher. Joe had pitched great, but we couldn't generate much offense against Chicago left-hander Ed Smith, so we were trailing, 2-1, when I stepped in to hit. I'd love to tell you that I hit a 2-run homer, but that wasn't the case. Still, I did my job — I moved a base-runner up with a sacrifice, then returned to my spot on the bench. The runner was left stranded, however, and we lost the game, 3-1, but I was happy to have finally made a small contribution to a game.

JULY 27, 1946: Generating offense, our problem with the White Sox two days earlier, wasn't usually a problem with the high-powered 1946 Red Sox, and that was again evident as we whipped my old team, the Brownies, 13-6, at Sportsman's Park on this day. Ted Williams, as I've mentioned, was the main man in our offensive attack, but another key man with the bat in 1946 was Rudy York. He, like me, was late in his career, but Rudy was still strong as a bull and very smart. He'd been a staple of the Tigers' line-up for nearly a decade, but the Red Sox had acquired him in a trade prior to this year's spring training. He was tailor-made for Fenway Park, and the trade would prove to be a good one for Boston. Rudy was a heavy drinker, so one of the gambles of the deal was whether Joe Cronin could manage York's drinking and still be able to get a productive season out of him. Joe proved to be up to the task, and under his guidance York hit .276 for us with 17 homers and 119 runs driven in. A big chunk of that offensive output came on this day, too, as he walloped not one, but two grand slam home runs. He finished with 10 RBIs on the day, and even had a chance for more when he batted with one on in the 7th and two aboard in the 9th. Rudy's two grand slams matched a feat accomplished only twice before. Incidentally, this was the second game of our 3-game set with the Browns in St. Louis. It was my first trip to Sportsman's Park since I'd played my last game there as a member of the Brownies the year before. There were mixed emotions at returning there. I had only the warmest of feelings for the players, coaches, executives, and fans of the Browns. They had treated me well during my four years there, and we'd parted on the best of terms. So it was strange to now be an adversary, but that's the business of baseball — then and now. No matter what, though, the St. Louis Browns would always be special to me.

JULY 31, 1946: *FIREBALLER WHIFFS NINE AS RED SOX TUMBLE.* That was the Associated Press headline describing Bob Feller's dominant performance as we lost to the Indians, 4-1, at Cleveland on this day. "Rudy York," the article text wrote, "hefty Boston first baseman whose heavy hitting has been a feature of the league leaders' pennant drive, went down swinging three times on Bob's fastball, and Feller humbled Williams in the 4th frame. Other strikeout victims of Feller were Dominic DiMaggio, losing pitcher Mickey Harris, John Lazor, Wally Moses, and Don Gutteridge." That's right, Feller got me, too. In just my second appearance in a game for the Red Sox, I had to face Rapid Robert as a pinch-hitter in the 8th inning. Since playing opportunities were few and far between for me, I really wanted to come through with a hit in that situation, but there was no shame in striking out against Feller. Even at this point in his career, he was a great pitcher.

AUGUST 3, 1946: I began this day on the bench as we played the second of a 3-game series against the Tigers at Briggs Stadium. Pinky Higgins had begun the game at third base, but he got spiked pretty badly when George Kell slid hard into him in the bottom of the 1st inning. I went in and did okay, getting one hit in three at-bats. "Walks to Ted Williams and Rudy York and Don Gutteridge's two-bagger made it 4-0 in the 5th before the Tigers made their bid," wrote the Associated Press in describing my run-scoring double. On the mound for us in this game was Dave "Boo" Ferriss. Boo was one of the best examples of the gentlemanly style of the 1946 Red Sox. He'd been in the service for a few years, but a sinus condition had returned him to the Red Sox in time for the 1945 season whereupon Boo went out and won 21 ballgames. He'd post an even better season in '46. Boo was a classy fellow and a good Christian gentleman. He always had a smile and a good word for everybody. In the clubhouse, we all looked up to him. He was very intelligent, so we all asked him lots of questions. And he was a truly fine pitcher. Boo wasn't overbearingly fast, but he had excellent control with a very good slider. He always had to pitch against all the other clubs' best pitchers, yet he still won regularly. That speaks volumes about his ability. He was absolutely one of the best pitcher's I'd seen, and there were none better than him in 1946. Boo went the distance in our game on this day to earn a 5-3 victory — his 18th of the season — and I was very happy to have played a small role in helping him get the win.

Substituting at third base for Pinky Higgins who'd left in the 1st inning after getting spiked by George Kell, I had the opportunity to exact a little revenge on George, putting him out here in our 5-3 win over Detroit at Briggs Stadium on August 3rd, 1946.

AUGUST 6, 1946: We opened a series against the Athletics at Shibe Park on this day, and I got my second start in a row at third base while Pinky Higgins' spike wound was healing. Joe Cronin had started me the day after Pinky got spiked, but I drew an 0-for-4 against Tigers pitchers Hal Newhouser, George Caster (now with Detroit), and Johnny Gorsica. To make matters worse, I made an error at third base. After being a regular player for the bulk of my career, I was getting a lesson in how tough it was to be ready to go in on a moment's notice and produce — at bat and on defense — when you spend so much time on the bench. No matter how many ground balls you take in pre-game workouts, and no matter how much batting practice you take, nothing can simulate real game conditions. I had a new appreciation for utility players! In any case, I was hoping to do better in our game against Philadelphia on this day. Well, things don't always go as you hope, as my TWO errors in the field can attest. But I did manage to get a hit, described by the Associated Press this way — "Don Gutteridge doubled to the leftfield corner in the 5th and took third as Johnny Pesky desperately tried to beat out an infield grounder. It was on this play that Pesky turned his ankle. Gutteridge scored after Wally Moses flied out to Tuck Stainback in deep right center." Johnny's ankle would be fine, and my errors were not costly thanks to great pitching by Tex Hughson. He shut out the A's for a 5-2 win, his 12th victory of the year.

AUGUST 17, 1946: Boo Ferriss did it all on this day and got his 21st win, a 7-4 victory over the Yankees at Fenway Park. He was really money in the bank during this time — as reliable as any pitcher has ever been. Boo went the full nine while adding two base hits to his mound accomplishments. Another amazing statistic about this win was that it was Boo's 13th consecutive complete game. It wasn't just about getting wins in those days, it was also about finishing what you started. Pitchers were expected to throw complete games, and guys looked down upon those who couldn't. Boo was one of the game's best at going the distance. Also of note in this game was the fact the Joe DiMaggio played leftfield. He'd thrown out his arm in the game before, so they moved him to left for this game in an effort to reduce the strain of making the long throw from center. He was again in leftfield for our doubleheader on August 18th, the last games of our 4-game series against New York. Johnny Lindell played center for Joe while he was nursing his sore arm in left.

AUGUST 25, 1946: We swept a doubleheader from Cleveland at Fenway Park on this day. I did not play — in fact, the only action I'd seen over the last three weeks had been one pinch-hitting and one pinch-running appearance — but that's not to say that there wasn't plenty of action to keep me interested. Boo Ferriss won his 23rd game in the opener — another complete game, and Joe Dobson combined with Earl Johnson to win the nightcap. To be honest, the games provided all the entertainment I needed, but on this day there was the added attraction of Jackie Price. He was a longtime minor league infielder who also doubled as a baseball clown. Bill Veeck, a baseball showman himself, had purchased the Indians a couple of months

earlier. Price was a perfect fit for Veeck, so Bill soon added Jackie to the Indians roster. Price got in a handful of games, but his main purpose for being on the ballclub
was for his act. Unlike Al Schacht and Max Patkin, the other famous baseball
clowns, Price was more of a stuntman. He amazed people by performing zany stunts
utilizing his baseball skills. For example, he would hang by his ankles from the batting cage and take batting practice upside down. He'd hit balls from the right and
left side while in this inverted position. He'd throw three balls at one time in three
different directions perfectly on target to three different infielders. He'd catch fungos behind his back, between his legs, or in his uniform jersey. He could hit two
balls with a fungo bat at the same time in different directions. One of his most popular tricks was to use an air gun to fire a ball high into the air, then jump into a jeep
and speed to the outfield and catch the ball before it landed. All of these tricks and
more were on display between the games of our doubleheader on this day, but so
was another of Price's popular gags — and this time it landed a couple of fans in
the hospital. Here's how it was written up by the Associated Press...

"A bleacherite was knocked unconscious accidentally today by a baseball slung
by Johnny Price, Cleveland Indian stuntman, between games of a doubleheader
between the Indians and Red Sox at Fenway Park. A companion, struck by the same
ball, suffered a head contusion. Eugene Sullivan, 19, married, of Somerville, was
revived at City Hospital. Doctors said he suffered a brain concussion. His companion, Edward Hutchins, 21, single, also of Somerville, was struck a glancing blow and
was allowed to go home after treatment at the hospital. Before the start of the doubleheader, Price, using a sling, had heaved a baseball completely out of the ball park,
a stunt he has performed elsewhere. He tried it again just before the start of the second game and the ball flew into the rightfield bleachers from in front of the
Cleveland dugout. Red Sox spokesmen quoted Hutchins as saying, 'We were looking at our scorecards and the next I knew the ball hit us.' " I learned my lesson that
day — always keep your eye on Jackie Price while he was out there doing his act!

AUGUST 26, 1946: We completed a series sweep of the Indians with a 5-1 win on
this day at Fenway Park. I did not appear in the game, but I was on my toes. After
the Jackie Price incident of the day before, I was on the lookout for more craziness
from Bill Veeck's Indians. Sure enough, they delivered the goods. Lou Boudreau was
still using his "Williams Shift" whenever Ted went up to hit, but on one occasion
there was an added twist. Here's how it was described in *The Sporting News* —
"VOLUNTEER TENTH FIELDER AIDS INDIANS AGAINST TED. When the
Indians again used their 'Cleveland Shift' against Ted Williams of the Red Sox here,
August 26, they found themselves with an uninvited tenth man on the field, taking
over the unoccupied third base position. The extra man was Marco Songini, a three-
foot midget and local vaudeville performer. Leaving his box seat, Songini dashed to
third base, picked up Pinky Higgins' glove and stationed himself at the far corner. As
umpire Hal Weafer ordered the intruder off the field, manager Lou Boudreau shouted, 'Let him stay there— we need him, too!' " We were all in stitches at the sight of

the midget at third base. Some even recalled the incident a few years later when Bill Veeck sent midget Eddie Gaedel up to pinch-hit in a Browns-Tigers game. I don't know if Veeck put Songini up to running out on the field on this day, but if he didn't we now know where he probably got his Gaedel idea.

SEPTEMBER 5, 1946: The ballclub was on a real roll as we prepared to play the Senators on this day at Griffith Stadium. We'd won seven in a row, and in the process trimmed our "magic number" to five. That meant that any combination of five wins by us or five defeats by the 2nd-place Yankees would clinch the pennant for us. It was astounding considering that there was still over three weeks left in the season, but New York was a distant 16-1/2 games back. From my seat in the dugout that day I watched my teammates execute a crisply-played 1-0 victory. Jim Bagby, Jr. pitched very well for us to get the win. He was at the back end of his career after a couple of fine seasons with the Indians in the early-40s. He'd actually started his career with Boston in the late-30s, and he'd been brought back for the '46 season. He was used mostly as a reliever and occasional spot starter, and he did well, especially at the end of the season when he picked up a few of wins for us in August and September while spelling some of the regular starters.

SEPTEMBER 11, 1946: A week after Jim Bagby's win, we still had not clinched the pennant. We'd hit the skids, in fact, and had lost four in a row leading up to our game at Detroit on this day. The Yankees hadn't been much better, however, so despite the fact that we hadn't won a game in a week, our magic number was down to one. That meant that we'd be American League champions if we won on this day. The only action I'd seen during our losing streak was one pinch-running appearance, so I was thrilled when Joe Cronin informed me that I'd be starting at third base and leading off in our game against the Tigers. Memories of clinching the pennant with the Browns back in 1944 came to my mind, and I was excited at the prospect of being on the field to experience that joy again. The fact that Boo Ferriss was on the hill only fortified my belief that we'd get the job done because he was as close to a sure thing as there was in baseball at that time. But there are no sure things in baseball, and Boo was roughed up in the 1st inning. Eddie Lake and George Kell led off with singles, and then Hank Greenberg cleared the bags with a home run. The inning got worse when Detroit scored two additional runs on three more singles and an error by me. I felt sick about my mistake, but Boo was a real gentleman and never showed any anger about it. I took out my frustration at the plate, slamming a double off Tigers pitcher Dizzy Trout, but we lost the game, 7-3. Our plans to sew up the pennant would have to wait until tomorrow when we opened up a series against the Indians at Cleveland.

SEPTEMBER 12, 1946: The Indians' Bob Feller wasn't about to let us wrap up the A.L. championship on his dime and in his ballpark, so he bore down on this day and pitched us to our sixth straight defeat — a 4-1 loss. Our pennant-clinching plans would again have to be postponed until tomorrow. Despite my error the day before, Joe Cronin again gave me a start at third base, and I was grateful for the opportunity to be out there in a big game like this. I had an opportunity to drive in a run in the 2nd when I came up with Ted Williams on second base. Feller gave me a nice pitch to hit and I drove it into left for a clean single. In fact, I hit it so hard that it got to Indians leftfielder Pat Seerey very quickly. Williams had no intention of stopping at third, unfortunately, and Seerey made a great throw to cut Ted down at the plate. I came up with another RBI opportunity in the 7th, this time delivering the run with a sac fly — but that was all we could scrounge up on the day. Incidentally, I've mentioned a few incidents against Cleveland that reflected the nutty personality of their new owner, Bill Veeck. First, the midget who ran out and tried to play third base during the "Williams Shift." Then there was stuntman/infielder Jackie Price who landed two guys in the hospital when he catapulted a baseball into the stands. Well, Veeck had another comic attraction, a fellow who has since become a legend. Here's how the Associated Press wrote up that fellow's contribution to our game on this day — "Umpire Cal Hubbard scored the quickest and most loudly protested put-out of the game when he ejected Max Patkin, the Tribe's clown coach, from the first-base box in the second. Hubbard called a strike on Les Fleming and the first baseman protested. Patkin made a throat-cutting gesture, indicating the pitch was that high, and Hubbard thumbed him from the field while 5,365 jeered." Max Patkin, Jackie Price, midgets — you just had no idea what to expect when you played Cleveland.

SEPTEMBER 13, 1946: *WILLIAMS' HOMER TRIPS INDIANS, 1-0. BLOW TO LEFT IN FIRST INNING DECIDES, BRINGING FIRST FLAG TO BOSTON SINCE 1918.* The wait was over — for us and the fans of Boston. Tex Hughson pitched a dominating 3-hitter for his 18th win, and, more importantly, the pennant. Indians right-hander Red Embree was even more dominant, believe it or not. He held us to just two hits. I was again stationed at third base for this game, but I just couldn't do anything with Embree's offerings, going 0-for-2 with a sacrifice. Thank goodness Ted Williams came through, however, and you wouldn't believe the circumstances. Here's the Associated Press description of Ted's game-winning home run — "Picking on a 3-1 pitch with two out in the 1st, and the Cleveland outer works congregated in rightfield in the famous "Williams Shift," Ted belted a long fly to left. The ball soared over the head of leftfielder Pat Seerey, who was deployed just behind shortstop, rolled to the fence, and Ted slid across the plate." That's right — an inside-the-park home run. It was amazing. It was just the 1st inning, so we never thought that that would be the only run scored in the game, but when the last out was recorded it was Ted's inside-the-parker that stood up as the game-winner and flag-clincher.

Unlike the scene when we clinched with the Browns in 1944 — pure mayhem — the mood on the field here was subdued. There was virtually no handshaking or backslapping. This ballclub had a very professional, business-like attitude.

They took the pennant in a rout of the league, and they wanted the people in the stands and the writers in the pressbox to know that they were good and EXPECT-ED to win the flag. A wild celebration would not have conveyed that impression. Hence the muted on-field behavior. But once in the confines of our clubhouse it was a different situation. A quartet of guys immediately jumped into the showers and began harmonizing on "You Are My Sunshine." The rest of us then joined in, hooting, hollering, and simply enjoying the wonderful camaraderie of sharing in the achievement of accomplishing our goal. Some, like Ted Williams, Dom DiMaggio, Johnny Pesky, Boo Ferriss, and Tex Hughson, to name a few, played big roles in the ballclub's success. Others, like me, played only minor roles. But we all contributed, and we were a true team. That moment in Cleveland's visiting clubhouse was very special for me. I understood that it was different than what I experienced with the '44 Browns because I was just a role player with the Red Sox, but it was still special in its own way. It's a memory that I will always cherish.

SEPTEMBER 15, 1946: We split a twin bill with the White Sox at Comiskey Park on this day. Joe Cronin had decided to rest the regulars as much as possible after we clinched, so I saw a good deal of playing time through the remainder of the season, including the nightcap of this double-feature. The key for Joe was to try and get guys rest without taking the edge off them by sitting them too much. He did this by giving guys a day off here and there, and also by removing players midway through random games. I think Joe did a good job of resting guys for the Series without making anyone rusty. In any case, rest for the regulars meant more work for me, and I welcomed the opportunity to try and sharpen up a little in time for the Series. I sat out the opener and watched Boo Ferriss deliver yet another amazing complete game victory, his 25th of the season. The Sox's Johnny Rigney hung an 0-for-3 in the second game, but it felt good to get in the game. Don Kolloway, Chicago's big third baseman, helped me shake some of the rust loose with a good old fashioned football block — but it was just good clean fun!

Big Don Kolloway of the White Sox laid a nice roll block on me in our 6-0 loss to Chicago in the nightcap of a doubleheader split at Comiskey Park on September 15th, 1946.

SEPTEMBER 21, 1946: We downed the Senators on this day, 7-5, in an exciting game at Griffith Stadium. Buck Newsom and Boo Ferriss were both pitching very well through seven innings, but Newsom had a 2-1 edge as we opened the 8th inning. I had failed to hit in my two previous at-bats, but Newsom had gotten into a little trouble, allowing two men to reach just before as I stepped up to the plate. I really wanted to drive in at least one run to tie the game for Boo, but what happened was even better. I laid the fat of the bat on a Newsom pitch and the ball carried into the stands for a home run. I felt great rounding those bags knowing that I had contributed a big hit that might be enough to help Boo get his 26th win of the season. As fate would have it, though, the Nats came right back with three runs of their own in the home half of the 8th. I think Boo was a little fatigued. We were down a run and Boo was knocked out of the box. It wasn't all bad, however. We tied the game in the 9th, and then won it in the 11th. It was our 100th victory of the season, a win total I'd never reached with any big league club I'd ever been on.

SEPTEMBER 22, 1946: "Don Gutteridge's single and Johnny Pesky's double gave Boston a run in the 1st inning, and the Red Sox counted another in the third as Gutteridge scored on Ted Williams' infield out." That's how the Associated Press described the first two runs we scored against the Senators in our 4-1 win over them at Griffith Stadium on this day. It was fun to be in the middle of the action and I enjoyed every minute of it. I was 2-for-5 against Washington's Early Wynn, and I approached every at-bat as if it might be my last of the season. I knew and understood that I would soon return to my spot on the bench as we got closer to the Series.

This photo was shot before our game with the Washington Senators at Griffith Stadium on September 22nd, 1946. The caption read, "Here is Don Gutteridge, infielder for the Boston Red Sox, winners of the 1946 American League pennant." I liked the sound of that.

SEPTEMBER 29, 1946: We closed out the regular season with a 7-0 loss to the Senators at Fenway Park on this day. That finalized our record at 104 wins, 50 losses, and two ties — a very impressive campaign. My 2-hit day off Early Wynn a week earlier did, in fact, turn out to be my last start before Joe Cronin returned to playing the regulars longer. I'd been inserted as a late-inning replacement a couple times, and that's how I was used again today. I went in for Bobby Doerr late in the game and got one at-bat against Nats right-hander Ray Scarborough. He was sharp that day, so I was thrilled when I was able to rap a single off him. With that hit I felt I was ready for the Series should Joe Cronin call upon me.

OCTOBER 1, 1946: On this day, a day when we should have been kicking off the World Series, we were instead playing an exhibition game. It turned out that the National League pennant race had ended in a dead heat between the Dodgers and Cardinals, so they were going to have a best-of-three playoff to determine who would meet us in the Series. Meanwhile, Joe Cronin was faced with the dilemma of how to keep us sharp while we waited for the winner of the N.L. playoff. Joe and the front office brass didn't like the idea of relying solely on daily workouts, so they lined up a 3-game exhibition series with a team of big league all-stars, the games to be played at Fenway Park. The All-Stars had a good line-up featuring Luke Appling, Joe DiMaggio, Hank Greenberg, Hal Newhouser, Dizzy Trout and Ed Lopat to name a few. What harm could come from a little exhibition baseball, right?

A VALUABLE ARM IS HIT BY PITCHED BALL; WILLIAMS, STRUCK BY PITCH, SUFFERS BRUISED ELBOW IN EXHIBITION GAME; RED SOX STAR WILL MISS THE REST OF ALL-STAR CONTESTS, BUT IS EXPECTED TO BE READY FOR WORLD SERIES. That was the headline to the newspaper article covering game one of our exhibition series with the All-Stars. The fact that we won, 2-0, was an afterthought. What everyone in Boston was worried about was Ted and his right elbow. Here's how the text of the article described the pitch that hit Ted — "Williams batted in the 5th with Bobby Doerr on first base, and was hit when Washington port-sider Mickey Haefner's curve, intended to break sharply, dropped only about an inch. Williams, a keen student of every American League pitcher, was familiar with Haefner's stuff and was caught off guard when it became a slider." Ted came out of the game with an egg-sized lump on his elbow. He was taken to the hospital for X-rays where it was determined that nothing was broken, but it was a question as to how it would affect him in the Series — if he could play at all. We played all three of the exhibition games, winning the series two games to one. I appeared in the second game, replacing Bobby Doerr in the late innings and going 0-for-2. In the meantime, the Cardinals had won the first two games of their playoff against Brooklyn to advance to the Series, set to begin in two days.

OCTOBER 6, 1946: World Series Game One — *RED SOX VANQUISH*

CARDS IN 10TH, 3-2, ON HOMER BY YORK. That was the *New York Times* headline to John Drebinger's article reporting on Game One of the 1946 World Series played on this day at Sportsman's Park. The '46 Series is now considered a classic for reasons I will recount here, and it started building that legendary reputation right away with an incredible Game One. Despite weather reports to the contrary, we had a great day to open the Series. Warm temperatures in the 80's, and sunny. The old place looked great — just like in 1944 — trimmed in bunting and packed to the rafters with excited fans. Looking across the field at the Cardinals I couldn't help but think back to 1944. There had been considerable turnover in their roster since the war had ended, but there was still a handful of familiar faces — faces of men who had played key roles in ending my 1944 dream of a world title. Still around from '44 was Whitey Kurowski, Stan Musial, Enos Slaughter, Marty Marion, Ted Wilks, and Harry Brecheen. That was a great core of players, and they were bolstered by new names like Red Schoendienst, Joe Garagiola, Harry Walker, Del Rice, Erv Dusak, Terry Moore (in the service during the '44 Series), and pitchers Murry Dickson, George Munger, Howie Pollet, Al Brazle, Dick Sisler, Nippy Jones, and Johnny Beazley. It was a formidable roster, and although we were heavily favored, we knew it would take a complete effort to win it.

Opening festivities were somewhat minimal as baseball commissioner Happy Chandler tossed out the first pitch, after which we quickly got the game underway. I took in the bulk of the game from my seat on the bench, entering the game late, however, as a pinch-runner. Tex Hughson drew starting chores for us and southpaw Howie Pollet got the nod from Cardinal manager Eddie Dyer. Both guys pitched great, really bearing down in the pinches, but we were able to get on the scoreboard first, scratching out a lone run in the 2nd. It was during that inning that we also learned that the Cardinals were going to apply their own version of the "Williams Shift" on Ted despite the fact that Dyer had told reporters that he would not put a shift on Williams. Ted led off the 2nd and would have had a sure single between a normally-positioned first baseman and second baseman, but Cards second baseman Schoendienst was right there to take Ted's smash and easily throw him out. But then Pollet faltered just a bit, hitting Rudy York with a pitch and then walking Bobby Doerr. Pinky Higgins then rapped a solid single to score Rudy, but that was all we ended up getting.

The score remained 1-0 until the bottom of the 6th when Musial tied the game with an RBI double off the rightfield wall. The score was still tied, 1-1, when we got a bad break in the bottom of the 8th. Kurowski got it started with a single down the leftfield line. Then Garagiola drove a long fly to center — a ball that Dom DiMaggio had to run back to get, but a ball that he easily handles 99 times out of 100. Here's how Drebinger described the play in his article — "It was quite a clout. But the youngest of the DiMaggio boys spun around at the crack of the bat and it looked like a certain out. For the bespectacled 'Little Professor,' as they call him, is regarded as one of the surest ball hawks in the game. But as he turned around to make the catch it became apparent that he had lost the ball in the sun. An instant later he resighted it and reached for it frantically, but the ball slipped through his fingers for a hit." The play got complicated from there. Kurowski raced all the way home from first, but BEFORE he crossed the plate Garagiola was tagged out for the third out trying to stretch his double into a triple. A bitter protest erupted when we realized that plate umpire Lee Ballanfant was allowing the run, but Joe Cronin backed off when he was informed that the run was being allowed because of interference. Apparently, our third baseman, Pinky Higgins, had been in Kurowski's way as he rounded third, and third base ump Charlie Berry had immediately ruled interference even before the play had concluded.

So we headed into the top of the 9th in a heap of trouble, trailing 2-1. That's when the tables turned and we got a lucky break. With one out, Higgins hit a routine ground ball to Marion at short. Poised to easily gather the grounder and toss out Pinky, the ball suddenly took a bad hop right through Marion's legs. The crowd couldn't believe it. We couldn't either — now we had a chance. Cronin told me to go in and run for Pinky, so I jumped up and sprinted out to first. I know pinch-running is way down on the list of pressure-packed baseball activities, but believe me, there was tension involved in doing it in a situation of this magnitude. I was coming into the game stone cold, yet I had to be acutely aware once I got on that bag. I had to be careful not to get picked off by Pollet's left-handed move. I had to be smart not to try something risky that might get me thrown out, but at the same time I had to try anything necessary to score and tie the game. Rip Russell made my job an easy one, however, lining a clean single to center and moving me up to third. I never considered trying to score on the play — not with just one out and the third base coach waving the stop sign. Roy Partee was sent up to pinch-hit for Tex Hughson, meaning that we would have to go to the bullpen if we were able to tie the game. It was tough duty for Roy and he struck out. Rightfielder Tom McBride was our last hope. Pollet got two strikes on Tom and was one strike away from victory when McBride hit a sharp single between Marion and Kurowski. I streaked home with the tying run and greeted my happy teammates in the dugout — relieved! Johnny Pesky now stepped up with a chance to win the game for us with a hit, but he flied to Slaughter to end the inning. After 8-1/2 innings we were tied, 2-2, and our pitching fate was now handed over to reliever Earl Johnson.

Earl was a tall, thin left-hander who had pitched very well for us out of the bullpen throughout the season. Any worries that Earl might not have been up to the pressure of the situation could easily have been laid to rest if you knew his background. He'd enlisted in the Army right after Pearl Harbor, and just a year and a half prior to taking the mound on this day he'd been fighting in the Battle of the Bulge. He'd emerged from combat with a Bronze Star, a Silver Star, and an Oak Leaf Cluster for heroism — so World Series pressure was not going to faze Earl. That was confirmed when "Lefty" coolly retired the Cardinals 1-2-3 in the bottom of the 9th. It appeared as if we, too, would go down 1-2-3 when we came up to hit in the top of the 10th. Dom quickly grounded out and Ted followed with a foul pop-out to Musial at first. Rudy York hit next, working Pollet to a count of two balls and no strikes. Rudy had often told me that he was a guess hitter, and he never guessed better than he did on the next pitch. Pollet came in with a fastball and Rudy belted it into the last row of the leftfield bleachers. We mobbed the big guy as he came into the dugout, confident that we were now on our way to victory. That was all we got, though, so it was up to Earl to hold the lead and nail down the win — and that's just what he did. An error put a runner in scoring position with just one out, so Cronin went out to talk to Earl. After the game Joe told reporters that he went out and asked Earl, "What was that battle you were in on the other side?" Earl reminded Joe that it was the Battle of the Bulge. Grinning, Joe said, "This isn't that tough," then he strolled back to the dugout. Joe was right, too, this was just baseball — not life and death. Still, I imagine that Earl felt pressure, but a different thing altogether than what he felt in battle. If he felt any pressure, though, he didn't show it. In fact, as the saying goes, he had ice water in his veins, easily retiring future Hall-of-Famers Stan Musial and Enos Slaughter to sew up Game One.

One final note on Earl Johnson, the winning pitcher of Game One of the 1946 World Series. He'd been very good for the Red Sox before I joined them in July, but he'd tapered off considerably in the second half. With the season over and our club playing those pre-World Series exhibition games against the American League all-stars, Hank Greenberg came over to our bench. He told Earl that he'd been "telegraphing" his pitches and that's why everybody in the league had been "teeing off" on him for the past two months. Then Hank proceeded to tell Earl how he was tipping his pitches. It was a wonderful gesture on Hank's part. Hank knew there was a chance he would still have to bat against Earl in the future, but he had American League pride and he wanted to do whatever he could to help our club win.

It was a jubilant scene in the clubhouse after the game. Being one strike from defeat only to come back and win the game on a dramatic extra-inning homer brings out the kid in a fellow. There was yelling and shouting all over the place, guys jumping up on trunks and whooping it up. A chant of "three more to go, three more to go, three more to go" rose up above the melee. It was quite a scene for our usually buttoned-down ballclub. Cronin was holding court to the reporters, praising Howie Pollet, but lavishing even more praise on his guys. "That boy from the Belgian Bulge looked pretty good out there, didn't he?" Joe asked. "That Johnson's not bad for a guy who had 190 straight days of combat service. He really came along with some superb pitching — just when we needed it. Hughson pitched smartly and strongly all the way. He gave Pollet a battle until we needed some hitting and I had to send up Roy Partee in the 9th."

It's true that we caught a lucky break when Pinky's bad hop grounder went through Marion's legs. Arthur Daley of the *New York Times* made a point of emphasizing that when he wrote, "Hitting and fielding weren't all the Bosox had today. They also had horseshoes, four-leafed clover, rabbits' feet, and the leprechauns whispering into Joe Cronin's ear. Never were truer words spoken than Lefty Gomez' classic line, 'I'd rather be lucky than good.' " That was all true, but what Daley failed to say was that you have to be in position to take advantage of your good luck. Had we been losing 5-0 when that ball hopped through Marion's legs, no one would have mentioned our good luck. But we played well and stayed close, then capitalized on our lucky break. So, after our win on this day we were on top of the world because we believed we were both lucky AND good — a combination that would be tough for anyone to beat.

OCTOBER 7, 1946: World Series Game Two — *CARDS EVEN SERIES WITH RED SOX, 3-0, AS BRECHEEN STARS.* I'd gotten a good look at how tough Harry Brecheen was when he'd beaten my Browns back in Game Four of the 1944 Series. It was like deja-vu on this day, only he was even better than he was in the '44 Series, this time allowing just four hits while shutting us out with his impressive array of fastballs and curves. But his bread-n-butter pitch in this game was, once again, a screwball, which he used to perfection to repeatedly baffle our guys. I took in this game entirely from the sidelines — not even a pinch-hitting or pinch-running appearance — so I had a great view of Brecheen's dominance, and it was something to behold. He was a heck of a competitor, especially in the pinches.

Sometimes the best way to beat a good pitcher is to get to him early, before he settles into a good rhythm. That's what we were hoping would result from rightfielder Tom McBride's lead-off single against Brecheen, but Harry proved to be too good to let that happen. He struck out Johnny Pesky, our next batter, then got Dom DiMaggio to ground into a double-play to end the inning. I knew right then and there that we were probably going to have to battle to get anything going against Brecheen. Pitching for us was Mickey Harris, a left-hander who'd had a very good year for us by winning 17 ballgames. 1946 was Mickey's first season back from four years in the Army, and that made his performance in '46 that much more impressive. It was the kind of day on which Mickey liked to pitch — sunny and unseasonably warm, in the 80's — and he certainly pitched admirably in allowing just six Cardinals hits, but he simply had the misfortune of being matched up against a very hot Brecheen. Neither pitcher had allowed a run through 2-1/2 innings, but the Cardinals broke through with a single run in the bottom of the 3rd. And wouldn't you know it — it was Brecheen who delivered the run. He was determined to beat us in every way that day. Cards catcher Del Rice led off with a double off the leftfield wall, then Brecheen sent him across with a clean single to right.

That run turned out to be all that Brecheen would need to beat us that day, but the Cards added two more insurance runs in the bottom of the 5th. Rice was again the catalyst, leading off the inning with a long single to leftfield. Brecheen then bunted down the third base line to try and move Rice into scoring position. Pinky Higgins fielded the ball, wheeled around and fired it to second to try and force Rice. Even though Rice didn't run particularly well, Higgins had to rush his throw, and in doing so he threw wild to second where Pesky was covering. Johnny got his glove on it, but he couldn't come up with the peg and it glanced off his mitt and rolled out to center. Rice went to third and Brecheen moved up to second. Both runners failed to score when Red Schoendienst, the next batter, grounded to Bobby Doerr who held them and flipped to first for the out. But we weren't so lucky when the next man up, Terry Moore, hit a much hotter shot to Doerr. Bobby made a nice effort on the grounder, but it glanced off his glove and rolled into right-center for a run-scoring single, and Brecheen moved up to third. Harry then scored when Musial grounded to Doerr who threw to Pesky at second. They forced Moore, but their relay was too late to turn two on Musial running to first. As this inning illustrates, baseball's a game of inches. Three plays, all decided by inches, now had us down, 3-0.

The last four innings were played without us ever really threatening to score. Brecheen only seemed to get stronger, only once allowing us to get a man to first base. That came in the 9th inning, and for a moment it gave us hope. Dom led off the inning by hitting a slow bounder along the third base line. Whitey Kurowski came in on it fast, but his throw was too late to get Dom who ran very well. The big guns of our order were up now — Williams, York and Doerr — just the guys you'd want up there with the game on the line, but we'd apparently spent all our magic on the game before. First Ted went down easily on a foul pop to shortstop Marty Marion. That's right — a foul pop to the shortstop! Third baseman Kurowski was way over on the right side because the Cardinals were playing the "Williams Shift," so Marion had to leg it all the way to foul territory from his spot near second base to snag the ball. Then Rudy flied out to Enos Slaughter in shallow right. Doerr, our last hope, hit a long drive to the left-field wall, but it settled into Harry Walker's glove for the last out and the Cards had evened the Series, 1-1.

Ted Williams fouling out to Kurowski with the game on the line contributed to an unfortunate World Series subplot that began to take shape on this day. The sportswriters started getting on Ted for "not hitting in the clutch" and for "being selfish" by not hitting the opposite way against the "Williams Shift." Ted and the sportswriters already had an ongoing well-publicized adversarial relationship. Ted simply hated the writers, so they in turn wrote negative stories about him. Ted was a wonderful guy — great to be around in the clubhouse. But let a writer come in and the mood would completely change. Seeing how the writers pounced on him as soon as the chips were down made me believe that the sportswriters were hoping all along that Ted would flop in the Series. It would give them something juicy to write about. Ted had been held to one quiet single in Game One, but that had not been not enough to let the dogs loose. But when he struggled in Game Two against Harry Brecheen, the writers seized the opportunity to start ripping him. They couldn't question his regular season productivity because Ted had produced prolific numbers every year of his career. Part of the reason our club ran away with the 1946 pennant was because of the incredible season Ted had posted. He'd hit .342 with 38 home runs and 123 RBI, and was named the American League MVP. But with Ted now struggling in his first World Series, the writers felt his post-season productivity, or lack thereof, was fair game for criticism.

There's no denying that Ted was frustrated on two counts by the Cardinals in Game Two. Count one, Harry Brecheen; and count two, the "Williams Shift." Batting against the shift every time in Game Two, Ted struggled. In his first at-bat he'd hit a bounder to Musial, stationed on the first base line, well out of his normal position. Stan easily beat Ted to the bag for the out. The St. Louis crowd went wild when Brecheen struck out Ted on three pitches in Williams' second at-bat. The shift robbed Ted of a sure hit in his third at-bat when he hit a screaming line drive right to Schoendienst who was positioned well in back of first base — also way out of his normal spot. And, as I mentioned, Ted popped-out foul in his final at-bat of the day. John Drebinger of the *New York Times,* certainly NOT one of Ted's sportswriter adversaries, still carried a bit of a negative and sarcastic tone when he wrote, "The prestige of the fabulous Mr. Williams suffered a blow, too." After recounting Ted's failed at-bats, Drebinger concluded by saying, "It was scarcely an impressive showing by Boston's Thumping Theodore." That was mild — the real attacks on Ted came from the Boston writers, particularly Dave Egan of the *Record.*

I mentioned that "selfishness" was one of the claims that the writers made about Ted. They claimed that Ted could have singled against the shift at anytime if he would just hit to leftfield or bunt. Ted was strong-willed, however, and he wanted to beat the shift with his strength — pull-hitting. "I know that those wide open spaces in left look inviting," he told reporters, "but with that short rightfield fence, the percentages are still in my favor hitting to right." When the writers heard Ted say that, they felt he wasn't a team guy. I know he was, though. Ted was for the team all the way, and he was convinced that the best way to help our club beat the opponent was by continuing to pull the ball. Folks can debate whether he was wrong or not on this point, but his decision to continue to pull was not a selfish one. He did it because he truly believed it was his best chance to be productive at the plate — and a productive Ted Williams was good for the entire Boston Red Sox team.

Unfortunately, the writers had the last laugh as far as Ted and the World Series was concerned. Ted ended up having a miserable Series at the plate, batting just .200, and the writers feasted on him. Because Ted failed in the 1946 Series, many writers have concluded that Ted Williams couldn't hit in the clutch. In my mind, that's unfair and not true. Ted refused to use his elbow injury as an excuse for his bad Series, but I'm telling you here — there's no question it hampered his effectiveness. I'm sure Ted was confident that he'd have another chance to prove the writers wrong in the future, but Ted never got back to the World Series. For a career as great as his, it's unfortunate that so much has been made of his poor performance in the '46 Series. One World Series is not enough of a sample to gauge whether a player is a "choker" or not, and it hurt Ted when some writers labeled him that way. I once read an interview with Ted where the writer asked him what in his career he would do over if given the chance. Ted, in his mid-70's at the time, got a little choked up when he answered, "1946 — I wish I had done better in the World Series." The writers may have had the last laugh on Ted as far as the World Series was concerned, but Ted had the last laugh in life. He was a great ballplayer, a great American, and simply a great guy. I'm proud to have been his friend.

As you'd expect, it was quite a different scene in our clubhouse after our Game Two loss as opposed to our Game One win. We all filed by the disconsolate Mickey Harris to pat him on the back and let him know that he'd pitched a great game and it wasn't his fault. Still, we weren't too low. We knew we were heading back to Fenway Park where we played very well. Getting out of St. Louis with a split was actually a pretty good deal considering how good a ballclub the Cardinals were. Joe Cronin deserved a great deal of credit, too, for keeping us from getting down on ourselves after our loss. He didn't point any fingers or yell and scream, he simply praised Brecheen for a job well done and then looked ahead to the future. "He had plenty of stuff today," Joe told reporters. "Mickey Harris had a lot of stuff, too, but we couldn't do a thing with those screwballs Brecheen was tossing up there. We couldn't get any runs today because we couldn't hit Brecheen. He was a great pitcher out there. But I'll use Ferriss in the first game at Boston, and maybe I'll come back with Hughson in the second game there." Boo Ferriss and Tex Hughson — that sounded like two wins to me.

OCTOBER 9, 1946: World Series Game Three — *YORK 3-RUN HOMER DEFEATS CARDINALS FOR RED SOX, 4 TO 0. FERRISS GIVES TEAM 2-1 LEAD IN GAMES WITH 50TH SHUTOUT IN WORLD SERIES HISTORY.* There you have it — the *New York Times* headline to our second win in the 1946 World Series on this day. My services were not required for this game, so I sat it out in the dugout. And from what I observed, the services of our entire team were not needed all that much — all we really needed were the outstanding efforts of Boo Ferriss and Rudy York. Unlike the Indian summer that St. Louis had for Games One and Two, it was a typical crisp fall day with blue skies for Game Three in Boston. The Boston Red Sox had not hosted a World Series game since 1918 when Babe Ruth was their star pitcher, so the entire city was really juiced up for the event. In fact, they were starved for a champion. On hand were a couple of legendary representatives from the old 1918 ballclub — centerfielder Tris Speaker and manager Ed Barrow.

Early arrivals to the ballpark were treated to a band as well as a brand new comedy routine from baseball clown Al Schacht. Every seat in the place was filled by the time the game was ready to begin. Peppered throughout the high-dollar box seats were powerful politicians like Governor Tobin and Mayor Curley, and movie and radio stars. There was also a special section behind home plate filled with wounded veterans in their wheel chairs. It was truly an electric atmosphere. Commissioner Happy Chandler threw out the ceremonial first pitch, just like he'd done in St. Louis, and then Boo got to work. The big guy made short work of Red Schoendienst and Terry Moore, but pitched carefully to Stan Musial and walked him. Musial stole second, but then committed the first of two key Cardinals base-running mistakes by getting picked off to end the inning.

Little right-hander Murry Dickson got the start for the Cardinals. He was far from overpowering, but he was crafty. Dickson threw such a wide array of pitches that Cards catcher Joe Garagiola once said that he didn't have enough fingers to signal them all. Dickson was a tough competitor, too, a characteristic he may have developed while serving in World War II. He, like our own Earl Johnson, was highly decorated, having fought in the Battle of the Bulge and having landed at Omaha Beach on D-Day. So we knew we would have our work cut out for us just like we had with Harry Brecheen. Wally Moses led off for us but was easily retired on a fly ball to Harry Walker in left. Johnny Pesky batted next, and he was due for a hit. He'd gone hitless in Games One and Two, but he came through this time with a single down the third base line. Johnny moved to second on Dom DiMaggio's ground out to Musial, so that brought up Ted Williams with two outs. Had they pitched to Ted, who knows — maybe Ted would have come through with a big hit to forever change his World Series reputation for the better. But Cardinals manager Eddie Dyer instead had Dickson walk Ted to get to Rudy York. It may have looked good on paper, but it didn't work out so good for St. Louis.

The game had only been going for about 15 minutes and there was still a lot of standing-room-only people still filing into the park. In other words, a great deal of folks at the game that day never saw Rudy unload on a 3-2 Dickson curveball and send it screaming over the left-centerfield wall for a 3-run homer. Here's how John Drebinger described Rudy's big round-tripper in the *New York Times* — "Gaining momentum as it zoomed through the air, it cleared the high barrier some 350 feet from home plate and fell into the netting just beyond. The purpose of this netting is to protect the windows in the buildings across the street from just such drives. But there was nothing it could do to protect the unfortunate Cardinals on this occasion and the gathering whooped it up." And Drebinger was right — we whooped it up. We were very confident that those three runs were all that we'd need to win because we had Boo Ferriss on the mound. He was undefeated at Fenway Park in 1946 — 13 wins and no losses.

The score was still 3-0 when there was finally some excitement in the bottom of the 3rd inning. As usual, it was Ted who was at the center of the attention. He went up to hit with two outs and the Cardinals defense playing the "Williams Shift." Then Ted did the unthinkable — he bunted! Here's how

Drebinger described the play — "Williams deftly met the first pitch for a roller that hugged the third base line as though operated on a string, and by the time shortstop Marty Marion came dashing over to intercept the ball, Williams, chuckling like a youngster who had just pulled the chair out from under the teacher, was on first base with a single to his credit. The fans howled with glee." Needless to say, all of us on the bench were laughing, too.

With the exception of the mistake he'd thrown to Rudy in the 1st inning, Dickson was matching Boo out for out through five innings. He'd even exacted a measure of revenge for Williams' bunt single by striking Ted out looking in the bottom of the 5th. Then Dickson even tried to spark the St. Louis offense when he doubled into the leftfield corner to open the 6th, but, as with Musial earlier, a base-running mistake erased him. Schoendienst, batting after Dickson, blooped one into shallow center. Dickson, meanwhile, had wandered off second base as Dom sped in after the ball, frozen by the spectacle of DiMaggio's desperate chase for the ball. Murry should have been on the bag, so when Dom came up with a shoestring catch he was easily able to double-up Dickson. That really put a damper on any ideas of a rally, then Boo struck out Moore to end the inning. Amazingly, that was Boo's first strikeout of the game, and he ended up with only two. When one looks at how dominant he was that day you might think he had to be blowing guys away, but that wasn't his style. He did it with pinpoint control and his great slider.

Dyer sent up a pinch-hitter for Dickson in the top of the 8th, so Ted Wilks replaced him on the slab in the bottom of the inning. Ted was one of the few Cardinal pitchers that we'd roughed up in the 1944 Series when I was with the Browns, and he wasn't treated so well on this day, either. After retiring Williams on a line shot to Enos Slaughter in right, Wilks gave up a single to York and a double to Bobby Doerr. Pinky Higgins was out on a come-backer, which held the runners at second and third, but Rudy then scored when Schoendienst fumbled Hal Wagner's easy roller for an error. Wagner's insurance run ran the score to 4-0, which is how it ended — but not without a minor scare in the bottom of the 9th. Boo quickly got two outs on a ground ball by Schoendienst and a fly ball off the bat of Moore. But then Musial hit a triple to the rightfield wall just in front of our bullpen. That brought up a tough out in Slaughter, but with the drama building Boo struck out Enos with a slider on the outside corner to end the game. Everyone rushed to congratulate Boo on the great job he'd just completed. Before he disappeared into the clubhouse he went up to his mother who was sitting in back of first base. He handed her the ball which had struck out Slaughter and told her to take care of it for him. It would be added to the collection of balls on display back at the Ferriss home in Shaw, Mississippi. You see, Boo had grabbed the last-out ball from all 47 of his big league victories, but no doubt about it — this ball would be the most prized. I couldn't have been happier for him, and from the smile on his face you could see that he was about as happy as any fellow could be.

In the clubhouse Boo, sitting in front of his locker, was surrounded by reporters and well-wishers, and he shared some of his thoughts about the game. "My first big league game was a shutout over Bobo Newsom early last year and, until now, that was the happiest day of my life," Boo said. "But today tops everything. I'm just the happiest guy in the world, thanks to Rudy and that homer. I never felt any nervousness before the game." It was true, too. In fact, Boo walked by Boston sportswriter Johnny Drohan just before the start of the game, slapped a friendly pat on Drohan's back, and said, "Don't be so nervous, John — It's just another ballgame." That said, Boo did recognize the enormity of the game, and he said as much when he told reporters, "But I was a bit on edge, I guess. It was my first World Series game, my biggest assignment, and I felt keyed up to it as I warmed up, but once I put my foot on that rubber it was just another ball game. They were just another ballclub, and I just fired it across there, doing my best. Rudy and the rest of the boys made sure my best was good enough. I never felt tired. I was strong all the way and just mixed them up pretty good with fast ones, curves and a change-of-pace ball. York's homer made me feel pretty comfortable after the 1st inning."

It was a mob scene around Rudy's locker, too, but he was a little less talkative about his big moment. "I hit a curveball for that homer and met it pretty good," he told the throng around him. When asked if it was a "hanging" curve, Rudy smiled and said, "The only place it 'hung' was on the shelf over the scoreboard." Joe Cronin was also nearby speaking to the writers. Handed a quick 3-run lead with one of the league's best hurlers on the mound, Joe had about as easy a day as a manager will ever get, and he told the reporters so. "Of course, it was York and Ferriss today," said Joe. "There wasn't much else to it. I thought the boys looked like a different ballclub, a better club. Ferriss pitched a whale of a game. I was tickled to see him come through in his first World Series start, and York's homer just about settled the issue."

One final note of interest about the Game Three. Ted Williams, the man that so many Boston writers were crucifying as selfish for his refusal to hit to left, gave them what they wanted when he laid one down the third base line. That still wasn't enough to call all the dogs off. I guess they wanted him to do it every time. Still, some might have changed their tune if they'd seen that Ted was the first one at the ballpark that day, working diligently on hitting and bunting to leftfield — just in case it was needed of him in the game. He quickly ducked into the clubhouse just when the Cardinals appeared so as not to clue them in on the fact that he was considering hitting the other way. And believe me — it would have been big news had it gotten out early. Everything Ted did was big news. It's hard to imagine now, 60 years after the fact, but Ted was so charismatic that writers, players and fans were more interested in his battle against the shift than almost anything else — including Rudy York, a man who'd already hit two game-winning World Series homers. Arthur Daley of the *New York Times* captured this phenomena best when he wrote, "Somehow or other, the husky first baseman is not quite the glamour boy that Williams is. Even the crowd, which thankfully roared in approbation when he lofted one over the barrier, watched York disinterestedly the rest of the way while every time the Kid stepped up to the plate there was an instant ripple of excitement. There's just no way to explain it. Magnetism and personality are something you have or haven't. Ted has it." Daley was right on that one — Ted definitely had magnetism and personality, and the game of baseball was the better for it.

OCTOBER 10, 1946: World Series Game Four — *CARDS, WITH RECORD-TYING 20 HITS, ROUT RED SOX, 12-3, TO EVEN SERIES.* The prognosticators had been predicting some heavy-hitting in this World Series, slugging that had yet to materialize, but they'd been saying it would come from us, not St. Louis. But that's why they play the game, as the old saying goes — because no one really knows what'll happen on the ballfield once the ump hollers, "Play ball!" And on this day the St. Louis Cardinals handed us an old fashioned butt whipping to square the Series at two games apiece. Midway through the top of the 9th inning Bobby Doerr had to leave the game because of a violent migraine headache, so I went in to replace him. But other than that brief participation in the action, I observed the events of this game from my perch on the bench.

It was slightly warmer than it had been for the previous game, but folks were still bundled up against the cold air. It was a festive atmosphere prior to the game with the early arriving fans being treated to popular tunes played by Chet Nelson's 20-piece circus band. Lots of players including myself roamed around the field, many of us taking home movies. Rudy York was a real camera fiend and he was filming, too. Rudy, catching a glimpse of Harry Brecheen, bellowed, "Let's get a shot of you throwing that blankety-blank screwball!" Brecheen shook his head no and said, "I can't." Rudy hollered back, "Yes, you can!" And when big Rudy hollers, you listen! So Brecheen smiled and did as he was told, demonstrating his delivery for Rudy's movie camera. Incidentally, I shot a lot of home movies that season. A number of years ago HBO produced a great program entitled *When It was a Game.* It was comprised entirely of beautiful color home movies shot by players. If you ever get a chance to see it, I recommend it highly. Plus, it features a bit of film I shot of Ted Williams and his picture-perfect swing.

In addition to the band and the players milling about the field, there was also the usual assortment of political, sports, and show business celebrities there to excite the fans. Mrs. Grace Coolidge, the widow of President Calvin Coolidge, was in a box with a group of friends, and she garnered some pointing, but it was box seat holders Joe Louis, current world heavyweight champion, and Joe DiMaggio that received the most attention. Clusters of autograph seekers crowded around them right up until the time that the game began, at which point they scurried to their seats. Once seated, the Red Sox fans were witness to an inning that may have given them a false sense of confidence — at least as far as the effectiveness of our pitching was concerned. Tex Hughson, our 20-game winner who had pitched so well in the opener, got the starting assignment and he looked good setting down Red Schoendienst, Terry Moore, and Stan Musial for a 1-2-3 top of the 1st. When Cards right-hander George Munger responded by retiring us in order in the home half of the inning, it looked as if another pitching duel might be in the works.

But that was as good as it got for us that day. From that point on, poor pitching, poor fielding, and poor hitting doomed us to an historic defeat, and this inning encompassed all three elements. In essence, the top of the 2nd was a microcosm of what befell us in the field in Game Four. It began with Enos Slaughter opening the inning with a home run, a powerfully belted line drive shot against the wind and into the rightfield seats about 375 feet away. That was the Cards' only long ball of the day, however. From then on they racked up their runs with singles and doubles — and errors. Slaughter's homer was the first run that St. Louis had scored in 14 innings, but they quickly made up for their scoring drought. Whitey Kurowski whacked a double off the leftfield wall, and Harry Walker later singled him home. Tex was struggling. He was pitching on just three days rest, something that had proven to be somewhat problematic for him during the season. He'd lost only one game all season when pitching on four days rest, but he'd lost ten games when hurling on three days rest. At any rate, even when we did something right it would go bad, and that probably did more to hurt Tex than the fact that he was pitching on short rest. For example, Hal Wagner, our catcher, caught the Cardinals in a hit and run. He called for a pitch-out and fired the ball to Johnny Pesky at second. We had Walker hung up — an easy out. Harry desperately scrambled back to the first base bag, but Johnny's throw to Rudy went in the dugout. Walker moved up to third and then scored on a squeeze bunt by Marty Marion. We finally got out of the inning when Tex struck out Munger, but St. Louis had tacked three quick runs on the scoreboard.

The Cards not only whipped us with their bats, they did it with the leather, too. Slaughter had made a fine running grab on a long drive by Dom DiMaggio in the 1st inning. Then in the bottom of the 2nd Enos made another excellent running catch on a long clout that Pinky Higgins hit in the right-center gap. That same frame provided the defensive play of the day when Terry Moore made a spectacular diving catch off a smash that Rudy York hit deep into right-center-field. Terry was a great centerfielder, and I'd seen him play incredible defense since our old days with the Gas House Gang, but his legs were not what they'd once been. None of us expected him to get that shot that Rudy hit, but he did — and it was one of the best catches you'll ever see in a World Series. Helped by his defense, Munger hung another goose egg on us in the bottom of the inning.

This combination of great Cardinal pitching/hitting/fielding versus our poor pitching/hitting/fielding repeated itself throughout the day. St. Louis scored three more in the top of the 3rd through a few hits and another throwing error. Before the inning was over, Tex was gone — replaced by Jim Bagby. We finally cracked the scoreboard with a single run in the 4th when Ted singled and scored on a double by York. We scratched out our only other runs in the 8th when Doerr slugged a 2-run homer over the leftfield screen. Meanwhile, St. Louis added single runs in the 5th and 7th innings as Bagby gave way to Bill Zuber and then Mace Brown. The score was 8-3 as we opened the last inning, but the game was actually more one-sided than the score indicated. But that anomaly was erased when the Cardinals tallied four more times. Slaughter opened the inning with a single to center. Kurowski bunted down the third base line and Pinky threw wild to first. Joe Garagiola singled — his fourth hit of the day. Joe Cronin trudged out to the mound again and replaced Mace with 40-year old Mike Ryba. Mike was with me on the Cardinals back in the Gas House Gang years. I'm sure he'd fully expected to pitch in the Series with some of those clubs we were on in St. Louis, but it never came to fruition. So Mike must have been shocked to finally find himself in a World Series game at this stage in his career — especially considering that he'd only pitched about a dozen innings for us in '46.

It didn't go well for Ryba. With runners on first and second and none out, Walker moved them along with a sacrifice. Marion then drove in both runs with a double to the leftfield corner. Next, Marty advanced to third when Munger grounded out. Schoendienst hit what looked like the last out of the inning when he bounced one to York. Rudy tossed to Ryba, but Mike missed the bag with his foot and Red was safe. Ryba was charged with an error and Marion scored on the play. It was at this point where Doerr had to leave the game because his migraine headache became intolerable. It'd be funny to say how the cumulative effect of our poor play in the field gave all of us a headache, but Bobby's migraine was a serious situation for him. He was a tough competitor — I've already explained how he'd played with a broken finger when I joined the ballclub — and the last thing he wanted to do was come out of that game here in the 9th inning. But he had no choice, so I grabbed my glove and trotted out to second base, wishing Bobby well as we passed. We resumed the game, and Mike Ryba's trouble resumed, too. Terry Moore, the only Cardinal who'd failed to hit safely to that point, singled. Then Ryba walked Musial to load the bases. Cronin came out to the mound again and pulled Mike, replacing him with an even more unlikely guy — left-hander Clem Dreisewerd.

Clem was a 30-year old farm boy from Old Monroe, Missouri. He'd labored for many years in the minor league systems of the Giants and Cardinals, finally making his big league debut in a handful of games with the 1944 Red Sox. At 29 years of age and with the war almost over, Clem figured to be with Sox again in 1945, but he was drafted and only appeared in a couple of games for them before reporting to the Navy. Clem pitched while in the Navy, but he also stayed sharp by pitching to his wife, Edna. That's right — his wife! For years Edna acted as Clem's offseason catcher. In the 1970's she wrote a book about their baseball experiences entitled *The Catcher Was a Lady*. In any case, Clem had been discharged in time for the 1946 season and had logged only about 50 innings for us, mostly in relief except for one spot start in July. He was a good fellow, though, very congenial, and he never complained about not pitching very much. Clem was always upbeat and happy to contribute in any way that he could. Despite pitching fairly well when called upon, Clem had recently found himself reduced almost exclusively to the role of batting practice pitcher — yet here he was in the World Series for the first time in his life. Granted, it was a forgettable game as far as the Red Sox legacy was concerned, but it was World Series history nonetheless. In fact, Clem had become the punchline to one of Cronin's standing jokes. Throughout the season when reporters would ask Joe who was starting the next day's game, a grinning Cronin would always respond, "Dreisewerd." But pitching in the Series was no joke to Clem, even if he was a mop-up man in a 12-3 blowout. He was proud to be there, and he looked determined as he toed the rubber to face an equally determined Slaughter. When Enos stepped up to the plate to face Clem, home plate umpire Charlie Berry reminded Slaughter that his four hits had tied a World Series record. One more hit would break the record. So Enos was giving it his all as he faced Clem, but Dreisewerd got Slaughter to pop up to end the inning. Clem only pitched in two more games in the majors, appearing twice for the 1948 Browns. He would always reflect upon his one World Series appearance — 1/3 perfect innings of work — as the highlight of his career.

No one on our ballclub — not even Clem — was thinking about personal highlights after the game. Munger slammed the door on us in the 9th inning by retiring Wagner, Leon Culberson and Pesky. Just a year earlier Munger had been part of the U.S. Army occupation in Germany, and now he was a World Series hero for the St. Louis Cardinals. We hit him hard early, but those great catches by Slaughter and Moore helped him stick around long enough to get in a groove. The Cards were respectful as we all filed off the field, keeping their celebration in check. You see, passage to both clubhouses at Fenway Park was through the Red Sox dugout and then down the same tunnel. But once in their clubhouse, we could hear them whoop it up. Our clubhouse, on the other hand, was very quiet. Cronin was a bit down, but he tried to put on a smile as he talked to the writers. "It just wasn't our day," he said. "It was their show entirely. Nothing went right for us. Our pitching didn't stand up; we didn't hit; nor did we field well. We just had a very bad day. That was all." But Joe made sure to end on a positive note, telling the reporters, "The Cards were the ball team today — we were not, but my club is far from beaten."

Ted tried to look at our blowout loss from the "glass half full" perspective, saying, "I'd rather lose that way than by 3 to 2 in 15 innings." There was some truth to that, but the bottom line was that a loss was a loss. Ted did have a small victory in that the Cardinals abandoned the full blown "Williams Shift" for the game. They still had everyone shift to the right, but they left Kurowski at third base. We had reason to believe that St. Louis was going to modify their shift because of a conversation Ryba had had with Marion the night before the game. "That screwy shift on Williams is out," Marty told Mike. "We're not going to give him those bunt hits any more. We're going to make him work for them, brother." We had no way of knowing whether Marion's leak was fact or fiction until the game and Ted's first at-bat, but it didn't really matter anyway because of the lopsided results. What did matter, however, was our dire need to win the final game at Fenway Park tomorrow because we knew it would be tough to go back to St. Louis down three games to two and needing to sweep the final two at Sportsman's Park.

OCTOBER 11, 1946: World Series Game Five — *RED SOX TAKE 3-2 LEAD IN SERIES WITH DOBSON BEATING CARDS, 6-3.* That was the *New York Times* headline reporting on our crucial Game Five victory over the St. Louis Cardinals on this day at Fenway Park in Boston. John Drebinger of the *Times* said it best when he wrote, "Bouncing back from adversity apparently is not a commodity peculiar to National League teams in general and the Cardinals of St. Louis in particular. For on this clear, sunny afternoon Joe Cronin and his Red Sox put it on display and they really bounced around in convincing fashion. Surging back in a remarkable recovery after the crushing defeat they had suffered the previous day, the Bosox, responding heroically to the cheers of 35,982 onlookers, decisively whipped Eddie Dyer's Redbirds in the 5th game of the current World Series, 6 to 3."

Drebinger was right — our Game Five win really was a bounce-back victory for us. Our Game Four loss was the worst defeat we'd suffered in all of 1946. I'm not referring to it being the worst defeat because of the importance of the game, I'm mean it was LITERALLY our worst loss. At no point in the season had we suffered a more lopsided loss, so it was unclear as to how we would respond. The uncertainty of whether we could bounce back was further clouded by the line-up that Joe Cronin put on the field. The second-guessers were very surprised when Cronin announced that he would start right-hander Joe Dobson. They felt that Cronin should have gone by the book and returned to Mickey Harris, but Joe was playing a hunch by starting Dobson. Many of the second-guessers felt that Cronin was repeating a mistake he'd made while managing the Senators in the 1933 World Series when he'd held his best pitcher, Earl Whitehill, until Game Three — and blew the Series. But when Cronin got a hunch, he wasn't to be persuaded by second-guessers, so Dobson got the ball — and he wouldn't disappoint. Joe had been around since 1939, and he'd logged a couple of nice seasons with the Red Sox before going off to serve two years in the Army during World War II. 1946 was his first season back and it had been his best ever as he pitched to a 13-7 record, but he had been very unpredictable as of late. Dobson had started the season like a house afire, but slowed considerably in the second half of the campaign. Cronin seemed to have restored confidence in Dobson, however, after a couple of wins that Joe notched in late September.

The other new additions to the line-up that had the second-guessers concerned were stationed in rightfield and at second base. Out in right was Leon Culberson, a solid outfielder who swung a pretty decent stick when called upon, but he'd batted less than 200 times in 1946. The problem was that he was replacing veteran Wally Moses. Wally had come to us mid-season, then hit well below his once excellent reputation. But he was now swinging a hot bat, having collected four hits in our game the previous day, so many folks wanted to see him in there again. The second baseman who Fenway fans were not too thrilled to see starting the game was... me! Bobby Doerr was still ailing from his migraine, so Joe Cronin had let me know early in the day that I'd be playing second and batting lead off. The Red Sox fans didn't have anything against me, it's just that they were disappointed that Bobby could not play. His bat was crucial to our success in 1946, and the fans knew that his absence from the line-up did not bode well for our chances to generate some offense. I was, as I'm sure Dobson and Culberson were, too, determined to come through for our club in its time of need.

It didn't take long for us to start making good on Cronin's hunches, but there was an early moment of trepidation. Dobson chucked his last warm-up pitch and then catcher Roy Partee gunned it down to second, after which we threw it around the infield and then tossed it back to Joe. Then from my spot between first and second I watched Joe step on the rubber and fire the first pitch of the game to Cardinals lead-off man Red Schoendienst. Red took it, but then rifled Joe's next pitch into rightfield for a single. You could sense the uneasiness in the crowd. It was as if they were thinking, "Oh no — they're picking up where they left off yesterday!" Cronin must have sensed it, too, because he immediately had Harris and Earl Johnson start warming up in the pen. But Dobson remained cool, rebounding with two quick outs when he struck out Terry Moore while Partee threw out Schoendienst trying to steal. Strike 'em out, throw 'em out. The crowd breathed a sigh of relief when Dobson ended the inning by retiring Stan Musial on a fly ball to Ted Williams.

From the on deck circle I watched Howie Pollet warm up as I got set to lead off our half of the 1st inning. Dyer had gone back to the little left-hander for the first time since his heartbreaking 10-inning loss in Game One. I didn't want to fall behind in the count and have to face Pollet's vast array of change-ups and curves, so I decided to swing at the first pitch if it was a strike. Howie came in with a strike and I hit a smash to Musial that bounded off his glove and into rightfield for a single. I was tickled to have come through with a lead-off hit for us, and I noticed off in the distance that Eddie Dyer had left-hander Al Brazle hurriedly start warming up. Obviously both managers wanted badly to win this ballgame. I moved up to second base when Johnny Pesky banged a single to right. The crowd was buzzing as Dom DiMaggio stepped in to hit, but their spirits were doused a bit when Dom grounded to Whitey Kurowski who stepped on the third base bag to force me. The fans came alive again, however, when Ted took his place in the batter's box. The Cardinals did not implement the "Williams Shift," and Ted made them pay by ramming a run-scoring single into rightfield. The crowd went wild, smelling blood, and their enthusiasm only increased as they watched Eddie Dyer go out to the mound to remove Pollet. I'm sure it pained Eddie to have to pull Pollet so quickly. They were great friends, and for years Howie would work in the offseasons at Eddie's insurance agency. But, as we later learned, Pollet was hurt, suffering arm and side pain from the heavy workload he had carried in 1946. The crowd's excitement turned to disappointment, however, when our golden opportunity to hang a crooked number on the scoreboard evaporated due to some crafty pitching by Brazle who wiggled out of the trouble he'd inherited.

The mood got even darker when we allowed the Cards to tie the game at 1-1 in the top of the 2nd. Enos Slaughter led off the inning with a ground ball to me, which I handled just fine, then throwing him out at first. I was glad to get a play under my belt. Kurowski then popped out to Rudy York, but not without a little drama. Rudy temporarily lost the ball in the sun, but recovered just in time to snag the ball in the webbing of his mitt. Joe Garagiola batted next, and it looked like he hit a sure third out when he slapped a grass-cutter to Pesky, but it went through Johnny for an error. Sure enough, Harry Walker took immediate advantage of our mistake when he doubled to score Garagiola. Dobson did not let it fluster him, though, and he kept his focus, ending the inning by getting Marion to fly out to right.

The bottom of the 2nd opened with a lead-off hit into centerfield by Partee. Dobson then laid down a sac bunt, but both he and Partee were safe when Kurowski tried to force Roy at second instead of taking the sure out at first. Whitey's throw was late, so there were runners on first and second as I came up to hit for the second time. Here's how John Drebinger of the *New York Times* described what happened next — "Up stepped substitute second baseman Don Gutteridge. Oddly, facing the Cardinals in the World Series is no novelty to Don. Two years ago he opposed them as a member of the St. Louis Browns. So, without further ado, he promptly slapped a single into center for his second straight hit, and on the wings of that shot Partee scooted home with what, to all intents and purposes, was the ball game." What a feeling it was to come through with that RBI single. I was high as a kite. When Drebinger wrote it was "the ball game," I guess it kind of was. What he meant was that my RBI gave is a lead that we never relinquished. Both clubs scored more runs, but we always led after my run-scoring hit, and that made me feel really wonderful. But that's all hindsight — my RBI only put us ahead by 2-1, and we knew that there was still a lot of baseball left to play on this day. But there would be no more playing until Garagiola had a heated run-in with home plate umpire Lee Ballanfant about my RBI. After I hit my single to centerfield, Terry Moore fielded it quickly and fired it home. We knew the play would be close, so on-deck man Pesky was desperately signaling for Partee to slide, which he did. Garagiola took the throw and applied the tag, but we all agreed with Ballanfant — the tag was AFTER Roy had touched the plate. Garagiola, who is a good friend of mine, vehemently protested, even showing Ballanfant the spike marks on his right arm as evidence that he had blocked the plate. Dyer joined in with the protest, but Ballanfant's call stood. If you ever see Garagiola on the street, ask him about the play. I'm sure he'll still say Roy was out!

The score remained 2-1 until the bottom of the 6th. That's when the third newcomer to Cronin's line-up came through big. Dobson was still proving Cronin's hunch to be a good one by limiting St. Louis to just one run through six innings. It certainly wasn't a Joe Cronin hunch that landed me at second base in this game — it was Doerr's illness — but I had at least validated Cronin's faith in me by coming through with a couple of hits and an RBI. Now it was Leon Culberson's turn. Leading off the home half of the inning, Leon hit a majestic home run against the leftfield screen directly over the scoreboard. He had a wide smile on his face as he came into the dugout amidst many congratulations and slaps on the back, knowing that he had just rewarded Cronin's vote of confidence in him. It was a great moment. We ran the score to 6-3 in the next inning when we added three more runs to our total. In that frame we got an RBI double by Pinky Higgins, and then two more runs when Marion took a bases-loaded grounder from Partee and threw the ball into rightfield trying to force Culberson at second in an attempted double-play.

My hitting streak ended after my hits in the 1st and 2nd innings. I was out on a bounder to Marion in the 4th; I hit a fielder's choice to Marion in the 6th; and I flied out to Moore in the 8th. My fly-out to Terry turned out to be the last World Series at-bat of my career. I didn't think about it at the time, but that's how it ended for me. I feel blessed, though. Most fellows never make it to the majors. Of the ones that do, very few make it to the World Series. I did both, and I have a great appreciation for my good fortune. The game wasn't over after my fly-out in the 8th, though. We still had to take the field for one last inning, and with the way Dobson was cruising, our 6-1 lead looked insurmountable. But, as the saying goes, you shouldn't count your chickens before they're hatched — and the feisty Cardinals were still sitting on a few eggs. Musial walked to open the 9th, Dobson's first walk of the game. Joe came back, though, striking out Erv Dusak. He was Dobson's eighth strikeout victim of the day. I have to admit I detected some uneasiness in the stands when Kurowski, the next batter, hit a roller to Pesky, which Johnny fumbled for an error. All hands were safe as Garagiola stepped up to hit with Johnson and Bob Klinger scrambling to get up in the bullpen. Garagiola then grounded to Rudy for the second out, Kurowski moving up to second and Musial holding at third. With that, believe it or not, many people began to head for the exits — but they were stopped dead in their tracks when Harry Walker smacked a single to left scoring Stan and Whitey. It was now 6-3 with a runner on first and Marion at the plate. The Red Sox fans' anxiety was relieved, however, when Dobson got Marty to pop up. Pesky camped out directly on second base and waited for the ball to come down. When it slammed into his glove for the final out, we all descended on Joe to offer congratulations for a job well done. Were it not for a couple of infield errors, Joe would have likely pitched a shutout.

With the see-saw Series advantage now back in our court, it was our turn to again have the happy locker room. Everyone was whooping it up, jumping around, and exchanging smiles and congratulations. As soon as we got into the clubhouse, Cronin pushed through the swirling crowd of writers, guests, and celebrating players and grabbed Culberson by the shoulders. He smiled at Leon and said, "Great hitting, kid. Be sure to tell the right pitch you hit when these newspaper wolves ask you." Then, addressing the reporters, Cronin admitted, "I had Culberson in right as a defensive move. He's really a centerfielder, but he covers a lot of ground. The move proved to be a good one." Next, Cronin made his way over to Dobson who was already surrounded by a large group praising his effort. Standing next to Dobson, Cronin said, "Dobson pitched a great game. He was no surprise pick, either. I had him in mind as part of my pitching sequence right along. It was his turn and he came through marvelously." Then Cronin addressed my contribution. "Bobby Doerr couldn't play, but he's going with us to St. Louis. If his headaches are still bothering him on Sunday, Gutteridge will be ready. Don played a swell game today." I took in the scene, delighting in every moment. Having joined the team at the season's midpoint, it took a while for me to feel like I completely belonged. It's not that my new teammates hadn't welcomed me into the fold immediately — they did. But I still felt like I needed to make a measurable contribution on the field to complete the deal. That's hard to do when you don't play very much. But, in a way, this wonderful game was the last thing that, in my mind, completed my role as a member the 1946 Boston Red Sox team.

Dobson, at first, was so overcome with the swarm of congratulations he was receiving that he couldn't speak. He had gone into the game under a cloud of worry. His wife was scheduled to have a serious operation at the conclusion of the series and that weighed heavily on his mind. But he didn't let it hinder him once he took the hill, and he pitched a whale of a game. As soon as the swarm around Joe subsided, he found his voice, almost sounding a bit like Ol' Diz. "I threw my atom ball at them," he told the writers. "Yep, that old atom ball destroyed 'em. Just wiped 'em out. A wonderful feeling, too. I never started a Series game before. I've been in on relief, but this was my first start. I'm happier than I can say right now. Never had too much trouble. Didn't get tired, except in the last inning. Then my arm was cold and I couldn't loosen it up. But I didn't worry because I knew we could hold a good lead. I fooled them all along with curves, a fast one, a change-of-pace ball, a slider, and the old atom ball."

Above the racket of the noisy clubhouse, Johnny Orlando, our assistant trainer, could be heard hollering at the top of his voice, "Pack the caps and gloves! The caps and gloves, pack 'em! Don't forget!" He was in high gear, hustling to get ready for the plane to St. Louis. While we were eating dinner, he had bags to ship and trunks to be packed and hauled down to the railraod station. It was an exciting scene. And all I could think was that it would all come to a head in St. Louis — just like it had in 1944. I just hoped that this time, when it was all said and done, I'd be celebrating a World Series championship.

OCTOBER 13, 1946: World Series Game Six — *CARDS DOWN RED SOX, 4-1, FORCE SERIES TO SEVEN GAMES.* That was the *New York Times* headline reporting that the St. Louis Cardinals had evened the 1946 World Series at three games apiece on this day. Just like that, the whole season came down to one game to be played in 48 hours — winner take all. The travel day allowed for Bobby Doerr's migraine headache to subside, so he was back at second base for Game Six. That meant that I was back at my spot on the bench, and it was from there that I took in all of the day's action. It had been cold and raw in St. Louis when we'd arrived the day before, but that front had moved out and it was clear and warm at game time. The pitching match-up featured Harry "The Cat" Brecheen against Mickey Harris. The Red Sox second-guessers were at it again with Joe Cronin's announcement that he was going with Harris. Many felt that Joe should have chosen Tex Hughson because of his capability to be overpowering. Some even thought that Cronin should have gone for the immediate kill by using our ace, Boo Ferriss, even though he'd only had three days rest. But Joe opted for Mickey and decided to let the chips fall where they may.

With our return to Sportsman's Park there was a bit of a resurgence of complaining by our players about the conditions at the old ballpark. I was well aware of the shortcomings of the stadium after so many years with the Cardinals and Browns, so I was used to it. It's not that the poor field conditions were a revelation to the Red Sox players — they knew all about it from playing the Browns in St. Louis during the regular season. But the stakes weren't as high in the regular season, so it wasn't as much of an issue. But it irked some of our fellows to have to play the deciding game or games of the World Series on a field with a subpar playing surface. It's the infield that was the real problem, so hard that it was dubbed "the rockpile" or the "granite quarry." More of a problem, however, was the tricky hitting background. Many of the guys said it blurred their vision. Just when reporters started to chastise us for whining about something that was of equal detriment to each club, Ted Williams said, "It's strange to us because whenever we played the Browns there was no crowd in the bleachers." It was a good point. The Cardinals drew very well and were therefore used to hitting with fans in the centerfield bleachers. The Brownies drew poorly, so the empty centerfield bleachers always provided a good hitting backdrop.

It didn't seem to matter what backdrop Ted had, or whether they shifted on him or not, he was still struggling at the plate. Before Game Five he was in front of his locker fiddling with his bats and mumbling, "I gotta get me some hits. This can't go on forever." It did get worse for Ted, though. He got only one hit in five at-bats, and he struck out twice. Many of the writers seemed to enjoy watching Ted continue to struggle and gleefully reported on his trouble at the plate. Even compliments directed at Ted were of the backhanded variety, one Boston scribe writing that "Theodore the Great" seemed to be more civil to the writers of late. "Ted's improving," he wrote. "Some day he may be as charming as the modest, capable Stanley Musial." Another columnist speculated that Ted was already pining for the offseason, writing, "Williams can't wait for this Series to get over so that he can go hunting and fishing in South Dakota, far from the maddening crowd. Thus far in the Series the only fishing he's done has been fishing after third strikes, and his hunting has consisted principally of hunting for base hits. Neither appeals to Temperamental Ted." The final dig at Ted was when the writer concluded by reporting, "Mr. Theodore Samuel Williams pulled up his average to a rousing .238. Just thought you might like to know." Is it any wonder why Ted hated sportswriters?

As the 1st inning got underway it appeared that Brecheen was not as sharp as he'd been when he shut us down in Game Two. He fanned Leon Culberson to open the game, but he then gave up singles to Johnny Pesky and Dom DiMaggio. Next, Harry issued a pass to Ted to load the bases with only one out. That brought up Rudy York, giving him another chance to be a hero for us. But it didn't work out this time as Rudy hit a smash to Whitey Kurowski at third, and Whitey turned a lightning 5-4-3 double-play to end the inning.

After Mickey set the Cards down in order in the bottom of the 1st, we then found ourselves with another great opportunity to score in the top of the 2nd. First, Doerr singled off Kurowski's glove to lead off the inning. Pinky Higgins followed with another single, this one lashed into left-center. It looked like Bobby could easily advance to third base on the hit, but Erv Dusak, playing left-field only because the southpaw Harris was pitching, quickly got to the ball and nailed a sliding Doerr with a perfect rifle throw. Seemingly energized by his club's great defense, Brecheen knuckled down, ending the threat by striking out Roy Partee and popping up Harris. After coming up empty in two straight innings, I couldn't help but wonder how many more opportunities this good — if any — we'd get throughout the rest of the game.

Unlike us, the Cardinals made the most of their first scoring opportunity when it presented itself in the bottom of the 3rd. Mickey had held them hitless through two innings, but his luck changed when Del Rice singled sharply over Pesky's head to start the inning. Rice, like Dusak, was only in the game to face Mickey's left-handed offerings, and he apparently liked what he was seeing from Harris. In fact, Mickey had yet to retire Rice because Del was 2-for-2 against Harris back in Game Two. Rice was erased when he was forced at second on an attempted sacrifice by Brecheen, but then Red Schoendienst followed with a double down the rightfield line that placed runners at second and third with one out. Then St. Louis pushed across their first run of the day when Terry Moore hit a fly ball to Culberson in right. In a heartbeat, the Cards scored twice more off consecutive singles by Musial, Kurowski and Enos Slaughter. That did it for Mickey. Cronin came out and took the ball from him, motioning to the bullpen for Tex Hughson. I felt bad for Mickey as I watched him walk of the mound very dejectedly. He'd failed to finish in both of his World Series starts, and I know it really ate at him. With Tex throwing from the right side, Cards manager Eddie Dyer sent Harry Walker to the plate in place of Dusak. It looked like more trouble when Walker laid into one, sending it on a line to center, but Dom kept us in the game with a tremendous running catch just off the grass to end the inning. It was one of the best grabs of the entire series.

Tex pitched admirably for the next three innings, but we couldn't get him any runs. After escaping with his life in the 1st and 2nd innings, Brecheen had settled into a groove. Harry was nicknamed "The Cat" because he was such an agile fielder — cat-like in the way he pounced on the ball. But with the way he had repeatedly slithered out of danger early in the game, I was now wondering if his nickname referred to the fact that "The Cat" seemed to have nine lives! We were still trailing, 3-0, when we finally got to Brecheen for a run in the top of the 7th inning. Rudy nearly hit his third homer of the series when he led off the inning with a powerful drive to center, but it didn't have quite enough to leave the yard and it slammed off the wall for a triple. Doerr drove in Rudy with a long fly to leftfield, but our rally was halted there when Brecheen popped up Higgins and Partee.

The Cardinals picked up another run in the bottom of the 8th when Marty Marion doubled off Earl Johnson to score Walker. Cronin had sent Tom McBride in to pinch-hit for Tex in the top of the 8th in a futile attempt to generate some offense, so Earl took the mound after that. He allowed only that one run, but it turned out not to hurt us because we failed to rally in the 9th. We had one out when Ted broke through with his first hit of the day. That raised some optimism in our dugout, but St. Louis quickly stifled our hope with a game-ending double-play off the bat of Rudy — Marion to Schoendienst to Musial. Game Six was in the history books.

The air in our clubhouse was heavy with disappointment. No one was more upset than Mickey Harris who was denied a World Series win for the second time. As we entered the clubhouse, Mickey slammed his cap and glove into his locker, then kicked his shirt, trousers, and windbreaker onto the locker room floor. We offered sympathy, but Mickey was inconsolable. Cronin, too, was struggling to put on a brave face. He didn't even want to discuss the happenings of the game, but he reluctantly offered some thoughts for the gathering of sportswriters. "One more hit in that 1st inning," he said, almost inaudibly, "just one more hit. One out, the bases loaded and York swinging. And they come up with a double-play. In the 2nd Dusak comes up with a perfect throw — it had to be perfect — and nails Doerr going into third. Instead of two runners on and none out, we have a man on first and one out. Harris had a lot of stuff, great stuff. [Homeplate umpire] Cal Hubbard told me he never saw him better any time this season. But that hit by Schoendienst was the tough one, that double that shot right along first out of reach of York, in the 3rd. That was the ball game. Brecheen pitched a good game after the 2nd inning. But a couple of runs would have made all the difference in the world. Just one more hit. One more. Ah, well, now we're down to the clincher. It will be Ferriss for Tuesday and..." Before he finished his thought, Joe turned to coach Del Baker and whispered something.

Rudy busted in at this point and tried to pick up the mood. "We'll get 'em next time, boys," he shouted, "we'll get 'em Tuesday!" Tex, slapping his glove on his locker shelf, joined in and added, "It's our turn to win the next one! Every other day — every other day! Say, one game in this Series is a winning streak!" And Tex was right — if the trend played itself out again in Game Seven, then we'd be celebrating a world championship in a mere 48 hours.

OCTOBER 15, 1946: World Series Game Seven — *CARDS TAKE SERIES AS BRECHEEN BEATS RED SOX THIRD TIME, 4-3.* That was the headline from the *New York Times* article recounting our loss in the seventh and deciding game of the 1946 World Series. From our perspective, it was a real heartbreaker. The dramatic and unbelievable way in which the game finished ended up making the Series an instant classic — truly one for the ages. The story of that climactic game has been told countless times, but I'll do my best to tell it one more time here — the way I saw it from my front row seat in the Red Sox dugout.

The mood before the game was not one of impending doom. We had no reason to believe that we'd lose. In fact, we were confident that we'd prevail. We had our best pitcher handling the mound chores in big Boo Ferriss. We had the ongoing trend of winning every other game on our side. Plus, half-baked theories like the "Curse of the Bambino" had yet to develop amongst the Boston sportswriters, so we weren't operating under a cloud previous failures. But Ted Williams was still down over his inability to get started. Joe Cronin tried to lighten Ted's mood, however, by presenting Ted with a gift just before we left the clubhouse. Everyone knew that Ted always looked forward to the end of the season so he could go fishing, but this year Ted was particularly anxious to see the season end because of the miserable Series he was having. So Joe presented him with a book entitled, *The Hell with Fishing.* Everyone got a good chuckle out of it, then we took to the field for batting practice.

Murry Dickson drew the starting assignment for the Cardinals, his first appearance since his tough-luck loss in Game Three. Dickson looked focused as he took his final warm-up tosses, but so did Wally Moses, our lead-off man who was swinging a few bats while watching coolly from the on-deck circle. Moses made a believer of me when he singled right up the middle. Wally then went to third when the next man up, Johnny Pesky, hit a bounding single over second base, just out of Marty Marion's outstretched glove. We were quickly in business with runners at the corners and none out. Dom DiMaggio followed with a fly ball that scored Wally, then Ted stepped up with a chance to do some real damage. He hit a towering smash into deep center, and here's how John Drebinger of the *New York Times* described the ensuing action — "It was pretty much unprotected territory, for in the Card outer defenses against Thumping Ted two fielders played far to the right and only Harry Walker remained on the left side. But Terry Moore, forgetting his years and racing with all the speed he could get out of his aging legs, caught the ball with a final lunge. Pesky, who had gone all the way to second, confident this would be a hit, had to do some tall stepping back to first." When Rudy York popped out to end the inning, we knew we had let a great opportunity slip through our fingers.

The Cardinals did a little threatening of their own, too, in the bottom of the 1st when they also banged out two hits, one a double by Stan Musial. But they, too, came up empty thanks to some nifty pitching by Boo and a great throw by Ted to nail Red Schoendienst trying to stretch a single into a double. Dickson was again in trouble in the top of the 2nd when he found himself facing a situation with Bobby Doerr on third and only one out, but he seemed to get tougher when in a jam, and he wriggled out without allowing us to add to our 1-0 lead. The crowd really cheered Dickson as he walked off the mound, then they were really given something to applaud when St. Louis tied the game with a run in the home half of the inning. Whitey Kurowski opened with a two-bagger to left-center, then advanced to third on a ground-out by Joe Garagiola. He then scored when Walker flied out to Ted in deep leftfield.

The score remained knotted at 1-1 until the bottom of the 5th when something unthinkable to us happened — Boo Ferriss got knocked out of the game. Here's Drebinger's description of the events — "As had been the case so many times this year, the Cardinal attack began quietly enough. Walker opened with a single, but when manager Eddie Dyer cautiously ordered Marion to sacrifice this didn't presage an overwhelming assault. In fact, it wasn't a move many managers would have made with the pitcher the next batter. But Dickson is cast along slightly different lines. Like nearly all Cardinals, whether they be pitchers, catchers, or bat boys, this slim native Missourian is a versatile ballplayer and an extremely dangerous hitter when a blow really means something. Hadn't he helped win a big game from the Cubs in that sizzling pennant race with a single? He certainly had, although the Sox seemed to have forgotten about it. This time Dickson did even better. He drove a two-bagger down the leftfield line and the crowd really turned it on as Walker rounded third and dashed for home to put the St. Louisans ahead."

Continuing, Drebinger wrote, "Scarcely had the Sox recovered from this shock when Schoendienst gave them another when he larruped a single into center to drive in Dickson. The stands were in a terrific uproar and there was no abatement when Moore followed with another single to center. That was all for Ferriss, and Joe Dobson, who had won the 5th game for the Sox with a surprisingly fine effort, left the bullpen. Joe still had a few surprises left, and he brought the Redbird attack to an end." I was sad to see Boo get knocked out of that game.

He was such a great person that I would have just loved to see him win that game — and the Series — for all of Boston. He was pitching well enough to win, but everything the Cards hit that inning just seemed to have eyes.

Murry Dickson, now pitching with a 3-1 lead, kept our bats in check for the next two innings. He did it with great control as well as a few sparkling defensive plays by Moore and Walker. Dobson was Murry's equal, however, also allowing no more Cardinal scoring through the 6th and 7th innings. But with time running out, we made a run in the top of the 8th. Cronin sent Glen Russell in to hit for Hal Wagner, and Rip responded with a lead-off hit to centerfield. Cronin went to the well again, this time sending George Metkovich in to pinch-hit for Dobson. Catfish came through with a ringing double to left, putting runners on second and third with nobody out. Dyer then went out and removed Dickson from the mound. Murry, furious about being pulled while still holding the lead, walked off the field in obvious disgust.

Our glee at knocking Dickson out of the box was tempered somewhat when we saw his replacement — Harry Brecheen. Harry had had our number in two Series games already, so we were just hoping that the law of averages would finally swing in our favor. That didn't appear to be the case at first, however, when Brecheen quickly retired Moses on a strikeout and Pesky on a shallow fly to Enos Slaughter. But Harry's luck seemed to finally run out when Dom hit what looked like a possible 3-run homer. The ball didn't have quite enough to leave the park, however, but it slammed off the rightfield wall for a 2-run double. The good news was that the score was now tied 3-3, but the bad news was that Dom pulled up lame while sprinting into second base. He'd severely pulled a leg muscle and had to come out of the game, Leon Culberson trotting out to take his place. I later learned that Dickson, in the clubhouse and hearing his lead erased, was so angry at the turn of events that he left the stadium. He listened to the rest of the game on his car radio while driving around St. Louis.

At this point Ted stepped up to hit. This at-bat turned out to be the final indignity in his World Series nightmare. With first base open and two outs, it wasn't a stretch to figure that Dyer might have Brecheen walk Ted to set up an easy force-out at any bag. But Harry had owned Ted throughout the Series, so they decided to pitch to him instead of giving Rudy a chance to deliver more of his home run heroics. Brecheen delivered a pitch to Ted and Williams took a terrific swing. He fouled the pitch straight back, the ball ricocheting off Garagiola's bare hand and splitting one of his fingers open. Joe had to come out, Del Rice replacing him. The delay didn't help Ted come up with a strategy to hit Brecheen, and he eventually popped out to Schoendienst to end the inning, disappointment written all over his face. Ted would never again bat in a World Series.

Our guys ran out to their positions for the bottom of the 8th, recharged now that the score was deadlocked at three apiece. We had a new life. Culberson was now in center, Roy Partee replaced Wagner behind the plate, and replacing

Dobson on the mound was right-hander Bob Klinger who was making his first appearance in the Series. Bob was an older guy, about 38 in 1946. He'd had some decent years as a starting pitcher with the Pirates in the late-30's and early-40's. Then he was off to serve in the Navy during World War II. 1946 was his first year back in baseball and he'd landed with Boston where he was used almost exclusively as a reliever, pitching very well for us in that capacity. So there was no reason to think that he would not be up to the situation at hand, but the second-guessers will forever question Cronin's decision to go with Klinger instead of calling on Tex Hughson.

Slaughter opened the inning by slapping a single to center, bringing all of us in the dugout to the edge of our seats on the bench. We were calmed a bit when Kurowski, the next batter, failed in his effort to move Enos to second, instead popping his bunt attempt right to Klinger. Even more of the stress was relieved when Rice then flied to Williams in left for the second out, Slaughter remaining on first base. But then all hell broke loose. Here's how John Drebinger saw it — "Patiently Slaughter waited on first while Klinger retired Kurowski and Rice. But Harry Walker followed with a line drive double into left-center, and for the next few seconds the gathering was to witness an electrifying spurt that doubtless will linger for many years with those who saw it. At first it didn't seem possible that Slaughter could score on the hit, but the Carolinian they call "Country" ran as perhaps he never had run before. He rounded second, third, and then sped for home while a bewildered Boston shortstop, handling the relay from the outfield, spun around to make a futile throw to the plate."

Slaughter was easily safe on the play, and the run gave the Cards a 4-3 lead. Everyone in the place, except Enos, was shocked as he dashed for home on Walker's hit. It caught everyone off guard — even Cardinals third base coach Mike Gonzales. Mike was waving Slaughter around second and on to third, but Gonzales hesitated as Enos approached third. Slaughter, however, didn't hesitate. He tore around third and streaked home, sliding across the plate well in front of Pesky's relay. With two outs and first base open, Cronin had Klinger intentionally pass Marty Marion. Then Joe removed Klinger, bringing in Earl Johnson to try and get the final out. The next batter was Harry Brecheen. With a slim 1-run lead and two runners on, it would not have been much of a reach to think that Dyer would go for the knockout punch by sending someone up to pinch-hit for Brecheen. But he didn't. That's how hot a hand Brecheen had at that time. Dyer had so much confidence in Harry that he liked his chances better with Brecheen pitching the 9th with a 1-run lead than his chances with someone else pitching with a 2 or 3-run cushion. Johnson got Harry to bounce out, so our guys piled into the dugout for the final inning.

Before I recount our final at-bat of 1946, let me take a moment to reflect on the catastrophic events of the bottom of the 8th inning. It started with an ironic twist when DiMaggio tied the game with his 2-run double in the top of the 8th. There would have been no need for "Slaughter's Mad Dash" had Dom not tied the game. But when Dom pulled a muscle and had to leave the game on the play, we lost a great advantage on defense in center. Culberson was certainly an adequate centerfielder, and this is not intended to be a knock against him, but he was no Dom DiMaggio. Heck, nobody was. Dom was simply as good as it got at that very important position. And that's where our problems on the play began — in centerfield. Drebinger was right when he wrote, "it didn't seem possible that Slaughter could score on the hit." That's because Drebinger was used to seeing DiMaggio quickly cut off hits like that, thus preventing the runners from taking the extra base.

But it was Culberson who fielded Walker's hit, not Dom. And Leon did not exactly get to the ball and get it in very quickly. Drebinger summed it up this way — "While Culberson fielded it well enough, little Dominic might have managed it better and kept Slaughter on third." Enos was certainly aware that Dom was no longer in the outfield, and there's no doubt that he factored that into his decision to round third and continue to home. Plus, at that stage of the Series, Slaughter was simply a man on a mission. In addition to his many great catches in rightfield, he'd hit the ball very well. But his Series almost came to an end when he was hit on the elbow by a pitch in Game Five. Enos was forced out of that game because of the injury, but he played through severe pain in order to be in the line-up for Games Six and Seven — and it paid off. Slaughter, in the locker room after the game, described the desperation he felt to score when he said, "I just had to run, that's all. I just dug in and tore for home. I had to make it. It was the Sox's responsibility to head me off. The odds were riding with me."

The last major ingredient of the play was Pesky's relay home. In the *New York Times'* play-by-play description of the play, they wrote, "Apparently, not thinking that Slaughter would try for home, Pesky hesitated with the ball long enough for Slaughter to slide ahead of his frenzied delayed throw to the plate." Johnny was a standup guy in the clubhouse after the game, and he tried to accept full responsibility for allowing Enos to score. "I'm the goat," he told reporters, "I never expected he'd try to score. I couldn't hear anybody hollering at me above the noise of the crowd. I gave Slaughter at least six strides with the delay. I know I could have nailed him if I had suspected he would try for the plate. I'm the goat, make no mistake about that."

Believe me, the sportswriters wasted no time in taking Johnny up on his offer to label him the goat. They took the theme and ran with it, implanting the notion in the mind of every Red Sox fan from that point on. The old films support the assertion that Johnny hesitated before throwing, but I think he was being overly noble when he accepted full responsibility. One can not undervalue Johnny's comment that he, taking the relay with his back to the infield, could not hear anything due to the crowd noise. Had he heard a teammate hollering, "CUT HOME!" then perhaps he could have turned and instantly fired a strike to the plate. Of course, Partee, fresh in the game after sitting out the first seven innings, would have then had to block the plate, catch the ball, and apply the tag. That's what it would have taken to get Slaughter — a perfect catch, a perfect throw, and a perfect tag — none of which were guaranteed even had Johnny made the throw without delay. We know no one in the ballpark expected Slaughter to run for home. Knowing that, and knowing that Johnny could not hear the commands of his teammates if any were being yelled at all, how can anyone expect Johnny to have been ready to immediately fire the ball to the plate upon spinning and visually assessing the scenario? He had to visually process what was going on and THEN throw home — hence the delay — and by the time he did that, it was too late. I guess what I'm getting at is that on that play Johnny was between the proverbial rock and a hard place. There's no way he should ever have had to wear the goat horns by himself.

Nope, it was a total team effort. Boo shares responsibility by not pitching a shutout. Klinger shares responsibility for allowing Slaughter to open the inning with a single. Dom shares responsibility for getting hurt. Culberson shares responsibility for not being as good as DiMaggio. Johnny shares responsibility for not nailing Enos at the plate. And, most importantly, the whole club shares responsibility for not scoring enough runs so that it didn't come down to this. I share some responsibility, too. Sure, I was sitting on the bench, but maybe I could have noticed something that could have helped us get another run here or there. Maybe I could have spotted something in Brecheen's delivery — something that could help a teammate get a key hit. But I didn't. In that respect, it was a total team breakdown — in addition to the Cardinals simply getting the job done — that put us in the predicament of trailing by a run as we headed into the last inning of Game Seven of the 1946 World Series.

Harry Brecheen, now in a position to win his third game of the Series, was still on the mound as we opened up the top of the 9th. And it looked for a moment as if Dyer may have gone to the well one too many times when he stayed with Brecheen. Rudy led off by bouncing a single past Kurowski into left-field. That represented the tying run, so the situation called for Cronin to insert a pinch-runner for the slow-running York. I anticipated that Joe might call on me, and I was ready, but he instead opted to send in Paul Campbell, a first baseman who could stay in the game in place of Rudy should we tie the score. Doerr hit next, singling into left with Campbell stopping at second. Pinky Higgins attempted to sacrifice next, but Kurowski was able to force Doerr at second. With runners at first and third with just one out, we were now in a great position to at least tie the score. But Brecheen was up to the task, and he got Partee to pop out to Musial in foul territory. The pitcher's slot was the next up, so Cronin sent Tom McBride up to pinch-hit for Johnson. Representing our last chance, McBride rolled to Schoendienst who tossed underhand to Marion covering second to force Higgins — ending the Series.

A roar went up from the St. Louis fans as the Cardinal players rushed to Brecheen and lifted him on their shoulders and carried him from the field. The whole ballpark was a scene of total joy and celebration. Almost total. Quietly, our ballclub retreated to the clubhouse under a mood of complete desolation. Cronin was downcast and in no mood to hide his feelings. He did his best, however, to be gracious to the sportswriters, saying, "We were beaten by a good ballclub. I have no alibis. We played our best and it just wasn't good enough. That about explains it. They're a great defensive ballclub. That Slaughter, Moore, and Walker are about the best outfield around right now. Three catches beat us today. Moore made two of them, one on Williams in the 1st and the other on Higgins in the 5th. Walker made the other on Williams in the 4th. Any one of them was good for three bases if it got through. Ferriss had stuff, he was all right. Maybe he didn't have the stuff he had in Boston, but we couldn't get a hit when we needed it."

After speaking his piece, Joe headed over to the Cardinals clubhouse to offer his congratulations to Dyer. Meanwhile, Red Sox general manager Eddie Collins, the once-great player for the White Sox and Athletics, came in and tried to cheer us up. Team owner Tom Yawkey came in, too, also attempting to lift our spirits. We were inconsolable, though. Losing that Series in that way was just too bitter. It was a heart-wrenching feeling that only the passing of time would ease. While we all shared feelings of great loss, my emotions were probably a bit different than those of the rest of the guys. I'd felt the pain of a World Series loss just two years earlier with the Browns, but it was much different. Sure, we were upset at losing the 1944 Series, but the feeling wasn't quite the same as the depth of the pain here. The Browns were so happy just to be in the '44 Series that our loss didn't carry the same impact as the Boston loss. In fact, beating the Yankees for the American League pennant in 1944 was actually bigger to the Browns than the World Series itself, if you can believe that. That was much different with the 1946 Sox. We'd run away with the pennant and were heavily favored in the Series. The Boston fans were desperate for a title, and our failure to deliver it weighed heavily.

Still, we appreciated Collins and Mr. Yawkey's efforts to make us feel better. In fact, it was Mr. Yawkey for whom I felt particularly bad about losing the Series. He was a wonderful man and all of the players really loved him. He wanted a winning ballclub and was willing to pay for it. The 1946 Red Sox were the culmination of that. Mr. Yawkey had paid his players well — like REAL ballplayers should be paid. Many critics would say that he overpaid his players. They said that the players' contentment led to complacency and softness, something that would never allow the Red Sox to win a championship under Mr. Yawkey. I was disappointed that our loss in the Series would lead the critics to continue their criticism of Mr. Yawkey's style. The critics' theory was preposterous in my opinion. I believe that Mr. Yawkey's generosity had the complete opposite effect on players — we played even harder for him because we cared for him. I stand as a case in point. A full World Series share for our club was $2,052 per man. The team voted me a half share since I hadn't joined them until July. I felt that was perfectly fair, so I was absolutely happy with my $1,026 Series check. Do you know that on the first opportunity he had, Mr. Yawkey called me into his office and wrote me a personal check for the other half share? He said, "Don, you worked hard and you deserve it." How could you not want to do anything for a man like that? And that's how everybody felt about Mr. Yawkey, but unfortunately he never got his World Series.

Boston, on the other hand, did eventually get their World Series title — but not until 58 years later in 2004. It's hard to imagine that it took that long. And while Boston waited all those years for its title, Johnny Pesky waited, too. Year in and year out, he had to listen to people continually bringing up his "held ball." Still, Johnny never got bitter or jaded. He did everything the Boston franchise asked of him, from coaching to managing to hitting fungos. And he did all — and still does it — because he loves the Boston Red Sox. Hopefully, now that Boston finally has a champion, people will forget about Johnny's held ball of 1946 and simply remember him for the great player he was and the fine person that he is.

That's me placing the tag on Phil Rizzuto who'd gotten hung up in a rundown. Helping me on the play is shortstop Johnny Pesky, a great ballplayer and a great guy. Johnny is one of the fellows who made my years in Boston so enjoyable.

1 9 4 7

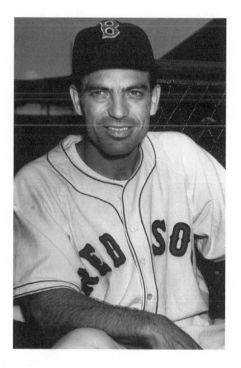

APRIL 15, 1947: I was 34 years of age when we closed out the 1946 season, so there was doubt in my mind as to whether I would be back with the Red Sox — or any big league club, for that mater — in 1947. But here I was on this day, again a member of the Red Sox as we got set to open up the season with a home game against the Senators. I knew my role on the team would be limited, but I was, nonetheless, thrilled to still be a player in the big show. I knew my days were numbered, so I was determined to enjoy every remaining moment that I had as a big leaguer.

As would be the case in about two-thirds of the games from our '47 campaign, I would not play in this game. But it was opening day and I could enjoy it from the dugout. Opening day was always something I loved because it signi-fied the end of the cold, dreary winter, and the beginning of a warm summer of baseball. It was usually NOT warm on opening day, but the beginning of the baseball season let everyone know that summer was right around the corner. There was still a chill in the Boston air as we got ready to start the game, but there was still the matter of some pre-game festivities. Following some musical entertainment from a local band, a Marine guard hoisted the American flag up the centerfield flagpole. That received only polite applause from the 31,000 Sox fans in attendance. In what could only be classified as out-of-kilter priorities, Old Glory was then out-cheered by Joe Cronin raising the big blue and white pennant symbolic of our 1946 American League championship. It was proof to anyone who ever doubted that Boston fans take their Red Sox very seriously. But those fans had waited a long time for this ceremony, the last time coming on opening day of the 1919 season. Those same fans, however, were known to be somewhat superstitious. While the Stars and Stripes had slid smoothly up the pole, Cronin had a bit of trouble with the pennant banner. It got all caught up in its own stubborn folds as Joe wrestled with it, trying to shake it loose. It was

I was happy when Joe Cronin, Red Sox general manager, informed me that I was a part of their 1947 plans, so I went to spring training and did my usual thing — hustle. Here, in a spring training game against the Yankees in Sarasota, Florida, I hustled after hitting a ground ball, but I was still out as Snuffy Stirnweiss turned the double-play. That's Eddie Pellagrini sliding into second, and the umpire is Bill Grieve.

on the unsightly side as it attempted to unfurl, and some of the superstitious fans joked that it was a bad omen for the 1947 season. Maybe they were right, as the season would prove to be a frustration for us.

There was no frustration for us on this day, however. After Governor Robert Bradford threw out the first pitch, we rewarded our fans with an exciting 7-6 win. Tex Hughson looked to be in midseason form, setting down the first 15 Nats he faced. In the meantime, we'd jumped on the scoreboard with a 2nd inning solo homer from Eddie Pellagrini. Eddie was a funny, friendly and out-going guy. He was little — smaller than me — so he wasn't really a long ball threat, but he'd homered in his first major league at-bat with the Red Sox early in the 1946 season. He only appeared in a few more games before being shipped back down to the minors that year, but he was back with the big club for anoth-er trial in 1947. Pinky Higgins had retired in the offseason, so the front office was hoping that Eddie would be able to replace Pinky at third base. And if Eddie would have had more games like this one, he probably would have been a main-stay in the Red Sox line-up for many years. Tex got knocked out of the box in the 8th, and a 4-run Washington rally in the top of the 9th tied the score at 6-6. But Eddie opened the bottom of the 9th by beating out an infield hit. He then went to second on a sacrifice by Johnny Pesky, moved to third on a wild pitch, and scored the winning run on a long fly to center by Dom DiMaggio. It was a great way to kick off our defense of our American League title.

APRIL 20, 1947: We'd won three more games in a row following our opening day victory, so we were feeling pretty good about ourselves as we arrived in Washington on this day to play the Senators. We'd played two games in Philadelphia prior to coming to D.C., and while in Philly Bobby Doerr had come down with the flu. So I got my feet wet on this day for the first time in '47, leading off and playing second base for Bobby. On the mound we had a promising young left-hander from New Orleans named Mel Parnell. It was his big league debut. Mel demonstrated all the stuff that would make him a great pitcher in the future, but not until after he had been nicked for three 1st-inning runs. He regained his composure, though, and pitched through the 7th inning. All in all, and considering the nervousness that comes with making your first appearance in the majors, I'd say it was a fine effort on Mel's part. He took the loss, 3-1, but mainly because we couldn't get any runs for him. The man on the hill for the Senators was right-hander Walt Masterson. Some of the guys called him "Frog Eyes" because he wore glasses, but ol' Frog Eyes had the last laugh on this day as he held us to just three hits. I wish I could say that I had one of our three safeties, but I didn't. I was 0-for-4 on the day.

APRIL 22, 1947: Bobby Doerr was still out with the flu, so I got a second straight start at second base as we opened up a 3-game set at Yankee Stadium. We got homers from Ted Williams, Sam Mele, and Rudy York while Joe

Dobson, Earl Johnson, and Harry Dorish combined to limit the Yankees to just three hits. Only one of those Yankee hits made it past the infield — yet we managed to lose the ballgame, 5-4. That's baseball for you. It's really no mystery, I guess. Poorly timed walks and a poorly timed error are what did us in. They'll kill you almost every time. Our bats had still not caught up with the pitching at this early point of the season, and we collected just seven hits in this game. My bat definitely had not caught up yet, and for the second game in a row I went hitless — 0-for-4 again. It was frustrating to be given a chance to help out in Bobby's absence, yet come up empty — a frustration made all the more painful when Joe Cronin felt the need to have Wally Moses pinch-hit for me in the 9th.

Incidentally, this game featured our first look at the Yankees utilizing the "Williams Shift." We'd seen it in the Philadelphia series prior to coming to New York, and believe me, Ted wasn't happy to see this thing spreading. First Cleveland, then the Cardinals in the 1946 World Series, and now the Athletics and Yankees. The shift robbed him of a hit on this day, too, in the 5th inning, but it was useless against Ted's mammoth wallop into the upper rightfield deck in the 3rd inning. Ted spoke to reporters about the shift following the game, saying, "I'm much more relaxed about the shift than I was a year ago. It bothered me, to put it frankly, but it doesn't anymore. Now I think it's a lot of fun. They tried it in Philadelphia and I cracked two doubles right where someone should have been playing but wasn't. I'll hit to left on them to make them honest. I tried to beat down the challenge last year, but this season I'll outsmart it." Hearing that, a smiling Rudy York skeptically said, "The reformation of Ted Williams." Ted, also laughing, validated Rudy's skepticism by saying, "But every time I look at the 294-foot sign on that rightfield stand out there I weaken slightly in my good resolutions." Hearing the discussion and knowing that Ted Williams would never bow to the shift, Dom DiMaggio closed the topic by saying, "The same old Ted Williams."

APRIL 23, 1947: For the third straight game, I started in place of Bobby Doerr who was still sick with the flu — and once again I was collared with an 0-for-4. It was frustrating. After opening the season with a 4-game winning streak, we'd now followed with three straight defeats as we again lost to New York on this day, shutout by a score of 3-0 at Yankee Stadium. I'm sure it was just coincidence, but our 3-game losing streak directly coincided with my three starts. On the one hand I wanted Bobby to hurry up and get healthy because he was a key element in our offense getting off the ground, but at the same time I wanted another chance to try and atone for my lack of hitting in my three games. It was a dilemma common to utility players like me. In order for a utility man to get a chance, a frontline player must go down. But if a frontline player goes down, then your team's line-up has decreased potential. It was sort of a catch-22. At any rate, it wasn't just me who was not hitting in this game. In fact, the Yanks' Allie

Reynolds was so dominant that he allowed just two hits on the day — both collected by Rudy York.

With Bobby Doerr sick with the flu, I got my third straight start at second base in this game, a 3-0 loss to New York at Yankee Stadium on April 23rd, 1947. This play took place in the bottom of the 8th. George McQuinn, my old Brownie teammate, was now playing with the Yanks, and he'd singled to the corner in rightfield. George tried to stretch it to a double, but Same Mele made a great throw and I tagged him out. The umpire making the call is Art Passarella.

APRIL 26, 1947: Speaking of Rudy York, he had quite a day on April 26, 1947. We'd returned home to Boston the day before to open a 3-game series against the Philadelphia A's at Fenway Park. After dropping the opener, 11-7, we were hoping to get a win in the second tilt on this day. Rudy, legendary in his ability to tilt the bottle, had done just that in the evening following our loss in the series opener. He'd returned to our hotel in the wee hours of the morning, then proceeded to do what he always did at that time — sit on his bed and smoke a cigarette until he got sleepy. The problem was that Rudy sometimes wasn't finished with his cigarette when he fell asleep. Because of that he'd been setting small hotel fires since his days with the Tigers back in the 1930's. But the fire he set on this early morning wasn't small. He didn't burn down the hotel, but he came darn close. Here's what the United Press wrote about it — "YORK SMOKED OUT BY FIRE. Rudy York, the Boston Red Sox's slugging first baseman, nearly was overcome by smoke and 450 guests were routed from their beds at the Myles Standish Hotel early today when fire swept the player's room. Dazed by the smoke, York staggered toward the door of his chamber and was led to safety by Benjamin Petruzzi, night engineer of the apartment hotel. Petruzzi had been notified by a guest that there was the odor of smoke in the building and made his way to the second floor. A doctor was summoned and said that York had suffered only slight smoke inhalation and was not burned. Believed to have started from a smoldering cigarette, the flames destroyed virtually everything in York's room."

Rudy was a tough guy, so he wasn't about to let a little thing like nearly getting killed in a hotel fire keep him out of our game on this day. He even man-aged to get a hit, the Associated Press writing, "Rudy York, who was let out of his smoke-filled room early in the morning, got one of the six Boston hits, a sharp single in the 9th." Even a tough guy like Rudy needed a break, however, so Joe Cronin pulled him out and sent me in to pinch-run for him. I was left stranded and we lost the game, 5-2, but it was really a day to remember. Some time later I was in the hotel lobby with Helen and our son, Don Jr., when we ran into Rudy. To the shock of Helen and me, Don Jr. asked him, "Mr. York, did you get yourself burned when you set the hotel on fire?" Don Jr. was just an innocent 4-year old, so he had no idea of the awkwardness of his question, but Helen and I just about fainted. Rudy was good-natured, though, so he took no offense, telling Don Jr., "No, son, I got out okay."

APRIL 30, 1947: Joe Dobson plunked Bobby Doerr on the elbow during bat-ting practice prior to our game against Detroit at Briggs Stadium on this day. Joe Cronin told me that Bobby couldn't play, so he was putting me in there to fill in. I had yet to get another at-bat since my three straight 0-for-4 games, so I was hoping that I would break out of it today. It didn't happen. Batting out of the number seven slot, I went 0-for-5 against Hal Newhouser and Art Houtteman. Now I was 0-for-17 on the season and desperate to get a hit — any kind of hit. As with most slumps, it was a combination of being "off" as well as suffering bad luck. In that 0-for-17 there were strikeouts, pop-ups and dribblers, but there were also a few hard hit balls that went right to defenders. It didn't matter, though. All anyone remembered at the end of the day was that you were 0-fer. It wasn't all bad, though. We got back in the win column for the first time in five games. Also in the win column for the first time in his career was Mel Parnell who pitched beautifully, a complete game 7-1 victory. Mel would go on to win 122 more games in his 10-year career, all with the Sox. He would lose just 75.

MAY 13, 1947: Bobby Doerr's bad elbow forced him to miss only the April 30th game, so my services weren't needed for quite some time. In fact, it would be nearly one month before I would get into another game in any capacity. In the meantime, I tried to stay ready while taking in the action from the bench. If you like offense, our game on this day against the White Sox at Fenway Park was one for the ages. Our bats had recently come to life, slugging us to six wins in our last seven games, but we really outdid ourselves on this day, pounding Chicago, 19-6. It was the most runs we'd score in any game all season. Everybody in our line-up got in on the hitting action except for poor Hal Wagner and relief pitch-er Bill Zuber. Particularly prolific was Doerr who hit for the cycle and Eddie Pellagrini who drove in four runs.

It was a Ted Williams subplot, however, that really had the people buzzing. Ted and Joe Dobson had visited an 11-year old youngster in Malden Hospital before the game. The boy's name was Glenny Brann, and he was recovering from a horrific accident that had resulted in the amputation of both of his legs. Ted and Joe chatted with the boy, then gave him a ball and bat to try and lift his spirits. As they were leaving the boy asked Ted to hit a home run. An 11-year old in pain has no idea how difficult it is for a ballplayer — even one of Ted's ability — to hit a home run on command. Certainly this young boy had heard stories about Babe Ruth doing it, so why not Ted? "I'll try, Glenny," Ted told him, "and if I do you'll know I hit it for you." What Glenny didn't know was that Ted had actually pulled off the feat just a month and a half earlier as we were wrapping up spring training. We were in Chattanooga to play the Reds in an exhibition game as we worked our way north for the opening of the regular season. While there Ted had promised another boy that he'd do his best to hit a homer for him — and Ted delivered.

It wasn't widely known at that time just how much Ted loved visiting hospitalized children. He did it quite often because it made him feel good to put a smile on the face of a sick child. Amazingly, Ted liked to keep it out of the public eye. Despite the fact that many of the sportswriters had painted him as a selfish problem child, Ted did not want his hospital visits used as a tool to rehabilitate his image. But even Ted couldn't keep his visit to Glenny Brann out of the papers — especially after he hit not one but two homers in our game on this day. Someone, knowing that this accomplishment was something truly special, leaked the story to the writers and then it was all over the sportspages. I know it sounds like a Hollywood movie, but it really happened. I'm sure there were probably many occasions when an ailing youngster asked Ted to hit a home run for him and Ted couldn't do it. But on this day it was a dream come true for a sick kid — and Ted Williams, whose broad smile could be seen all over Fenway Park as he triumphantly rounded the bases following his two round-trippers for Glenny Brann.

MAY 25, 1947: The New York Yankees put a real whipping on us on this day at Yankee Stadium, defeating us by a score of 17-2. It was an all-around terrible team effort in all phases of the game — offense, defense, and pitching. With a thumping like this taking place, Joe Cronin figured it was as good a time as any to give me a little playing time while giving Bobby Doerr a rest. He probably regretted his decision. I had not played in the last 19 ballgames, and my rust showed itself immediately as I added a throwing error to the other four errors committed by my teammates. It had been a long time since I'd batted, but I still had that 0-for-17 hanging over my head. By the time the game ended my slump had been extended to 0-for-18. Yes, it was definitely a rough time I was going through here in 1947, but the good news was that I had bottomed out and things would soon turn better for me.

MAY 29, 1947: As we loosened up to play the Athletics in the final game of a 3-game series at Shibe Park on this day, Joe Cronin informed me that I would be starting at second base in place of Bobby Doerr who had wrenched his back the day before. Me and my 0-for-18, batting seventh and playing second base. As I sat in the dugout watching tall Philadelphia right-hander Bob Savage fire his warmup pitches into the mitt of his catcher Buddy Rosar, I couldn't help but think of my hitting woes so far. I was due — big time. All I needed was one hit — any kind of hit. A bloop, a flair, a Texas Leaguer, a seeing-eye grounder — it didn't matter. I just needed a hit and I didn't care what kind. Savage retired me my first time up to run my slump to 0-for-19. But I felt good as I ran back to the dugout because I had seen the ball well. When I faced Savage again in the 5th, I unloaded a month-and-a-half's worth of frustration on one of his fastballs — a long solo homer into the Shibe Park seats. It felt like a great weight had been lifted off my shoulders as I circled the bases. I was disappointed that we lost the game, wasting a good pitching performance by Harry Dorish, but on a personal level I felt good about the way I had swung the bat that day and I felt it boded well for me down the road.

One of my key responsibilities with the Red Sox was to be ready in the event that our star second baseman, Bobby Doerr, needed me to spell him for whatever reason. In this photo I can be seen trotting out to replace Bobby after he'd been hit in the elbow by a pitched ball.

MAY 30, 1947: Bobby Doerr's bad back kept him out of the next five games, and I subbed for him at second in each game starting with our twin bill against the Senators at Griffith Stadium on this day. In fact, our game the day before kicked off a period in which I would start 25 consecutive games. I didn't know it at the time, but it would amount to the last significant period of playing time for me in my big league career. As I mentioned, Bobby only missed six games with his back spasms. The rest of my run as a starter came as Joe Cronin tried to shake up the line-up a bit. I hit in all six games that I subbed for Bobby, so Joe wanted to keep my bat in the line-up while it was hot. Earlier in the month Joe had moved Eddie Pellagrini to short while shifting Johnny Pesky over to third. But Eddie failed to hit consistently in either spot, so Joe benched him, sending Johnny back to short and inserting Rip Russell at third. But Rip had also failed to hit, so when Bobby's back was well enough that he was able play, Joe moved me over to third and benched Rip. It was like musical chairs, but it ended up allowing me to play regularly.

So, back to our doubleheader against the Nats on this day. It didn't go well as we got swept, 13-6 and 5-3. Tex Hughson and Mel Parnell got knocked around in the opener, and Joe Dobson, Earl Johnson, and Johnny Murphy got roughed up in the nightcap. After singling and scoring in four at-bats out of the number seven slot in the first game, Joe moved me to the lead-off spot in the second game — and I picked up another single. I remained in my familiar lead-off spot for the duration of my month-long stay as a regular — it was like old times.

Eddie Pellagrini spent the bulk of his playing time in 1947 at third base, but he was occasionally used at shortstop, as was the case here where we combined on a double-play. The Yankee baserunner is Joe DiMaggio.

JUNE 2, 1947: We split a doubleheader with the White Sox at Comiskey Park on this day. Boo Ferriss was his usual rock-solid self in the opener, pitching us to a 6-2 victory. He helped us win the game with his bat, too, which wasn't uncommon for him. Boo was a big, strong, strapping guy — a solid 6-foot-2 and 210-pounds. He swung such a potent stick that he was often called on to pinch-hit in games when he wasn't pitching. He pinch-hit in this day's nightcap, in fact. But it was in the opener that he wrecked havoc on the White Sox pitching staff with his lumber, banging out a single and a 3-run triple to catapult him to his fourth triumph of the season. I chipped in a single and a run to help Boo's cause, but as you can see, when Boo was right he didn't need much help.

The nightcap was a little more eventful, as least as far as my involvement was concerned, but not all of my action was of the good variety. I'd walked to open the game, then scored on a double by Wally Moses. But in the bottom of the 1st I allowed a run to score when I threw wide of first base while trying to turn a double-play. I have to admit that it was taking me a while to shake off the rust from my defensive game, and my wild heave meant that I'd now erred in three of my last four games. I added a single and a stolen base in my next at-bat, and we were tied, 4-4, when things got interesting in the bottom of the 5th. It's at that point that a football game broke out at second base as I again tried to turn a double-play. And when you weigh only 165 pounds, such as I did, you usually lose in a football game. Here's how Irving Vaughan of the *Chicago Tribune* described the play — "With one out in the home half of the 5th, Thurman Tucker walked and Jack Wallesa exploded a two-bagger, after which Dave Philley was purposely walked. Jake Jones grounded to Johnny Pesky, who tossed to Don Gutteridge for a force play. Gutteridge started to throw for a double-play, but just then something upset him. It was Philley. By the time Gutteridge picked himself up off the seat of his pants, Wallesa had followed Tucker across the plate for a 6 to 4 lead." Philley was a big guy when compared to me, and his "slide" just about knocked me into the outfield grass. The Associated Press described the play a little better when they wrote, "The Chicago rookie slid hard and put a football block on Gutteridge, grounding the Boston infielder as Tucker and Wallesa hurried home." Those turned out to be the winning runs for Chicago. We scored once more in the 7th inning, but lost the game, 6-5. Never let anyone ever tell you that baseball's not a contact sport.

JUNE 3, 1947: Our ballclub, at 20 wins and 20 losses, was languishing when compared to our 1946 team, and it was games like the one we played on this day that were the reason. We opened up a series against the Browns at Sportsman's Park, and St. Louis was the type of second division club that we should have gotten fat on. They had only a couple of guys who could really hurt you — my old teammate Vern Stephens and an up-and-coming kid named Bob Dillinger. Well, Tex Hughson had held both of them in check for eight innings, but with the bases loaded Tex found himself clinging to a 3-2 lead and facing Dillinger with the bases loaded. Forced to come in to Dillinger with a hitter's pitch, Dillinger lined a hit to left scoring the tying and the winning runs. It was a disheartening loss — the type of game that, more often than not, we would have won in 1946. Incidentally, this was my last day subbing for the injured Bobby Doerr, and I extended my VERY modest hitting streak to six games with a 1-for-2 against Brownie right-hander Ellis Kinder.

JUNE 4, 1947: Bobby Doerr returned to the line-up on this day for the second game of our Browns series, so I slid over to the hot corner for my 19 consecutive game stint as our regular third baseman. My mini-hitting streak came to an end, however, as I went 0-for-4 against Bob Muncrief and Browns reliever Glen Moulder, but the upside was that we won the ballgame. In fact, we did very well during my stay at third base, winning 13 of the 19 games in which I was stationed there, including eight in a row at one point. I'm sure the fact that we were winning during the time I was at third was just a coincidence, but I did manage to hit in 10 of the 19 games while committing no errors except for a rough day on June 22nd when I committed three miscues in a doubleheader against Cleveland at Fenway Park.

JUNE 8, 1947: Despite my 0-for-4 against St. Louis, I had continued to swing the bat well in that game. Bad weather kept us off the ballfield for the next three days, something that I hated to see happen when I was seeing the ball well, but the skies cleared on this day just in time for our game at Detroit. Hal Newhouser's stuff looked electric as I watched him warm up, but when I stepped in to lead off the game I was happy to find that I was still picking up the ball very well. Still, Newhouser retired me, but I tagged him for a long two-bagger the next time I faced him in the 3rd inning. The rest of the guys weren't so lucky that day, however, and Newhouser was really mowing them down. By the time I came up again in the 8th inning, we were down, 5-0, and Prince Hal had only allowed three hits. I touched him for another hit in that inning, but then he slammed the door on us to notch a complete game 4-hit shutout.

JUNE 9, 1947: The next day we were in Cleveland to open a 3-game series against the Indians. We came out on top in a slugfest, the Associated Press describing it like this — "The game developed into a home run battle with Sam Mele, Don Gutteridge and Bobby Doerr slamming four-baggers for the Sox and Hal Peck and manager Lou Boudreau hitting homers for the tribe. Indians starter Don Black was the victim of most of Boston's heavy hitting. Black was removed in the 3rd after giving up five runs and five hits, including the homers by Gutteridge and Doerr." That turned out to be my last big league home run, something I had no way of knowing as I stepped on Municipal Stadium's home plate after making my circuit. It had been a long time since I'd hit my first home run against Brooklyn's Max Butcher way back in 1936, and while I'd hit only 38 more since that first one, they were all very special. There are many different things that gave me immense pleasure in baseball — making a great defensive play or stealing a base, just to name a couple. But it's hard to top the feeling that surges through your body when you know you've just connected for a round-tripper. I guess that's why, thanks to Babe Ruth, the home run has come to be baseball's most glamorous accomplishment. Who knows — had I known this was my last career 4-bagger, I may have bent down and kissed the plate. Probably not, though — putting on a spectacle like would have definitely landed me on my backside the next time I came up to hit!

JUNE 15, 1947: The White Sox had come to Boston for a 3-game series two days earlier. I took an 0-for-4 collar as we beat them in the opener, 5-3, then we were rained out the next day. The day off gave Chicago general manager Leslie O'Connor, who'd accompanied the White Sox to Boston, a chance to pow-wow with Red Sox general manager Eddie Collins. O'Connor wanted power, Collins wanted speed. By the time we took the field for a doubleheader on this day, Rudy York was wearing the road gray of the Chisox and Jake Jones was sporting the home whites of the Boston Red Sox. All they did was change clubhouses. Rudy was struggling at the plate this year, hitting just a tad over .200 with only few home runs. Joe Cronin thought Rudy would be served well by a change of scenery, telling reporters, "It's funny how human nature is. Last year I took York in the expectation of getting only one year out of him. But he did so well that I started to hope that perhaps I could squeeze still another good season out of him. But then I began to doubt it. The big Indian just wasn't going to repeat." It's always kind of sad to see a teammate go, but you get used to it in baseball. When I heard about the trade I couldn't help but think of how we would miss Rudy's bat. What we wouldn't miss, however, were the hotel fires!

Once the twin bill got under way, Jake Jones did his best to make everyone at Fenway forget about the loss of Rudy's power. While I was struggling at the plate, collecting just one hit in eight at-bats, Jake had a field day. Supposedly brought in to add to our team speed, Jake showed that he was bringing some pop, too, as he hit home runs in both ends of the doubleheader. In the 7th inning of the opener he lifted an Orval Grove pitch into the leftfield screen as we won, 7-3. He outdid himself in the nightcap, however, when he socked a 2-out 9th-inning grand slam that provided the margin of victory as we again won, 8-4. He finished with six RBIs in the game. It was amazing. What a debut. He was truly the hero of the city — for a day, at least. Jake was an American hero, too — he'd been a fighter pilot in World War II. From what I heard, Jake had bagged six Japanese planes in combat, four of them coming during the Battle of Tokyo while he was serving on the carrier Enterprise.

JUNE 17, 1947: I came up with a 2-hit game against the Browns as we edged them, 6-5, on this day. While it had been just 2-1/2 short years since I had celebrated an American League pennant with them, there were just two of the old guys left in their starting line-up — Vern Stephens and Al Zarilla. The new faces weren't helping the situation there, either, and the Brownies had sunk back down to their losing ways. Denny Galehouse entered the game as a reliever in the 3rd inning, and it was he who served up my two hits — a double and a single. My old ballclub got even with me the next day, however, as Bob Muncrief and Ellis Kinder combined to saddle me with a 1-for-8. That'll put a hurting on your average real quick. Fortunately, we won the game — a 15-inning 6-5 thriller.

JUNE 21, 1947: There's nothing like a multi-hit game to help you forget the agony of going 0-fer the day before. That's what happened on this day as I collected two hits while scoring two runs in our 9-1 romp over Cleveland. The day before I was hitless as we lost, 3-2. My action was described this way by the Associated Press — "Doerr's four-run wallop came in the 1st after Don Gutteridge opened with a single to left and Feller jammed the sacks by passing Johnny Pesky and Ted Williams. Gutteridge started off the 4th with another safe drive into left and scored on a Pesky two-bagger." Joe Dobson, incidentally, was in top form while going the distance.

JUNE 23, 1947: We continued to play good ball, surging into 2nd place as we defeated the Tigers, 8-2, at Fenway. The whole team hit well in this game, and I threw in two singles, a stolen base, and four runs scored. "The eighth and final run came in the 5th," wrote the Associated Press, "when Don Gutteridge singled, stole second, and sped home on Sam Mele's rightfield hit." Reading that — hit, steal, score — almost made me feel like I was 10 years younger and back with the Gas House Gang.

JUNE 27, 1947: Like the month of March, my run as an everyday player with the 1947 Boston Red Sox came in like a lion and went out like a lamb. My bat had quieted a bit in the second half of my 25-game stint, and our game against the Senators at Griffith Stadium on this day was my last as a regular. I drew an 0-for-3 off Nats starter Mickey Haefner, and we lost the game, 3-0. The next day Joe Cronin would return to Eddie Pellagrini as his man at third base — and I would return to the bench.

JULY 14, 1947: I played the role of Red Sox fan on this day as I, from my seat on the bench, cheered on my ballclub to what turned out be perhaps one of the most bittersweet Boston victories ever. Boo Ferriss, the 25-year old young man with the bright present and even brighter future, the fellow who'd been so dominant in 1945 and 1946, was gunning for his eighth victory as we took on the Indians at Municipal Stadium in Cleveland. It would be no easy task for big Boo, though, because he was matched up against maybe the hottest pitcher in baseball — Don Black, the tribe right-hander who'd no-hit the Philadelphia Athletics a few days earlier in his previous start. The game delivered what it had promised — a classic pitcher's duel. Both guys went the distance, but Boo came out on top with a 1-0 win thanks to a dramatic 9th-inning solo homer by Bobby Doerr.

It was a heroic performance by Boo, especially considering the circumstances NOT shown in the box score. Despite the fact that it was mid-July, it was a chilly and damp night at Cleveland's huge stadium next to Lake Erie. It's possible that the weather may have played a role in what happened. Boo was cruising along when he suddenly found himself in a jam with two outs, runners on, and Indians rightfielder Catfish Metkovich the batter. Metkovich worked the count full, then waited to see what Boo was going to throw him. Everyone waited. All the players, ushers, coaches, groundskeepers — you name it, not to mention the 20,789 fans who'd paid to get in. Boo was so good that he could throw any pitch for a strike in any count. Metkovich, however, was sitting dead red, and when Boo surprised him with his overhand curve, Catfish went down on strikes.

We all offered praise to Boo for getting out of the fix when he sat down in the dugout, but he did not look happy. In fact, he seemed preoccupied, working his arm around with a concerned look on his face. When asked what was the matter, Boo said that he'd felt a "snap" in his shoulder as he threw the overhand curve to Metkovich. He said pain shot through his arm, and then it went numb. So what did he do? The same thing 99 percent of all pitchers back then would have done — he went back out and completed the game. Boo wasn't the same, though. He was in trouble again in the 8th and 9th, surviving both scares on sheer guts and smarts. Boo got his eighth win on this day, but it was a costly one. He'd won 54 games in his short 2-1/2-year career up through his 1-0 win over Cleveland, but he would win only 11 more big league ballgames.

Boo's shoulder injury, something that could have been easily repaired in today's age of advanced orthopedic surgery, turned out to be the only foe that the big guy couldn't whip. They futilely massaged Boo's arm with rubbing alcohol after the game and told him to "wear a coat." Boo couldn't even lift his arm the next day. Still, despite his pain, he continued to take his turn in the rotation, but he no longer had that hop on his fastball. "You either pitched or you went home," he said, "and I was where I wanted to be. I wasn't ready to go home." And that's how most guys thought back then. You knew you were expendable, so you played through injuries. Boo was able to scratch out four more wins before finally being forced out of the rotation from late-August through the season's end. He struggled to a 7-and-3 record with the 1948 Sox, then spent a couple years trying to hang on in the minors. Boo dealt with his bad break like the true gentleman he was. He showed no bitterness, and eventually resigned himself to the reality of his predicament by hanging up his spikes. He forged ahead with a job as Red Sox pitching coach, and then proved what a winner he was by taking on a job as athletic director and baseball coach at Delta State University in Cleveland, Mississippi. He built their baseball program from nothing, literally carving their stadium out of a bean field — a stadium that now bears his name. He coached there for 26 years, winning 639 games against 387 defeats. I was thrilled when I heard that Delta State won the 2004 NCAA Division-II national championship — and even more thrilled when I heard that Boo was in the stands to see it in person. Dave Boo Ferriss was, and still is, a class individual.

AUGUST 28, 1947: Baseball, unlike, say, working at a filling station (something I did during the off-season one year), can raise your emotions like nothing else, and our game against the Tigers at Briggs Stadium on this day illustrates it to perfection. I didn't play, but from my seat in the dugout I saw Hal Newhouser break one of baseball's unwritten rules — DO NOT openly challenge the manager's authority in front of a stadium full of onlookers. The game was tied, 1-1, in the 3rd inning when the trouble began for Prince Hal. All of a sudden, he couldn't get anyone out. With two outs and five runs in, Detroit manager Steve O'Neill had seen enough. As was his method, O'Neill signaled from the dugout that Newhouser was through for the day. As was also their custom, third baseman George Kell then went over to Newhouser to take the ball while the reliever came in from the pen. It's then that Newhouser snapped. He suddenly asked plate umpire Joe Rue for anther ball, and Rue tossed him one. Newhouser then began rubbing the ball down as he walked back to the rubber. At that moment, in a rage, O'Neill, came charging out of the dugout. O'Neill was usually a low-key type, but he had managed a long time in addition to having played 17 years in the majors, so he knew this flagrant display of insubordination had to be dealt with harshly.

Newhouser had always had a reputation as being temperamental ever since he'd broken in back in 1939, but his brilliant run from 1944 through '46, seasons in which he'd won 29, 25, and 26 games respectively, had relegated discussion of his tantrums to the backburner. But he was having a tough season in 1947, and that brought about the occasional return of his once-famous temper. Upon reaching the mound, O'Neill and Newhouser engaged in a long, heated discussion. It went on and on — O'Neil demanding that Newhouser give him the ball and head to the showers, and Newhouser stubbornly refusing. In the dugout, we couldn't believe what we were seeing. Finally, Newhouser relinquished, and stormed off to the clubhouse. It was a display that just could not be allowed, and O'Neill dealt with it quickly, announcing immediately after the game that Newhouser would be fined. The next morning's papers fleshed out the situation, reporting that O'Neill had fined Newhouser $250 for "indifference," a serious charge that accused the pitcher of not trying his best. "Hal insisted that he was trying out there," O'Neill told reporters, "but it didn't look like it to me. He was certainly pitching inferior ball. I had to take the ball away from him and get him out of there, but he simply wasn't going to leave. It didn't look good to see him arguing about being summoned to the dugout. I told him I ought to fine him $250 for the way he was acting, but he continued to argue. There wasn't anything for me to do but hang it on him." As I said, the fierce competition of baseball can make even mild-mannered guys lose their self-control, so you can imagine what it can do to someone like Newhouser, a guy already predisposed to outbursts of temper. No one held it against him. O'Neill dealt with it as he should have, and then everyone moved on — and Hal Newhouser CALMLY entered the Hall of Fame in 1992.

SEPTEMBER 5, 1947: "Don Gutteridge, subbing for Bobby Doerr who had a recurrence of his old severe headache, fumbled Elmer Valo's groundout with two out in the bottom of the 1st." That snippet is from the Associated Press' article about our 9-7 loss to the Philadelphia Athletics at Shibe Park on this day. Obviously, it's not always fun to see your name in the papers. My "fumble" led to four Athletics runs, wiping out a 1-0 lead we'd taken in the top half of the inning. I'm sure it had nothing to do with my error, but this game ended up being the last time I would ever start for the Red Sox. I appeared in just five of our last 25 games, always as a pinch-hitter, pinch-runner, or late-inning substitute. Also, I went 1-for-4 in our loss on this day, and my hit turned out to be the last one I would notch for the season. In fact, it ended up being the last safety of my big league career — hit number 1,075.

SEPTEMBER 12, 1947: We got pounded by the Indians, 11-6, in front of baseball royalty at Fenway Park on this day. There was a king on hand — the home run king himself, Babe Ruth. The Babe was in Boston, the scene of his early triumphs as a great pitcher, to present Boston University scholarships to six youths from the American Legion Junior baseball program. Everyone knew that Ruth was very ill, but he had been forging courageously ahead. Babe, once so strapping but now looking very thin and frail, made the presentations before the game, then posed for pictures with Sox general manager Eddie Collins, one of his greatest on-field adversaries, and Ted Williams, heir to his slugging crown. It was the last time I saw Ruth alive, because he died just eleven months later. I'm glad to have gotten in the game on this day, entering as a late-inning substitute for Bobby Doerr. Even today, nearly 60 years after The Bambino's passing, no one has ever surpassed the greatness of Babe Ruth.

SEPTEMBER 15, 1947: I watched us split a twin bill with the White Sox on this day at Fenway Park. Our loss in the opener made official what we'd known for a while was inevitable — we would not repeat as American League champions. With our defeat, the Yankees clinched the A.L. flag for the first time since 1943, then went on to defeat the Dodgers in the World Series, four games to three. The loser in the first game was Boo Ferriss. It was just his second start in the last three weeks, and it was tough to watch Boo struggle through his shoulder trouble. He was one tough competitor, though, and he gutted his way through eight innings, but he just didn't have anything on the ball and the White

Sox tagged him for 15 hits and six runs.

SEPTEMBER 28, 1947: We prepared to close the '47 with a game against the Senators at Griffith Stadium on this day, and I hadn't played in the last 16 games, save one appearance as a pinch-runner 10 days earlier. Our record stood at 83-and-70, a full 20 games worse than we were a year earlier prior to our last game of the '46 season. The front office could hardly be accused of standing pat following our 1946 pennant. There were at least 17 players from our '46 roster who did not return in 1947, not to mention a few who were traded or released during the course of the '47 campaign. That said, however, we went in to '47 relying on the same core of guys that had led us to the flag in '46. But, when you got right down to it, we simply did not play as well in 1947 as we had in 1946 in all facets of the game, and our record reflected the drop-off in our performance. We lost the final game of '47, 5-1, stifled by Washington's Mickey Haefner. I went into the game as a late-inning sub for Bobby Doerr at second base, and failed to hit Haefner in my only at-bat. Had I known what the future held for me as I changed in the clubhouse following the game, I might have stuffed my number 10 road jersey into my bag. This game turned out to be the last one in which I would play for the Boston Red Sox.

1948

APRIL 19, 1948: As I took my seat on the dugout bench on this day, I considered that it was the 10th time in my big league career that I was on a major league roster and there to witness the opening of a new baseball season. It was always a special day, full of hope and optimism, and I, as always, again felt the pull of those emotions — but things were a little different this year. When I looked down at the front of my gray road jersey, I saw the still unfamiliar black and yellow letters that spelled out "PITTSBURGH." I had yet to became completely acclimated to the new look because I had been wearing Pittsburgh togs for only a few weeks.

Backtracking a bit, in early February of 1948 I took a few days off from my winter job of officiating college basketball games to travel to Boston to meet with Red Sox general manager Joe Cronin about my 1948 contract. We had a nice get-together, and I signed my contract. Granted — there were no guarantees in baseball back then, especially for 35-year old role players like me, but I left Joe's office fairly comfortable that I would again be with the Sox in my customary utility role for the 1948 campaign. My sense of security was even bolstered when upon my return home to Kansas I read this in *The Sporting News* — *LITTLE DON 'FULL OF PEP.'* "Don Gutteridge, who played a utility role with the Red Sox last season, took time between his collegiate officiating duties to sign his '48 contract. 'I am feeling fine,' wrote Don, 'am full of pep and ready to go.' When general manager Joe Cronin read the note, he smiled and said, 'I never saw him any other way. He's a great little guy to have around, if only for his spirit and hustle.' "

I'm fully aware that you need more than just spirit and hustle to stay in the majors, but my discussion with Joe when I signed my contract left me confident that I'd be in the Red Sox fold come opening day. So I went to spring training with Boston and was really giving it my all, as usual. On March 26th, with just a few days left before we were scheduled to start our trek north to Boston to open the season, Joe called me into his office. He then explained to me that the Pittsburgh Pirates needed a utility infielder, so I had been sold to them and I was to immediately join them in Arizona as they traveled back east from their training camp in San Bernardino, California.

I couldn't believe it. I was very appreciative to Joe and the Red Sox for giving me another opportunity to extend my big league playing career when they bought me from Toledo back in July of 1946, but I was very resentful about the timing of my sale to Pittsburgh. I had worked very hard for them, and I now needed just 30 more days in the majors to be a 10-year man. Just like that, I had to pull up stakes and try and make it with a new ballclub with just a few weeks before the opening of a new season. I knew it would be difficult, and, more than anything, I was afraid that this might kill my chance at becoming a 10-year man. Being a 10-year man was very important to me at that time. The pension plan was just underway, and being a 10-year man meant that you were entitled to a FULL pension. That meant $100-per-month for the rest of my life after I turned 55 years old. At that time, believe it or not, I felt that if I could get that $100-per-month then I would be set for life. I sure got fooled on that, didn't I?

What I also got fooled on was the idea that you'd be taken care of by your team. I learned that there were no guarantees, so I decided to head to Arizona and take my best shot with the Pirates. I wasted no time after joining the club, immediately demonstrating my hard-working style, my energy, and my hustling tendencies. The Pirates' infield was far from being set, and the addition of me to the mix only added to the confusion. Les Biederman, Pirates beat writer, wrote, "When 35-year old Don Gutteridge came to the Pirates on waivers last week, he placed a couple of the Buc infielders squarely on the hot seat. Gutteridge isn't going to win any pennant for the Pirates, and he isn't going to figure in the regular plans for manager Billy Meyer, but no doubt he'll stick around as a handyman."

Biederman was exactly right — Meyer decided to keep me as a utility infielder, so I took gladly took my place on the Buc bench as we got set to open the season with our game against the Reds at Crosley Field on this day. What I saw was as wild an opening day ballgame as I could remember. It included tight pitching, rousing home runs, and a free-for-all scuffle. 6-foot-6-inch 195-pound right-hander Ewell "Blackie" Blackwell, the National League's leading winner in 1947, went for the Reds, while we threw former Dodger right-hander Hal Gregg. Seemingly overmatched, Hal instead did very well, leaving for a pinch-hitter in the top of the 7th while trailing 2-1. Hank Sauer opened up the Reds lead to 4-1, however, when he launched a 2-run homer onto the laundry out beyond the leftfield fence off Hal's replacement, Vic Lombardi, in the 8th.

It was the next play that saw all hell break loose. Cincinnati first baseman Babe Young followed Sauer's long ball with a booming double off the rightfield fence. Here's how the Associated Press described what happened next — "Eight feet from second base the Redleg ran into Stan Rojek, Pittsburgh shortstop. Both went down. Young scrambled to his feet, touched the bag, and then grabbed Rojek. Both started swinging, but no one was hit. Teammates tried to pull them apart, and photographers swarmed to the scene. Beans Reardon, umpire in chief, ordered the photographers from the playing field. Umpire Jocko Conlan and one camera clicker scuffled near third before the photographer, grumbling, departed. A tall, hatless spectator leaped from the stands, swinging his fists. Reardon swung his mask, but missed, and his mates, Larry Goetz and Conlan, came up to offer aid. Police escorted the offending spectator, who appeared to think the game was a bottle-opener, from the park. Rightfield bleacherites flooded the field with bottles. Time was called, the field cleared of debris, and the game went on. During the fighting Dixie Walker heaved the ball to the infield. Lombardi picked it up, touched Young as the latter scuffled with Rojek, and Young was out."

The Reds failed to score any more runs once the brawl was ended, but we also failed to score in our last at-bat, so we dropped the game by a final score of 4-1. I made a brief appearance as a pinch-hitter in the 7th inning, and it did not go well. Our catcher, Clyde Kluttz — the same Clyde Kluttz who had crushed my toe back in 1941 when I was with the Sacramento Solons — hit a 1-out single, then advanced to second on a hit by Rojek. Lombardi went down on strikes for the second out, then Myer told me to go in and run for Kluttz. Here's how *The Sporting News* described what happened next — "Don had hardly been announced before Blackie spun around on the mound, fired the ball to Virgil Stallcup, and Gutteridge was caught off the keystone, ending the inning and breaking up a possible Pirate rally." Although I'd watched another veteran, Dixie Walker, get picked off by Blackwell's sneaky move back in the 4th inning, I was still shocked when he turned the trick on me. Needless to say, it was a terrible way to start my career with the Pirates — a bad omen for things to come.

APRIL 20, 1948: A year-and-a-half earlier I had watched Rip Sewell serve up one too many blooper pitches to Ted Williams in the 1946 All Star Game. Ted deposited the eephus pitch into the Fenway Park stands, and with that "The Blooper Man" was forever sealed in baseball lore. But when you looked beyond Sewell's clownish blooper ball, what you really saw was an excellent pitcher. He'd dominated during the war, winning 21 games in 1943 and 1944. His win totals decreased in each of the following three years, but he put together a nice comeback season in 1948 — a comeback that would help lead the Pirates to a 4th-place finish. 4th place may not sound like anything to brag about, but the Pirates had been one of the worst franchises in baseball over the last few years, and a 1st-division finish was something worth celebrating in Pittsburgh. And on this day Rip's fine pitching led our team to its first win of the campaign, a 3-2 victory over the Cubs at Forbes Field in Pittsburgh.

The place was sold out for our home opener, and the crowd was treated to a dandy of a ballgame. I sat it out in its entirety. My pinch-running blunder of the day before probably didn't help my chances at getting back in a ballgame any time soon, but I enjoyed watching the crisply played game. Rip was trading scoreless innings with Cubs right-hander Russ "The Mad Monk" Meyer until he took matters into his own hands by clobbering a towering solo homer in the bottom of the 3rd inning to put us up, 1-0. A 2-run shot by Phil Cavarretta in the 4th put the Cubs ahead, 2-1, then we tied it with a run in the bottom of the 5th. Monty Basgall, our rookie second baseman, won the game for us with a bases-empty round-tripper in the 6th — the first home run of his career. Monty chose a great time to hit his first of just four career homers. He did it in front of Pirates co-owner — and Hollywood legend — Bing Crosby.

APRIL 25, 1948: We were an even .500 — 3 wins and 3 losses — prior to a doubleheader against the Reds at Crosley Field on this day. As you may have guessed, we split the twin bill to remain at .500. There was a pretty big crowd there to watch, too, as nearly 30,000 fans turned out to see this Sunday double-feature. What they got in return for their paid admission was plenty of offensive firepower. The first game featured Reds veteran Bucky Walters matched up against our Mel Queen, a right-hander who'd pitched pretty well with the Yankees back when I was with the Browns in 1944. Neither pitcher was around very long in this game, however, and the score was tied, 6-6, in the bottom of the 9th when Hank Sauer put an end to the drama by belting a 400-foot game-winning home run off Vic Lombardi. Sauer was back at it in the nightcap, too, hitting two more round-trippers. It wasn't enough, though, as our guys out-bombed Cincy to get us a 13-10 victory. It's funny, but more than Sauer's fireworks, I remember the five walks drawn by our rightfielder, Max West, in the second game. His batting line is as unusual a line as you'll ever see — 0-for-0 with three runs scored. His five walks tied a National League record.

I made pinch-hitting appearances in both games, and I did not help myself in my efforts to win the good graces of Billy Meyer. In the opener, Meyer sent me in to hit for reliever Nick Strincevich in the 5th inning, and I struck out. It was the same story in the second game as Meyer sent me in to bat for starting pitcher Hal Gregg in the 6th. I again fanned, and that bat felt mighty heavy as I carried it back to the dugout. It's not unusual to strike out in consecutive pinch-hit appearances, but the timing of my failures was not very good. Coming on the heels of my base-running miscue in my only other game appearance so far this season, my two strikeouts just magnified the difficult spot I was in as far as trying to prove myself quickly before I ran out of opportunities.

MAY 2, 1948: I hadn't been with the Pirates very long yet, but I'd been there long enough to see that they had an incredible talent in Ralph Kiner. He'd broke in with a bang by hitting 23 homers for the Pirates back in 1946, then poled an amazing 51 long balls in his sophomore season of 1947. Ralph looked like he was on his way to another big year on this day, too, as I watched him act like a one-man wrecking crew, hitting two homers and driving in four runs in our 6-4 win over the Reds at Forbes Field. Both of Ralph's homers on this day landed in the screened-in bullpen located down in the leftfield corner. The Pirates had built the bullpen when they'd acquired Hank Greenberg back in 1947. It shortened Forbes' leftfield dimension by some 30 feet, and the Pirates' hope was that Hank would take advantage of the new, inviting target. It was Ralph, however, who took full advantage of the decreased leftfield dimension. Ralph was a dead-pull hitter, and the shortened leftfield dimension allowed him to more than double his home run output in its first year of existence. Originally named "Greenberg Gardens," the bullpen area was re-christened "Kiner's Korner" following Greenberg's retirement prior to the '48 season. Ralph continued to pepper that bullpen with homers long after I was gone. Some say he rode Kiner's Korner right into the Hall of Fame.

MAY 6, 1948: The Giants arrived in Pittsburgh on this day for a 2-game series at Forbes Field. Prior to their arrival, our club had gotten hot, winning our last five in a row. It was early yet, but our winning streak had put us at the top of the National League heap and taken everyone in baseball by surprise. However, from my seat on the Pirate bench I watched our streak snapped — thanks, for the most part, to the actions of an old pal of mine from the days of the Gas House Gang — Johnny Mize. He was coming off a 51-homer season for the '47 Giants, and from the looks of his swing on this day, he appeared to be headed to another big year with the bat. He banged home the first Giant tally in the top of the 1st to open the game's scoring, then drove in another run with a booming double in the 3rd. He topped off his big day by crushing a solo homer into the upper rightfield deck in the 7th. We never recovered from his onslaught, and we lost the game, 9-2. When big John was on his game — whether it was with the 1936 St. Louis Cardinals or the 1948 New York Giants — he was a force to be reckoned with.

MAY 9, 1948: On this day I appeared in my last ballgame as a big league player. At this stage in my major league career I was certainly well aware that the end of my playing days was near, but I in no way imagined that I was about to play in my final game as we took the field for a doubleheader against the Brooklyn Dodgers at Forbes Field. We were trailing, 3-1, in the opener when Billy Meyer sent me in to run for Max West in the 7th inning. I was left stranded when the inning ended, so I trotted off the field for what ended up being the final time. The game got out of control and we lost in a blowout, 14-2. Then we dropped the nightcap, 10-8. I did not play. I was in uniform for our game the next day, a 4-2 victory over the Dodgers, but again I did not play. We did not play the next day, May the 11th, so the front office guys took that opportunity to present me with the bad news — they were sending me down to Indianapolis of the American Association.

The news hit me like a punch in the face, and I was mad about it. When I went over to Pittsburgh I thoroughly discussed my number one priority — staying with them for the entire 30 days I needed in order to become a 10-year man. They promised that they would keep me for at least those 30 days, but now they were releasing me after just 20 days. I still needed 10 days to qualify for the increased pension that came with being a 10-year man, and I knew that it was very unlikely that I'd ever get another opportunity to pick up those 10 days. They didn't care, though, and they said the deal was done. It was either go to Indianapolis or go home. I told them I had no intention of going to Indianapolis — at least not without my 10 days — so I packed my bags and headed home to Kansas, completely unsure of what I would now do to earn a living.

1959

SEPTEMBER 22, 1959: On this evening at 10:45 PM at Cleveland's Municipal Stadium, Indians' second baseman Vic Power hit a 1-out, 9th-inning, bases-loaded grass cutter to White Sox shortstop Luis Aparicio. Moving to his left, Luis scooped up the ball, dashed for second, stepped on the bag with his right foot, then fired to first to complete the twin killing. A split second after the ball had come to rest in the mitt of Sox first baseman Ted Kluszewski, all hell broke loose.

The Cleveland players headed for their dugout in despair as the Sox players bolted for the pitcher's mound where right-handed reliever Gerry Staley stood waiting to receive his teammates in joyous celebration. Amidst the 54,293 mostly-Indians fans in attendance were a contingent of White Sox fans, and they poured onto the field to join in OUR celebration. I say "our" celebration because I was right in the middle of it all. In fact, I was the fifth White Sox team member to reach Staley, trailing only Sherm Lollar, Dick Donovan, Nellie Fox, and manager Al Lopez. The reason for all the commotion was simple — Aparicio's double-play had just clinched the 1959 American League pennant for our ballclub, the first A.L. title for the Chicago White Sox since 1919. Despite the fact that my big league playing days had ended over a decade earlier, this moment was as thrilling as any I'd ever had as a player. You see, I was the first base coach for this over-achieving group of guys, and I couldn't have been any happier at this moment had I won this game with a home run.

A lot had gone on in my life between the day I was released by the Pirates back on May 11th, 1948, and this day. There were unanticipated twists that I was, at the time, unhappy about, followed by equally unanticipated turns that appeared to be strokes of great luck. Looking now at the sum total of those twists and turns with the aid of 20-20 hindsight, I would venture to speculate that every one of those events, good or bad, was absolutely necessary to bring me to the place I was on this day — bound, once again, for a World Series. And it doesn't get any better than that.

Still angry about the Pirates not fulfilling their promise to keep me on their '48 roster long enough for me to achieve full 10-year status, I'd returned home to Pittsburg, Kansas, to consider my options for the future. The Pirates wanted me to go to their American Association farm club in Indianapolis, but I refused to accept the assignment. I wanted to be strong and stick to my principles, but as I thought through my opportunities for employment, none of them included baseball. I guess I just wasn't ready to walk away from the game because in short order I decided to report to Indianapolis. Deciding to go to Indianapolis turned out to be one of the best decisions I ever made. Leading the Indianapolis Indians was Al Lopez, the once-great catcher who was then on his way to becoming a great manager. I already knew Al pretty well from playing against him when I was with the Cardinals, so I was looking forward to playing for him. It turned out that the relationship I cultivated with Al in 1948 paved the way for me to enter a long career in the big leagues as coach, manager, and scout.

I played third base for Al's 1948 Indianapolis Indians, and we did very well. We ended up winning the Little World Series, the championship held annually between the winners of the American Association and the International League. It was quite a prestigious thing as far as minor leaguers were concerned. I returned to Indianapolis in 1949, this time as a player-coach for Al, and I was back in the same capacity in 1950. Al's success in those years at Indianapolis earned him a call-up to the big leagues where he assumed the managerial reins of the 1951 Cleveland Indians. With Al's move to Cleveland, I was named manager of the '51 Indianapolis Indians. 1951 marked the first time in 19 years that I was not an active player. Instead, I acted strictly as a manager, forever abandoning my role as a player. For me, no longer playing was less traumatic than one might think. I guess my transition to full-time manager was made smoother because I eased into it by first being a player-coach — a sort of interim stage.

I spent 1948 through 1951 with the Indianapolis Indians of the American Association in capacities varying from player, player-coach, and manager.

The Indianapolis club was sold after the '51 season, and I found myself out of a job as the new owners brought in their own men. I traveled to the winter meetings to see if there were any openings, and it was there that I accepted an offer from the White Sox to manage the Sky Sox, Chicago's Colorado Springs affiliate. 1952 was an exciting season for us in Colorado Springs as we played well but lost the pennant by a half game on the last day of the season. We bounced back in 1953, however, this time winning the flag on the season's final day. I felt I was ready to move up, so that winter I told White Sox general manager Frank Lane that I really wanted to coach in the major leagues. He promised to work on that for me if I would do him a favor — manage the Memphis

Chicks in 1954. I agreed, so I went down to Memphis where we turned in a pretty good season despite losing in the playoffs.

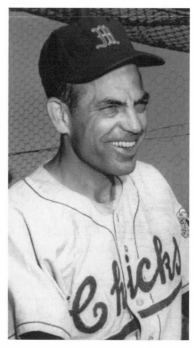

My travels saw me manage the Colorado Springs Sky Sox in 1952 and '53, then the Memphis Chicks in 1954. I joined the coaching staff of the Chicago White Sox for the tail end of the '54 season after we finished our season in Memphis. That began a long career for me with Chicago.

I was all set to return home for the off-season when I heard news that White Sox manager Paul Richards had just resigned to take a job as general manager with the Baltimore Orioles. Marty Marion, one of Richard's coaches, was promoted to manager. It was September 13th. Almost immediately I received a call from Lane asking me to come to Chicago for an organizational meeting with the rest of the managers in the Sox farm system. Once there I was called in to see Marty and White Sox front office executive Ed Short. "You still want to be a coach in the major leagues?" Marty asked me. With adrenaline pumping I replied, "You're damn right I do!"

Cutting in with a smile and a handshake, Ed said, "Okay — as of tonight you are officially a coach for the Chicago White Sox." Then Marty said, "Tonight you start, Don." It was all so sudden that I couldn't believe it. I had to borrow a sweatshirt, shoes, and everything because I didn't have anything with me. Then they did the most amazing thing for me. They back-dated my contract 10 days, righting the wrong that Pittsburgh had done me back in '48. The minute I put my name on the contract, I was officially a 10-year man and now eligible for a full pension no matter what happened from here on. It turned out to be an unnecessary gesture of goodwill on their part, however, because I would go on to spend many years with the White Sox as a coach and manager, easily qualifying for a full pension. But I didn't know that at the time, so I was very appreciative of their generosity.

White Sox management must have liked what they saw in Marty because they brought him back for the 1955 season, and Marty asked me to return, too. We had a fine team that season, winning 91 games and finishing in 3rd place, five behind the pennant-winning Yankees. We were all back for the '56 season and again finished 3rd. But we won six fewer games than the previous season, finishing a distant 12 games in back of the American League champion Yanks. It was frustrating, but our club just wasn't quite ready to be a real pennant contender. We had some good ballplayers like Walt Dropo, Nellie Fox, George Kell, Chico Carrasquel, and Billy Pierce, to name a few, but we just hadn't yet come completely together as a unit. At any rate, we were hoping that it might happen the next season, so we felt very optimistic as we packed up and prepared to leave for the off-season. Marty, speaking to me and the rest of the coaching staff, said, "I want you all back with me next year, so consider yourselves rehired. I'll have the secretary send you contracts to make it official." It was a great feeling to head home for the winter knowing for sure where you were going to be next spring.

Helen and I were enjoying a nice breakfast one morning in late October just a few weeks after returning home. I was sipping a cup of coffee and listening to the 8:00 morning news on the radio when I heard the announcer say, "Marty Marion, manager of the Chicago White Sox, has announced his resignation. Also out is Marion's entire coaching staff." I tell you, I nearly bit a chunk out of my coffee cup! I couldn't believe it, and I wondered what I was going to do now. My spirits were lifted about three hours later when I received a phone call from the White Sox. They told me that the new manager was going to be Al Lopez, and they were pretty sure that he would rehire Marty's entire coaching staff.

Officially, Marty resigned, but the truth of the matter is that he was forced out. After managing the Cleveland Indians from 1951-56, Al had voluntarily stepped down. He'd finished second to the Yankees in each of those seasons except the 1954 campaign when his Indians won the flag. Despite always fielding a winner, there were rumblings in Cleveland about him always finishing second. Al didn't need that aggravation, so he quit. As soon as the White Sox heard that he was available, they snapped him up. The guy on the short end of the stick was Marty. He'd done a good job with what he had, but our club had slipped back a bit in '56 after our 91-win season in '55. I think they used that against him so they could bring in Al, the man they really wanted. It was too bad, too, because Marty deserved better. I was glad that I was there with him, and I'm proud of the job we did.

Sure enough, Al kept me on his coaching staff just as the front office had speculated. Aside from the varied general coaching tasks I would perform, my number one duty was to be Al's first base coach. I eventually became sort of his second in command. If a player had a complaint, for example, I would act as the intermediary between the player and Al. It worked out well. Al was a great manager and his influence was felt immediately as the team rose to 2nd place in the final 1957 standings with a 90-win season. It was, of course, the Yankees to whom we were runner-up. It was the same story in 1958 as we again placed 2nd to New York. We were not overly frustrated by our second banana status, however, because we all could see that we were a club on the rise. So as we headed home for the off-season following the 1958 campaign, we felt great about our chances for possibly unseating the Yankees in 1959.

Don't let Al's surname "Lopez" throw you — he was an all-American boy. His parents were from Spain, but Al was born in Tampa, Florida. He broke in with Brooklyn in 1928, but didn't arrive on the scene to stay until 1930. And when I say he stayed, I mean it. Al played his last season in the big leagues in 1947, and when it was over he had caught 1,918 games. At the time it was more than any other catcher in major league history, and the record stood for over 40 years. The *New York Times'* Arthur Daley accurately described Al, the player, when he wrote, "He was like a cat as a catcher, slick and agile. He was deadly on bunts and deadly on pop-ups. His arm was strong and swift. Runners ran on him at their peril. He was superlative at calling pitches, and wasn't a bad hitter, either."

Al, while catching in all those games, soaked up every bit of information he saw around him. And he had some great managers to learn from, too. The legendary Uncle Wilbert Robinson was still at the helm of the Dodgers when Al first came up. Then he had Casey Stengel to learn from while Casey managed Al at Brooklyn and Boston. Not all of Al's managers were great, though, but he learned from them, too. Upon moving into the managerial ranks with our 1948 Indianapolis Indians, Al began to implement all that he'd learned. The result was a pennant, and he just kept rolling from there.

It'd take a book much longer than mine to detail all the things that made Al a great manager, but there are a few key items that stand out. Al was a great handler of men, one of a manager's most crucial qualifications. He was a very engaging fellow with a truly magnetic personality, and that helped him get guys to listen to him. He was very fair. He was great at instilling confidence in players. Despite being self-deprecating, Al projected the unmistakable fact that he was indisputably THE one in charge. He was the boss. He was subtle and serene in his authority, but not weak. He tried to play down the way he handled his players, telling people, "I just leave them alone." That was an intentional oversimplification on his part. He did leave them alone, but only AFTER he had everything in place the way he wanted it.

Al's managerial style would have served him equally well had he been running a business. His were just sound, solid managerial techniques whether it be on the ballfield or in the corporate world. But when added to the baseball knowledge he brought to the table, Al became a real force to be reckoned with. Al had a keen eye with pitchers. He could spot the most subtle problems of a pitcher, point them out, and reap immediate rewards once the guy implemented Al's change. Not only was Al great with pitchers, he was one of those managers who was always ahead of the game. He always had something in mind two plays ahead of everyone else. I enjoyed watching him pull the strings like only he could. Perhaps the trait that served Al the greatest, however, was his adaptability. He believed that he needed to tailor his philosophy to the players he had. In Cleveland he'd had a team of sluggers, so he played for the home run. They'd wait for the big inning and get it, and that's why he won with the Indians. When Al came over to the Sox, he saw the giant dimensions of Comiskey Park and the lack of power on the club, so he changed his approach, instead focusing on good defense, good pitching, and speed on the bases. He used to say, "You have to build your club according to your park. You play 77 games at home. Power-hitters die at Comiskey Park." It was the complete antithesis of how he'd won in Cleveland, yet he won in Chicago, too. It was amazing.

So here we were, jumping up and down like a bunch of school kids, celebrating the fruits of Al's great managerial ability — the 1959 American League pennant. When we began the game on this day, the Indians were the only team left with a chance to challenge us for the pennant. They were in 2nd place, 3-1/2 games behind us with just four left to play. The next nearest team was the Yankees, and they trailed by double digits. Just two weeks earlier it looked like we would be able to clinch the flag relatively easily, but we hit a period of mediocre play and the Indians hit a stretch where they played very well. All that said, it still would have taken a near miracle for the Indians to overtake us, but stranger things have happened in baseball. So for that reason we wanted to immediately put an end to the suspense by beating the Tribe on this day.

The pitching match-up featured Cleveland's good looking rookie right-hander Jim Perry against our ace, 39-year old right-hander Early Wynn. Early was a great choice as the guy to try and nail down the pennant for us. He was having one of his best seasons ever — and he'd had a lot of great seasons. Early's victory for us on this day would be his 21st of the year, and he'd notch one more before we moved on to the Series. Both pitchers traded goose eggs for the first two innings, but then our guys staked Early to a 2-0 lead in the top of the 3rd after run-scoring doubles by Luis Aparicio and our third baseman, Billy Goodman. Based on Al's philosophy, that should have been enough to win. He was perfectly contented to win every game 1-0. He expected his players to get on base by any means necessary — hit, walk, error — whatever. Once on base, he expected them to manufacture a run via the steal, the hit-and-run, the bunt, the sacrifice, or any other means available. Once the run was across, Al would turn to the pitcher and say, "There's your lead — now hold it." And with quality pitchers like Early, Billy Pierce, Dick Donovan, Bob Shaw, and a bunch of others, they were usually able to do as Al commanded. This scrappy style of play had seen the club nicknamed "The Go-Go Sox," a term that actually went as far back as Paul Richards' 1951 Sox. They, too, played a style similar to our club, and the nickname was spawned from the Chisox crowd hollering, "Go! Go! Go!" as they watched their boys tearing around the basepaths. While the nickname may have originated years before, it was our '59 ballclub with which the nickname will forever be associated.

The Indians drew to within one run after they scored in the bottom of the 5th, but we responded by beating Cleveland at their own game — the long ball. 6th-inning solo homers by our leftfielder, Al Smith, and our rightfielder, Jim Rivera, extended our lead to 4-1, but Early was not at his best on this day. He allowed another Indian run to score in the bottom half of the inning before leaving the game for reliever Shaw with two outs. Bob closed out the inning with no further damage, then pitched scoreless ball for the 7th and 8th innings.

Our guys, led by Shaw, took the field for the bottom of the 9th, leading, 4-1, just three outs from the pennant. Then it got tense. Indians lead-off hitter Woody Held made a quick out, but Jim Baxes then lined a single off Shaw's shin. While the crowd roared its approval, Indians manager Joe Gordon sent Ray Webster in to pinch-run for Baxes. Then Gordon sent Jack Harshman in to pinch-hit, and he delivered a sharp single to left. Jimmy Piersall was next up, and he drilled a liner to Nellie Fox at second. The shot nearly knocked Nellie into rightfield. He couldn't hold it, and the bases were loaded with just one out. That sent Al out to the mound where he called on his 39-year old right-handed relief specialist, Gerry Staley.

Gerry had been a big winner with the Cardinals in the early 1950's, but he'd fallen on hard times in the middle of the decade. His career apparently through, Gerry had come over to the Sox partway through the '56 season. It was then that Marty Marion converted Gerry to a reliever, giving Staley a new lease on his career. Gerry's solid work out of the pen, along with that of fellow reliever Turk Lown, was a key ingredient in our ability to win the 1959 pennant, and it culminated with his performance in this game. Facing incredible pressure, Gerry calmly took the ball from Al and threw one pitch, inducing Vic Power into his game-ending double-play.

Incidentally, 1959 was obviously the last year of the decade of the 1950's. Winning this pennant was the culmination of a long battle to dethrone the Yankees. They had won eight of ten pennants in the 1950's, their only two failures coming at the hands of teams managed by Al — the '54 Indians and the '59 White Sox. Now all that was left was to play out the last three meaningless games of the regular season, then see if Lopez's '59 A.L. champs could do what his '54 model couldn't do — WIN the World Series.

SEPTEMBER 27, 1959: We closed out the 1959 regular season with a 6-4 victory over the Detroit Tigers at Comiskey Park on this day. We'd returned to Chicago after clinching the pennant in Cleveland five days earlier, then had two days off before the Tigers arrived at Comiskey for a season-ending 3-game series. The goal in our last three games was to rest guys, but not to the degree that we'd lose our edge. I think we accomplished that. We got rest for the regulars and playing time for the back-ups, all while still managing to win two of the three games against Detroit. Right-hander Bob Shaw worked five innings to get his 18th win in our season finale, but the most memorable moment came when our guys halted a 3rd-inning Tiger rally by turning a crazy triple play. Harvey Kuenn was on first and Tom Morgan was on third with none out when the play went down, and here's how it was recounted in the papers — "Gail Harris hit back to Shaw and he trapped Morgan off third. Third baseman Bubba Phillips tagged Morgan out and then ran to first where Harris, who had rounded the bag, was tagged out. Phillips threw to the plate and catcher John Romano's throw to Luis Aparicio covering third retired Kuenn." It was an exciting play, but not half as exciting as what went on after we clinched the flag five days earlier back in Cleveland.

The moment our ballclub's on-field celebration began in Cleveland, another celebration got under way back in Chicago. It had been a long, grueling, 40-year wait in between pennants for White Sox fans. Not only was it tough to have to wait so long, but it was made particularly difficult by the fact that the last White Sox pennant winner was the disgraced 1919 Black Sox. Fans of the beleaguered franchise, although in no way responsible for the events of 1919, still shouldered some of the burden of the scandal. A pennant seemed like just the tonic to cure what ailed them, so they were primed for a real celebration. So when the ball popped into Ted Kluszewski's mitt for last out of the flag-clincher, the people in Chicago's South Side cut loose in joyous celebration. In the streets, in bars, in homes — wherever — folks engaged in a raucous party. One aspect of the city's triumphant display actually caused a sort of "War of the Worlds" effect. The city's civil defense sirens began to blare as soon as the game was over. These sirens had been installed strictly for the purpose of warning people of an enemy attack. Thousands of people upon hearing the sirens did not associate them with our victory, so they flooded the phone company with calls, inquiring, "What's happening — are the Russians coming?"

We were coming, NOT the Russians, and once assured of that, the fans redirected their attention to our return from Cleveland. As we approached the airport in Chicago we could see that there were thousands of fans awaiting our plane. They were so crazed, some even spilling onto runways, that our plane was forced to circle the airport for quite some time while the police cleared the landing strips and restored order. We finally landed, but it was still such bedlam that our wives who were waiting at the airport were instructed to go home without us because it would be too difficult for us to navigate the throng to meet up with them. So the wives went home and a bus later delivered them their husbands.

There was one last bash before everyone finally turned their attention to the fact that we still had to play the meaningless season-ending series against Detroit and THEN the World Series. On September 24th the city threw us a huge tick-er-tape parade, and 700,000 fans swarmed over State and LaSalle streets to take part. Three marching bands led the procession, followed by a fleet of convert-ibles carrying players, coaches, and front office execs two to a car. The whole extravanganza came to a stop in front of city hall where there was a bunting-cov-ered reviewing stand situated below a big banner that read, "Hail to the Champs — Give Chicago the World's Title!" Everyone was introduced to great cheers from the crowd. It was a wonderful event and Sox president Bill Veeck captured many of our thoughts when he told the mob, "We're only half way home. The magic number for the White Sox is now four. And I hope you'll be as delighted with us AFTER we play the National League champions as you are now."

At the time Veeck spoke those words the National League had yet to crown a champion. In fact, the N.L. pennant race was a real dogfight. The San Francisco Giants, Milwaukee Braves, and Los Angeles Dodgers were battling tooth and nail, right down to the wire, and when it was all said and done, the Braves and Dodgers ended in a tie. A 3-game playoff was scheduled, but the Dodgers needed only two games to eliminate the Braves, clinching the N.L. flag on September 29th, two days after we'd completed our season and a full week after we'd clinched the A.L. pennant. The wait had been excruciating, but it was now over. We now knew that our World Series opponent would be the Los Angeles Dodgers, and we couldn't wait to get it started.

OCTOBER 1, 1959: World Series Game One — *WHITE SOX ROUT DODGERS IN SERIES OPENER, 11 TO 0.* That was the headline in the *New York Times* describing our Series-opening win against the Dodgers at Comiskey Park on this day. We were very excited to jump out in front in the Series, but a little shocked at the one-sidedness of the final score. The day started with the usual pomp of every World Series. The stands were filled with all types of peo-ple from the everyday fan to the politician; famous entertainers to sports celebri-ties; you name it. The White Sox players wives, most decked out in their finest furs and dresses, were a sight to behold in their third base box. Many of the wives were also wearing a red rose, one of 20,000 red roses that Bill Veeck had ushers give to all the ladies in attendance.

A throng of players, coaches, managers, executives, and reporters milled about the field before the game. One group was particularly boisterous, and that's because it was headed by Casey Stengel. As manager of the New York Yankees, Stengel was a regular at 8 of the 10 World Series held in the 1950's, but he attended this one as a correspondent for *Life* magazine. Sportswriters had always loved to follow him around to listen to his "Stengelese," and this day was no exception. Stengel worked his way over to Al Lopez in order to interview his old pal. Al was ready to steal the show by replying "no comment" to Casey's first question, but Stengel never gave him the chance. Casey, in his best unintelligi-ble Stengelese, asked Al a question, but then proceeded to answer it himself before Al could ever get a word in. All the while Casey made a show of repeatedly flashing a big World Series ring past Al's face. He eventually pointed at it and told Al that it was "number five." It was all good fun, and everyone, including Al, got a big laugh.

There was music and a host of other activities to add to the festive atmosphere as game time approached. One of the last ceremonies was the "first pitch," and this one featured a very interesting and symbolic pairing. Stepping onto the mound with a ball in his hand was 71-year old Red Faber, and behind the plate was 77-year old Ray Schalk. They represented the "clean Sox" of the 1919 Series, and their participation in the first-pitch ceremony was to symbolize a passing of the guard — a sort of cleansing process. So Faber wound up and delivered a strike to Schalk (some joked it was a spitter), and with that the Series was officially opened. Our guys, wearing brand new uniforms, tore out to their positions to begin the top of the 1st. While crisp, white, and new, the uniforms were exactly the same as the ones we'd been wearing all season long — except for the socks. All year we'd worn BLACK socks with red and white stripes, but these new socks were WHITE with red and black stripes. The decision to change to white socks had come from he front office. It was a switch they said would help people focus less of the "Black Sox" scandal of 1919. The overly superstitious players — and there are always quite a few on every ballclub — couldn't help but question the idea of changing ANYTHING at this point in the season, but their concerns were dismissed by the rationalists around them. Black socks didn't win games, they said — White Sox did!

The pitching match-up for Game One featured Early Wynn against the Dodgers' tall right-hander, Roger Craig. There was no doubt all along that Al would go with Early. Just like he'd wanted him to secure the pennant a week earlier, Al was now counting on Early to go out and get us a Game One win. Craig, on the other hand, was a bit of a surprise starter. The big guns in the Dodger rotation were Don Drysdale and Johnny Podres, but they were not ready to go because of the unexpected playoff games. Craig had nearly been given up on as a sore-armed pitcher back in 1958, but his return from the minors in mid-1959 bolstered the Los Angeles pitching staff as he pitched to an 11-and-5 record.

The first man Early faced was Dodgers third baseman Jim Gilliam, and he hit a routine grounder to Luis Aparicio at short for the first out. We faced a quick test, however, soon thereafter. The next batter, second baseman Charley Neal, singled. Left-fielder Wally Moon popped out, but then Neal stole second and Early walked centerfielder Duke Snider. Early, always seemingly aware of when to bear down, then snuffed the threat by getting rightfielder Norm Larker to fly out to right.

Roger Craig also suffered some 1st inning trouble, but by the time he got it under control our boys had scored two runs. Aparicio led off the inning with a pop-out to Dodger shortstop Maury Wills, but our next batter, second baseman Nellie Fox, then walked. That may sound insignificant, but not when it's the

1959 Go-Go Sox. With our club, a walk could often lead to a steal, a sac bunt, a scratch single, and a 1-0 victory. Knowing that, the crowd began to chant "Go! Go! Go!" as Nellie trotted down to first base. As centerfielder Jim Landis stepped in to hit, Al, as you'd expect, put on the hit-and-run. Craig delivered, Nellie took off, and Jim swung. It worked to perfection, Jim's ball getting through for a single, sending Nellie to third. Then Ted Kluszewski slammed a single through the right side, scoring Nellie with the first run of the Series and pushing Jim around to third. Sherm Lollar, our catcher, then fell in line by promptly lifting a sac fly to right, scoring Jim. Billy Goodman flied to center to end the inning, but when it was all said and done we'd executed a classic Go-Go Sox inning: two hits, a hit-and-run, a sacrifice fly — and two runs. As I headed back to the dugout from my first base coach's box I saw Al lean in and say something to Early. I was too far away to hear what was spoken, but knowing Al, he probably said, "There's your lead, Early — now go and hold it."

Early held the lead, hanging zeroes on the Dodgers in the 2nd and 3rd innings. Then, batting in the bottom of the 3rd, our guys gave Early a lead he could've held in his sleep. They piled on Craig for three runs, and then added four more in the same frame off right-handed reliever Chuck Churn. The damage could not all be laid at the feet of the Dodger pitchers, however. Los Angeles fell apart in the field, too. Moon and Snider collided while trying to catch a drive by Lollar, and Snider was charged with an error when he dropped the ball. That put Sherm on second, and he scored when Goodman, the next batter, singled. Then Al Smith doubled off the wall in left-center, sending Goodman to third. Smith, in his excitement, had his head down all the way, thinking three bags. Halfway to third base he looked up and was shocked to see Goodman occupying the bag. Smith hit the brakes and Goodman took off for home. Dodger first baseman Gil Hodges was in position to take Snider's throw, and Gil would have had his pick for an out because Smith and Goodman were sitting ducks, but Duke's throw was off line and Hodges couldn't handle it. It went down as another error for Snider, and Goodman scored while Smith moved up to third base. Jim Rivera batted next. He slapped a grounder to Neal, and Smith broke for home. Smith would have been nailed at the plate had Neal made a good throw, but Charley bounced the ball in front of catcher John Roseboro and Smith slid in safely.

I point out that comedy of errors for a reason. A key characteristic of the 1959 White Sox was that we did not beat ourselves, and we capitalized on the opponent's mistakes. Opposition ballclubs, knowing that our team was fast and liked to run, often made errors in their haste to make a play, and our club was great at making them pay for it. Our 7-run bottom of the 3rd is a great illustration of that. The catalyst for our big inning, however, was somewhat out of character for us — the long ball. With one out and a run in, Kluszewski stepped up to face Craig with a runner on first base. Big Klu then hit a towering shot that carried just enough to barely clear the wall in right, landing in the first row of seats for a 2-run homer.

We capped our scoring with two final runs in the 4th when Kluszewski, in his next at-bat after homering in the 3rd, went deep again. With Landis on first after singling, Ted unloaded on Churn, depositing the ball into the upper right-field stands. Ted was quite a happy fellow when he shook my hand as he rounded first base, and he deserved to be happy. After some huge power years with the Reds from 1953-56, Ted had hit hard times because of a bad back. Cincinnati shipped him off to Pittsburgh in 1958, and the White Sox acquired him on August 25th, 1959. Despite the fact that his back had been getting better, his power had really not returned. In fact, he'd hit just two homers for the '59 Pirates before coming over to our club, and then he'd homered only twice for us — until this day when he looked like the Klu of old.

Whether the old or new Klu, Ted was a big guy. He'd been a star defensive end at the University of Indiana before signing with the Reds. He was 6-foot-2 and 245 pounds when he joined us, but by playing every day he'd dropped a few of those pounds by the time the Series came around. And he still had those big, muscular arm sticking out of his cut-off sleeves. It was a very intimidating look, but Ted was not that type. He was soft-spoken — sort of a gentle giant. He played one more year for us in 1960, and he was a real pleasure to be around. One last thing about Ted's pair of homers. A local car dealership had promised a free Ford Falcon automobile to any White Sox player who hit a home run in the Series, so in the process of hitting his two long balls Ted had won himself two new Ford Falcons. As big as he was, it probably would have taken two Falcon's to carry Ted around town. At any rate, for reasons which I've never known, baseball commissioner Ford Frick stepped in and said "no" before Ted ever had a chance to claim his prize, so we never got an opportunity to see big Ted driving around the South Side in his two Ford Falcons.

As I mentioned, our guys didn't score anymore after our 2-run 4th — but neither did the Dodgers. Early was never really in any trouble, repeatedly setting down the Los Angeles hitters by expertly mixing his 5-pitch repertoire — fastball, change-up, curve, slider, and knuckleball. But Al had noticed something after Gilliam singled to open the 8th, so he went out to talk to Early. Wynn mentioned that his elbow was stiffening up, so Al, not wanting to take any chances, immediately removed Early from the game. Gerry Staley came in and, just like he'd done in the pennant-clincher, nailed down the 11-0 victory. Our on-field celebration was very restrained after the win, and that mood carried over to the clubhouse. Our guys knew that it was great to get the first win of the Series, but they also knew that our goal of winning it all was still a long way away, and their restraint simply reflected the demeanor of their leader, Al Lopez. Despite his happiness over winning the game, Al was predictably quiet, composed, and dignified as he spoke to reporters. That was saying something, too, considering that this win was his first in World Series competition. His 1954 Indians had been swept by the New York Giants, so Al had to wait five long years in order to sample the taste of victory that our Game One win provided. "They just had a bad day," Al told the reporters when sizing up the Dodgers' defeat. "That could happen to any team. Bob Shaw will pitch tomorrow."

OCTOBER 2, 1959: World Series Game Two — *DODGERS BEAT WHITE SOX, 4-3, AND TIE WORLD SERIES.* That was the *New York Times* headline describing our loss at Comiskey Park on this day. For a while it looked as if bad weather might postpone the game, and when the contest was over we wished it had. It was cool and rainy prior to the game — bad enough that it curtailed our batting practice. Al Lopez periodically climbed to the top step of the dugout and looked up at the gray skies, but his worries were later alleviated when the clouds cleared and warm sunlight broke through. Also, it can never be said that EVERYONE associated with the '59 World Series did not have every opportunity to be well fed on this Friday for Game Two. Why? Because Bill Veeck, the man who seemed to think of everything, received a dispensation from the Archbishop of Chicago so that meat could be eaten by all Roman Catholics among World Series personnel — players, umpires, executives, ushers, officials — and even the sportswriters!

Johnny Podres, hero of the 1955 World Series, was the Dodgers' choice to start, and Al chose to go with Bob Shaw. Bob had been very effective for us in 1959, winning 18 while losing only six. His tremendous success that season owed a great deal to the sound pitching advice he received from Al Lopez and Ray Berres, our pitching coach. Bob had a brief trial with Detroit in 1957 and was up with them in '58 when he was dealt to our ballclub that June. A right-hander who sometimes possessed the wacky mindset of a lefty, Bob also possessed considerable potential. Al and Ray felt that one of Bob's pitching quirks was preventing him from fully reaching that potential. You see, Bob threw overhand while pitching to left-handed hitters, but he liked to come from the side when facing right-handers. Al and Ray worked hard to convince Bob to change his style to where he threw overhand all the time. It was tough for Bob at first, but he did what they said, working diligently through the '58 season. It was great to see his faith in Al and Ray rewarded in 1959 when he reaped the benefits of his hard work.

Things started in much the same way that they had begun in Game One with the Dodgers threatening in the top of the 1st, but failing to score. Wally Moon hit a 2-out single to center, then stole second. We got a break, however, when the next batter, Duke Snider, hit a liner back at Shaw that looked like a sure run-scoring single. But Shaw got his glove on the smash, and then the ball caromed to Nellie Fox. Snider was able to reach safely, but Nellie pounced on the rebound, forcing Moon to hold at third instead of scoring. That play enabled Shaw to get out of the jam by inducing the next batter, Norm Larker, to fly out to right.

For those who believe in such things, our fortuitous escape in the top of the

1st could have been construed as a harbinger of good things to come. And anyone who thought that way seemed to have their beliefs validated in the home half of the 1st when our guys hung two runs on Podres, just as they'd done to Roger Craig in Game One. Also reminiscent of the first game was the fact that the Dodgers again helped us in our scoring with poor defense. Luis Aparicio opened the frame with a double down the rightfield line that was fair by inches. Nellie then moved Luis to third with a fly-out to deep right. Podres, looking somewhat aggravated by the way the inning was going, then walked Jim Landis. That brought up Ted Kluszewski, and he slammed a hard grounder to Charley Neal at second. It looked like a certain twin-killing, but Neal fumbled the ball. He recovered in time to force Klu at first, but Landis moved up to second and, more importantly, Luis scored. Sherm Lollar batted next, and he, too, hit to Neal. Charley was able to get his glove on the ball, but only enough to slow it down a bit. The ball rolled onto the outfield grass and Landis scored. Al Smith hit next and reached when Maury Wills fumbled his grounder for an error while Lollar moved to second. It was looking very bad for L.A., but Podres stopped the bleeding by popping up Bubba Phillips to end the inning.

Just as in Game One, the Dodgers were beating their own brains out — and our guys were taking full advantage of it. Staked to his lead, Shaw went out and pitched scoreless innings through the 4th, but Neal reached him for a solo homer in the top of the 5th to pull the Dodgers to within one run. The score remained 2-1 until Los Angeles exploded for three tallies in the top of the 7th. Shaw had retired the first two batters of the inning when Chuck Essegian appeared out of the dugout, entering the game as a pinch-hitter for Podres. With very little playing time and just one home run to his credit in 1959, Essegian was hardly viewed as a hitter to be overly feared. Maybe on the football field where he had been a halfback for Stanford University, but not on the baseball field. We knew Essegian had power, but his relatively minor role in the Dodgers' day-to-day activities had him way down on our scale of worries. But Essegian changed that thinking when he caught hold of a slider that Shaw left up in the zone, belting the pitch into the upper deck in left for a game-tying solo home run.

Looking at Bob, you could see that he was annoyed by this turn of events, and he walked the next batter, Jim Gilliam. That brought Neal back to the plate. Charley was very thin, 5-foot-10 and only about 155 pounds at that late stage of the long season. Well, he got every ounce of his slender self into a Bob Shaw fastball and put it into our centerfield bullpen about 415 feet away. It was quite a wallop, and a devastating blow to our chances to win. That was the end for Shaw on this day. It was tough to see him leave the game in that manner after he'd pitched so well all season, but that's just how it goes sometimes in baseball. Bob didn't pitch badly — the Dodgers just came up big when they needed to. And after the day before — they were due. Al called for right-handed reliever Turk Lown, and he got us out of the inning with no further scoring.

Now trailing, 4-2, our guys' backs were against the wall as they tried to claw their way back into the game. Right-hander Larry Sherry had come on for Podres and we quickly saw why he had been so valuable to Los Angeles' run at the pennant in the second half of the '59 campaign. He was only 24 years old, but he'd been brought up at mid-season when the Dodgers really needed pitching help. Working as a starter as well as out of the pen, Sherry mixed an excellent fastball with a very effective slider, a combination that propelled him to 7-and-2 mark. He'd won the first playoff game against the Braves, and now he was giving our guys a first-hand look at why he'd been so successful as he set us down easily, 1-2-3, in the 7th.

The 8th inning provided our best opportunity, but also our biggest disappointment. Kluszewski reached Sherry for a single to center to open the home half. Lollar followed with another hit, moving Klu up to second base. Our ballclub was known for its speed on the basepaths, but with Sherm and Ted you were looking at a couple of the slowest guys in the league! Lopez remedied that a bit when he sent Earl Torgeson in to run for Lollar as Al Smith prepared to step in to bat. Smith then belted a 2-bagger off the left-centerfield wall. Earl tore around third and scored easily, followed shortly thereafter by Lollar — only Sherm didn't make it. Instead, he was gunned down at the plate with yards to spare on a perfect relay from Moon to Gilliam to John Roseboro. It was bad, but it didn't need to have been a death blow. The score was now 4-2, and we had Smith at third with just one out. But Sherry buckled down and ended the inning by striking out Billy Goodman and popping up Jim Rivera. With that you could almost hear the wind go out of the sails of the Comiskey Park crowd. We had one last shot to get to Sherry in the bottom of the 9th, but he was too good, retiring the side on three routine ground balls.

It was a frustrating loss. We'd been particularly adept at winning 1-run ballgames all season, so it was tough to be on the other end in such a crucial game. We were a resilient club, though, so I wasn't too worried about our fellows' ability to bounce back in Game Three. What I didn't like about the loss, however, was the finger-pointing that started as soon as the final out was recorded. We had quite a cohesive group, so there was none of that amongst the team — it was the sportswriters who were looking to lay blame somewhere. In the perfect vision that is hindsight, they immediately started blaming third base coach Tony Cuccinello for the poor decision to send Lollar home on Smith's double. Despite the fact that we still had the tying run on third base with just one out following Lollar being put out at home, they laid the blame on Tony for our failure to tie or take the lead.

I felt bad for Tony because he was a class guy and didn't deserve that treatment. But he was a standup guy and accepted full responsibility even though it was unclear as to whether it was a bad decision to send Lollar home or whether Sherm had hesitated. "Yes, I waved Lollar in," Tony told the reporters in the clubhouse. "At first I didn't think the Dodgers had a chance to get him. After all, Smith swung on a 3-and-2 count and Lollar was running with the pitch. But after I had given Sherm the "go on" motions, I realized that things were not going to go well. Maybe it would have been different if Lollar hadn't stopped on his way to third. Looking back on the play, I can't say I would do it the same way all over again. It was my fault." Sherm, for his part, showed equal class and refused to allow Tony to be blamed, saying, "I broke stride. It was not Tony's fault at all." Still, the papers continued to point at Tony.

The whole thing just points out what a tough job it is being the third base coach. There's a lot riding on the decisions made there. That's why in the older days you'd usually see the manager out there himself. When John Drebinger of the *New York Times* approached me for my thoughts on the flap, I defended Tony's decision to send Lollar. "After all," I told Drebinger, "that's the way we've been playing it all year long. And if we hadn't played it that way all year, I don't think you'd be seeing us in this World Series. To win, our club has had to follow a type of play that calls for taking advantage of every scoring opportunity that comes. In the first game, it worked when Duke Snider's throw went through the infield. Yesterday, it failed because Wally Moon and Maury Wills came through with a perfect relay to the plate. Also," I said, summing up my point, "don't forget that after Lollar was tagged out, we still had a chance to tie it with a runner on third and only one out. But what did the next two batters do? One struck out and the other fouled out behind the plate. That's why, to win, we've HAD to take chances all year." In any case, as I watched the fateful play continue to be debated, I just hoped that we'd come back and win the Series so that, for Tony's sake, the whole thing would be forgotten. I did NOT want to see it turn into another deal like Johnny Pesky's play in the 1946 Series.

One other reason that we were particularly upset at letting the game get away from us was that the Series was now going to move to the Los Angeles Coliseum. We knew that we'd be at a disadvantage there just like we were at an advantage at Comiskey. Because Comiskey Park was so large, it played to our strengths — defense, speed, and spraying the ball around. The short leftfield wall at The Coliseum, on the other hand, invited players to swing for the homer. That would greatly benefit the Dodgers.

Another reason we liked to play at home was that the Comiskey Park surface itself was customized to our liking. Gene Bossard, our head groundskeeper, was a genius at this, and he began doing it at the urging of Lopez. Al told Gene that we needed to do something to help the guys on our team that liked to bunt, mainly Aparicio and Fox. So Gene built up the third base line just enough so it would keep fair any balls that hugged the chalk. He didn't stop there. Since our guys liked to run, Gene made the lead-off area at first base real hard so the fellows could get a good foothold from which to take off. We also kept Gene busy by making him adjust the height of the mound depending who was pitching. Early Wynn, for example, liked to pitch off a high mound, so Gene would build it up for him prior to his starts. Tailoring your field in these ways was not uncommon around the league, but Gene was one of the best at it. Everyone

This is me in my coach's box at first base. Batting helmets were still a difficult adjustment to many of the older guys on the club, so they often couldn't wait to rid themselves of their cumbersome headgear as soon as they reached base. That meant that I often found myself in possession of a batting helmet while I coached — and that wasn't always a bad thing with the pace at which line drive fouls and wild throws came up on me!

knew we did it, but we still tried to keep it hush-hush. Still, it somehow made its way into the papers prior to the start of the Series. Gene, following his natural inclination to be honest, told reporters, "Of course we have built a slight rise to the third base path. All clubs erect their fields so that they will be to their advantage. Why not us? This is nothing new." Probably realizing that he was divulging too much information, Gene back-pedaled a bit by concluding, "I haven't worked on it since last year." I had to laugh when I read that knowing that I had just seen Gene working away on his customizations that very morning.

Aside from questioning Gene's modifications to Comiskey Park's field, the writers also questioned the basic quality of Gene's infield. The Dodger players were complaining that it was a rough infield that was to blame for all of their errors in Games One and Two. Umpire Bill Summers agreed, saying that the infield at Comiskey was one of the worst. Well, they could accuse him of doctoring the baselines, but NO ONE questioned the quality of Gene's well manicured infield. Taking exception, Gene said, "It's no worse than any other infield. It's bank sand on a clay base and reacts just like the others." It was all a moot point — for the time being, at least — because we wouldn't play another game at home if we couldn't somehow manage to win at least one of the three upcoming games in Los Angeles.

OCTOBER 4, 1959: World Series Game Three — *92,294 SEE DODGERS WIN, 3-1, AND TAKE SERIES LEAD.* That was the headline in the *New York Times* following our tough loss to the Los Angeles Dodgers at the L.A. Coliseum in Game Three of the 1959 World Series on this day. The sportswriters couldn't point to ONE critical play for our defeat this time — something like the Tony Cuccinello/Sherm Lollar moment in our previous game. This time the Dodgers merely played slightly better baseball than us, and the result was a three games to one lead for them in the Series.

The Coliseum stadium itself was almost the bigger story as we spent a travel day flying from Chicago to Los Angeles as the Series shifted to California. Most people still had a tough time saying "Los Angeles Dodgers," so it was quite a concept to consider that this would be the first time ever that a World Series game was played on the west coast. It seemed like only yesterday that the Dodgers had finally broken through for the franchise's first-ever World Series championship — in BROOKLYN. Now, just four years later, Ebbets Field had been abandoned and the franchise was looking to capture its second title, but in its new home in sunny Los Angeles. Since relocating to L.A. in 1957, the Dodgers had been playing their home games in the Los Angeles Memorial Coliseum while their new stadium was being constructed in Chavez Ravine. The Coliseum was certainly suitable for football and track and field events, but it was a lousy place to try and fit a baseball diamond. Its problem was similar to that of the Polo Grounds, only worse. The long rectangular shape meant that the left-field wall was ridiculously close — 251 feet to be exact. To compensate they added a 42-foot tall wire mesh screen, starting from the leftfield foul pole and extending 145 feet towards left-center. The rest of the dimensions were relatively normal — 390 feet to left-center, 420 feet to dead-center, 375 feet to right-center, and 333 feet down the rightfield line. It was an odd-looking configuration to say the least, and, when viewed from high in the stands, the field definitely had the ill-fitting feel of a square peg in a round hole.

The leftfield screen posed a real problem, however, because it had a great capacity to lure teams who didn't play a power game — teams like us — away from their style as they instead aimed for the invitingly short leftfield fence. That had a real potential to affect our guys, so I was a little concerned about it as we took to the field for our first workout prior to the game. If Al Lopez was concerned, he didn't show it. Instead, he told the reporters, "Everyone says we are a club with a powder-puff punch. Maybe this is just the sort of field made to order for us."

Playing World Series games in Los Angeles did present a benefit never experienced before — predictably warm weather. Previously it had always been a crapshoot as to what the temperature would be in Series games. You might get lucky and have warm weather, but you could usually count on some cold and wet stuff, too. But in L.A. it was always sunny and hot — and that was the case on this day as the temperature on the sunken field was well into the 90's at the start of game time. I tell you, it was something to look around and see nearly 100,000 people in the stands. I'd played in front of some big crowds at Yankee Stadium and Cleveland's Municipal Stadium, but never anything like this. There was one last point of business to take care of before the game was to start — the ceremonial first pitch. Harking back to their past — their Flatbush past — the Dodgers had brand new Hall of Famer Zach Wheat do the honors. The old Brooklyn leftfielder then one-hopped a pitch over the plate, and the game was on.

On the mound the game pitted the Dodgers' right-handed side-armer, Don Drysdale, against our tall left-hander, Dick Donovan. After trials with the Braves and Tigers, Dick was purchased by our front office guys prior to the 1955 season. It turned out to be a great move because Dick broke through with an excellent 15-win season in '55. He continued to be very good for us winning another 43 games from 1956 through '58, but he'd been troubled by a sore arm through much of 1959. He'd gotten somewhat better late in the season after being out in August, but it was still uncertain how he would feel out there. But if Dick's arm was right, we knew we'd be fine. He had a very good slider that when working well made him tough to hit, and he fielded his position excellently, too.

Our efforts to jump on Drysdale quickly failed when he was able to wriggle out of a bases-loaded fix in the top of the 1st inning. He started out just fine, power-pitching his way to a called strikeout of Luis Aparicio, but he then walked Nellie Fox. If we'd have been back in Chicago you would have heard the chanting begin — "Go! Go! Go!" But we were a long way from home, so the sedate L.A. crowd remained peaceful. Jim Landis hit next and he lined a single over second, moving Nellie to third. That brought up Ted Kluszewski. Ted had barely gotten comfortable in the box when Landis stole second. I don't think Drysdale or John Roseboro were expecting it because they didn't even make an attempt to throw Jim out. With first base open, Drysdale issued an intentional pass to Ted. So here we were, bases loaded and one out — a tense moment for the Dodger fans who had hardly even settled in to their seats. But the moment passed as Lollar popped out foul behind third base, and Billy Goodman rolled out weakly down the first base line.

It was immediately apparent in the bottom of the 1st inning that Donovan was feeling good, and he looked great as he easily set down the first three Dodger hitters in order. Actually, I shouldn't say it was easy. Dodger lead-off man Jim Gilliam really tagged a Donovan pitch, sending a terrific low drive into left-center. It took a great running shoestring catch by Landis to make the out — but he made those catches all the time. In this case it was Landis that made it look easy for Donovan. Jim always made the tough ones look easy. He had great range and a good arm. Landis was one of four centerfielders I saw that I felt were truly great. I've already written in detail about one of them — Terry Moore. The other two were Joe and Dom DiMaggio. As I've mentioned, Terry, more than anyone, got the best jump on the ball. Joe, on the other hand, had long, smooth strides and looked like he wasn't really moving that fast, but he always got there in plenty of time to catch the ball with apparent ease. Dom went back on the ball better than anyone, so he was able to play very shallow. Once he knew that a ball was going over his head, he'd turn and be on his way. Landis was more of the Joe DiMaggio type because he could run so well. When the ball was hit, he was immediately on his horse. I think Landis could've outrun Joe, but we'll never really know, of course. But it's always fun to compare players from different eras. One thing we know for sure is that Landis couldn't out-hit Joe! Jim wasn't a very good hitter, especially early on. He tweaked his stance in 1958 and improved a great deal, but make no mistake about it — he was in the big leagues because of his stellar defense. Landis possessed a .989 fielding percentage at the time he wrapped up his big league career in 1967, and that was good enough to place him second all-time amongst outfielders.

We had another opportunity to get something going in the 2nd inning, but again failed to capitalize. Jim Rivera walked with one out, but was then cut down trying to steal. Roseboro had apparently seen enough after Landis' uncontested steal in the previous inning because he would not allow another steal on the day, nailing two more of our boys before the day was done. Donovan popped a single off the screen immediately after Rivera had been gunned down by Roseboro. It was the first time in the Series that the screen made its presence felt. It would have been a pop-out in every other big league park in baseball — most Little League fields, too — but at the Coliseum it was a hit. Aparicio followed Donovan with a walk, so we had two men on with two outs — but the rally died there when Fox grounded out to end the inning.

The 3rd inning looked like a repeat of the 2nd. Donovan set the Dodgers down 1-2-3, thanks in part to a double-play ball off the bat of centerfielder Don Demeter, then we proceeded to go down while again stranding two runners. Donovan and Drysdale continued to exchange scoreless innings for three more frames. In that time Dick had been much sharper than Drysdale, allowing just one hit to Drysdale's six, but the frustration was that the score was still 0-0. We picked up two more singles in the top of the 7th, but Drysdale rose to the occasion and again escaped unscathed. We weren't so lucky in the bottom half of the inning. With one out, Charley Neal got things going for the Dodgers by hitting a single off the screen. Neal moved up to second when the next batter, Wally Moon, grounded out. With two outs and a man on second base, Donovan was still in control of the situation. He had not issued a base-on-balls all day, but all of a sudden he couldn't find the plate and walked Norm Larker. Then he walked Gil Hodges to load them up.

That was enough for Lopez. Al got up and made a slow walk to the mound, along the way signaling for Gerry Staley. Al hated to take Dick out — heck, he'd given up only two hits — but Lopez had a great feel for when to pull the strings. Plus, he had at the ready one of the year's best relievers in Staley, so why not use him. While Staley came out to loosen up, the manager in the other dugout pulled his own strings, recalling Demeter and sending 37-year old Carl Furillo in to pinch hit. The "other" manager was none other than Walt Alston, my one-big-league-at-bat teammate from way back in 1936 with the Cardinals. Walt was in his sixth season as Dodger manager, and he'd done quite well in that short period of time. This was already his third appearance in the World Series, and he will be forever remembered in Brooklyn as the ONLY man ever to lead their since-departed franchise to a World Series championship, which he did in 1955.

In spite of the fond feelings Brooklynites may have had for Alston, there was, at the moment, no love loss for Walt as far as the White Sox fans were concerned since they'd read in the papers that he'd called their beloved Go-Go Sox "a bunch of second-raters." Walt vehemently refuted the assertion that he'd slurred our club, but the fans weren't buying his denial. We didn't particularly care one way or the other — we were just hoping that Lopez's hunch to remove Donovan would trump Aston's hunch to bat Furillo. Walt, however, was on a roll as far as recent hunches were concerned. Days earlier Alston had sent Furillo in to pinch hit in the 12th inning of their second playoff game against the Braves, and Carl came through with a game-winning, playoff-ending single. Then, against us in Game Two of the Series, Alston raised some eyebrows when he pinch hit Chuck Essegian instead of Furillo — but Walt again hit pay-dirt when Essegian homered.

Well, Walt hit pay-dirt again. Staley threw a slider and Furillo got good wood on the ball. It was hit to Aparicio's left, and it looked like Luis was going to get it as he made a lunge — but then the ball took a hop right over his outstretched glove and into the outfield for a single. The huge crowd, which had been very quiet for the entire game, suddenly let out a roar as Neal and Larker scored. Staley got the next man to end the inning, but we were now trailing, 2-0, as we headed into the 8th.

Our 1959 ballclub was a team that just didn't quit. They kept coming at you. In an obviously desperate situation, Kluszewski led off the top of the 8th with a single to left. Then Lollar singled to right, moving Ted up to second. That's when Alston went with the hot hand of Larry Sherry, bringing him in to replace Drysdale. Sherry had been flawless, but he stumbled a bit here by hitting Goodman to load the bases with none out. Then, in a flash, Al Smith hit into a 6-4-3 double-play. A run scored on the play, but that was a small consolation when the inning ended as Rivera, the next batter, popped out.

Los Angeles pushed their lead back to two when they got to Staley for a run in the bottom of the 8th, so our guys had one last chance as they got set to face Sherry for the top of the 9th. It was no use — Sherry's stuff was electric. Masterfully mixing his fastball, curve, and slider, he first fanned pinch-hitter Norm Cash swinging, then he got Aparicio looking. Fox worked him for a single, but then Sherry blew his fastball by Landis for the last out of the game. A steam whistle mounted atop the stadium immediately blasted, signaling a Los Angeles victory, and the Dodger players converged in the middle of the field to share congratulatory backslaps and handshakes. Needless to say, we were disheartened as we headed to the clubhouse.

Once inside, Lopez, wearing a weary smile, faced the sportswriters. They asked him how it felt to lose after a lousy break like Furillo's bad-hop grounder. "We had a few of them during the season, too," Al said. He pointed out that it wasn't really the bad hop that did us in, it was our inability to score when presented with golden opportunities. He mentioned that we had out-hit the Dodgers 12 to 5, yet still managed to score only one run. In fact, we had beaten Los Angeles at their own game — "screeno." That was what they had come to call hitting the ball off the leftfield screen. We had five "screenos" to their one. "We always do it the hard way," Al said. "We'll have to do it that way again."

One reporter asked Al if he thought that the Dodgers had stolen our "steal" sign because Roseboro had thrown out three of four stealers. Al just laughed it off, saying, "I really don't know." Then, pretending to get up, he added, "I think I'll go over there and find out!" The possibility that the Dodgers had stolen our steal sign certainly was not out of the question. Chuck Dressen, one of the best all-time sign stealers, was a coach with the Dodgers, so it was certainly possible. Sign stealing wasn't against the rules, so we just changed our signals prior to the next game as a precautionary measure.

As soon as the first team started using signs in the early days of baseball, other teams started trying to steal them. It was, and still is, common practice — even with our Go-Go Sox. In fact, the whole war of sign stealing reached heights that even I'd never seen earlier in the season. We'd suspected that the Indians were somehow stealing our signs whenever we played them at Municipal Stadium. We'd all heard rumors that the 1951 Giants had stolen signs by placing a guy with a telescope in the faraway clubhouse in dead-center at the Polo Grounds. Supposedly, he would look at the catcher's fingers, then send the decoded sign to the dugout via a hidden buzzer. Then a signal would be flashed to the hitter. Some feel that this helped the Giants overcome the 13-1/2 game deficit in the '51 pennant race — and some even think that Bobby Thomson was tipped as to what pitch Ralph Branca was going to throw prior to his "Home Run Heard 'Round the World." Well, we finally discovered that the Indians did, in fact, have a guy with a telescope in their scoreboard, and he'd relay our signals to their hitters with a light.

We kept quiet about our discovery and decided to give them a taste of their own medicine the next time they came to Comiskey Park. Soon thereafter, the Indians rolled into Chicago and Early Wynn sneaked out to our scoreboard with a big telescope in hand. Let me tell you, Lollar and some other guys really enjoyed teeing off when they got the signal of what was coming. Still, most of our hitters did not want to be tipped off. They were leery of the whole thing. They thought they could get beaned if Wynn got the signs crossed. Our scoreboard stealing operation was such a success that it continued right into the 1960 season with blessings from Lopez and Bill Veeck. It got a little sticky, though, when Al Worthington, a right-handed pitcher, joined the club in the middle of the '60 campaign. He was sort of a righteous guy and didn't like the whole scoreboard deception scam. He went to Lopez and expressed his disapproval, but Lopez told him he had to abide by it. Not liking Lopez's orders, Worthington went up the chain of command — all the way to the top. He went to see Veeck, only poor old Worthington had no way of knowing that the sign-stealing scam had come from Veeck himself. Bill simply told Worthington to obey his manager. When the season was over, Worthington chose to quit baseball rather than continue to play for a club he felt was competing dishonestly. I could see Worthington's point, but I thought his was an extreme position to take. As far as I was concerned, it was just baseball. But for guys like Worthington, it posed a serious moral dilemma. 1960 wasn't the first time Worthington had faced this problem, either. In fact, he'd faced the same issue late in the 1959 season as the San Francisco Giants chased the Dodgers and the Braves for the pennant. The Giants had resumed their scoreboard sign-stealing program and pulled to within just a few games of Milwaukee and Los Angeles. But then Worthington, at that time a pitcher with San Francisco, went to management and complained about the scam. The Giants supposedly then abandoned the whole operation and ultimately faded from the race. Then Worthington was shipped off to Boston just before the start of the 1960 season.

In any case, it was going to take more than a stolen steal sign to beat us in the Series. We still had confidence in our ability to come back, and Lopez reflected that when he wrapped up his post-game chat with the reporters by saying, "It will be Wynn tomorrow — then WIN all the way!"

OCTOBER 5, 1959: World Series Game Four — *DODGERS SET BACK*

WHITE SOX, 5 TO 4, ON HODGES' HOMER. There you have it — the *New York Times* headline summarizing our Game Four loss at the Los Angeles Memorial Coliseum on this day. One of the biggest stars of the game turned out to be the tall screen in the Coliseum's leftfield corner. In an article titled *A GAME CALLED SCREENO, Times* columnist Arthur Daley artfully described the screen's first real moment as a factor in the 1959 World Series. "Like a monster that emerged alive from one of those Hollywood horror movies," wrote Daley, "The Thing gave shudders and thrills today to the largest crowd in World Series history. The Thing is the grotesque screen at the leftfield end of the misshapen ballfield laid out in the Coliseum. It's been terrifying pitchers since the Dodgers moved to this never-never land from Brooklyn. It frightened Roger Craig in the 7th inning just as he seemed to have the game easily won, then it gave Gerry Staley the screaming-meemies in the 8th." Clever descriptives not withstanding, we were now in a real jam as the defeat put us behind in the Series, three games to one. The contest would feature a familiar pattern to us as of late — threatening early but failing to capitalize. The ironic twist, however, would be the failure of our usually-airtight defense up the middle.

Throughout the season, "strength down the middle" had become a commonly spoke phrase when describing the success of our 1959 ballclub. In building this team, Al Lopez's belief was that we had to be strong in that all-important "line down the middle" — and I have to agree that he was right. With Comiskey Park being so big, middle strength was the key in controlling the opponents' offensive output. Al always explained it like this — "If you don't let THEM score that run, and instead YOU score it — you'll win." It sounds like stating the obvious, but he really meant it. The essence of it was that if you had strength down the middle then you could rely on your ballclub to win the close games. You didn't NEED a 3-run cushion to win, just a 1-run lead. Our 1959 record proved Al correct, too. Of the 46 1-run games we played in '59, we won 33 of them. We also won 11 of the 15 extra-inning contests we played.

Even as we were racking up wins in '59, people had a hard time believing that you could get all the way to a pennant by playing a style like ours. Casey Stengel, who in the meantime was watching his defending champs get nickel-and-dimed right out of their A.L. title, tried to make believers out of folks by saying, "People used to tell me they couldn't keep it up, winning by one run and getting no hits. Why can't they? You get one run, they get two. You get eight runs, they get nine. You make a mistake against this club and you lose a game." Bill Veeck, who's previous clubs had usually relied heavily on offense, once told a reporter, "This team may change the entire concept of baseball. Who ever thought a team could win so many games without a big RBI-man, the number-3 or number-4 hitter who drives in runs?"

Al's "strength down the middle" philosophy began with the pitching. Our starting rotation was strong at its core with Early Wynn and Bob Shaw. The rest of the rotation — Billy Pierce, Dick Donovan, and Barry Latman — was not quite up to the level of Wynn and Shaw, so we needed a solid group of relievers to help them out when necessary, and we had that in Gerry Staley and Turk Lown. Once the ball left the pitcher's hand, the rest of the middle-strength guys came into play — the catcher, shortstop, second baseman, and centerfielder. I've already mentioned Jim Landis' great ability in center, but I've yet to detail the talents of his down-the-middle cohorts.

Sherm Lollar was a fine defensive catcher. In fact, his .992 career fielding percentage is in the top five of all time. Equally as important, Sherm was very good at handling the pitchers and really called a good game back there. Like most catchers, however, he was slow as the dickens — but he was a clutch man with the bat. Aside from his penchant to deliver the key hit, Sherm could hit the long ball. Only two men on our '59 club compiled double-digit home run totals — Al Smith with 17 and Sherm with 22. That turned out to be a single-season career high for him. He was a quiet leader on our ballclub.

At shortstop we had Luis Aparicio, and I really think he was one of the best I've ever seen at that position. He had great range and a very strong arm. Luis could do more things right than anybody. I never saw him make mistakes or be in the wrong place on a relay play. He was great with the relay — probably one of the best ones ever. In fact, Luis' arm was so strong that we had him go into the outfield to take all the relay throws in 1959 while Nellie Fox covered the base — Aparicio's arm was that powerful. Luis, after taking over the starting job from Chico Carrasquel in 1956, seemingly always led the league in fielding his position. He literally dominated A.L. shortstops. He came to the states already well-schooled in the position because his father had also been a great shortstop back home in Venezuela. They'd even played together on the same team in the Venezuelan League, 16-year old Luis eventually replacing his father at short when Dad, getting up in age, could no longer outfield his phenom-son. Luis' greatness at shortstop was only bolstered when he joined the Sox in '56 and was mentored by Marty Marion, one of the position's truly great ones.

Marty also worked with Luis on his hitting. Marion tweaked Aparicio's stance by having him bring his feet closer together so he could stride into the pitch. There was an immediate improvement and Luis hit .266 while leading the league in steals on his way to being named rookie of the year. He was pretty good at drawing walks, too, and this only helped his base stealing numbers as he went on to lead the league in swipes for the next eight seasons. By 1959 the writers began writing of the "Aparicio Double," which was a walk and a stolen base. Luis was a great player and a great person, and I was very happy to see him make the Hall of Fame.

Rounding out our "strength down the middle" group was Nellie Fox. Everybody knows what a great second baseman he was. Like Luis, Nellie's in the Hall of Fame, and deservedly so. He should've gotten there a little sooner, in my opinion. He passed away in 1975, and two years later the veteran's committee put him in the Hall — two years too late for Nellie to enjoy it while he was living. That was a shame. In any case, with Nellie and Luis, we were as good as any middle infield has ever been, and that's a very important start to establishing a strong defense. The White Sox acquired Nellie from the Philadelphia Athletics shortly after the conclusion of the 1948 season. He was just a boy, so there was no way to know what a fine player he'd develop in to. He was a starter by 1950, and he continued to anchor the White Sox infield through the 1963 season.

Nellie was well-established by the time I joined the Sox coaching staff in 1954, but I was quickly even more impressed by him once I got to see him up close. He wasn't gifted with natural physical ability. For starters, he was only about 5-foot-9 and 150 pounds. He was not fast, and he lacked arm strength. What he had, however, was a work ethic that was far superior to that of most players I'd seen. Through his hard work he turned himself into a great fielder, one who could make all the plays. One of my jobs as a White Sox coach was to hit infield. Nellie wasn't satisfied with the amount of work he got in during our regular practice sessions, so he would ask me to hit him extra balls practically every day that the club was at home in Chicago. I'd hit him about 45-50 balls. He'd want me to hit them to the right, then to the left, and then back. After that, I'd hit line drives right at him. He just wanted to get better. Nellie Fox did more with his limited ability than anybody I've ever seen. What he accomplished should be an inspiration to anyone who considers himself an underdog.

Nellie's hard work eventually lifted him to the position of leader of our infield, and our infield was the strength of our '59 club. He didn't lead by being a rah-rah type of guy — he was, instead, a quiet leader, strong in character. He led by example. The younger guys would see how he operated, and they respected what they saw. And not only did they see a great fielder, they saw a fine hitter, too. Through great persistence, Nellie made himself a very good contact hitter. He always hit around .300, and rarely struck out. In fact, he averaged only about 15 strikeouts a year, repeatedly leading the league in that category. Nellie did all of this — the great fielding and the great batting — he did it all while setting records for durability, at one time playing in 628 consecutive games. Nellie really was a catalyst for the great season we had in '59, and his achievement was recognized when he was named 1959 American League MVP.

Strength down the middle would not be enough to win a pennant without a solid cast filling out the rest of the lineup. Billy Goodman and Bubba Phillips were our third basemen. They alternated and made up a fine tandem. Complimenting Landis in the outfield were Al Smith and Jim Rivera — both good ball players. There were other fellows, too, like Ron Jackson, Earl Torgeson, and Jim McAnany, to name a few. They all made valuable contributions to us finally reaching our goal of unseating our arch rivals, the New York Yankees, in 1959. Every year we'd try to beat them, and we'd come close, but we just couldn't cross that threshold until we finally broke through in '59. That's why we were so thrilled the day we won the pennant — because we'd finally beat the Yankees! However, as was the case with my 1944 St. Louis Browns, the enormous achievement of dethroning the Yankees sometimes overshadowed the ultimate task of winning the World Series. Now, after our loss to the Dodgers on this day, we trailed in the Series, three games to one, and were in serious danger of suffering the same fate as my '44 Brownies.

There was one fellow who was as good a choice as any to be the man who could get us pointed in the right direction. That was Early Wynn, and it was he who drew the starting assignment on this day in a rematch of Game One when he faced Roger Craig. Early had just the right mound disposition — mean and scowling — to let the Dodgers know that we meant business and were not about to concede anything. It's funny, but Early's pitching approach was the complete opposite of his off-field personality. When not pitching, Early was a laid-back, happy-go-lucky type — even to the point of being the occasional practical joker. But when on the mound, he was all business. In fact, he used to say that the mound was his "office." And when working at his office, Early was an intimidating force who was feared by hitters. Years before he'd told sportswriters that he'd knock down his own grandmother if she dug in on him. The quote stuck with him forever, and batters who tried to get a good toe-hold soon found out he wasn't kidding. We'd hoped that Early's tough, grim-faced approach might be just the thing to get us back in the win column — just like it had already done on 22 other occasions in '59.

Standing in my first base coach's box, I watched Craig throw his last warm-up pitch as Landis strode to the plate to lead-off the game. What I thought about at that moment was that Early would be good, NO doubt — we could count on that. It was our BATS that needed to come alive today. We'd scored only one run in our previous game, the big problem being that we had not hit with runners in scoring position. Well, our prospects for turning around that trend did not look good after we loaded the bases and failed to score — just like we'd done in the last game. Landis made a quick out by flying to center, but then Aparicio walked and stole second — our first "Aparicio Double" of the Series. Nellie followed with a bloop double to right, but Luis only reached third on the hit because he had to stay near second base until he was sure that Dodger rightfielder Wally Moon was not going to catch Fox's flare. Craig issued an intentional pass to Ted Kluszewski to load the bases with one out, and that move paid off for them when Lollar hit into a 6-4-3 double-play.

Early seemed to validate everyone's confidence in him when he looked good while retiring the Dodgers in the bottom of the 1st inning. He gave up a 2-out single to Moon in the frame, but then quickly slammed the door shut on any idea of a rally by striking out Norm Larker. We got a 1-out single from Smith in the top of the 2nd, but Craig, too, snuffed any thoughts of a rally by getting Rivera to fly to right and popping up Wynn. Los Angeles had an interesting bottom of the 2nd when they looked more like the Go-Go Sox than the Dodgers. Don Demeter, playing his second game in center in place of the injured Duke Snider, legged a 1-out infield hit to shortstop. Next, he took second on a deep fly-out by John Roseboro. Then Maury Wills duplicated Demeter's feat with another scratch infield hit to short. The hit moved Demeter up to third base, then Wills prompt-ly stole second. It looked like we were watching ourselves in Dodger uniforms. But, unfortunately for L.A., their Go-Go Sox impersonation was so good that they failed to score when Craig went down on strikes to end the threat.

We looked to have something going in the top of the 3rd when we got 1-out singles from Aparicio and Fox, but it netted nothing when Kluszewski hit into an inning-ending twin-killing. The Dodgers, too, would threaten in their half of the 3rd, but they made good on their opportunity by hanging four runs on us. The shocker of the Dodger onslaught was that their runs came largely as a result of a breakdown in our vaunted "strength down the middle." Early seemed to be cruising along just fine as he set down the first two batters of the inning — Jim Gilliam on a pop to Fox, and Charley Neal on a come-backer. Then Moon reached Early for his second single of the game.

That brought up Larker with two outs and a man on first. Norm smacked a single to centerfield, and Moon motored right around second with designs on reaching third. Landis tried to peg Moon out at third, but his throw was wild and got by Goodman. By the time Early recovered the ball, Moon had scored and Larker had moved up to second. Gil Hodges immediately made us pay fur-ther for Landis' error by singling to left to drive in Larker with the second tally of the inning. Then Demeter singled to center while Hodges went all the way around to third. Next, Early was working to Roseboro when Lollar let a pitch go through him for a passed ball. The miscue allowed Hodges to score easily while Demeter moved up to second. Again, the Dodgers made us pay for our mistake when Roseboro singled to right, allowing Demeter to score uncontested. As Rivera gathered the ball on the play, Roseboro rounded first to try and stretch his single into a double. Aparicio was covering second as Rivera's throw came in — and Roseboro would have been out — but Luis dropped the ball. Roseboro was safe on Aparicio's error. It was unbelievable. Almost the entire "strength down the middle" unit had faltered in the inning — Early wasn't fooling anyone anymore; Aparicio and Landis had erred; and Lollar allowed a passed ball. The only member of our "strength down the middle" unit who emerged from the inning unscathed was Fox. These guys were human, of course, and everyone made mistakes from time to time, but they were so good that you just never expected to see this type of wholesale breakdown happen all at once. And the results were devastating as we now trailed, 4-0 — and we still needed an out to get out of the inning.

Lopez trudged out to the mound to remove Early, waving in Lown from the bullpen, and Turk put a merciful end to the inning when he got Wills to ground out to Fox. Our guys were now in a tough position as they staggered off the field. We weren't built to come from behind, but that's what we were now facing. Our comeback did not go well from the 4th through the 6th innings, either, as Craig mowed our fellows down without allowing any runs. The good news was that we weren't falling any further behind because Pierce had come on in relief in the 4th and pitched scoreless ball through the 6th.

We finally broke out of our scoreless malaise in the top of the 7th inning. Torgeson, pinch-hitting for Pierce, grounded out to open the frame, but Landis followed with a sharp single to left. Aparicio then tried to bunt for a hit, but he pushed it too hard right back to Craig and was thrown out at first base. Landis moved up to second, so Luis got credit for a sacrifice, but he was definitely trying for a hit. The rally looked to be wilting with Luis' failure to bunt for a hit, but Fox then lined a single off Craig's glove, advancing Landis to third. Ted Kluszewski heated things up by poking a solid single to right, scoring Landis with our first run of the day and sending Fox to third.

Walt Alston went out to talk to Craig, then returned to the dugout without making a pitching change. It seemed like all of Alston's decisions up to that point had been the right ones, but his choice to leave in Craig would quickly prove bad for his ballclub. No sooner had Alston stepped back into the Dodger dugout when there was a crack of a bat and the sound of fans yelling, "Screeno! Screeno!" What Alston turned to see was that Lollar had gotten a hold of a slider away and popped it over the leftfield screen for a game-tying 3-run homer. Lollar's pop would have been an easy out back home at Comiskey Park, but here at O'Malley's Chinese Theater (a derogatory nickname the Coliseum had taken on due to its notoriety for the "cheap" home run), Lollar's pop-fly was as good as any tape-measure shot ever hit. Craig finished the inning by striking out Goodman, but he would not return for the 8th. Finally, one of Alston's hunches had gone wrong.

Staley took the mound for us in the bottom of the 7th and looked good as he retired the side in order. The down-side to knocking Craig out of the game was that it meant that Alston brought in his red-hot reliever Larry Sherry. And he looked great in setting us down in the top of the 8th, getting all three outs on ground balls. So, it was still tied, 4-4, when the Dodgers came up to hit in the bottom of the 8th. Our guys had barely finished throwing the ball around the infield to start the inning when Gil Hodges, the first Dodger batter of the inning, hammered a Staley sinker over the far end of the screen for a solo "screeno." Gil's homer was a devastating blow to us — a real morale breaker. Gerry pitched lights-out for the rest of the inning, getting Demeter, Roseboro, and Wills in order, but the damage had been done.

Our guys certainly did not give up, but they faced a tough task in trying to score on Sherry in the top of the 9th. He was on the kind of roll that you don't see pitchers get on very often. The momentum he'd built up in the regular season had carried right into the Series, and he already had saves in Games Two and Three. Sherry looked absolutely confident as he took the mound to start the 9th. I'd read where Dodger coach Chuck Dressen had said, "Larry just comes in to take charge. He thinks he can do it — he doesn't care who's batting. Larry has the best assortment of stuff on the staff." Apparently, Dressen wasn't kidding. Sherry took control of the inning from the first pitch to Aparicio. Luis quickly grounded out, followed by another ground-out off the bat of Fox. Down to our last out, we had a fighting chance with the powerful Ted Kluszewski batting, but Sherry got Ted to pop out to left to end the game.

For good reason, it was like a tomb in our clubhouse. Lollar, without whose clutch 3-run homer we would not even have had a chance, was the picture of dejection as he sat slumped in front of his locker talking to reporters. At that moment he could have cared less about his big homer — it was his critical passed ball that he was lamenting. But that's the kind of team player he was. Lopez was also speaking to the sportswriters, trying to put on a brave face. "It'll be Bob Shaw tomorrow," he said, "then we're GOING to take this Series back to Chicago." Al was trying to speak with bravado, but there was almost a hint of incredulity in his words as he added, "The Dodgers are a good team, but they're not THAT good."

Better than any of the other writers, Arthur Daley best summed up why we lost Game Four when he wrote, "This was an odd ballgame. In the third, the Sox came unraveled. They just came apart. The team that scrounged and scrimped and never gave anything away all season long suddenly became as wildly extravagant as a big shot executive with an unlimited expense account. They gave away runs and that's entirely contrary to their parsimonious nature. Two errors, slipshod play, and unprepossessing Dodger hits suddenly totaled four runs. Thus have the rags-to-riches Dodgers moved another step toward the grand climax of what Hollywood would describe as a Cinderella-type picture. They need only one more victory and there will be no tomorrow for the profligate and wasteful minions of Al Lopez. This town will go crazier than usual and the Go-Go boys will depart quietly for home to spend a cold winter berating themselves for their profligacy." They were sobering words for us, but we knew that they were absolutely true.

OCTOBER 6, 1959: World Series Game Five — *WHITE SOX WIN, 1-0, CUT DODGER LEAD FOR SERIES TO 3-2.* That was the headline in the *New York Times* on this day as we fended off elimination by squeaking out a narrow win at the Coliseum in Los Angeles. Our victory meant that we would win or lose the Series back home in Chicago where we were at our most comfortable. Our team was built for the confines of Comiskey Park, so we were very happy to be seeing the last of the Coliseum. Arthur Daley of the *Times* captured our sentiments exactly when he wrote, "With one convulsive shudder the White Sox freed themselves from the snake pit today. They climbed clear of the horrors of Walter O'Malley's Chinese torture chamber as a result of one unprepossessing run in the 4th inning. But they were tormented fiendishly in the 8th before completing their escape to the sanity of Chicago. So this great post-season carnival now leaves this land of magic and make-believe for the colder and more prosaic site of Chicago, with the White Sox still alive, and kicking with unexpected vigor."

It was classic Go-Go Sox baseball that allowed us to escape Los Angeles with a fighting chance to still win the Series. We scratched out an ugly run, played solid defense, pitched very well, and outsmarted the opponent on the managerial level. Plus — we wore BLACK socks! Ed Froelich, our trainer, had seen just about enough of us struggling since switching to white socks at the beginning of the Series. To heck with the rationalists who were not superstitious about our pre-Series sock switch, said Ed. We needed some luck — NOW, and Ed thought going back to the black socks was just the thing to bring us some. Al Lopez gave Ed his blessing to switch us back to our black socks for the rest of the Series — regardless of whether they reminded anyone of the 1919 Black Sox scandal. So, sporting our old black socks, we won. Who knows — maybe Ed was on to something!

Bob Shaw was Lopez's choice to start Game Five. This gave Bob a chance to avenge his tough loss in Game Two, but he had his work cut out for him in that he was facing Dodger left-hander Sandy Koufax. Sandy was still a couple years removed from really finding himself as a pitcher and coming into his own, but he still flashed his future greatness on occasion. In fact, Koufax had made head-lines about a month earlier when he'd struck out 18 San Francisco Giants in one game, tying Bob Feller's 21-year old record. From my first base coach's box I watched Koufax take his warm-up pitches prior to the start of the 1st inning. He looked very good — and even better when the inning actually began. Koufax appeared overpowering as he set our guys down in order — Luis Aparicio on a strikeout looking; Nellie Fox on a weak pop to short; and Jim Landis on a strike-out swinging.

Los Angeles mounted a minor threat in the bottom of the 1st when Jim Gilliam led off with a single to center. Charley Neal hit next, and he lifted a pop fly into foul territory on the left side. Aparicio, leftfielder Jim McAnany, and third baseman Bubba Phillips all tore off after the ball. It looked like no one would get to it, but then Luis made a great catch with his back to the infield. Gilliam was able to tag and go to second on the play, but Shaw put out the fire by getting both Wally Moon and Norm Larker on come-backers.

Both pitchers continued to look strong in the 2nd, each retiring the oppo-sition in order. Our fellows generated our first scoring opportunity of the day in the top half of the 3rd, however. Phillips got things going by reaching Koufax for our first hit of the game, a well-hit single off the leftfield screen. McAnany fol-lowed with a pop-out to first, and then Shaw moved Bubba up to second base with a sac bunt. Next up was Aparicio, and he lashed a sharp single to leftfield. Bubba moved up to third on the hit, making a big turn but holding. Meanwhile, Larker scooped up the ball in left and fired it in the direction of home plate. Seeing that, Aparicio took off for second base — but Gilliam cut off Larker's throw and made a quick peg to Charley Neal at second. It was great fundamen-tal baseball, and Luis was a dead duck. It was the type of aggressive base-running we'd done all year long. It was part of the reason why we were able to win the pennant. Aparicio's gamble killed the rally, but we had no regrets about his gam-ble in that situation.

The Dodgers made a little offensive noise of their own when they touched

Shaw for back-to-back singles with two out in the bottom of the 3rd inning. But they, too, failed to push anything across when Moon grounded into an inning-ending force-out. Our guys, on the other hand, finally broke through with a run in the top of the 4th — but it wasn't exactly a thing of beauty. Fox led off the inning with a single to right. Landis followed with a single to center, sending Nellie to third. That brought up Sherm Lollar and visions of another 3-run "screeno" like he'd hit in the previous game, but any ideas of a big inning fizzled, however, when Sherm instead hit into a 4-3 double-play. The bright side, though, was that Nellie had scored on the play. Koufax avoided further damage by squashing the rally when he retired our next batter, Ted Kluszewski, on a fly ball to center.

It seemed like the Dodgers were always knocking on the door, before and after we took our 1-0 lead. With one out in the bottom of the 4th, Gil Hodges stroked a 400-foot triple to right-center, but Shaw recovered from the scare by getting Don Demeter to bounce back to the mound and then retiring John Roseboro on a pop to short. Los Angeles threatened again the next inning when Gilliam singled and stole second with two outs. But Shaw again dodged the bullet by popping up Neal to end the inning. We had a very close call with two outs in the 6th when Hodges ripped a shot off the screen in left. It was a line drive that would have been a home run in almost any big league park, but it never got high enough to clear the mesh. Plus, Hodges hit it so hard that he only got a single out of it, then he was left stranded when Demeter ended the inning by hitting into a force play.

Our slim lead faced another challenge in the 7th, but our guys again avoided disaster — this time thanks to a heads-up move by Lopez. With two outs and Dodger runners on first and second, Lopez called time and made a defensive change. McAnany, playing leftfield, came out of the game. Al Smith, playing rightfield, shifted over to left. Jim Rivera, an excellent fly-chaser with a very good arm, went in to play right. Al said he made the move to give us more throwing power in this key situation, but it was Rivera's great range that turned out to be what saved us. As soon as everyone was situated in their new positions, Shaw, facing Neal, uncorked a wild pitch that allowed both runners to advance one bag. So now the situation was even more dire with the tying AND winning runs in scoring position. Bob came in to Charley on the next pitch, and Neal launched it to the far reaches of right-centerfield. With two outs, the runners were off at the crack of the bat, destined to score with ease. At the same time, Jim took off after the ball in mad pursuit — and hauled it in about 10 feet from the fence. It was a great catch, an over-the-shoulder grab very similar to the one made by Willie Mays in the 1954 World Series. I couldn't help but wonder if Lopez, seeing Rivera's great snag, had a flashback to Mays' rally-killing catch because it came against Al's '54 Indians club.

The *Times'* Arthur Daley recounted the sequence in his column the next day. "But in the 7th, when the straining Dodgers got two men on with two out, the Lopez generator began giving off sparks," wrote Daley. "He placed Jim Rivera

in rightfield, and Jungle Jim justified that faith by running almost to the peri-
style to catch Charley Neal's blast. Al Smith, the man Rivera replaced, couldn't
have got close." Later, Lopez would tell reporters, "It was as great a catch as I've
seen him make all year. He made me look good, didn't he?"

We were right back in hot water in the bottom of the 8th and, again, it was
Lopez who deserves a great deal of credit for our escape. The inning opened with
Landis dropping a towering fly ball off the bat of Moon. The ball went into the
sun at the last minute and Jim just couldn't follow it. He was also hampered by
the impossible background of white-shirted Dodger fans. This actually made it
very difficult to pick up the ball from anywhere in the Coliseum. Because of the
extreme heat at the uncovered Coliseum, the Dodgers played most of their home
games at night when the temperatures were cooler. For that reason, even THEY
were surprised at the difficulty in tracking the flight of the ball when we played
Games Three, Four, and Five during the day at the Coliseum. In any case, after
Landis' muff, Larker flied out to right, bringing Hodges up to the plate. Gil was
obviously picking up the ball very well from Shaw. He'd tripled in his first at-bat,
then singled off the screen in his second trip. Now, again, he unloaded on Shaw,
sending a smoking shot over the screen in left — foul by inches. It was a close
call, and we felt lucky when Shaw proceeded to hold Hodges to a mere single
when he resumed his at-bat, but Moon advanced to third on Hodges' hit and Gil
was able to go to second as the throw came in to third. So, we had one out with
runners on second and third, and that's when the Al Lopez-Walt Alston chess
match broke out.

You may need to take notes to keep up here. Seeing a chance to possibly
break the game open against Shaw, a right-hander, Alston removed the right-
handed swinging Demeter in favor of left-handed pinch-hitter Ron Fairly. Seeing
that, Lopez went to the pen and called for our southpaw, Billy Pierce. Alston
countered by recalling Fairly, opting instead for the right-handed hitting Rip
Repulski. Many Dodger fans who had witnessed the recent pinch-hitting heroics of Carl Furillo wondered why Alston would go with Repulski instead of
Furillo in this situation. Furillo, like Repulski, was a right-handed swinger, yet
Furillo had the hot bat. All you needed to do to find the answer to this question
was look 90 feet down the first base line at the vacant first base bag. Alston knew
that Lopez would order an intentional pass in this situation, so Walt didn't want
to waste Furillo for that purpose. Sure enough, Lopez signaled Pierce to walk
Repulski, so Pierce put him on, loading the bases.

Now we had the bases loaded with one out and the left-handed hitting
Roseboro set to face Pierce. This gave Alston the chance to get the match-up he
wanted — the right-handed swinging Furillo against the lefty Pierce — so Alston
sent Furillo in to hit for Roseboro. With that, Lopez removed Pierce, replacing
him with right-hander Dick Donovan. So here we were, umpteen moves later,
with a right-handed hitter facing a right-handed reliever. The match-up would
appear to favor the pitcher, but both managers at this point believed that they had

the guy in there that they wanted in this situation. Lopez won the battle of wits, however, when Donovan got Furillo on an infield pop. Then Donovan ended the inning by getting Don Zimmer to fly out to left. It was high drama for everyone. For me, it was always a pleasure to watch Lopez work in this manner.

The 9th inning provided us one last opportunity to try and pad our lead, but our fellows went down 1-2-3 against the Dodgers' big reliever, right-hander Stan Williams, who'd taken over for Koufax in the 8th. Donovan had his one run, and now he was going to have to protect the lead — our Series fate riding on his right arm. Dick was unflustered by the situation, however, and coolly strolled out to the hill for the bottom of the 9th. The first batter he faced was pinch-hitter Larry Sherry. That's right — Larry Sherry! Out of options from all his earlier maneuvers, Alston needed someone with some pop in his bat — and he had no one to turn to except Sherry. Although Sherry had been a serious thorn in our side for the three previous games, that had been in his role as a pitcher. As a pinch-hitter, however, Sherry was not quite so intimidating, and Donovan easily retired him on a ground ball to third. Continuing to expertly mix his well-located assortment of sliders and fastballs, Dick then shut the door with ground ball outs off the bats of Gilliam and Neal.

We converged around Donovan for subdued congratulations as the disappointed Los Angeles fans quietly filed out of the Coliseum. They knew they'd seen the last of their Dodgers for 1959, and if their boys were going to win the Series, they'd have to do it at Comiskey Park. Our happy clubhouse was a stark contrast to its mood following the three previous losses. It wasn't wildly out of control, just quietly upbeat and buzzing. "Now we're going to win this thing," a smiling Lopez told a crowd of sportswriters, players, and other assorted people. "I told the boys if we won this one, we'd take the Series." Someone off in the distance hollered, "Now we'll get 'em back in our own backyard!"

Donovan and Shaw shared a heartfelt bear hug for the photographers' cameras. Shaw was beaming because he'd now gotten a key win after suffering the frustrating loss in Game Two. Donovan was coming off an equally frustrating loss as the pitcher of record in Game Three, but his face was more reserved like the big man himself. "I thought I pitched a much better game today than I did in Game Two," Shaw told the reporters. "I put the ball where I wanted to. Sure, Hodges and Neal got their hits — they are good hitters — but I kept the ball away, so they didn't overpower me this time." The reporters then turned to Donovan to ask him if he was really as cool as he looked out there in the 8th and 9th. "I was keyed up," Dick said with genuine honesty. "I wasn't whistling 'Yankee Doodle Dandy,' I can tell you." Then a cameraman asked Dick to smile, at which Donovan replied, "I won't be able to smile for three days." Then, as best he could, Dick smiled.

Rivera, of course, was also a very popular guy with the sportwriters that day because of his big game-saving catch. Recounting his grab of Neal's 365-foot drive, Rivera told the reporters, "I knew if I didn't get it, the game was over. I ran like hell and stretched out as far as I could — and the ball stuck." Also speaking with the writers was Aparicio. He had a nice 2-hit day, one of his hits coming in our run-scoring 4th inning. Luis didn't want to discuss that, though, all he cared to comment on was the Coliseum infield. Maybe he was doing it on behalf of Gene Bossard, our groundskeeper whose reputation the Dodgers had sullied when they complained about Gene's infield following Game Two. "I can recall only one worse infield than the Coliseum's," Luis said. "Back in Venezuela we had a field full of rocks." A short time later we boarded a jet and took off for Chicago, leaving behind the Coliseum's white-shirted fans, its 42-foot tall monstrosity of a leftfield screen, its oppressive heat... and its lousy infield.

OCTOBER 8, 1959: World Series Game Six — *DODGERS WIN WORLD SERIES BY BEATING WHITE SOX, 9 TO 3, IN THE SIXTH CONTEST.* That was the dreaded *New York Times* headline summarizing our defeat in the sixth and deciding game of the 1959 World Series on this day at Comiskey Park in Chicago. Our boys were loaded with confidence as we flew back to Chicago for our Thursday date with the Dodgers for Game Six. We liked our chances at evening the Series on our own ballfield behind Early Wynn, who Al Lopez had decided would start. Early had been great in the Series-opener, but he was bounced from Game Four in the 3rd inning. Early had been so good in 1959 that we had every reason to believe that he would not have back-to-back bad outings in the World Series, so he seemed to be a natural pick to start the critical Game Six. There's one fellow who might have disagreed in Lopez's choice to use Wynn in Game Six, however, and that was Billy Pierce — and he had good reason.

The left-handed Pierce had been the anchor of the White Sox pitching staff since coming to the club in a legendarily one-sided deal after the '48 season. That trade saw the Detroit Tigers send Pierce to the White Sox in exchange for Aaron Robinson. The Tigers even threw in $10,000! To their defense, though, the Tigers had not been able to get Pierce to achieve his full potential while in their farm system. However, once under the tutelage of then-Sox manager Paul Richards and pitching coach Ray Berres — two of the best at developing pitchers — Pierce hit his stride. He won 76 games for the Sox from 1949 through 1954 when I joined the club late in the season. The only problem was that he'd lost 79 games in that same time span. It wasn't because he didn't pitch well, however. In fact, he always pitched well in those years, but his won-loss record was usually negatively affected by the fact that the White Sox were notorious for not scoring runs — not to mention the fact that as the ace of the staff Pierce was always matched up against the opposition's ace. That meant he faced Whitey Ford when playing the Yankees, Bob Lemon when playing the Indians, and so on and so on.

1955 was my first full year with the White Sox, so it was my first close look at Pierce. What I saw was a hard-working kid with real talent. His career took a quantum leap forward that season. He went 15-and-10 with a league-leading 1.97 ERA. He was amazing that season and would have certainly been a 20-game winner had we scored more runs for him. Pierce became a 20-game winner the very next season, however, and repeated the feat in 1957. He slipped to 17 wins in 1958, but it wasn't because he'd lost anything. In fact, he probably pitched better in '58 than he did in '57, finishing with a 2.68 ERA. He had it all working in 1958, and on one occasion he nearly threw a perfect game. It was late-June against the Senators at Comiskey Park. Pierce was on fire and he retired the first 26 Nats hitters in a row. Then, with two outs in the top of the 9th and us leading, 3-0, Washington manager Cookie Lavagetto sent up Ed Fitz Gerald to pinch-hit. We were really on the edge of our seats. Then Fitz Gerald got lucky and caught one of Billy's curveballs, looping it down the rightfield line for a double. Pierce struck out the next batter, Albie Pearson, to end the game, but he'd lost the perfect game and no-hitter. I was really pulling for him to get it, too.

Billy's 1959 season had not gone as well as his previous years. By today's standards it was a great season — 14-and-15 with a 3.62 ERA in 33 starts — but it was a marked step back for Pierce. Billy was 32 in 1959, so he wasn't over the hill by any stretch of the imagination, but he just wasn't at his best. Plus, a torn hip muscle had forced him out of action for most of August, and it had hindered his performance upon his return to the rotation later that month. That left him as sort of the odd man out when the World Series rolled around. He'd pitched three scoreless innings in relief during our Game Four loss, and he'd been used "for strategic purposes" when Lopez brought him in to intentionally walk Rip Repulski in our Game Five victory. Pierce wasn't pouting about his situation, but he was obviously feeling a little bit hurt. When, prior to our game on this day, reporters asked him why he had yet to start a game in the Series, Pierce, in a defeated tone, said, "1959 was a lousy year for me. Early Wynn and Bob Shaw have pitched great ball for us all year, so I think it's only natural that they should have started the first two games. Then we go to Los Angeles, and you know all about that leftfield fence there. It's supposed to be death on left-handed pitchers. It makes good sense to start right-handers there."

Lopez had already announced that Donovan was the likely starter should the Series go seven games. If Pierce was bitter about not getting a starting assignment, his classy demeanor did not show it publicly. Instead, he simply said, "Naturally, I'd like to start. But if Al can use me the way he's done so far and win, fine. I have no complaints." When the reporters looked at him skeptically, Pierce gave them a heartfelt, "Honest — I mean it." I felt compassion for Pierce and his situation. He'd been such a key man during the building years, yet here he was unable to help the team in the way that he wanted to. For that reason I was very happy when the San Francisco Giants made it to the World Series in 1962. By then Pierce was pitching for the Giants, and his 16-and-6 season helped San Francisco to the '62 pennant. The Giants lost the Series to the Yankees, four games to three, but Pierce started two of the games and pitched well in both, even getting the complete-game victory in Game Six.

Even Billy Pierce at his best may not have been able to help us win Game

Six of the '59 Series despite how good we felt about our club as we prepared for the game. I really can't overstate how positive we felt about bringing the Series back to the comforts of Comiskey Park. The sportswriters understood it, and they wrote about our advantage when playing there. There was even a photo that ran in the papers emphasizing the point. The photo was taken prior to a light practice we had on the off-day before Game Six. The picture showed me, Tony Cuccinello, and Lopez grinning as groundskeeper Gene Bossard knelt in front of us on the Comiskey Park infield, lovingly caressing the grass. Simply put, we LOVED playing on Gene's custom-manicured field.

In spite of our confidence and the fact that the odds-makers had favored us to win the ballgame, there were some hefty obstacles impeding our path to victory. Only two teams had ever won the Series after trailing three games to one — the 1925 Pirates and the 1958 Yankees. The Dodgers were also getting back the services of their slugger, Duke Snider, whose bad knee had kept him out of the previous three games. So, at 2:00 P.M. on a sunny and warm Thursday afternoon in Chicago's South Side, Early Wynn fired the first pitch to Dodger lead-off man Jim Gilliam, and Game Six was under way. Gilliam was quickly called out on strikes, but Charley Neal assured that we would not get out of the 1st without sweating a bit when he followed with a single to centerfield. Wally Moon flied out for the second out, but then Snider drew a free pass. With two on and two out, it took a great defensive play to get us out of the inning. Gil Hodges hit the ball hard in the direction of Bubba Phillips at third. The smash looked destined to find its way through the infield for at least one run, but Phillips streaked to his left and scooped up the ball. Then in one fluid motion he flipped the ball to Nellie Fox at second for the force-out. It was a great play — just what we needed to set the defensive tone for the day.

Walt Alston had selected Johnny Podres as his starter, and his choice looked like a good one when Podres got out of the 1st with no real difficulty except a 2-out single by Jim Landis. Early walked the Dodger lead-off man in the top of the 2nd, but he, too, escaped with relative ease by getting John Roseboro on a fly to right; Maury Wills on a grounder to second; and Podres on a fly to left. Our difficulty in scoring runs continued in the bottom half of the inning when Podres retired the side in order.

The game looked like it was developing into one of our typical low-scoring affairs, the type we'd won in Game Five, but the Dodger half of the 3rd brought an end to that speculation. The inning began uneventfully with Gilliam flying out and Neal following with a strikeout, but then Early walked Moon, bringing up the dangerous Snider. With the count 1-and-1, Early threw a "waste" pitch, high and away. In the tradition of Yogi Berra, Duke chased the bad ball, belting it 400 feet into the densely-packed stands near the centerfield bullpen. Let me tell you, it was as quiet as a funeral in that ballpark as Snider and Moon rounded those bases. Early regrouped after that and ended the inning by popping up Hodges, but Wynn was mad as hell as he walked off Bossard's extra-high mound and made his way to our dugout.

2-0 was certainly not an insurmountable deficit to overcome, but with the way we had NOT been scoring of late, it was still a formidable task. We didn't help our cause, either, when our guys went down 1-2-3 in the bottom of the 3rd. The difficulty of our comeback effort increased beyond comprehension, however, after the events of the top of the 4th. Norm Larker opened the inning with a single to center, then left the game for pinch-runner Don Demeter. Roseboro, batting next, moved Demeter up to second with a sacrifice bunt. That brought up Wills, and he rapped another single to center. Landis bobbled Wills' bounder, allowing Demeter to score easily. It was a minor fumble and didn't even register as an error, but Landis was no doubt a little embarrassed when the next batter, the light-hitting Podres, doubled over his head, scoring Wills.

At this point Lopez slowly made his way to the mound to give Early the hook, and Wynn handed the ball to Al without incident. Early had come along way in this respect. As recently as 1958, Early's first year with the Sox, he still had occasional trouble controlling his emotions in situations like this. For example, the very first time Al went to the mound to relieve Early in '58, things didn't go smoothly. Al thought Early needed to come out of the game, but Wynn, because of his competitive nature, wasn't ready to go to the showers. So Early displayed his anger by showing up Al in front of a whole stadium full of people. Wynn angrily walked right by Lopez and tossed the ball into Al's belly as Lopez let out an "Oof!" Al, however, was used to Early's intensity from their days together in Cleveland, so he knew just how to handle Wynn. Instead of blowing up at Early, Al calmly told him, "Don't throw at me — throw at the batters." Over time, Al's understated managerial style chipped away at Early until he eventually gave Lopez the respect he deserved. And that respect was evident on this day as Early contained his rage as he walked off the field while his replacement, Dick Donovan, walked on. Meanwhile, the White Sox band tried to lighten the mood of doom and gloom by playing the old Judy Garland song, "Look for a Silver Lining." Losing by a score of 4-0, however, made it tough to see a silver lining anywhere — and it got even tougher when Donovan walked Gilliam. Neal followed with a 2-run double, and then Moon cleared the bags with a homer into the lower right stands. That did it for Donovan, and Lopez headed back out to the mound remove him. Turk Lown came in and got the last two outs of the inning, but as our guys made their way to the dugout we were now trailing, 8-0.

There wasn't any quit in our boys. They'd clawed and scratched for every win they'd gotten this year, and they weren't going to give up now. You could see it on their faces. But the bottom of the 4th turned out to be the last gasp of our 1959 White Sox — then Larry Sherry came in and choked the life out of us. Fox led off the inning, but popped out to short. Then Podres let one get away from him and he beaned Landis right on the noggin. Landis avoided injury because he was wearing one of the new, still-novel "protective helmets." Not everyone was wearing them yet despite the fact that they'd now been around since the early 50's. But those who were wearing them, especially guys who got plunked on the head, were thankful for the newfangled plastic resin helmet — and that included Landis as he trotted down to first base. Once Landis reached first base I checked to see if he was okay. He assured me that he was fine, and that got me to thinking — what would it have been like to have faced Roy "Tarzan" Parmelee with a helmet on my head? It still would have been a scary proposition, but a lot less so than it was with nothing but a wool cap protecting your skull from a wild 100-MPH Parmelee fastball! In any case, Podres continued to struggle with his control by walking the next batter, Sherm Lollar. The dejected crowd perked up a little and began to chant, "Go! Go! Go!" as Ted Kluszewski stepped up to the plate. Ted's pull-hitting power had been negated by the huge rightfield dimensions at the Coliseum, so he now looked very comfortable as he dug a toe-hold here in the comfortable surroundings of Comiskey Park. With an 8-run lead, Podres did not want to nibble, so he challenged Ted. In a flash, Kluszewski sent a towering drive to right, the ball crashing into the upper deck for a 3-run homer.

Once our runners had completed their circuits, Alston beat a hasty path to the mound to confer with Podres. Since his heroic performance in the Dodgers' 1955 breakthrough World Series win, Podres had been viewed with deserved reverence. That, combined with the fact that Los Angeles still led by five runs, probably influenced Alston to leave Podres in the game. But when Podres walked our next batter, Al Smith, Alston followed with a quick hook. Alston signaled the Dodger pen, and out jogged the guy whose brilliant relief work had carried their ballclub to three wins in the Series — Larry Sherry. Part of me thought, "This guy's on a roll — we do NOT want to see him in this critical situation." But part of me thought, "He CAN'T keep it up — we're due to get to him." Initially it looked as if the first of my two theories might be correct as Phillips greeted Sherry with a single. Sherry struck out our next batter, pinch-hitter Billy Goodman, but then he walked Earl Torgeson who had come in as a pinch-hitter for Lown. That loaded the bases with two outs and the top of our order coming up, but Sherry seized control of the situation right there and ended the inning by getting Luis Aparicio to pop out to short.

The rest of the game can be summed up in two words — Larry Sherry. He pitched the remainder of the contest and was dominant. From the 5th inning through the 9th, Sherry allowed just three hits — a double by Fox in the 5th, a single by Aparicio in the 7th, and a double by Kluszewski in the 9th. Despite those two doubles, we were never really a serious threat to score on Sherry. Since his mid-season call-up to the Dodgers, Sherry had constantly pitched in pressure-packed situations — and he just kept on delivering. While he always looked cool and collected in these do-or-die games, others weren't necessarily able to remain so calm — particularly Red Corriden, the scout who discovered Sherry. Corriden had been a scrappy, seldom-used little infielder with the Browns, Tigers, and White Sox in the early-teens. After his playing days he became a coach, and eventually managed the White Sox for the bulk of the 1950 season after Chicago fired Jack Onslow. By 1951 Corriden had become a scout with the Dodgers, and it was in that capacity that he discovered Sherry.

The Dodger front office brass had grappled with the idea of keeping Sherry with the club at the beginning of the '59 season, but they opted against it out of fear that Sherry was not quite ready. However, desperate for pitching help by mid-season, they placed a call to Corriden and asked him what he thought. "Do you really want my opinion, Lollypop?" asked Corriden of the man on the other end of the telephone line, Dodger general manager Buzzy Bavasi. Corriden apparently called everyone "Lollypop" for some reason. "Grab him fast," said Corriden with unwavering confidence. Bavasi listened to Corriden's advice, and Sherry made Red look good by providing the Dodgers with the push they need-ed to end the season in a 1st-place tie with the Braves.

Tragedy struck in the first game of the Dodgers-Braves playoff series, and it could potentially be blamed on the stress that came with watching Sherry pitch under extreme pressure. Dodger starter Danny McDevitt got in trouble in the bottom of the 2nd inning. With one out, runners on first and second, and the score tied 1-1, Alston brought Sherry in to relieve McDevitt. Sherry got a ground ball from the first man he faced, Braves pitcher Carl Willey, but Wills erred on the play and the sacks were loaded. Bobby Avila batted next and Sherry got him, too, to ground to Wills. This time Maury fielded the ball cleanly and tossed it to second for a force-out, but the Braves took a 2-1 lead on the play. Then Eddie Mathews grounded out to end the inning. Sherry pitched the rest of the game, and the Braves never scored again. Each inning was soaked with tension, howev-er. The Dodgers tied the game in the 3rd, then took a 1-run lead in the 6th. The score was still 3-2 in the 8th inning when Red Corriden died of a heart attack while watching his discovery pitch on the televised broadcast of the game from his home in Indiana. It was an incredibly ironic — and sad — happening.

But, to the best of my knowledge, no one else died during Sherry's run through the '59 post-season. The only thing that died was everyone's hopes that the Go-Go Sox could bring the South Side its first Series title since 1917. There was one more play of note before the game ended. The game was well out of hand by then so it had no real significance other than the fact that it had never before happened. Neither team had scored since the explosive 4th inning, so the score was still 8-3 when Alston sent Chuck Essegian up to pinch-hit for Snider to lead off the top of the 9th. Gerry Staley had pitched scoreless ball from the 5th through the 7th innings, then Pierce had pitched a scoreless 8th. Ray Moore, a right-handed fastballer who had pitched pretty well for us out of the bullpen in 1959, had yet to see any action in the Series, so Lopez sent him out to pitch the 9th. Essegian greeted Moore by ripping a fastball into the lower leftfield stands for his second pinch-homer of the series. It was amazing — a feat never before accomplished and never since eclipsed, although Bernie Carbo equaled it in the 1975 World Series. Moore settled down after that and easily retired the next three Dodger hitters in order.

Our guys came in for one last chance. It would've taken one hell of a rally, but Sherry wasn't going to allow it. Goodman led off the inning with a come-backer for out number one. Lopez sent Norm Cash in to pinch-hit for Moore, and Cash lined out to center. Down to our last out, Aparicio stepped in to hit. The skies, so sunny at the game's beginning, had now changed. Arthur Daley of the *New York Times* described it beautifully when he wrote, "The sun beamed down cheerfully at the start of the game. By the time it was over even Chicago's sky had donned mourning of dark black. In the last half of the 9th the tears, a sprinkle of rain, came. The beloved White Sox had lost the World Series." Luis sent a fly ball to left that landed in Moon's glove for the final out. As the Dodgers descended upon Sherry for a glorious team celebration, our boys sadly made their way to the clubhouse, the Series now a part of history.

Like everyone with the White Sox organization, I had my own personal feelings of disappointment at our loss, but I felt particularly compassionate for our players as they filed into our clubhouse. I knew exactly how they felt based on my having been a player on losing ballclubs in the 1944 and 1946 World Series. Listening to the guys and their conversations with the sportswriters, it seemed that they were in agreement that it was really just a matter of too much Sherry, Hodges, and Neal. One of our players accurately told a writer that our loss was simply a case of "missed opportunities by us — and I can't help but feel that we might have done better than we did against the Dodgers." Fox, in a foul mood over our loss, was a little less diplomatic about things as he stripped off his uniform, saying, "The Dodgers got the breaks; we didn't get any."

In the meantime, Lopez had gone over to the Dodgers clubhouse to congratulate them on "a helluva victory." Upon his return to our clubhouse, Lopez told reporters, "They played good ball — real good ball — and Alston did an extra-fine job of managing. They had momentum carried over from their closing series with the Giants, Cardinals, and Cubs. They had Sherry and Neal, too. We hurt ourselves mainly because we didn't hit with men on the bases in the games at Los Angeles. That hurt us, and our defense was bad in the games there, too." I mirrored Lopez's assertions when asked by the sportswriters for my opinions on our loss. I wasn't ready to concede that the Dodgers were a better team than us, but they certainly were the better ballclub during the week of the Series, and that's all that really mattered. When you got right down to it, they simply beat us at our own game. Dodger coach Chuck Dressen said it best when he told reporters, "We out-ran 'em, out-pitched 'em, and out-fielded 'em." That was about the size of it.

For me, it was a disappointment to again be on the losing end of the World Series. It had been 13 years since I'd last been involved in a Series, and despite the fact that I knew we had a good group of players returning in 1960, there were no guarantees that we'd ever win another pennant. In fact, I considered myself lucky to have already been a part of three World Series teams. I knew a heck of a lot of other fellows who were NEVER a part of a pennant winner. People always ask me to name the highlights of my career, and being with the 1959 White Sox is always one of the things I point out. It's right up there with other moments like my first big league call-up; the big day I had as a rookie at Ebbets Field in 1936; winning the A.L. Pennant against the Yankees on the last day of the 1944 season; and helping the Red Sox to a pennant in 1946. Being a coach with the White Sox was quite different than being a player for the Cardinals, Browns, and Red Sox, but I still felt like I'd really contributed a great deal to our '59 team.

One by one, the players exited the clubhouse on their way to homes scattered all over the country. Finally, one writer asked Lopez the inevitable question of what he thought about our chances in 1960. "This club," Al said, "with only a little bit of help, maybe in rightfield, is good enough to win the pennant again. Kluszewski has won the job at first base; there's nothing wrong with the men at second, short, third, or two of the outfield positions." Just then Bubba Phillips walked past and said, "See you at spring training skipper."

"Yeah," said Al, "see you at spring training." I guess that's when it really set in — our wonderful season was really over.

The 1959 White Sox were a special bunch of guys, and I am very proud to have helped them achieve their goal of making it to the World Series. Helen's father, Sidney McGlothlin, knew what a special year we were having, and he got to witness it first-hand when he came to Chicago to see us play. Here in this photo he swapped hats with Nellie Fox and posed for a snapshot. From left to right is Jim Rivera, Nellie, Sidney, me, and Bubba Phillips.

1 9 6 9

MAY 3, 1969: *GUTTERIDGE'S DEBUT RUINED; KILLEBREW AND TWINS SINK SOX, 3-1.* That was the *Chicago Tribune* headline recapping my first game as manager of the Chicago White Sox on this day. The text of the article went on to say, "The debut of Don Gutteridge, new White Sox manager, ended in another major disappointment for the skidding Chicagoans today, but only because Gary Peters couldn't keep his gopher ball out of Harmon Killebrew's contact zone. Gutteridge, the 56-year old freshman pilot, took the defeat admirably. No tears. No beefs. 'I thought Peters pitched well again,' he said. 'The ball Killebrew hit into the seats was a sinker away from him. Killebrew just went with the pitch. He's so strong he can hit those out of the park.' Only last Sunday, Killebrew hit a home run in the 1st inning while the free-swinging Twins proceeded to administer the first of three 1-run defeats absorbed by the Sox in the closing days of Al Lopez's last managerial fling. If Gutteridge didn't accomplish anything else today, he at least saw an end to the 1-run annoyance."

Despite the fact that the 1969 season was just a few weeks old, that one little paragraph from the *Tribune* said an awful lot about our ballclub. With an overall record of eight wins and ten losses, we were hardly out of contention, but our loss on this day was our fifth consecutive defeat, and we were definitely "skidding." Yes, it was true that I led our troops to a 2-run loss in my debut, breaking the "1-run annoyance" trend, but we quickly returned to the "1-run annoyance" trend in my second game as manager. In fact, losing by one run was something that would plague us throughout the '69 season. As I said in the old *Tribune* article, Gary Peters, a left-hander, did pitch well on this day — well enough to win — but he got no offensive support. That was another season-long trend for our starters in '69. Our starting rotation had talent, but they were erratic. Unfortunately, when they were on their game the bats often seemed to go quiet. Peters, like a couple of our other starters, was often a victim of this phenomenon. He'd had a few brief trials with us from 1959 through 1962, but he stuck for good in 1963 when he won 19 games, led the league in ERA, and was named rookie of the year. He had a 20-win season in 1964, but arm troubles slowed him a bit for the next few years. He pitched through it, though, and continued to be a mainstay in our rotation, but 1969 would test his inner strength. Lastly, the *Tribune* article mentioned the disappointment involved in losing on this day — the day I debuted as Sox manager. It wasn't the fact that we lost in my first game as skipper that disappointed me. I was simply disappointed to lose — period. In my mind, this day wasn't about ME — it was about the Chicago White Sox. Sadly, though, I would have to get used to the disappointment of losing because we would do it on 84 more occasions under my leadership in 1969.

MAY 4, 1969: *SOX SWOON BEFORE BIG CROWD; SLOPPY PLAY SETS UP 4-3 TWINS VICTORY.* That was the *Chicago Tribune* headline on this day as we lost again at Minnesota's Metropolitan Stadium in my second game as Sox manager. "Sloppy play" would be a recurring theme with my 1969 Sox. We were leading, 3-2, as we headed into the bottom of the 8th. Right-hander Bob Locker was the third pitcher I'd used in the game when I sent him in for the 7th inning, and he'd done a fine job of holding the lead until he gave up a game-tying solo homer to Twins rookie Graig Nettles on a sinker in the 8th. Locker had served up a homer to Nettles on the same pitch just nine days earlier, so we were all pretty surprised to see Bob throw it again in this situation. Later, in the clubhouse, Locker would explain it this way — "The sinker is my best pitch, but apparently he hits it better than I throw it. I'd better get a new book on him." That was a very funny way of putting it, I thought.

In any case, while Locker was thinking about how to pitch Nettles the next time, our defense slipped up and gave the game away. With the score now tied, 3-

3, more trouble started when Locker walked Chuck Manuel. The next batter, Ted Uhlaender, hit a double-play ball to second baseman Ron Hansen, but he threw the ball wide of shortstop Luis Aparicio, allowing the runners to advance to second and third. I had Locker intentionally walk pinch-hitter Rich Reese, and my strategy seemed to work when the next batter, Cesar Tovar, grounded sharply to third baseman Bill Melton. But Melton was just a kid in only his second season, and, for the second time on the current road-trip, he froze for a moment after fielding the ball, unsure of where to go with the throw. By the time Bill made up hid mind, Manuel had easily scored the winning run. When the sportswriters later asked me about the play, all I could say was, "He made an honest mistake." I felt bad for him. So, two days into my new job as White Sox manager and I was 0-and-2. I had to think about it for a while, too, because we were off the next day as we traveled to Baltimore to open a series against the Orioles. That, too, didn't bode well for my prospects of getting a win. The Orioles were a great team, already well on their way to an ill-fated place in the history books as the heavily-favored powerhouse who would lose to the Miracle Mets in the 1969 World Series.

"White Sox manager Don Gutteridge" — no one was more surprised by the sound of that than me. In no way was I expecting that when I took my place in the first base coach's box the day we opened the '69 season at Oakland against the Athletics. In fact, I was just getting re-acclimated to my job as first base coach when we opened the 1969 season. This was because I'd only been back at my post as White Sox coach since July 16th of 1968 — that after spending 1967 and the first half of '68 off doing other things. To explain this, let me take you back to the 1959 season. Following our loss in the 1959 World Series, Al sent the players and coaches home with best wishes for an enjoyable off-season. While disappointed at coming up short in the Series, we were all very excited at the prospect of coming back in 1960 and building on our success of '59. The entire coaching staff — me, Ray Berres, Johnny Cooney, and Tony Cuccinello — were all asked to come back. Al liked the idea of keeping the coaching staff intact because we'd been together ever since he came to the club in 1957. We were a tight-knit group and we worked very well together. It was unusual for a coaching staff to stay together like we did, and for that reason we were envied by quite a few other coaches around the majors. So, we all came back in 1960 — except Johnny, our bench coach. He decided he was ready to enter the next phase of his life — fishing — so he happily retired to the waters of Sarasota, Florida.

The White Sox coaching staff in 1960 — left to right is Berres, Cuccinello, Lopez, Cooney and me.

We had great success in the early to mid 1960's, yet we were never able to get back to the World Series. We finished 3rd with a record of 87 wins and 67 losses while defending our A.L. Pennant in 1960. We were 86-and-76 with one tie in 1961, good for a 4th-place finish; then we finished 5th in '62 with a mark of 85-and-77. We got it in high gear in 1963 and put together a 94-win season, but that was only good enough for 2nd place as the Yankees won the flag with 104 victories. We were even better in 1964, winning 98 games — but the Yankees again won the pennant by winning 99 games. We finished 2nd in the American League in 1965 with a record of 95 wins and 67 defeats, but this time it was the upstart Minnesota Twins that beat us out for the pennant. It was very frustrating to get so close while continuing to come up short. At the same time, however, it was a great time to be with the Sox. We had good ballplayers come and go during that period, and we just kept on winning. We'd lose an Al Smith at third base, then along would come a Pete Ward. That's why the ballclub was so attractive. We always had good talent. Lopez knew ability and was particularly good at recognizing when a player was starting to decline — before it was obvious to the rest of the league. Then he'd trade that guy for a player who could help the club. We had great fan support during that time, too. We had sell-outs practically every game, especially in September when the pennant race got really hot.

That's me, the amateur photographer, directing the action in the dugout with my trusty Polaroid.

Shortly after the 1965 season ended, Lopez stunned everyone when he announced that he was retiring. As long as I'd known Al, he'd had stomach problems. Doctors never really seemed to know exactly what was at the root of his discomfort, so they filed it under "nervous stomach," the generic terminology of the time. They prescribed pills for him, put him on a bland diet, and told him to try and keep from getting overly stressed. All three things were particularly difficult for a big league manager to do. The pills made Al feel "dopey," so he didn't like to take them when we had games — which was nearly every day for six months out of the year. The bland diet was tough to maintain when you're eating on the road so often. As for keeping down the stress level, well, it's just silly to even suggest that to a major league manager. Al's inability to stick to the doctors regimen meant that his condition got progressively worse every year until he couldn't take it anymore, so he resigned on November 4th, 1965.

Al stayed with the White Sox in an executive capacity, and Eddie Stanky was brought in to manage in 1966. Stanky was a hard-boiled type, and that style served him well throughout his playing career, but it wasn't the best personality trait when it came to being told he had to keep Al's coaching staff. I guess it made Stanky feel like an outsider because Cuccinello, Berres, and I had been there so long and were so close. The bottom line was that we weren't his men, so he didn't like us. So he made it difficult, and he and I simply did not get along. His abrasive personality had earned him the nickname "The Brat," but Helen and I had our own nickname for him — "Stinky Stanky." It's not very original, but we used to get a chuckle out of it. We plummeted to 4th place in 1966 under Stanky, winning 12 fewer games than we'd won in '65. Ray and Tony had had enough by the time the '66 season ended, so they both announced their retirement. Now by myself, I was an easy mark for Stanky, so he fired me. Believe it or not, life was so miserable under Stanky that it was a relief to get let go. The front office asked me to go back to Indianapolis to manage, and I gladly accepted the assignment. I never thought it possible, but I was actually happy to leave the majors and return to the minors, something I never thought I'd say back in 1953 when I told Frank Lane that I wanted to coach in the major leagues — but it was that bad under Stanky.

We had a pretty good year at Indianapolis in '67, finishing the season in 2nd place. I was all set to return there again in '68 when word came down from the front office that the club was being relocated to Honolulu. I kind of liked the idea of going there to manage, but Helen was dead set against it. She did not like the idea of me flying back and forth over the Pacific Ocean eight times a year, so I decided to quit. I went back to Kansas and got a job as a publicity man with a new bank in Pittsburg. It didn't take me very long to realize that this was not the life for me, so I started thinking about how I could get back into baseball. Kansas City had finally realized a longtime dream of having a major league franchise when the Philadelphia Athletics moved there in 1955, but the A's only stayed through the 1967 season before leaving for Oakland prior to the '68 campaign.

Kansas City, however, was promised a new franchise in 1969 when the league was planning to expand. I knew they were heavy into preparations for the new club, so I went over to see if they could use me for anything. I was elated when they hired me as their head scout.

My primary duty was to travel all over the country and look over the players that each big league team was making available for the upcoming expansion draft — we would be drafting two players from each team. So, that's what I was doing when I got a phone call from Sox general manager Ed Short in early July of 1968. "Don, how do you like your job scouting?" he asked me. I told him, in all honesty, that I loved my new job as a scout. Ignoring that, he continued, "Well, I've got some news for you — we're getting rid of Stanky. Lopez is coming back to manage the club and he wants you to come back with him." Moments later, Al was on the line confirming everything that Short had just told me. "What could I do? Here's a guy who gave me a job for years and years, so I felt an allegiance to him. I wasn't looking forward to doing it, but I went back to Kansas City and told the Royals executives about my decision to go back to the White Sox. They showed real class and told me that they completely understood my decision. They even promised me my job back should things not work out with the Sox. They were truly a classy organization.

With that business taken care of, I hustled off to Chicago to join Lopez and the team. Al had brought back Cuccinello and Berres, too, so the reunion was a very happy one with all of us back together. Stanky's run with the Sox was almost a success story after he fired us — ALMOST. In an effort to win right away, Stanky got the front office to change their philosophy. They began trading away their good young prospects instead of waiting for them to develop. It seemed to work as the 1967 season unfolded, and the Sox were in pennant contention for most of the year — but they faltered badly at the end. With just five games left in the season, the Sox had a chance to take sole possession of the A.L. Lead by sweeping a twin bill from the Kansas City Athletics. They not only lost both games to the A's, they went on to drop the last three games to the Senators. Instead of winning the flag, they finished 4th, three games back.

Stanky's "win now" philosophy caught up with the club in a big way as the '68 season got under way. The White Sox lost their first 10 games of the season, and stood at a disappointing 34-and-47 when Stanky "resigned" on July 12th, 1968. While Al, Tony, Ray, and I were very happy to be back together, we were very taken aback at how fast the team had gone downhill. We knew it was not going to be easy to turn things around — if we could turn it around at all. The team responded well to Al's return, winning their first three games under his leadership. There was a very positive mood in the air, but that all ended just ten games into Al's comeback when Lopez was rushed into surgery for an emergency appendectomy. It was quite a setback. Les Moss, a former catcher who had been on Stanky's coaching staff, had stayed on board when Al returned, so he took over as manager for the next 36 games while Lopez recuperated.

Appendicitis forced manager Al Lopez on the disabled list for 36 games in 1968, and coach Les Moss (right) managed in his absence. The man in the center is team owner John Allyn.

The ballclub didn't play very well while Al was recovering, and by the time he returned in late-August, we were well out of contention. We finished the season with 67 wins and 95 losses. That put us in 9th place in the American League, ahead of only the Washington Senators. It was uncharted territory for an Al Lopez team. In all his years as a big league manager, Al never had a team that didn't finish in the first division — until the '68 season. But no one held that against him because they all recognized that he was just mopping up the mess that Stanky had left. But 1969 was another thing altogether. It was understood that it would take a near miracle to get this group of players to finish in the first division, but people had such high expectations of Al that they felt good about his chances of again working his magic.

The only person that didn't feel good was Al. Quietly, as usual, he was suffering his stomach trouble every since resuming his managerial career. He looked thin and sick in spring training prior to the '69 season, but he forged ahead. We opened the season with a 5-2 loss at Oakland, but then we won eight of our next 12. Then we dropped four straight, the last three in particularly gut-wrenching fashion. "Gut-wrenching" is the best way to describe it, too, because it was those four losses that took a final toll on Al's nervous stomach — the last one in particular, a 12-inning 5-4 defeat to the Royals in Kansas City. Al knew he was quitting prior to that last loss, though. In fact, he'd called me, Tony, and Ray into his office the morning of that game — it was May 1st, 1969. "I'm sick, guys," Al told us. "I can't do this — I just can't take it anymore. I want one of you three to take over managing the club for me."

We were all well aware of Al's precarious health, so we'd known for quite some time that this was a possibility. Still, it was a shock to see it actually come to this, so we all just sat there in silence for a few moments. Finally, Tony spoke up. "I don't want that damn job," he proclaimed, "I'm no manager."

"I wouldn't have that job," Ray added.

"I don't want the job," I said, "I'm a COACH."

"Hey, one of you has got to take the job," Al pleaded, "I've had all I can take."

Then Tony looked at me and said, "Gutteridge, you're the youngest and you can stand it better than we can."

"Yeah, Don, you take it," Ray chimed in.

"No," I declared, "NO!"

After that, we got down to a serious discussion of the situation. Like me, Ray and Tony had come back to the White Sox as a favor to Al when he returned in mid-1968. Neither of them had planned on being around too long, but they told me that they'd stay with the team for the rest of the season if I'd take the job. They said that I'd have to take responsibility for all the final decisions, but they would help me in my transition. That was very important to me, so I agreed to take the post. We informed Short of our decision, then Ed and I worked out the details of the contract. My only key demand was that I wanted to be guaranteed another year after 1969. I knew it would take time to get our club back on the right track — more time than I had in 1969. My hope was that by the end of 1970 there might be signs that our ballclub was headed in the right direction, and that might lead to an extension of my contract. Short was agreeable, so he had the contact drafted, and I made it official with my signature on the dotted line. As soon as this was completed, I called Helen. "Guess what?" I asked mysteriously, "you're speaking to the new manager of the Chicago White Sox."

"Are you crazy?" she asked.

"No," I said, "these guys kind of forced me into it." Then I explained the situation to her. As usual, Helen gladly went along with it, just like she'd always done with all the twists and turns of my baseball career — except Honolulu! She always joked that she'd married a baseball, anyway, and for the most part, she was right.

The next afternoon we arrived in Minneapolis the day before we were to start a series with the Twins. Later that evening, in the Lilac Room of the Leamington Hotel, Al gave a somber press conference to announce that he was retiring. Short was there, as were Ray, Tony, and me. "I was trying to stick it out," he told the reporters. "I've been on pills continually since last November when I had a terrific pain in my stomach. It doesn't seem to get any better, and I feel dopey all the time. I've got to get off these pills, and I guess this is the only way I can do it." Then, forcing a laugh, Al added, "Maybe it's these last few games, too. I don't know."

When Short then informed the reporters that I was Al's successor, the questions turned to me. "I'm a Lopez man all the way," I said. "I want to manage as close to the way Lopez did, but still be Don Gutteridge. I never really thought about managing, but when they offered me the job I figured, what the heck, I've done everything else, why not? I think Luke Sewell always thought I'd be a manager because he used to sit next to me and tell me things, you know, explain things like how important it was to always have your pitcher ready. Things like that. I learned some things from all my managers — Frankie Frisch, Joe Cronin, Sewell, but I guess you have to say that Lopez influenced me most. After all, I was with him 17 years, and I guess it's bound to be that way. It would be a big mistake for me to try to be somebody else, though. You have to be yourself first of all. You're not going to do everything your hero did because you're bound to have a few ideas that are different. But I was with Lopez a long time and I usually agreed with his theories."

Continuing, I told the reporters, "A manager's biggest job is getting the players mentally ready to play. By that I mean, preparing them to play your style of baseball and getting them into a state of mind where they'll enjoy playing. I think the other part — the strategy — is pretty cut and dried. If you were to take the 12 American League managers and line them up side-by-side on the bench, they'd all probably make the same moves. Another thing of great importance is knowing your material. If I have a lot of speed on my club I can play a running game, but it's foolish to try it if I don't. If you have a man who's a good hit-and-run man you'll bat him one place in the line-up, and if he's not good at it you'll want him someplace else."

The press conference ended shortly thereafter, and the reporters left to write their stories. Short asked Al, Ray, Tony, and me to join him for a farewell dinner, but Al wasn't in the mood, so he told us to go ahead without him. We bid him farewell, and watched him head back to his room. It was a sad sight to see because Al loved to manage, and this is not the way he wanted to go out. Without a lick of fanfare, Al slipped out of the hotel by himself at seven o'clock the next morning and caught a flight home to Tampa. It took a period of time for him to adapt to life outside the dugout, but he eventually was better off for having left the game. His stomach condition became much more manageable, and Al lived a long and happy life. We always stayed in touch, too, right up until he passed away in October of 2005. He was a great friend and I miss him very much.

So, here I was, an 0-and-2 big league manager in search of my first victory. Looking back now, I know that I wasn't really ready to MANAGE. It would take me a little time to find myself as to where I should be as a manager. I wasn't very good at the start, but as time went on, of course, I got better. But that's the wisdom of hindsight talking. The only thing I was thinking about on this day, however, was how difficult it was going to be to try and beat the Baltimore Orioles tomorrow.

MAY 6, 1969: The wait was over as I got my first victory as White Sox manager on this day. We edged the Orioles, 1-0, at Baltimore's Memorial Stadium, and the win came in typical Sox fashion — good pitching, good defense, and MINIMAL hitting. Joe Horlen, our 31-year old right-handed starter, tossed a complete game 5-hitter and really shut down the powerful Orioles attack. His opposition on the mound was no slouch, either — future Hall of Famer Jim Palmer. Palmer was very sharp in the game, too, allowing just four hits, but one of them was a run scoring single by Luis Aparicio in the 3rd inning — and that was the difference in the game. The run looked like a throwback to the days of the Go-Go Sox. I'd made very few changes in the line-up that Al had been running out there, but one of my changes paid off for us in this game. I elevated our speedy second baseman, Sandy Alomar, to the lead-off spot for the first time this season. He took the change seriously, and was rewarded in the 3rd when he patiently worked a 2-out walk from Palmer. Alomar's big lead distracted Palmer to the point where he tried several pick-off attempts, but as soon as he delivered to the plate, Alomar swiped second base. Aparicio, about our only hot hitter at the time, then followed with a single to right, scoring Alomar with the game's only run.

Maybe Horlen heard echoes of Al Lopez's mantra, "There's your lead — now go hold it," because he was terrific and had made our lone run stand up. He really bore down in the pinches and got the job done, snapping our 6-game losing skein while also ending the Orioles' 4-game winning streak. The key to Horlen's success that day was a subtle change he made in the grip on his curveball. He and Ray Berres had been working on loosening his grip when throwing the curve. We'd noticed that Horlen's curve would break much more sharply when he threw it with a loose grip. It worked to perfection on this day, and he consistently got his curve over for strikes. That, of course, helped him get more out of his fastball. Horlen had been a fine pitcher and a key man in the Sox rotation since the early 60's. He was always good for 10 to 15 wins per year, but he also seemed to suffer a lot of tough-luck losses. I remember one in particular. It was in Washington in late July of 1963. We were leading, 1-0, as Horlen took the mound for the bottom of the 9th — three outs away from a no-hit masterpiece. He got Jim King, the lead-off man, to ground out, but then Chuck Hinton spoiled the no-hitter with a squibber to center. Horlen regrouped and got the next man, but then came the killer — Don Lock ended the game with a 2-run homer. Horlen eventually got his no-hitter, though. In 1967, the year I was managing at Indianapolis, Joe won 19 games and no-hit the Detroit Tigers late in the season. For me, the name of Joe Horlen will always be very meaningful because of his extraordinary performance in my first big league managerial win.

MAY 7, 1969: I had to wait only 24 hours to get my second win as we again beat the Orioles, 6-4, at Memorial Stadium on this day. Also with the win came the first hint of second-guessing by a sportswriter, something I would quickly become very accustomed to. This was a VERY minor case of second-guessing compared to what would come later, but it hinted at the future. We were leading, 6-3, as our boys headed out for the bottom of the 9th with our left-handed starter, Gary Peters, still in the ballgame. At 1-and-4 going into the game, Peters was having a tough season up to that point, but he was a very good pitcher. He, like Joe Horlen the day before, had been a staple to our rotation for many years. Peters had great success early on when he won 19 games in 1963, earning him rookie-of-the-year honors. He followed that season with a 20-win campaign in 1964, but then arm trouble slowed him a little. In any case, Peters was really battling out there on this day, and I wanted him to be able to finish the game if at all possible. But Orioles centerfielder Paul Blair kicked off the inning with a round-tripper, so I went out to relieve Peters. The next day the papers recalled it this way — "Manager Don Gutteridge, who exhibited an extreme reluctance to relieve Peters, finally did it when Paul Blair hit his sixth home run to open the Oriole 9th." I knew right then and there that my every move was going to be questioned. It came with the territory of being a big league manager, though. I knew that going in, but I'd never noticed it to the degree that I would now that I was the one in the hot seat. At any rate, right-hander Bob Locker came in to save the game for us, nailing down the 6-4 win. On offense we were helped by three hits and an RBI from our catcher Duane Josephson, two hits and three RBIs from our third baseman Bill Melton, and three hits including a solo homer from our rookie leftfielder Carlos May.

MAY 10, 1969: I had my first official managerial winning streak as we won our third straight game, 4-0, over the Indians at Cleveland's Municipal Stadium on this day. It was, to say the very least, a modest streak at best, but it equaled our longest win streak of the short season to date. Right-hander Tommy John was the man on the mound for this one, and he did a fine job. John relied on good control and a sinker that resulted in lots of ground balls. He got 14 Indians hitters to ground out in this game — two of them hitting into double-plays, another fringe benefit of John's good sinker. Along with Joe Horlen and Gary Peters, John was the other key man in our starting rotation. We would spend the entire season looking for a reliable 4th starter, to no avail. John had been a very good starter for the Sox since 1965 when he went 14-and-7 with a 2.62 ERA. He pitched very well in '68 when he went 10-and-5 with a 1.98 ERA, but this season would not go as well. John would only win nine games in '69. Sometimes he was not at his best, but, more often than not, he pitched well and lost due to poor offensive or defensive support. He also suffered, as did a lot of our players from the '69 team, from constantly having to leave the team to fulfill National Guard duties. John was in the Indiana Air National Guard. I know that definitely took guys out of their playing rhythm. Later in the season, John started to have trouble with his pitching elbow. It was diagnosed as tendonitis. His elbow got so bad years later that John underwent a very revolutionary surgical procedure where a ligament was removed from his left arm and transplanted into his right arm, replacing the damaged ligament. It's become very common nowadays, and it saves a lot of careers that at one time would have been ended. The procedure was immediately dubbed "Tommy John Surgery," and every time I hear someone say it I can't help but think back to my '69 ballclub.

The second-guessers were back at it in the top of the 8th of this game. We were nursing a 4-0 lead when John came up to hit with two on and two out. AFTER seeing how events played out, here's what the *Chicago Tribune's* Richard Dozer wrote — "Manager Don Gutteridge declined the use of a pinch-hitter in this inviting situation, and John made the final out of the inning against Horatio Piña. John then went to the mound, surrendered a single to Max Alvis, and yielded a double with two out to Hawk Harrelson. Gutteridge, the reluctant manager, finally brought in Bob Locker to retire Tony Horton." What Dozer failed to mention in describing this scenario was that John already had one single in the game, so he was certainly capable of getting the occasional hit. Sure, as a batter he was not on par with some of the fellows we had on the bench, but I wanted John back on the mound to try and finish what he started. This is no knock against our guys in the bullpen, although they struggled mightily in 1969, but John was a starter because he was one of our best pitchers. So I always wanted to go with our best as long as possible. John occasionally hit the long ball, too, so there was always an outside chance that he'd get a hold of one. If John would have hit a 3-run homer in that situation instead of grounding out, I'd have been hailed as a genius for leaving him in. It mattered not in the end — this time — because Locker came in and closed the door on the Indians the rest of the way.

MAY 11, 1969: Still searching for that elusive fourth starter, I gave right-hander Sammy Ellis the assignment on this day. It didn't go so well for him personally, but we were still able to get our fourth win in a row, a 7-5 victory over the Indians in Cleveland. Here's how the papers described Ellis' trouble while also continuing to state their opinion about my early tendency to stay with my starters too long — "The latest experiment with Sammy Ellis as a starting pitcher lasted until the 5th inning. Today he got away without taking a defeat, but the toll against him was nine hits and two walks before the extreme patience of Don Gutteridge finally ended with two on base and the score tied." We'd acquired Ellis from the Angels prior to the season with hopes that Ray Berres we could get him back to the form he'd had in 1965 when he'd won 22 games for the Reds, but it never happened for us and we ended up selling him to Portland in June. Unfortunately, it never happened anywhere for Ellis, and he never again appeared in the big leagues after we sold him. In any case, when I "finally" relieved Ellis, it was our left-handed knuckleballer Wilbur Wood who got the call. He'd done a great job in 1968, but he was having a little trouble getting it going at this point in '69, and his problems continued as he came in and walked Vern Fuller, then hitting about .125. Fuller eventually came around to score, so

I again went to Bob Locker with us trailing, 4-3. Locker pitched one scoreless inning, and by virtue of good timing was the winning pitcher because Sandy Alomar hit a clutch 3-run double in the top of the 8th. Right-hander Danny Osinski pitched the last two innings. He was a little shaky and gave up a run, but he was good enough to get the save and extend our winning streak to four straight.

MAY 13, 1969: Plans for my Hall of Fame managerial plaque were put on hold as our 4-game winning streak was snapped on this day by a 3-1 loss to Detroit at Tiger Stadium. Joe Horlen was pitching very well, protecting a 1-0 lead, until a 1-hour rain delay in the 7th inning. The Tigers had a man on first with none out and Willie Horton batting when the rains came. During the delay Horlen told me that his arm got stiff, so I sent Bob Locker to the mound when the game resumed. The sportswriters, still perplexed by my desire to stay with my starters, noted this by reporting, "Horlen felt his arm stiffening during the long delay and was replaced without hesitation by manager Don Gutteridge, who remembered vividly the loss of effectiveness by Tommy John under similar circumstances in Cleveland last Saturday." Once the writers got a look at our bullpen blowing Horlen's 1-0 lead, maybe they better understood my reluctance to give our starters the hook. The game resumed with an 0-and-2 count on Horton. Locker struck out the Tiger slugger with his first pitch, but Jim Northrup hit Locker's very next pitch into the upper deck for a 2-run homer, wiping out what moments before had been Horlen's 3-hit shutout. Wilbur Wood came in shortly thereafter and proceeded to walk in another run. There you have it. A struggling bullpen and a struggling offense — problems that would hound us all year long, ended our 4-game winning streak and what the papers called "the charmed life of Don Gutteridge."

MAY 16, 1969: I wasn't the only one new to the managerial ranks in 1969. There were others, but the only one anybody really wanted to talk about was my old Red Sox teammate, Ted Williams. Ted had been completely out of baseball since his retirement following the 1960 season. Then, completely out of the blue, he came back to the big leagues as manager of the '69 Washington Senators. Ted was great at everything he ever tried — whether it was hitting a baseball, fly-fishing, or piloting jet-fighters. Now, just to prove that he could do it, Ted decided to take a crack at managing. But Ted wasn't about to work his way up the ranks as a coach or a minor league manager. No, he was going to start right at the top — in the major leagues. And, as if managing ANY big league club wasn't a tough enough task, Ted decided to give it a go with one of the major leagues' worst franchises — the Senators. They hadn't finished a season over .500 since 1945, and they hadn't been to the World Series since 1933. None of that scared Ted, though, and it was really big news around the country when he accepted the post. And it was really big news when Ted and his Nats made their first trip to

Comiskey Park on this day.

Once the game began, however, it was the ballplayers who were the focus, and one of Ted's players upstaged everybody on the ballfield — including the Splendid Splinter. Senators first baseman Mike Epstein, a true disciple of Ted's theory on the science of hitting, clubbed my pitchers for three home runs on the day. Amazingly, Epstein's three long balls did not equal a victory for Washington. Thanks to a tie-breaking home run in the 7th by Carlos May, we won the game, 7-6. Don't feel too bad for Ted, though. His already-legendary reputation only got better because of what he did with the '69 Senators. They finished with a record of 86-and-76, a 21-game improvement from the previous season. And all of his everyday players saw a marked improvement in their batting averages thanks to hitting instruction from perhaps the best hitter of all time. Citing his poor relationship with the media and his limited patience with "ordinary" ballplayers, Ted's critics doubted his ability to succeed with the Nats. But they didn't know Ted. From personal experience, I knew Ted was an excellent teacher — and in 1969 he proved his critics wrong... again.

Ted didn't limit his teaching to just the players on his ballclub. When it came to talking about hitting and sharing his insight with players, Ted would teach ANYONE who asked for help. Heck, if you were a softball player in a beer league and you somehow stumbled upon Ted, he'd help you with your swing if you just asked. He simply loved to talk about hitting. I was well aware of this after playing with him in 1946 and 1947, but I was reminded of it as our paths crossed repeatedly in 1969. Whenever we were playing the Senators throughout the season I would often see my own players ask Ted for advice. "Hey, Ted," one of my players would ask him, "what do you think I'm dong wrong?" In spite of the fact that his insight might help one of my players hit better against his team, Ted would help. He'd say, "Come out at 10:00 tomorrow morning and we'll work on it." And he would. That's the kind of guy Ted Williams was — he wanted to help anyone who was sincere about wanting help.

MAY 22, 1969: There was some off-the-field turbulence with the White Sox during the '69 season — mainly personnel shifting in the front office and uncertainty as to whether the team was for sale. The ownership question was the weightier issue of the two, and one of the side effects of this problem was the fact that we had to play 11 of our home games ON THE ROAD. That's right, we played each American League club one time at Milwaukee's County Stadium, the former home of the Milwaukee Braves who had since relocated to Atlanta. Ownership claimed that they were doing it to expand the White Sox fan base, but everyone knew that it was really a way of testing the waters for a possible relocation of the Sox to Milwaukee. White Sox attendance had nose-dived since the days when we were always challenging for the pennant. Some said the attendance drop-off was because the South Side neighborhood had gone "bad," but some said it was because the team had gone bad. In any case, the Sox had played nine games in

Milwaukee in 1968, and the results were good on all fronts. They drew very well and they seemed to win more often than not at County Stadium. So they upped the schedule to 11 games for '69, and the result was that we had to pack up and go when we should have been able to be at home with our families.

But, we just followed orders and reported to County Stadium when told to do so. We'd played there just once in '69 prior to our game on this day, a 7-1 victory over the California Angels back on May 23rd while Al Lopez was still at the helm. And we won again on this day as we knocked off Detroit by a score of 7-3. I tried not to get too caught up in the fate of the Sox in Chicago, but I have to admit that I found it hard to imagine the White Sox moving to Milwaukee. Winning there was a double-edged sword, too — the better we did in Milwaukee, the better the chance that the club might be moved there. It was quite a quandary. It turns out that it any fear of the Sox moving to Milwaukee was wasted anxiety. Plans for shifting the franchise to Milwaukee were abandoned after the '69 season, and the Sox never again played any home games there. Fortunately, Milwaukee fans were awarded with an expansion team, the Brewers, in 1971.

MAY 30, 1969: We split a double-header with the Senators at RFK Stadium in Washington on this day. We were lucky to win even one of the two games due to breakdowns in hitting, fielding, pitching — and managing, too, if you believe the second-guessing of the sportswriters. "There was strong evidence of White Sox bungling today," wrote Richard Dozer of the *Chicago Tribune,* "from the manager's seat to the field, and to that barren area known as the White Sox bullpen." Here's the situation that Dozer felt I bungled — we were leading, 4-3, with the Nats batting in the bottom of the 8th. There were two outs with a runner on third base and the Senators' power-hitting right-handed swinger, Frank Howard, stepping up to the plate. Pitching for us was the left-handed Wilbur Wood. I went out to the mound to talk to Wood about what we were going to do, then trotted back to the dugout, leaving Wood in to pitch to Howard. The Senators' on-deck hitter was the left-handed swinging Mike Epstein, so some thought that I should have Wood walk Howard to get to Epstein — a lefty-lefty match-up. The Nats had no right-handed pinch-hitters left on their bench.

Of course, "The Book" says you DO NOT walk the go-ahead run in this situation. To be honest, I wasn't necessarily following "The Book" when I told Wood to pitch to Howard. I simply liked our chances with Wood against Howard. Big Frank struck out a lot, and we also had a Ted Williams-type shift on him because he was a dead-pull hitter. So I thought we had an excellent chance to get him out and end the threat. But, Howard squeezed through a seeing-eye single to tie the score. My strategy failed. We then lost in the 10th when Ed Stroud hit a dribbler in front of the plate with two out and Epstein on second base. By the time our catcher, Ed Herrmann, got to the ball, the speedy Stroud looked like he was going to beat it out for an infield hit. But Herrmann was a rookie and maybe didn't use the best of judgment when he tried to throw Stroud out at first. Stroud was safe when Herrmann's throw hit him in the back, and in the meantime Epstein raced all the way home from second with the winning run. When looking for the ultimate reason for our defeat, Dozer looked past our problems on the field and wrote, "The White Sox lived by 'The Book' — then died by it in the 10th." I point this out as an illustration of how different my life had become in a short period of time. Every little decision I now made was open to scrutiny, but that was the life of a big league manager and I was quickly adjusting to it.

The real news of that day wasn't my managerial moves, however — it was the incredible performance of our new second baseman, Bobby Knoop. Two weeks earlier we'd traded Sandy Alomar to the Angels in exchange for Knoop. We liked Bobby's great glove and really wanted him as a complement to Luis Aparicio at shortstop. We knew Knoop didn't usually hit too much, but we felt his excellent defense was worth the offensive sacrifice. Well, not only did he not hit much when he came over — he didn't hit AT ALL! He was 0-for-twenty-something after joining us, and just 5-for-35 as we headed into our twin bill against the Senators on this day. But he broke out of it in a big way by hitting three homers in the double-header. His 3-run shot in the nightcap led us to an 8-5 victory, helping erase the memory of our bad loss in the opener. And let me tell you, that homer was not a cheapie. It was an upper deck job, possibly 420-feet or so. Knoop was thrilled in the clubhouse, telling reporters, "I never even hit two homers in one day." Knoop's three homers in our double-header equaled his entire long ball output of the previous year. He went back to his light-hitting ways once away from D.C., hitting just three more homers for us the rest of the season. Knoop put together a nice 14-game hitting streak in July, but he struggled to keep his batting average above .225. He was a tough kid, though. Bobby fractured an eye socket bone in July when the Orioles' Dave Johnson kneed him in the face while breaking up a double-play, but Knoop was right back in the line-up as soon as the swelling went down enough so he could see clearly. He had minor surgery on the eye a few weeks later, and even that only knocked him out of the line-up for a couple days. I really enjoyed having him play for me.

MAY 31, 1969: The Senators beat us, 7-5, on this day in Washington, and in doing so reminded me of two things. ONE: on any given day, even the weakest of hitters can have a career game. TWO: as a big league manager, you'd better know the rule book inside-out or face the possibility of serious embarrassment. On the first count, Senators catcher Paul Casanova batted .196 with four home runs in 1968, and he was right around the same mark when our game began on this day. Forgetting that he was NOT supposed to do damage with his bat, Casanova proceeded to drive in five runs with a single, a sacrifice fly, a 2-run homer, and finally bases-loaded hit in the 8th to push across the game-winning runs. He was, as the saying goes, a 1-man wrecking crew. On the second count, we played the game under protest for what I thought was an umpire's mistake in interpreting the rules. It turned out the mistake was mine. We were trailing, 4-3, when we opened the 8th with back-to-back singles by Luis Aparicio and Carlos May. Senators pitching coach Sid Hudson then went to the mound to talk with his right-handed starter, Joe Coleman. As soon as Hudson departed, I sent lefty-swinging Gail Hopkins up to pinch-hit for Ken Berry. Hudson then reappeared from the dugout and replaced Coleman with left-hander Darold Knowles. I was SURE that Coleman was obligated to face one batter after Hudson's first mound visit, so I was teed off when the ump said that Knowles was, in fact, allowed to enter the game. I informed the umps that we were playing the game under protest, then I sent Buddy Bradford in to pinch-hit for Hopkins. In the clubhouse after the game, I was fully prepared to file a formal protest until Ed Short showed me the rulebook clause explaining that what the Senators had done was completely within the rules. Needless to say, it was somewhat embarrassing, but part of the learning curve for me in my new job as manager.

JUNE 19, 1969: I turned 57 on this day, and my team gave me a win with which to celebrate my birthday — a 13-10 victory over the expansion Seattle Pilots. We hadn't won very much since our 4-game winning streak back in my first week as manager. To be exact, we'd won just 13 of 34 games prior to our win on this day against the Pilots at Comiskey Park, so this victory, despite the fact that we didn't exactly play very well, was quite welcome. There was only one manager in the American League West who suffered worse than me in 1969, and he was sitting over in the Pilots dugout — Joe Schultz. His club would finish last in our division, right behind my White Sox. Joe was used to suffering, however — he'd been a part-time catcher for some bad Pirates teams in the late-30's and early 40's. I got to know him pretty well when he joined my Brownies team in 1943. We used to call him "Mr. Budweiser" because he could drink more beer than anybody on our ballclub. Joe was up with our '44 team for only a few games, so he missed out on the bulk of the pennant fever of that season, but he was, nonetheless, a member of our championship club. There was a luncheon reunion of the 1944 Browns at Riccardo's restaurant while the Pilots were in town, and Joe was there. It was nice to catch up with him as well as the other guys who came to town for the get-together. Joe had a particularly tough job in trying to make a positive mark out of the mess that was the Seattle Pilots. They had stadium problems, financial problems, player problems, and front office problems. It was, in fact, so bad that the team left Seattle for Milwaukee after the '69 season. Jim Bouton's hugely successful book, *Ball Four,* was all about his year with the Pilots in 1969. While Bouton admitted that Joe was liked by his players, *Ball Four* didn't paint a very flattering portrait of Schultz as a manager, and it may have hurt his prospects down the road after he was fired by the Pilots. That was unfortunate because Joe was a good guy and a smart baseball man.

JUNE 20, 1969: Any leftover birthday goodwill was quickly jettisoned on this day as we lost the opener of a twin bill with the California Angels, 2-1, in 12 innings in Anaheim. Our old pal Sandy Alomar, who we'd traded not too long ago, beat us, and that just aggravated the second-guessers all the more. We were tied at 1-1 with two outs in the bottom of the 12th when Alomar came up to hit with the winning run at second. Here's what Richard Dozer of the *Chicago Tribune* wrote AFTER the game — "Manager Don Gutteridge easily could have chosen to prolong to opener of a double-header that was only one out from stretching into the 13th inning. But with first base open in the 12th inning and a man at second, Gutteridge somehow decided against the intentional walk to set up a play at any base and bring up a rookie named Jim Spencer, instead. Astonishingly, pitcher Danny Osinski then pitched to Sandy Alomar, who poked a single over second base to drive in Roger Repoz and break a 1 to 1 tie that had stood since the 5th inning." Looking at the old clipping now and seeing my reply to the questions about my "backfired" strategy, I can see that I had yet to develop the thick skin that a manager must have to survive in the league. That would come in time, though. When probed about why I didn't have Osinski walk Alomar in that situation, I defensively replied, "Because I didn't want to. We wanted to pitch him low and we didn't. I don't know anybody in the league I'd rather face in that spot than Alomar. What's he got — three runs batted in?" Dozer went on to sarcastically report that Alomar, in fact, had 12 RBIs prior to that at-bat. In any case, and this is not intended to be a slight against Sandy, Alomar just wasn't a hitter to be feared so we went after him — and we lost. That's just how it goes sometimes. Spencer, on the other hand, may have struck out had we walked Alomar to get to him — but, then again, maybe he would have homered. While he was just a rookie, he would go on to hit 146 home runs — 133 more long balls than Alomar would hit in his career.

Osinski, for his part, was one of our better relievers despite being victimized by Alomar's game-winning blooper on this day. "Danny Slats," as he was called, was pretty consistent out of the pen in a year when we had serious problems in that department. A right-hander, he had a very good fastball and a nice slider. Alomar beating him with a flare wasn't uncommon for Osinski. The "ping hitters," as he called them, were typically the kind of guys who gave him trouble, but he was very good against the big swingers. Osinski would go 5-and-5 with a 3.56 ERA in 51 appearances for us in 1969. He'd been in the big leagues since 1962, his best season probably being the '67 campaign when he helped the Red Sox win the A.L. flag. But he was near the end in '69 and only appeared in a handful of games for the 1970 Astros before being gone from the big leagues for good. It was a typical story for us. Our 1969 club was filled with very young guys with no experience or old guys on their way out, and that is the ultimate reason for the dismal 26-and-34 record we had at the end of this day.

JULY 7, 1969: Gary Peters, overcoming his 1969 tendency to fall behind hitters, pitched a beautiful 2-hit shutout against the Oakland Athletics on this day at

Milwaukee's County Stadium. A run-scoring single by Bill Melton and a run-scoring double by Gail Hopkins gave Peters just enough run support to get the 2-0 win. There was a big crowd of almost 30,000 people there to see the game, and it's hard to say what the draw was. Reggie Jackson was in his second full year with A's and he was on a real home run tear, so there were unquestionably many folks there to see him. On the other hand, it was "bat day," and 10,000 full-size bats were handed out as the fans filed into the park. It's quite possible that the bat give-away helped boost the attendance. As you've probably noticed, they don't do "bat day" around the major leagues anymore. I guess they eventually realized that it wasn't a very good idea to give bats to thousands of people, many of whom often drank heavily and sometimes became angry at umpires. One thing I know DIDN'T drive up the attendance — but would have had people known about it ahead of time — was the presence of Joe DiMaggio in the A's dugout. I still had not adjusted to the bright yellow and green uniforms of the Athletics, but it was particularly strange to see that newfangled color scheme on DiMaggio's frame. If you saw DiMaggio wearing a baseball uniform, you just expected it to be Yankee pinstripes. DiMaggio had joined the Athletics as an executive vice president in 1968 after the A's had moved to Oakland, not far from Joe's home in San Francisco. Joe would occasionally act as a coach, too, suiting up for spring training or for random games like the one on this day. It was a thrill for the young guys, and I always enjoyed saying hello to him, too. The sportswriters wanted to get Joe's opinion on Jackson, asking him if he thought Reggie could be the next Babe Ruth. It sounds silly now, but Jackson had really taken the league by storm and was on a pace to break Ruth's single-season homer mark. Joe calmed them down, though, telling them that it was too early to make predictions like that, and that it was unfair to Jackson. Reggie's home run pace cooled later in the season and he finished with 47, well short of Ruth's mark.

JULY 17, 1969: We were in Minnesota on this day to wrap up an 8-game road trip against the Twins. The trip had been a disaster with us losing six of seven games prior to this day, so I told everyone to report to the ballpark one hour earlier than usual for a little "extra" work. The sportswriters wanted to know what was up, so I told them, "I just want us there early to get our minds on baseball. I don't want this losing complex to develop further, so this is just a stab at shaking us out of it." Once there, we all sat in the dugout and watched the Twins take batting practice. Minnesota was leading the American League West and playing great baseball. They would eventually win the division title, but lose to the Orioles in the A.L. Championship Series. We just sat there and watched them work out, talking baseball. We discussed all the little things that we were doing poorly — or not doing at all. You see, our team was very young and I thought they could benefit from this type of thing. We didn't need this type of intervention when I was a kid coming up with the Cardinals, however. In those days we traveled by pullman from city to city, and sometimes we'd be on the train together for up to 24 hours. That meant that we were hanging around each other a lot. The older players took that time to teach the younger players what they needed to know. We would actually sit there and discuss what to do in different game situations. By 1969, of course, we were traveling by jet, so the players simply were not spending that much time together anymore, and I think it hurt them.

I knew it would take a lot more than one of these dugout sessions to cure our problems, but I figured every little bit would help. In the end, however, the Twins were just too good for us on this day, and we lost our fourth in a row, 8-5. We jumped out to a 1-0 lead in the top of the first off Twins left-hander Jim Kaat, but then all our defensive shortcomings reared up in the Minnesota half of the inning. Cesar Tovar led off the inning with a single off Joe Horlen. We knew Tovar was going to try and steal, so we had a pitch-out called. Sure enough, Tovar took off, but we still failed to throw him out, Don Pavletich's throw arriving too late. Then another walk. Then Walt Williams got a poor jump on a ball he should have caught in leftfield and it went for a single. A few more walks, a few more hits, and by the time the boys came off the field we were trailing, 6-1. We even had trouble capitalizing on opportunities handed to us by other ballclubs. This game provided a great example of that. Kaat was a great fielding pitcher and had won seven straight Gold Glove Awards prior to 1969. He had only one error in all of 1968, so if it's one thing we were sure of it was that Kaat would NOT hand us the game by fielding his position poorly. And, to add irony to the situation, if you need any, Rawlings had presented Kaat with his 1968 Gold Glove Award just 24 hours before our game on this day. By the 6th inning, however, Kaat had committed THREE errors, yet we failed to make him pay for his mistakes to the degree that he should have. Such was our plight in 1969.

JULY 20, 1969: We kicked off an 8-game losing streak on this day as we dropped both ends of a double-header to the Royals at Comiskey Park. That's a pretty bad day at the ballpark, but even on your worse day at the ballpark there will always be something that'll make you smile. We were trailing, 5-4, in the opener when Walt Williams stepped up to open the bottom of the 7th. Right-hander Don O'Riley delivered to Williams, then Walt delivered a mighty blow — an infield hit to second base. Well, you'd have thought it was a mighty blow because as soon as Williams stepped on the first base bag, Comiskey Park's exploding scoreboard sent pinwheels spinning, sparks flying, and made noise worthy of the most majestic tape measure homer. It turns out it was not in celebration of Williams' leg hit; it was, instead, in commemoration of Apollo 11 making the first-ever moon landing. Apparently, the White Sox brass had prearranged to have the scoreboard operator let loose with the pyrotechnics at the very moment the astronauts touched down on the moon. So, that's what he did, and it just happened to be at the very instant Williams got his "moon shot." It was a funny moment, especially Williams' surprised reaction. Then the game was stopped as the announcement was made, and everyone in the ballpark bowed their heads in a prayer for Neil Armstrong and his crew. We made two quick outs once play resumed, but then we scored twice on back-to-back doubles by Gail Hopkins and Bill Melton. Our bullpen couldn't hold the lead, though, and gave up three runs in the top of the 8th, and we lost the game, 8-6. Incidentally, the "exploding" scoreboard was one Bill Veeck's innovations dating back to his short run as Sox owner from 1959 through 1961.

Our loss in the nightcap was particularly painful, especially for our catcher, Don Pavletich. We lost, 3-2, in 11 innings, in a game filled with errors and base-running mistakes. It's too bad, too, because it wasted a great pitching effort by Joe Horlen. In any case, the crowd was in a foul mood after our defeat in the opener, and our poor play in the nightcap only increased their ire — and they unfairly exacted their frustration on Pavletich. The game was scoreless in the top of the 2nd when Bob Oliver opened the inning with a double. Jerry Adair then laid down a sacrifice bunt which Horlen threw away, allowing Oliver to score. That started the crowd booing. Chuck Harrison grounded out next, advancing Adair to third. Bill Butler, the Royals pitcher, then missed on a suicide squeeze, and we had Adair dead to rights, but Pavletich dropped the ball while making the easy tag. The booing started again, only much louder than before. We were trailing, 2-0, when we finally got out of the inning, and, wouldn't you know it, Pavletich was slated to lead off the home half of the inning. He was booed unmercifully as he stepped to the plate, and it only got worse when he struck out. He fanned twice more in the game and the crowd was increasingly more brutal each time. I think they got in his head that day. It is certainly understandable. We got Pavletich from the Reds prior to the '69 season with hopes that he could add some experience to our young catching corps, as well as play a little first base. Don had been in the league since the early 60's, and he'd had a few nice seasons in Cincinnati. I'm sure he wasn't expecting this type of treatment when he came to Chicago. He did okay for us and was certainly not deserving of the treatment he received from the Sox fans on this day. But Don knew, as did all of us, that you took the good with the bad in baseball — but you didn't have to like it.

On hand to witness our unfortunate double-defeat on this day was a large chunk of the Sox championship team of 1959 — 17 players plus the entire coaching staff. The coaching staff part was easy — Tony Cuccinello, Ray Berres, and I were still with the Sox, but Johnny Cooney had to be torn away from his fishing boat down in Sarasota. The front office execs had decided weeks earlier to use this entire weekend to celebrate the 10th anniversary of the old Go-Go Sox. We were honored in between the games of our double-header, giving the Sox fans something to cheer about before they embarked on their assault of Pavletich in the nightcap. Al Lopez was there, too, looking great after having gained back a few of the pounds he'd lost while suffering his stomach troubles of the early spring. There was only one player on our 1969 roster who could tell the rest of the guys what it was like to wear a White Sox uniform in the World Series, and that was Luis Aparicio. He'd taken a 5-year repose from the Sox while he played in Baltimore from 1963 through '67, but our front office re-acquired him prior to the 1968 season. In the meantime, Aparicio had helped the Orioles to a World Series championship in 1966. It must have been a real shock for Luis to see the state of our once-great ballclub when he returned. We were a shell of what we'd once been, something that must have looked even more pronounced after having recently played for some great Orioles clubs. He didn't let it adversely affect him, though, picking right up where he'd left off with terrific glove-work at short. As far as his hitting went, Aparicio was actually better than he'd ever been. He hit a career high .280 in 1969, then topped that by hitting .313 in 1970. We were lucky to have got him back from Baltimore.

AUGUST 11, 1969: Our tough season rolled on as we dropped our sixth consecutive game on this day, a 5-2 loss to the Red Sox at Comiskey Park. Paul Edmondson, a tall, skinny, 27-year old right-handed rookie from California, started the game, but he didn't make it out of the second inning. He just didn't have it on this day, and the Red Sox jumped on him for four runs in the 1st and another run in the 2nd before I had to get him out of there. The loss dropped Edmondson to 1-and-5, but on the whole he'd pitched much better than his record indicated. I gave him 13 starts, and, with the exception of our game on this day, he always did very well. His record was 1-and-6 when the season ended, but he had a very solid 3.70 ERA. Edmondson could have very easily ended up with a record of 5-and-1 or 6-and-1, but he, like a lot of our '69 starters, had some tough luck. He didn't lean on the "tough luck" excuse, though. "When you're in the minors," he once said, "the parent club looks at you as an individual. If you pitch a good game and lose, well, they don't hold that against you. But when you're in the majors, everything is winning. You can pitch a 4-hitter and lose and you're considered a bum." Edmondson had a harsh view of the big leagues, but there was some truth to what he said. Still, we realized that despite his bad record, Paul was no bum. He'd pitched at San Fernando State College before spending five years in our minor league system. He threw a no-hitter for Columbus on May 23rd of '69, and that prompted us to bring him up for a trial in June. He looked so good that we kept him with the club for the rest of the season — and we had big plans for him to be in our '70 rotation until tragedy struck. Just a few weeks before spring training of 1970, Edmondson and his girlfriend were killed in a horrific car crash on a rain-slicked road in Santa Barbara, California. It was a shock to everyone in the organization, and Paul's death left a sad void in our 1970 ballclub.

In typical backwards fashion, our usually beleaguered bullpen had one of its better days in relief of Edmondson, but it went for naught. We hung two runs on Red Sox starter Mike Nagy with a 7th-inning rally that drew us to within three, but then Sparky Lyle came in and shut us down the rest of the way. I had a phone call waiting for me in my office when we entered the clubhouse, and that was usually NOT a good thing. On the line were Sox executives Ed Short and Leo Breen, and they had bad news — Carlos May, our rookie outfielder and the club's best hitter, had the top half of his right thumb torn off in a training accident with his Marine National Guard Reserve unit out in California. It was shocking news. Not only was this a bad blow for our ballclub, but also sounded like it could be a career-ender for May. Carlos had been up with us for a few games in 1968, but he'd come on like gangbusters in 1969. In the 100 games he'd played for us so far in 1969, he'd hit .281 with 18 home runs and 62 runs driven in. With the pace he was setting for himself prior to his accident, May was looking like a lock to win American League rookie of the year. Like his brother Lee, Carlos had power. He liked to pull the ball, but he also had opposite-field power when pitched away. The only down side to him was that he was only average, at best, as an outfielder. He tended to play too deep, which allowed a lot of hits to drop in front of him. But with a bat like his, his defensive liabilities would always be overlooked.

May was only 21 years old in 1969, and, like a lot of kids, he had the occasional lapse in good judgment. Back on July 27th we'd gotten throttled by the Orioles, 17-0, and May had a rare bad day with the bat. May's frustration boiled over in the 4th inning when plate ump Russ Goetz rung up him on a bad pitch. May lost his cool and threw his bat and batting helmet at Goetz. That got May immediately ejected, and we had to sweat it out for a couple days while we waited to find out if A.L. president Joe Cronin was going to suspend him. Maybe Cronin felt sorry for me because he decided not to suspend May, instead just fining him. I was glad because I didn't think the incident was indicative of the kind of kid May was. He could be a little sulky, but I think he was basically a good fellow — he just let his temper get the best of him.

Carlos was on a 2-week training session with his Guard unit at Camp Pendleton when the accident happened. He was cleaning a mortar which had supposedly been fired, but it actually still had a live round in it. The cleaning rod jammed the shell against the triggering mechanism, instantly ejecting the shell. As the shell left the mortar it ripped off half of May's thumb, while jamming the remaining portion down into his wrist. Needless to say, it was a grisly injury. Early on there was a fear that the doctors might need to amputate the rest of his thumb, and that would certainly have ended his career, but Carlos responded well to multiple surgeries and grueling physical therapy. He was, of course, lost to us for the rest of the season, but the good news was that he was able to continue his career in 1970. I think the injury robbed May of a great deal of his ability to hit the long ball, but he was still a fine hitter. However, none of that was yet known to me as I hung up the phone after my conversation with Short and Breen. All I knew on this day was that my best hitter was gone for the season, maybe never to play again, and that made for one fitful night's sleep.

AUGUST 31, 1969: It wasn't all bad in 1969. This day provided us with a good win and some cheers for Don Pavletich who the fans had treated so roughly about a month earlier. Edward Prell of the *Chicago Tribune* described our good day like this — "When the White Sox can survive a 4-run inning and still win, come out of the woodwork, you fans. They came up with this deft show of leger-demain in the 9th inning yesterday, scoring three times to whip the Cleveland Indians, 7 to 6, in a sweep of the 3-game series." Our three straight wins meant that we'd won six of our last eight, and when you're having the kind of season that we were having, six of eight was something to celebrate. Pavletich, for his part, saw to it personally that we'd win our third in a row with his 3-for-5 day at the plate. First, he tied the game at 2 apiece with a solo homer off Dick Ellsworth to open the 4th inning. Then Pavletich broke the tie in the 6th with an RBI single. Finally, he ended the game with a single to the wall that drove in Luis Aparicio with the winning run in the bottom of the 9th. I was happy to see a big smile on Don's face after that hit — he deserved it.

Incidentally, Edward Prell, as I mentioned, wrote the article recapping our win on this day. The *Chicago Tribune* periodically rotated their beat writers, and at this point in the season Prell was back covering our club. Prell and I, in fact, went way back together. Our paths first crossed was back in 1927 when I was in my first year of high school. Before I began playing for the Shop Team in the Old City League back in Pittsburg, Kansas, I kept score for them. I still wasn't grown enough to play with the big boys, but my time was fast coming. In the meantime, I learned the ropes as a scorekeeper/go-fer for the team. During the game I would take my hat off and pass it around the crowd, and the fans would drop money in it to pay the umpires and other expenses. At the end of the game I'd take the money, scores, and statistics up to the sportswriter — a Mr. Edward Prell. He'd take care of getting the money to the right people — but not until he took a quarter out of the hat and gave it to me. I always remembered and appreciated that. That's why I was so happy to watch Ed's rise through the sports-writing ranks, just like I know he was happy to see my rise to the major leagues. Ed eventually became the sports editor of the *Tribune,* and that's a long way removed from the Old City League in Pittsburg. But then again — so was managing the Chicago White Sox!

SEPTEMBER 19, 1969: Our solid play at the end of August did not continue into September, and we lost 9 of our first 15 games in the month. But then our fortunes turned around again, and we won five in a row culminating with our 7-0 victory over the Royals in Kansas City on this day. The winning streak was our longest of the season, and everyone had played well to make it happen. Tommy John got the complete game shutout and even chipped in two hits to help his own cause. The shutout was John's second of the season and his sixth complete game — something that was becoming a lost art by 1969. The 1960's officially ushered in the era of the relief specialist, and it's an approach that still exists today. They didn't think too much of relief pitching when I was playing in the

1930's. A starting pitcher was expected to go the full nine innings. He was looked down upon if he couldn't finish what he started. Because of that, starters paced themselves accordingly. If your club jumped out to a 4, 5, or 6-run lead, then your starter would let up a little bit to conserve his energy. That's why batting averages were higher back then. You'd get a couple of hits off him, but he would bear down when the game was on the line. Instead of winning the ballgame 5-0, he'd win 5-4. By 1969, it was not uncommon to expect your starter to go out there and give it his all for just five, six, or seven innings. Then a middle reliever might come in and throw as hard as he could for a couple innings. Then a set-up man, and finally a closer. That approach is one of the key factors that started bringing averages down. You get a fresh pitcher out there and it's a little tougher to hit. But Tommy John was from the old school, and he always wanted to go the distance if at all possible.

Right-fielder Walt Williams, catcher Ed Herrmann, and third baseman Bill Melton were the big guns on offense for us in our victory on this day. Williams was 2-for-5 with three RBIs. Williams had broken in with the Houston Colt .45's back in 1964, but he'd bounced around the minor leagues before coming to us in the winter of 1966. He was a little guy — only about 5-foot-6 and 185 pounds — but he had a quick bat with a very short stroke. Because of his size and his swing, Williams didn't hit for power, but he was a very good contact hitter in '69. He was fast, too, although he didn't steal many bases. I usually batted him first or second, but he hit particularly well in the lead-off slot. The only problem with Williams was that he wasn't the best outfielder. The only place I could play him was in rightfield, but he didn't really have a good enough arm to be out there. But his bat was too good not to be in our line-up, so I kept running him out there. Herrmann also had two hits in the game, the big blow being a 2-run homer off Dick Drago in the 4th inning. Herrmann was a rookie catcher, a tough assignment on any team, but particularly difficult when you had to deal with the constant challenge of blocking Wilbur Wood's unpredictable knuckleball. Needless to say, Herrmann led the league in passed balls on a number of occasions — but not for a lack of effort in trying to block Wood's knuckler. Ed always gave it 100%. Herrmann didn't hit for much of an average, but he had some pop in his bat, and he showed that with his homer against Drago on this day. He ended up batting .231 with 8 home runs and 31 RBIs in 102 games for us in 1969 — not a bad rookie season. He really broke out in 1970, however, when he hit .283 with 19 long balls. Melton was our best power hitter in 1969, however. He didn't go deep in our game on this day, but his two singles did help us get in the win column.

Melton had played in 34 games for us in 1968, but, for all intents and purposes, he, too, was essentially a rookie in 1969. With that said, you can only conclude that his first full season in the big leagues was a good one. He hit just .255, but he had great power, clubbing 23 homers while driving in 87. It was fun watching a talent like him develop right before my eyes. I remember how excited he was after he hit the first grand slam of his career. It was against Boston in late-May. He came back to the dugout wearing a big smile and said, "I've never hit a grand slam homer ANYWHERE before — PERIOD!" He struggled with his defense at third base at times, but that wasn't uncommon for a power-hitting third baseman. Despite his occasional defensive trouble at third, I specifically remember one game where he saved us with his glove — in rightfield. I used Melton as an emergency starter in right in a game against the Angels at Anaheim, and he cut down Sandy Alomar at third base with a great throw to preserve Billy Wynne's 1-0 shutout. A couple of days after that Melton hit three homers in a double-header at Seattle. As often happens, though, that big day seemed to make Bill start swinging for the fences instead of letting the round-trippers come naturally. He went into a bad slump and I had to bench him for a short period of time. He kept a positive attitude, however, and came back strong when I put him back in the line-up. Melton's power numbers really shot up in 1970 when he hit 33 homers. I was long gone from the Sox by the time that season ended, but Melton hit 33 home runs again in 1971, and that was good enough for the American League crown. I was glad to see him win the home run title, but I was not very happy to see some of the poor treatment he received from the Chicago fans and media over the next few years of his career. Melton missed half of the 1972 season with a herniated disc in his back and could never again hit home runs with quite the same regularity as he'd done before the injury. Robbed of much of his power, the criticism of his defense was stepped up, and Melton took it personally. I know he was happy when he finally got out of Chicago following the '75 season. I'll always remember Melton as a good fellow and one of the bright spots on our 1969 ballclub.

OCTOBER 2, 1969: *SOX END FRUSTRATING YEAR.* That was the headline to the *Chicago Tribune* article detailing our last game of the '69 season — a 6-5 loss to the Twins in Minnesota on this day. It seemed fitting, I guess, that we would lose our last game by one run, too, a problem that had plagued us from start to finish. The way we lost the game was also indicative of some of the trouble we'd had throughout the season — shaky starting and relief pitching, and defensive lapses. Danny Lazar was a rookie left-hander who I'd used in a handful of relief appearances, but I wanted to give him a shot to start once so I gave him the ball for this one. He may have been a little over excited, too, because he gave up a solo homer to Rich Reese, the second batter he faced. There's no shame in that, though — Reese was a good hitter. In any case, Lazar made it through six innings, but the Twins chipped away at him for four more runs, so we were tied at 5-5 as we headed into the 7th. We failed to score in the top of the inning, then our guys took the field for the Minnesota half of the inning. I sent Bart Johnson to the mound. He was about the only kid on the pitching staff with less experience than Lazar. Johnson was a tall, 19-year old power pitching right-hander from California. He'd only appeared in three previous games for us, and he'd shown some promise. Johnson struck out pinch-hitter Rick Renick to open the inning, but then he gave up back-to-back singles to Cesar Tovar and Rich Reese. Then, with Harmon Killebrew batting, Johnson and catcher Ed Herrmann got crossed up and allowed a passed ball. Tovar came in with what turned out to be the winning run. Losing our last game in that manner typified the frustrations we'd endured all season.

We finished the season with a record of 68 wins and 94 losses. That placed us 5th in the A.L. West, ahead of only Joe Schultz's Seattle Pilots. Our bad season was a tough pill for me to swallow, but I feel I did the best I could with what I had to work with. Picking out the causes for our failures was like shooting fish in a barrel. We were racked with injuries, with at least six or seven guys ending up on the disabled list at one time or another. We had eight or ten guys in the National Guard. Their constant coming and going made it difficult to establish any continuity in the line-up. The front office was in disarray, and that had a slight trickle-down effect to our club. All season long there were rumors that the team would be sold or moved. The rumors were repeatedly denied, but there proved to be some truth to the speculation when owner and president Arthur Allyn stepped down in September, handing over control of the club to his brother, John. Probably the most significant of all factors in our bad season was our inexperience. About half of the guys who took the field for us in '69 were in only their first or second seasons. Nowhere was that more of a detriment to us than in our pitching staff.

The youth on our team factored heavily in our tough year, but they also were our hope for the future, and that's the positive spin I tried to give everyone as we headed home for the off-season. "It wasn't all bad," I told reporters in the clubhouse after our last game, "we came up with some good young ballplayers." I pointed out position players like Bill Melton, Carlos May, Walt Williams, Gail Hopkins, Ed Herrmann, as well as pitchers Billy Wynne, Paul Edmondson, and Bart Johnson. "We used a lot of youngsters this season," I said, "and we're going to use even more next season. We're going to shoot the works on this youth movement."

It's possible that I, the rookie manager, had something to do with our poor record, but if I did I don't think it amounted to much. In fact, I don't think a manager can impact the overall record too much either way, good or bad. A good manager might be able to factor in on a handful of extra wins, and a bad manager might be responsible for a handful of losses. It ultimately comes down to the players, and we were just in a down cycle on that front. Long-time Chicago sportswriter Jerome Holtzman gave his assessment of my first season as Sox skipper, and I felt it was a fair look at the job I'd done. "Gutteridge is such a nice guy," Holtzman wrote, "that many people though he would nice-guy himself out of the league — that he would be too easy-going on his men. Gutteridge, thank heavens, will never be a Durocher, which is a plus for everyone. But Gutteridge won the complete respect of his players and worked beautifully with them — not too tough and not too easy, a difficult blend but one necessary for championship baseball. Like Al Lopez before him, Gutteridge also proved beyond a shadow of lingering doubt that he knows how to handle pitchers. Very often he saved games by taking a starting pitcher out while the starter still held the lead, and not later. Gutteridge also handled his bullpen beautifully and came up with a late-season sensation in Danny Murphy, who might have a big, big year next season." Next season. Having signed a 2-year deal, it was nice to know that there'd be a "next season" for me, but I knew I had to quickly show a marked improvement or it just might be my last.

1 9 7 0

APRIL 7, 1970: A new baseball season, fresh with hope and optimism, kicked off on this day, but those positive feelings were quickly buried beneath a 12-0 drubbing at the hands of the Minnesota Twins at Comiskey Park. With the exception of rookie first baseman John Matias and 2nd-year second baseman Syd O'Brien, everyone in our starting line-up had been a key part of the 1969 team. We had Walt Williams in right, Luis Aparicio at short, Carlos May in left, Bill Melton at third, Buddy Bradford in center, Duane Josephson at catcher, and Tommy John on the mound. The Twins jumped on us for three runs in the top of the 1st, and I'm sure many of our fans immediately began to worry that they were in for more of the same old stuff they'd seen in '69. John stuck around until the 5th when Brant Alyea unloaded a 3-run homer to put us down 6-0. I removed John and replaced him with right-hander Tommie Sisk who we'd gotten from Boston in a trade a month earlier. Sisk fared even worse than John, lasting only 1-2/3 innings and allowing three runs. So I went to Danny Murphy who'd done so well in the latter part of the '69 season. But he, too, struggled, allowing four runs without getting an out before I pulled him. The big blow against Murphy was another 3-run homer by Alyea. Meanwhile, as we were experiencing a complete pitching breakdown, our bats were almost non-existent, scratching out just six hits.

It was a tough way to open a new campaign, but, believe it or not, we had faith that this club was going to be much improved from our '69 team. The "we" being me and the White Sox front office. Knowing that most of our roster was the same as our 1969 roster — a conglomeration that had managed to lose 94 ballgames — it may seem hard to believe that we really had faith in these guys, but we really did. We felt that our youth movement had shown signs that pointed to a bright future. While it had yet to translate to wins, we knew that with patience we would be rewarded for choosing to go with youth. My job would be to try and keep these young fellows from losing their confidence as they faced the trials and tribulations involved with finding their way in the major leagues. Somehow I had to motivate these youngsters to keep playing at 100 percent despite the frustration that comes with losing, slumps, and benchings — things that all big leaguers will have to face at sometime in their early development. This task, something I had dealt with on numerous occasions in my minor league managing career, turned out to be one of the most difficult aspects of managing the '69 Sox.

Al Lopez, happily retired at the time, traveled up from his home in Tampa, Florida, to attend our opening day game against the Twins at Comiskey Park on April 7th, 1970.

APRIL 10, 1970: "Don Gutteridge trotted out a rookie pitcher for his first major league test yesterday, turned to more experienced help for support, and everything clicked perfectly." That was *Chicago Tribune* sportswriter George Langford's synopsis of how we got our first win of the season on this day, a 5-4 victory over the Milwaukee Brewers at Comiskey Park. Prior to our game with the Brewers on this day we'd suffered a second loss to Minnesota following our opening day embarrassment, but our guys had looked much better than they had in the opener. So it seemed to be a natural progression of performance — horrible, then decent, then good — for us to finally get a victory here in our third game. It took solid execution in all aspects of the game to get the win, and it began on the mound with rookie right-hander Jerry Janeski. The Twins got 10 hits in 7-1/3 innings off Janeski, but Jerry did a nice job of not allowing Minnesota to turn any of that offense into a big inning. We were leading, 5-2, with one out in the 8th when Janeski walked Ted Kubiak and Rich Rollins, so I took him out of the game. I brought in Wilbur Wood, and he immediately gave up a booming double to Tommy Harper. Kubiak scored easily, but a perfect relay from Carlos May to Luis Aparicio to Duane Josephson nailed Rollins at the plate. It was a great play and a real key to our victory. Although he allowed another run in the 9th, Wood was good enough to nail down the win, and Janeski had his first big league victory. The press had taken an immediate liking to Jerry from the moment we'd acquired him from Boston in early-March. He was a California boy who'd pitched his college ball at Cal Sate University. He brought with him that laid-back California attitude, a pedigree as a champion kite flyer, and a reputation as a physical cultist. The sportswriters loved these eccentricities, and they really had a ball when they got a look in Janeski's locker and saw the huge supply of vitamin pills, liver pills, oil pills, wheat germ, and other assorted health foods. They eventually took to calling him all sorts of descriptive nicknames, but "Mr. Wheat Germ" seems to be the one I remember being used most often.

All I cared about, however, was the fact that Mr. Wheat Germ had looked solid in his first major league start because that was good news for the ballclub. We needed Janeski to be good in 1970 because he had big shoes to fill — those of Gary Peters. Back in December we'd traded Peters and Don Pavletich to the Red Sox in exchange for second baseman Syd O'Brien and minor league pitching prospect Billy Farmer. It was part of our continued youth movement. Farmer had come up with a bad arm, however (he never did make it to the majors), so the Red Sox gave us a list of eight players to pick from as compensation for Farmer's failure to pass our physical. Janeski was on that list, so we grabbed him. He would go on to have an up-and-down season for us, finishing with a 10-and-17 record. Janeski's promising rookie season did not pan out for him in the long run, though, as he won only one more big league game after being traded to the Senators in 1971. Jerry pitched in a handful of games for the Rangers in their first season in Texas after moving there from Washington in 1972, but he never made it back to the majors after that. But on this day Jerry Janeski was king, and I was happy to see him get that first win under his belt.

APRIL 16, 1970: We lost to the Athletics on this day, 3-1, in Oakland. With the way we played, we were lucky the score wasn't worse. Tommy John continued to struggle, but he was, as usual, not very well supported in the field or on offense. We had the following defensive lapses in the 5th inning alone — Carlos May had a fly ball bounce off his chest for a double; Luis Aparicio did the unthinkable and misplayed two ground balls; and third baseman Bill Melton was duped into throwing to the wrong base, a mistake that allowed the go-ahead run to score. Our loss on this day came after two straight wins, but overall we had been playing terribly. Once in the clubhouse I let the guys know how disappointed I was with their effort, but they were getting used to hearing it.

We'd dropped three in a row after our first win of the season. Our pitchers were not bearing down on the guys they should be getting out. Danny Walton, for example. He was a rookie who wouldn't hit 30 homers in his entire career, yet we allowed him to go deep on us twice in one game as the Brewers beat us, 8-4, on April 11th. "We turned hero-makers again," I told reporters after the game. "We seem to make stars out of all the unknowns," I added, thinking back to Brant

We had a very young ballclub in 1969 and 1970, but Ken Berry, seen here with me, was one of our veterans. He was an excellent outfielder who could really go get 'em.

Alyea on opening day. The next day the Brewers swept us in a mistake-laden double-header, and I was fuming. "I'm not going to stand for this. There will be changes made. I don't know what they will be right now. But I told a lot of these players in spring training that making this team at the start meant ONLY that they were getting the first chance over over some other players in spring camp — and they've just about blown their first chance. Who's my number four starter? I wish somebody would tell me who my first two starters are. I'm not satisfied with anyone's performance on this team — pitchers, hitters, defense, all areas. I'm no loser and I'm not going to stand for this." As mad as I got, there really weren't a whole lot of changes I could make. When the youngsters were failing from pressing too hard, I would counter with a more veteran line-up. That usually meant changing to Ken Berry in center, Tom McCraw at first base, and Bobby Knoop at second, but neither approach was very successful.

APRIL 29, 1970: Something I came to dread during my run as White Sox manager was seeing the Baltimore Orioles on the schedule. They were a tremendous ballclub during that time, and they compiled excellent won-lost records the way most great teams do — by whipping up on the second division clubs. And the Orioles really had their way with us in 1969 and '70. They had come to Comiskey for a 3-game series, and on this day they beat us for the second day in a row, pounding us by a score of 18-2. It was an embarrassing defeat where five of our pitchers were knocked around for 20 hits while our batters managed just eight hits off Orioles right-hander Jim Palmer. Paul Blair led the Oriole attack with THREE home runs, but Boog Powell also hit a big 3-run round-tripper in the 5th inning. Blair's performance against us was an aberration, to say the least, but we were quite used to Powell beating up on us. He seemed to homer against us every time we played Baltimore. It didn't matter whether Powell was hot or slumping — when he played our club he was like Babe Ruth. He hit .459 against us in 1969, and continued to pound our pitchers, particularly Tommy John, in 1970. The Orioles always found a way to beat us. When they didn't clobber us by a score of 18-2, they'd edge us by one or two. One little bobble and they'd jump on it. They always had the extra inch.

MAY 1, 1970: We opened the month of May with a 13-6 win over the Tigers at Comiskey Park on this day. There was a benches-clearing brawl in the game, and maybe that helped shake our club from its malaise. I guess it's possible, because we won eight of our next 13 including our win on this day. Joe Horlen was shaky in the top of the 1st inning and he gave up two runs, but we responded by tying the game in the bottom half of the frame. The play that tied the game was the one that caused the melee. Bill Melton singled to drive in Luis Aparicio with the tying run, but Melton got caught off first base as the throw came in to the infield. Bill made for second and slid in high in an attempt to knock the ball out of Dick McAuliffe's glove. McAuliffe fell on Melton with his knees, and then the two squared off. As McAuliffe charged Melton, Bill landed a punch to the side of McAuliffe's head. McAuliffe swung and missed, then the two began to wrestle. Moments later, players and coaches from both clubs had charged to the scene. There isn't much more to report, just a bunch of crowding and hollering. Order was restored quickly with McAuliffe, Melton, and Tigers manager Mayo Smith the only ejections. Smith got tossed for arguing too vehemently. Sparked by the fight, our guys' bats seemed to get hot and they piled on the hits and runs. Our trouble with McAuliffe went back to the stretch run of the 1968 season. He'd charged Tommy John after a brush-back pitch in a game on August 22nd. The fight that ensued got McAuliffe suspended for five games, but it left John with a separated shoulder. McAuliffe was a very good player, but I did not like his quick temper. When the reporters asked me what I thought of McAuliffe, I tried to keep from inflaming the situation, saying only, "If I can't say something nice about him, I don't want to say anything."

MAY 16, 1970: It's amazing the difference two weeks can make. On this day we beat the Kansas City Royals, 6-1, at Comiskey Park, and the win brought our club to within two games of the .500-mark. At this moment our club was filled with positive feelings and boundless optimism. Two weeks earlier we had been abysmal in all facets of the game — except batting average. All year we'd had a very good team batting average, but not when it came to hitting with runners in scoring position. "It's nice that we can hit," I'd told the sportswriters who'd pointed out the fact that we had a number of guys hitting over .300, "but they don't pay off on hits. They pay off on runs, and those hits don't mean a thing if they don't drive in runs." But now our guys were driving in runs, too, and the results were showing in the win column. Our reversal of fortune had even lifted the spirits of Tommy John who had started the season 0-and-5. He pitched beautifully on this day, allowing just three hits while going the distance for his third victory. Our win on this day was our fourth in a row, and that, sadly, would turn out to be our longest winning streak of the season.

MAY 17, 1970: It's amazing the difference a day can make. Just a day before we were on cloud nine, poised to reach that elusive .500-mark, but on this day, just 24 hours later, our kids wore a defeated look on their faces. Bob Logan of the *Chicago Tribune* summed it up best when he wrote, "The White Sox took a ride on the wave of the future today at Comiskey Park, only to drown in the undertow. The Sox dropped both ends of a double-header in extra innings to the Kansas City Royals before the largest crowd to attend a regular-season game on their home grounds since June 23, 1968. They were within one out of extending their winning streak to five in the opener when the Royals rallied to tie it in the 9th inning and pushed over another in the 10th for a 3 to 2 victory. Then came the roughest blow. A rubber-armed sophomore southpaw, Jim Rooker, went the distance for Kansas City in the second game, beating the Sox, 8 to 4, in 11 innings." They were both disheartening losses, no doubt. A throwing error by third baseman Syd O'Brien opened the door for Kansas City to score the winning run in the 10th inning of the first game. Then we let Rooker beat us with a 2-run double in the 11th inning of the nightcap. They were both gut-wrenching defeats, but it was a time when, as the manager, I hoped the team wouldn't get too down. They needed to rally in that situation. But our youth hurt us there, I think. Instead of rallying, we went into a tailspin, losing 14 of our next 18 ballgames, and I guess I must accept part of the blame for failing to motivate them. Ironically, if you believe the post-game comments of the Kansas City players, instead of motivating my players, I actually motivated the ROYALS to their double-win. They told reporters that they were inspired by my previous days' comments when I said, "Yes, I'm very aware that we could reach .500 tomorrow if we win two games from Kansas City. And we'll be a .500 club tomorrow. I mean to win those two. They mean a lot." It ticked me off when the writers told me about how the Royals were spinning my words. They felt I was not giving them the respect they deserved. "I didn't say anything bad about their club," I snapped. "It's my job to steam up MY club, not THEIRS. If I ever walk on the field and don't feel we'll win, I'll forfeit." And I still believe that.

MAY 19, 1970: Rudy May of the California Angels beat us by pitching a 3-0 shutout at Comiskey Park on this day. May allowed only one hit through the first eight innings, and that lone hit was a cheap artificial turf single off the bat of Ken Berry that scooted under the outstretched glove of Angles shortstop Jim Fregosi in the 2nd. We got one more hit in the 9th, a looping single to rightfield by Walt Williams, but other than that we couldn't do anything against May.

If you were paying attention, you'll have noticed that I mentioned "Comiskey Park" and "artificial turf" in the same paragraph. It's painful to remember it now, but, believe it or not, Comiskey Park abandoned tradition and went with the latest craze and installed artificial turf prior to the 1969 season. The outfield was left as natural grass, but the infield was bulldozed, backfilled with a bed of crushed rock and concrete, then covered with an emerald rug made by Monsanto. Unlike some artificial turf fields, the skin of our infield remained dirt, but it was quite a shock to see groundskeeper Gene Bossard's beautiful grass infield take on the look of a pool table. The change was done for a number of reasons. It was cheaper to maintain, and for the cash-poor Sox of 1969 that was a big deal. It was "the future," or so we were told, so the Sox wanted to be on the front edge of the movement. Plus, they hoped it would generate more scoring for our offensively-challenged ballclub. Unfortunately, it also helped the opposition score. But, more offense supposedly put people in the seats, so there was no stopping it. Unfortunately, putting down artificial turf took away a real element of the character of Comiskey Park, especially as far as Bossard was concerned. No more soaking the infield to help our ground ball pitchers like Gene had always done for Dick Donovan, Tommy John, and Joe Horlen. We used to call it

"Bossard's Swamp" when he would do that. No more custom-trimming of the grass to help various infielders — i.e., leave the grass tall if in front of an infielder with poor range while cutting it short in front of a guy with good range. The days of the Go-Go Sox were long gone, but Luis Aparicio's bunting game suffered one final death-blow when the rug went in. "Now that the ball will have more bounce to the ounce," Aparicio said, "I'm not so sure that a bunt will be worth the risk." It had to pain Bossard to hear that after all the work he used to do to ensure that the third base line was ideally customized for Aparicio's bunting.

The infielders loved fielding on it, though, because its smoothness made for true bounces. Being from the old school, however, I had reservations about artificial turf and found it difficult to come up with any good reasons for installing it. Pressed by reporters for my input, all I could come up with was to say, "It bounces faster. This means more double-plays. And we have the boys to make them!" I don't know how convincing I sounded, but my words don't seem overly convincing as I read them nearly 40 years later. This story has a happy ending, though. Bill Veeck had been part of the Sox ownership very briefly from 1959 through mid-1961 when he sold his interest because of health problems. In that short time he installed Comiskey Park's famous exploding scoreboard amongst other interesting innovations. Well, Veeck bought back into the White Sox in December of 1975, and one of the first things he did was to have the artificial turf ripped out and replant grass prior to the 1976 season. That, I'm sure, was a happy day for Gene Bossard.

MAY 25, 1970: *SOX SUFFER 5TH STRAIGHT DEFEAT, 7-1.* That was the *Chicago Tribune* headline summing up our sad state of affairs following our loss to the Royals in Kansas City on this day. We were down, and when things are bad there are often stories of team unhappiness that make their way to the sportswriters — and that's what was going on with our club. "Any time you get into a streak like this, there are going to be 'stories,' " I told the reporters. "They really haven't been playing badly. They just haven't been hitting. But the manager has to take the blame. Sure, I'm at fault simply because it happens. What are you going to do? Hang me with a lasso rope? The problem is lack of hitting more than anything else. We just aren't scoring runs. We haven't got that spark. But this is the same club that was winning a week ago." Someone then asked me if I was able to get a good night's sleep when things were this bad. "No, you don't exactly sleep normally during something like this. But I'll catch up on my sleep when we win six in a row." Then I ended my chat with the reporters with this zinger — "The bus for early batting practice leaves at 10:00 am tomorrow!" That, more than anything, was the reason for most player discontent. They hated early workouts or off-day workouts. But the way I saw it, they were a necessary side effect of poor play. We simply needed more work to get better, and the only way to get the additional work was by having the OCCASIONAL extra practice session.

I can't think of anything that would have made me want to rip up my line-up card more than a 5-game losing streak like the one we were suffering when we lost to the Royals, 7-1, on May 25th, 1970.

MAY 30, 1970: The Red Sox beat us, 7-5, on this day at Fenway Park. It was a particularly frustrating loss as we let a weak-hitting pitcher beat us with his bat. The score was tied at 5-5 as we took the field for the bottom of the 6th. Jerry Crider had come on in relief the previous inning, so I sent him back out there for another frame. The first batter he faced in the inning was right-handed reliever Vicente Romo, one of the league's weakest hitting pitchers. Romo had been in the league three years and had exactly one RBI, but he pounced on Crider's first delivery and sent it 360 feet over the 37-foot high wall in left-center. I couldn't believe it. That was the difference in the game. The Red Sox added an insurance run later in the same inning, but Romo's shot was what killed us. Romo was in the majors for five more seasons and he NEVER homered again. This was his ONLY career round-tripper. His lifetime batting average stands at .149. I know that anomalies like Romo's home run happen in baseball, but they happened all too often to our ballclub. I attributed much of this problem to a lack of aggressiveness, and I explained that to the sportswriters in the clubhouse following the game. "There's no aggressiveness on this club," I said, still steamed over the defeat. "I wish I knew how to put some aggressiveness in them. They have got to want to win more than anything else. I'm still convinced they can play ball, but they are not convinced. I hope there is something I can do. You try to get somebody to do something, get something started, but they haven't been able to." My frustration over this defeat lasted through the night and into the next morning, leading me to call a team meeting before our game the next day.

MAY 31, 1970: "Don Gutteridge gathered his athletes together for a special little lecture before today's game because of his distress over 12 losses in 14 games. The White Sox hitters must have been deeply altered by their manager's remarks." That was the introduction to George Langford's *Chicago Tribune* article recounting our 22 to 13 win over the Red Sox on this day at Fenway Park. For a team like ours, one that had been hard pressed to score two or three runs per game over the previous two weeks, an offensive explosion like this was unfathomable. The pre-game meeting that Langford referred to was a short one. I told the team that I was disappointed in their lack of spirit. I told them that they lacked aggressiveness. I told them a few other criticisms, too, but the kicker was when I told them that we were going to have an early morning workout tomorrow when we arrived in Washington — and tomorrow was an off-day. As you can imagine, reaction to that was mixed. I don't know if their anger over having to practice on their off-day was what motivated them, but they took out their frustration on six Boston pitchers. It was a 24-hit barrage in which every position player except Buddy Bradford and John Matias got at least one hit and an RBI. The brutality began in the 1st inning off our former teammate Gary Peters. It was the first time we'd faced Peters since we dealt him to Boston. I actually felt bad for him as he was knocked around in the 1st inning. Peters didn't even make it out of the inning, but the story might have been different had Carl Yastrzemski not committed two errors — the big one being a dropped fly ball with two outs and the bases loaded that allowed all three runners to score. Peters was a class act, though. He and his wife still keep in touch with me. As the 22-13 score indicates, while our bats had come to life, our pitching didn't exactly show up. The combined score was just one shy of the record set back on July 29, 1950, when the Red Sox beat the Philadelphia Athletics by a score of 22-14. My experience had shown me long ago that weird things could happen at Fenway Park, and this game fits into that category. Incidentally, after the game I cancelled the off-day morning workout. I told the players that the 3-1/2 hour batting practice they'd just had was enough. Plus, I wasn't sure if they'd even be able to lift a bat the next day!

JUNE 3, 1970: We failed to maintain the momentum we had after our blowout over Boston. First, we suffered a 1-run loss to the Senators at RFK Stadium on June 2nd, then we let them edge us again on this day, 5-4. Nats catcher Paul Casanova, a .185-hitter who, like Boog Powell, always seemed to have his way against Tommy John, was at it again in this game. Casanova went 3-for-3 with two of those hits coming off John before he exited the game after seven innings. The big blow was Casanova's two run go-ahead double off John in the 4th inning. A bigger blow came after the game when Luis Aparicio, of all people, blew his top in the clubhouse. He threw an all-out tantrum, storming around the clubhouse scattering paper cups and whatever else got in his way. All the while he was airing every frustration that had built up in him so far that season. I never made a move to stop him. When a quiet guy like Aparicio blows his stack — a fellow who is respected as a ballplayer and a good man — sometimes it gets through to the players in a way the manager cannot. It was worth a try, at least. Plus, the sight of Luis tearing up the clubhouse was a once in a lifetime sight and I wasn't about to put an end to it!

JUNE 4, 1970: For a day, at least, our ballclub snapped out of the doldrums and played a good game, beating the Senators, 7-3, in Washington. We got adequate pitching from Jerry Crider and Danny Murphy. We were aggressive with the bat for a change, hitting in clutch situations. And we played smart, errorless ball in the field — even turning in a few exceptional plays. Maybe it was Luis Aparicio's tirade from the previous day that inspired the turnaround. Maybe it was just coincidence, too, but either way I think it was good that Aparicio, a veteran, let our youngsters know that the way they had been playing was unacceptable. Word of Aparicio's tantrum had leaked to the press, so Luis explained himself in the papers after our win on this day. "I just couldn't take it anymore," he said. "Every day. I know a lot of these players are young and haven't had a lot of major league experience, but they have a major league uniform on and there's just no excuse for the mistakes they have been making. Errors are one thing. Little mistakes are another. After last season I went home to Venezuela and I couldn't figure out how a team like ours could have lost so many games. I was sick. I lost my appetite. If it wasn't for the fans in Chicago who've treated me so good I don't know if I would've come back this year. But I owe them a lot and I intend to repay." I agreed wholeheartedly with everything Aparicio said. It's too bad that his great attitude toward the game and the fans was becoming an out-dated way of thinking, even way back in 1970. It's even more pronounced today, and that's too bad.

JUNE 23, 1970: As much as I admired Luis Aparicio's passionate attempt to reach his teammates with his June 3rd outburst, I knew that the effects of something like that were most likely going to be limited at best. When, and if, our young club ever broke out of their losing ways, it would be of their own volition — and it would be the result of them finally maturing as ballplayers. The positive results of Luis' tantrum lasted exactly one game, then we proceeded to lose 11 of our next 16 as we headed into our game against the Angels in California on this day. Frustrated with the way things were going, I made a major change that I hoped would help — and we won. The *Chicago Tribune* noted the move with a headline that said, *WHITE SOX LINE-UP CHANGE SUCCESSFUL; ANGELS FALL, 7-3.* The text went on to say, "Don Gutteridge, exhausting every possible move that might uncover the right combination for the White Sox, tried a line-up maneuver tonight involving Bill Melton and Syd O'Brien. The results were happy, if not conclusive. Melton, shifted from third base to rightfield, broke open a scoreless pitching match between Chicago's Jerry Janeski and California's Andy Messersmith with a 3-run homer in the 7th inning. Then O'Brien, who took Melton's place at third base, contributed a 3-run double in the 9th inning."

It was great because it worked — this time. My last gamble had failed miserably, and the writers jumped all over me. I stuck by my guns, however, telling them, "Sure it was a gamble, but I was a born gambler. If you're afraid, there's only one place for you — at home under the bed." Moving Melton to the outfield and bringing in O'Brien didn't seem like much of a gamble, though. Melton was having a very tough time on defense at third base. His troubles there hit an all-time low on June 8th when he was seriously injured when an infield pop ticked off the heel of his glove and hit him square in the face. The impact was vicious, breaking his nose and knocking him unconscious. After the game I told the sportswriters, "I thought he could play his way out of his fielding slump and I knew that when he did come out of it he would be a much better player than he's ever been. He's so damn wound up. But a man has to pull himself out of things like this. It's part of growing up." The problem, however, was that Melton did not seem to be separating himself from his defensive troubles. He had a great arm and had played outfield in the minors, so I thought it was a natural move to shift him to rightfield. Bill didn't like it, though, and that was one of the problems a manager faced when tinkering with his line-up in this way.

"I'm not happy playing the outfield," Melton told reporters. "I want to play third. It's bad to say it, but that's the way I feel. I know how I play the outfield — that's why they shifted me to third in the minors. I can't judge fly balls." I understood his feelings, but I kept running Melton out to right because I thought it was the best thing for the team. Bill ended up playing 71 games out there, yet he never again played outfield in any subsequent years of his career.

The down-side to my plan, however, was that Syd O'Brien wasn't much better on defense than Melton. He'd shown promise as a rookie with the Red Sox in 1969, hitting .243 with nine homers in 100 games. On defense he'd divided his time between third, second, and short, but the majority of his games were spent at the hot corner. The problem with that, though, was that it was at third where O'Brien committed most of his errors. We were hoping that he'd work himself out of his defensive troubles, but he committed 13 errors at third in 68 games. We used him at second and short in another 48 games, and he was a bit better there, but it was at third that we needed him so we stayed the course. While O'Brien could be the volatile type, he was good about our attempts to make it work with him at third. He hit decent enough, too, batting .247 with eight home runs in 441 at-bats, but he was dealt to the Angels following the season, and out of the big leagues for good following the 1972 season. In any case, Melton, O'Brien, and I were all in this thing together, so we were all going to do what was best for the team — and for the time being it was playing in this new configuration. "We're going to try this arrangement for at least two or three more games," I told the writers. "In our situation we can't just sit back day after day and do nothing. We have to try every possibility."

JULY 2, 1970: The Athletics whipped us, 10-6, on this day at Comiskey Park. Barry Moore was completely ineffective on the mound, and our guys committed four errors behind him. With our team struggling the way we were, what we all needed was a good laugh — and this game provided one. And I mean a BIG one. We were trailing, 10-4, in the bottom of the 7th when out of the stands bounded Morganna — The Kissing Bandit. Morganna was a former exotic dancer who had taken up a new hobby — interrupting big league baseball games by jumping onto the field, running up to one of the players, and planting a big kiss on him. She was quite a sight to see, too. She was blonde-haired and always wore a t-shirt and hot pants — and she was VERY well endowed. While it was considered a serious offense to trespass on a major league ballfield, Morganna was always gently ushered off the field and quietly arrested — always to the raucous cheers of the fans. In our game on this day, however, Morganna was no more than a few steps onto the field before it was absolutely apparent that this was NOT the real Morganna. This character was obviously wearing a bad blonde wig and cheap sunglasses, not to mention a hideous pants suit. Then there was the shape of the impersonator. Missing were the voluptuous curves of Morganna, replaced, instead, by the massive girth of a 260-pound man. Another dead give-away was the fact that the imposter was steadily puffing away on a stogie. Bad disguise and all, the Morganna impersonator made a bee-line for A's first base-man, Joe Rudi. Rudi took a defensive posture as the imposter drew near him, but Joe then smiled as he recognized the man beneath the get-up. Then David Condon, *Chicago Tribune* columnist, thoughtfully removed his cigar and plant-ed a kiss and a hug on Rudi. It was hilarious and we all got a good laugh out of it — and that was just what we needed to help ease our suffering.

JULY 12, 1970: We played our last game before the All-Star break on this day. We'd staggered to a record of 3-and-11 over our previous 14 games, but we went into the break on a good note by beating the Royals, 10-5, in Kansas City. Luis Aparicio was one of the keys to our victory as he went 3-for-5 with two RBIs. At 36 years of age, Aparicio was enjoying his finest season at bat, and his three hits put him at 102 at the midway point. Injuries slowed him down just a bit in the second half, but he still finished with a .313 average and 173 hits. Aparicio was our club's only representative for the All-Star game, which was held in Cincinnati. I watched it on TV. Luis started at short and hit lead-off, but he had a tough day at the plate, going 0-for-6. It was a memorable game, though, end-ing in the 12th when Pete Rose bowled over Ray Fosse to score the controversial game-winning run. The play was controversial because many felt that it was not necessary for Rose to go in so hard on Fosse. Fosse suffered a fractured shoulder and a broken finger in the collision, and while he continued to play, he never again displayed the power and consistency that he had shown prior to his All-Star injuries. I appreciate guys playing all-out in every game, but I've always felt that Rose should have slid in to home on that play instead of crashing into Fosse. It was an exhibition, after all, and the goal should be to win, but not at the expense of someone's well being.

JULY 17, 1970: The All-Star break failed to cure our ills as we dropped our first four games of the second half. Our 4-3 loss to the Tigers at Comiskey Park on this day was our second defeat in that streak. We were tied, 3-3, as we entered the 9th inning. Tommy John and Jerry Crider had combined to pitch the first eight innings, and I sent Wilbur Wood out to pitch the 9th. His knuckleball was really dancing, too, but that can be good AND bad. In this case, it was bad because he walked lead-off man Elliott Maddox. Cesar Gutierez replaced Maddox at first after forcing Elliott on a failed sacrifice, but then Gutierez stole second. I took my chances by having Wood continue to pitch to Detroit's right-handed hitting relief pitcher Tom Timmerman despite the fact that first base was open. Timmerman was about as weak-hitting a pitcher as you'd ever see, though, so it wasn't really much of a gamble. He'd finish the season 0-for-16 at the plate, and our strategy paid off for the moment as Wood struck out Timmerman. That brought up Detroit's dangerous right-handed swinging outfielder Mickey Stanley, so I had Wood walk him to get to the left-handed Dick McAuliffe. It all looked good on paper, but McAuliffe wrecked it for us with a single to right to push across the go-ahead run. We loaded the bags in the bottom of the 9th, but the runners were left stranded when Ed Herrmann hit a come-backer to end the game.

Denny McLain started the game for the Tigers. He pitched seven good innings before yielding to the bullpen, but before exiting the game he provided an intriguing moment. Herrmann singled to right with one out in the 6th. When the ball was returned to McLain, he began to fiddle with it, turning it over and over in his hand while sizing up its feel. He then called time and threw it out of the game. McLain then motioned to home plate umpire Jerry Neudecker to give him a new ball, which Neudecker did. But McLain didn't like the feel of that one either, so he asked Neudecker for another. And another. And another. Eventually, Neudecker sarcastically held out a whole handful of balls. McLain strolled over to the ump and very thoughtfully fondled the baseballs one at a time like a housewife squeezing the produce at the grocery store. He picked one. It must have been a good one, too, because he went back to the mound and proceeded to strike out Ken Berry with it. Reporters asked McLain about the incident after the game. "The balls felt cold, and some of them weren't rubbed up real well," McLain said. "You know, I've handled a lot of baseballs, and this is the one place I keep throwing them back."

While Denny McLain was one of the league's premier pitchers at that time, he was also somewhat flaky. Still, he may have been on to something in questioning the "feel" of the balls we provided for the game. In 1965 groundskeeper Gene Bossard had come up with a scheme to help our big three — Joe Horlen, Gary Peters, and Tommy John. They were suffering from a serious lack of offensive support, so Bossard implemented a covert operation of "freezing" the game balls. He wasn't actually freezing them, though. What he was really doing was soaking them. Down in the bowels of the stadium there was an old room where Bossard would run a humidifier for 24 hours a day, seven days a week. Bossard would leave the game balls in that room for 10 to 14 days and then bring out a batch prior to each home game. Gene claimed that they became a quarter to a half-ounce heavier, thereby restricting the flight of the ball by the opposing teams' power hitters. Later that season Harmon Killebrew walloped what should have been a sure home run, so he stood there admiring the flight of the ball. A split second later his admiration turned to panic as he saw the ball hit the wall — and Killebrew had to hustle just to get a single. In his next at-bat he told our catcher, J.C. Martin, "J.C., there's something wrong with those balls." Rumors eventually began to circulate about the White Sox's "frozen" baseballs, but no one was ever able to prove any wrong-doing. I was reminded of the whole thing a couple of years ago when the Colorado Rockies were accused of storing their game balls in a humidor. It was a little more sophisticated than Bossard's dungeon room with a rickety old humidifier, but it was the same idea. Bill Veeck used to believe that a "good" grounds crew was worth 10 to 12 wins a year. I'm not so sure the number would be that high — maybe a couple or three — but that could be the difference in a tight pennant race. Gene passed away back in 1998 at age 80 after 40 years with the White Sox. Whether you believe Veeck's numbers or mine, either way Bossard may have factored into a hell of a lot of Chicago White Sox victories.

JULY 31, 1970: It was stifling hot at Comiskey Park on this day. July had been a tough month for us, but we ended it with a good week, winning three of our last five games of the month culminating with our 5-4 win over the Cleveland Indians. Tommy John had braved the heat for 7-2/3 innings before he wilted and had to be relieved with the score tied, 3-3. Things looked bleak when Roy Foster opened the top of the 9th with a homer off Danny Murphy, but our guys rallied for two runs in the bottom half of the inning. Duane Josephson blooped a pinch-single to right to lead off the inning. Josephson was pretty slow, so I sent Tom McCraw in to pinch-run for him. McCraw was no longer the speed merchant he'd once been, either. He was almost 30 years old and had been suffering knee problems, but one of our true weaknesses in 1970 was a lack of overall team speed. Syd O'Brien then punched a hit through the middle, moving McCraw to second. Cleveland manager Al Dark sent right-hander Fred Lasher into the game to relieve Dick Ellsworth, but all hands were safe when Luis Aparicio, trying to bunt McCraw over to third base, sent a roller on the Comiskey Park artificial turf into no-man's land past the mound. At this point I sent up Gail Hopkins to pinch hit for Walt Williams, and Hopkins bounced a lucky infield hit past Lasher — a classic artificial turf single. McCraw scored the tying run on the play and O'Brien moved up to third base. Dark was desperate by this point, so he sent right-hander Phil Hennigan in to pitch to Bill Melton, but Melton lifted a sac fly to center, easily scoring O'Brien with the winning run. It was a great way to end the month.

Incidentally, I mentioned our lack of team speed in 1970. We were a far cry from the Go-Go Sox days when groundskeeper Gene Bossard would pack the lead-off area at first base so our base stealers could get a good jump. In fact, we were now having Bossard wet down the basepaths in order to slow opposition clubs down to our pace. Al Dark was a smart guy and he knew all about Bossard's reputation as a field customizer. He walked the grounds prior to the game, and his discovery prompted this blurb in the *Chicago Tribune* — "Alvin Dark, who manages Cleveland, did not appreciate the swamp-like condition of the base lines and asked to have them dried with sand before the game." Bossard complied, but I'm not so sure it really helped matters. Neither a swamp or a sand pit is very conducive to running.

AUGUST 6, 1970: *SOX BEAT BREWERS, VACATE CELLAR,* declared a *Chicago Tribune* headline following our victory at Comiskey Park on this day. When you're having the kind of season we had in 1970, you take baby steps on your road to improvement. And getting out of the basement of the American League West division was very important to us. We'd fallen into last place exactly four weeks earlier and it had been a struggle to climb out. But our 7-3 win over the Brewers was our third straight victory, and the win had "youth" written all over it. 24-year old Jerry Janeski got the win, breaking a personal 7-game losing streak. 25-year old Bill Melton hit his 20th home run of the season and was looking like a serious threat to topple the White Sox single-season homer mark of 29. 26-year old Syd O'Brien had a big triple and scored a key run. 22-year old Carlos May delivered an important RBI-single in the 5th inning that triggered our big 5-run rally. Seeing our youngsters starting to mature, I was feeling optimistic about the future of the White Sox despite our terrible 41-and-71 record.

AUGUST 12, 1970: It's not often that your 20-year old rookie pitcher goes 7-1/3 innings, allows just one run, gets three hits, beats the New York Yankees — and still gets chewed out by his manager. But that's what happened on this day as we beat New York at Yankee Stadium, 5-1, behind Bart Johnson. The *Chicago Tribune* headline summed it up this way — *JOHNSON BEATS YANKEES; 'LOSES TO GUTTERIDGE.'* That was a little harsh, but it is true that I addressed a couple of issues that arose during Johnson's big game — namely conditioning and fundamentals. These items weren't a matter of life or death, but they were important "little things" that players sometimes overlook. Johnson gave up his only run of the day in the bottom of the 6th inning when he surrendered a home run to Roy White that tied the game. I asked Bart if he was tired when he came in after the inning, and he assured me he was okay. Then he grabbed a bat and headed up to the plate to lead off the 7th inning. Johnson was already having a career day with the bat having singled to right in both of his previous plate appearances. Then he added another single by legging out an infield hit to second base. He culminated his mad dash to first with a head-first slide into the bag. From there we went on to score three runs in the inning, giving Johnson a 4-1 lead to work with as he headed out to the mound for the bottom half of the 7th.

But Johnson never headed out to the mound for the 7th. Instead, third base coach Bill Adair came up to me and said that Johnson had confided to him the he "was bushed" after running the bases in the top half of the inning. I sent Wilbur Wood in to finish the game, but I let Johnson know a few things about conditioning and fundamentals. I told him that I was happy about the great day he'd had on the hill and at bat, but I also told him that it was inexcusable that he was still having trouble with getting tired at this stage of the season. "If you were 35, that'd be different," I told him, adding, "plus, you'll run for 30 minutes tomorrow out here, and the next day you'll do the same thing in Washington. You're not in good enough shape to suit me." Then I turned my attention to one of the game's basic fundamentals, and I let the whole team hear. "I don't want anyone sliding into first base," I barked, "or taking that long last jump to get there. You make it there faster by just running normally through the bag — that's why the rules were set up to let you overrun first base. Sliding or lunging at first base only slows you down, not to mention that it can cause injuries." It may have seemed unfair to pick on Johnson that day — a great day for him at Yankee Stadium — but if a manager only chooses to make his points after a loss, sometimes those points don't make a lasting impression.

AUGUST 19, 1970: We hit the skids after Bart Johnson's big win at Yankee Stadium, losing our next six games in a row. We finally snapped the losing streak with a 13-5 win over the Red Sox on this day at Fenway Park. I couldn't have prescribed a better way to break out of the slump, either, than the way we did it — with an 11-run 9th-inning game-winning rally. We were trailing, 5-2, as we came up to hit in the top of the 9th. Bill Melton led off the inning with a single, and the party was on. We batted 16 men in the inning and racked up 11 runs on 10 hits. Our 11-run outburst tied a modern major league record for the most runs ever scored in a 9th inning, a record previously held solely by the 1951 Yankees. In a testament to our lack of power, there were no homers in our 11-run 9th. In fact, the only extra-base hit was a pinch-double by Luis Aparicio who didn't start the game due to a recurring stiff neck that had been plaguing him. When it was all said and done, however, it was just ONE win. "It gave us a little life," I told reporters who were wondering in what way I thought our comeback victory might help us break free of our losing ways. Still, I knew that the front office was getting very restless with our on-field results, so I ended my session with the reporters by saying, "Too bad it didn't happen earlier in the trip."

AUGUST 29, 1970: Our big comeback win in Boston did, in fact, somewhat turn around our fortunes, and we won six of our next nine including our 13-9 victory over the Red Sox on this day. Richard Dozer of the *Chicago Tribune* wrote, "Every 10 days or so — providing the Red Sox are the foe — the Chicago White Sox seem to score 13 runs. They did it again today, albeit with less 9th-inning sensationalism, and came from behind with an 8-run 6th to whip the Red Sox, 13 to 9, in Comiskey Park." The big blow for us was a grand slam homer by Ed Herrmann, his 17th round-tripper of the season. Bob Miller got the win in relief, although he struggled on the mound. It turns out that this was the last win in my career as White Sox manager. Much of the goodwill generated by this victory was erased the next day when Boston avenged their 13-9 defeat by beating us in both ends of a doubleheader. The opener was particularly embarrassing as we were trounced, 21-11. Very few of the 8,500 fans in attendance were still on hand to see the last out of the game. We were terrible in doubleheaders all season. We were swept in our first seven twin bills before we earned our first split. We managed to split four of our next seven doubleheaders while getting swept in the other three. We never swept an opponent in a twin bill in 1970. "We just always seem to be flat going into a doubleheader," I told the sportswriters. "I don't know if they don't get themselves ready or what, but there's no doubt they were flat. I can't understand it. I can't get them up for two games."

SEPTEMBER 1, 1970: The Athletics beat us, 6-5, in Oakland on this day, and the defeat contained many of the same elements that had dogged us throughout the season — errors and less than effective pitching, to name a few. Tommy John had labored through eight complete innings, walking eight batters, but we were still in the game, trailing by a score of 4-3 as we took our last at-bat in the top of the 9th. We got a little something going and had a man on first with one out and John due up, so I sent Gail Hopkins up to pinch hit for him. Hopkins then made me look like a genius by driving a 2-run homer into the Oakland Coliseum seats to give us a 5-4 lead. That was still the score as we took the field in the bottom of the 9th with Wilbur Wood assigned the job of holding the lead. He walked the lead-off man — a bad start. Then singles by Gene Tenace and Sal Bando tied the score. Don Mincher moved them up to second and third base with a sac bunt. I had Wood intentionally walk Reggie Jackson to load the bases so we could pitch to Tony LaRussa who was batting below the .200-mark. Then LaRussa hit a dribbler just out of reach of our third baseman Rich Morales. Tenace scored the winning run, and I went from genius to bum in a matter of minutes. That was the last baseball game I ever managed.

SEPTEMBER 2, 1970: *DON GUTTERIDGE RELEASED BY SOX.* That was the big headline in the *Chicago Tribune* sports section that on this day announced the end of my run as manager of the Chicago White Sox. At the very minute Tony LaRussa was beating us in Oakland with his dribbler the day before, things were getting shook up in the front office back in Chicago. Ed Short, currently serving as personnel director following his demotion from general manager midway through the 1969 season, was flat out fired. He'd been with the club for 20 years. Leo Breen, promoted from within as Short's successor in 1969, was now demoted to business manager and treasurer. Taking over general manager and executive vice president duties was Stu Holcomb, formerly the club's director of public relations. It was a real mess. When I heard the news of the shake-up later that evening, I had a feeling that my days as manager were numbered. Still, I was shocked at how fast my premonition came true. It was early afternoon and I was preparing to leave the hotel to go to the nearby Oakland Coliseum to get ready for our game that evening. I got a phone call from Holcomb. He'd told me that he'd flown into Oakland that morning and he wanted to meet with me at our team headquarters there in the hotel. I hung up the phone and headed down to see him. I was pretty sure that he wasn't calling me in to give me his vote of confidence, but I still held out hope.

The meeting took only a few minutes. Holcomb told me that the White Sox were not going to renew my contract for 1971. He said they had already picked a manager to replace me and a general manager to replace Breen. He said the old regime was completely out as the Sox tried to repair the beaten-down image of the franchise by bringing in new faces. Holcomb said that I could stay on until the end of the season if I wanted to, and he also mentioned that the club would like to keep me on in some capacity — possibly as a super scout. In spite of the fact that I saw it coming and knew it was simply the way things were done, I was mad. I declined Holcomb's offer to stay with the team through the remainder of the season, instead asking to be immediately relieved of my duties as field manager. I also declined to stay on with the team in any capacity. I decided then and there that this was the time to make a clean break with the White Sox. I went up to my room, quickly packed my things, and immediately checked out of the hotel. A short time later I was on a flight back to Chicago where I tied up a few loose ends before returning home to Pittsburg, Kansas. I saw in the paper that Bill Adair, our third base coach, was named to take over for me on an interim basis. I wished the best for him, but I knew it would be no picnic running the ballcub until the new manager arrived. It was a bit of a hollow assignment, but someone had to do it. The team lost its first game after my departure, a 2-1 defeat to the A's, and I couldn't help but feel for them.

The 1970 White Sox finished with a record of 56-and-106, by far the worst record in the major leagues that season. As the manager, I have to accept responsibility for that, and I do. My record is there in the books for all time, so it's undeniable. But the bottom line is that we simply did not have a good ballclub at that time. We had good ballplayers — but they had yet to gel as a good team, mostly because they were all very young. Most of them were inexperienced and brought up a little ahead of time because we didn't have anyone else to play at that point. So it was really tough. If I'd been able to stay there another year or two when all these good young players developed fully, I would have won some. Chuck Tanner arrived in time to manage the last 16 games of the 1970 season. It's a lot to ask of a guy to win immediately, so it shouldn't be surprising that the ballclub continued to struggle under Tanner, just as it had struggled under Adair's 10-game stint, and just as it had struggled under my tenure. The Sox won only three games while losing 13 under Tanner while finishing out the '70 season, but they made an impressive showing in 1971 as they won 79 games. Some credit should be given to Tanner for this turnaround, but the bulk of the Sox's success in 1971 is really a result of the young players finally maturing and then coming together as a team. Without taking anything away from Chuck Tanner, I feel that I helped lay the foundation for the success that the Sox achieved in 1971, as well as subsequent seasons — and I would have loved to have been there to share it with my players.

I reluctantly took the White Sox managerial job, but once in there I must admit that I enjoyed doing it in spite of the fact that it was a little bit tough. Aside from the on-field problems of our youth, there were off-field changes going on that made managing even more difficult at that time. The Viet Nam War, with guys constantly coming and going from National Guard duty, was not only affecting the continuity of your line-up, it was also changing the way your younger players thought. The mood of the whole United States was changing, so it's understandable that it would be reflected in baseball's young players. An off-shoot of that was the drug problem. It had been affecting regular kids for a couple of years, but now it was starting to seriously affect baseball. Other changes that complicated things were front office related. Players were now using agents to represent them in contract negotiations, and that changed the player-management relationship. While it may have been good for player salaries, it was not necessarily good for player-management relations. General managers were coming into full power and trying to run the clubs, thereby taking some decision-making powers away from the managers. As a manager, I didn't particularly like that. Being from the old school, I thought the manager should have the last say. As I walked away from the White Sox, I knew that the old way was gone for good. That's why I decided that this was a good time to hang up my coaching and managing spikes for good — and I never looked back.

2 0 0 7

JANUARY 1, 2007: I, like the rest of the world, welcomed a new year on this day. Unlike the rest of the world, however, most folks were not saying hello to their 94th New Year's Day. I feel blessed that I've been able to live such a long and happy life. Lord willing, I'll turn 95 years old on June 19th of this year, and I hope to be around to see a few more birthdays, too. Seeing the dawning of a new year while working on this book has given me the opportunity to look back on some of the things I did following my exit as White Sox manager back in 1970.

While I had no doubts about my readiness to permanently leave baseball as a coach and manager in 1970, I was definitely not ready to completely walk away from the game. Baseball was in my blood. And, at 58 years of age, I still needed to make a living. I'd learned my lesson back in 1967 when I'd tried to embark on a professional career outside of baseball — it didn't work. I needed to work in the game I loved. Fortunately, I didn't have to fret over it for very long because the New York Yankees called and offered me a job scouting for them. Clyde Kluttz, my old roommate from the Sacramento Solons — the same Clyde Kluttz who crushed my toe — was the farm director and he brought me on board. My area of coverage was Iowa, Nebraska, and parts of Kansas and Missouri. I scouted those areas for the Yankees from 1971 through 1974, and I really I enjoyed it. During those years I would also travel down to Florida and help with their minor leaguers in spring training. They had four or five clubs down there and I coordinated the schedule for them.

My run as a Yankee scout ended as a result of a big shake-up in the scouting system, but I immediately landed a new job scouting for the Los Angeles Dodgers. John Keenan was their scout supervisor, and he told me he needed somebody to help scout Kansas, Missouri, and Oklahoma. So I scouted for the Dodgers from that time until I retired at the end of 1992 season. I enjoyed scouting because I could sort of be my own boss — but it kept me away from home quite a bit and Helen didn't like that at all. As usual, however, she went right along with it because she knew I enjoyed it. It really is hard work to find a player that goes on to a good career in the majors. There are so many players and scouts out there that discovering a winner is like trying to find a needle in a haystack. Despite the fact that I spent the bulk of my scouting career with the Yankees and Dodgers, it was during my brief time scouting for Kansas City in 1967 where I turned up my best find — left-handed pitcher Paul Splittorff. I really liked what I saw in him while he was pitching for Morningside College, a small school in Sioux City, Iowa. He had great control and a fine sinkerball. I recommended Splittorff to the Kansas City front office, and they ended up taking him in the 25th round of the 1968 amateur draft. Splittorff ended up being the first player originally signed by the Royals to make it to the majors when he got his first trial in 1970. He put together a long career, all with the Royals, winning 166 games. That's not too shabby for a 25th round draft pick, and I was proud to have played a small role in his career.

There were all kinds of other fun things going on to keep me engaged and entertained during my years as a scout. Banquets, dinners, reunions, galas — you name it. For example, in August of 1971 the St. Louis Cardinals wanted to celebrate the 25th anniversary of their 1946 World Series title. They put an interesting twist on it, though. Instead of the typical reunion, they put on a re-enactment of the climactic Game Seven, which included staging a replay of Enos Slaughter's Mad Dash. The event took place right after a Cards game at Busch Stadium on August 8th. Lots of fellows who were involved in the '46 Series were there — George "Catfish" Metkovich, Ken Burkhart, Bob Klinger, Joe Dobson, Roy Partee, Joe Garagiola, Johnny Pesky, and Enos Slaughter himself, to name a few. I was there, too. While the re-enactment wasn't exactly a perfect replay of the original, it was a real hoot. Here's how the new version of Slaughter's Mad Dash went down: Dixie Walker, filling in for his brother Harry who was busy managing the Astros, stroked a hit to left rather than left-center as The Hat had originally done. Metkovich continued the deviation from the script, lobbing the ball to Pesky. Johnny, playing to the folks who believed he'd hesitated with the ball back in 1946, really poured it on, nonchalantly taking his time before throwing the ball home. Despite Pesky's exaggerated delay in getting the ball to home, Johnny's throw still reached Partee in ample time to nail Slaughter — but Partee's tag was late. "I couldn't tag Slaughter out because we wanted it to end the way it did in 1946," Partee said. But it didn't end quite the way it originally had. Somehow, inexplicably, WE won the game, 2-1. Pesky embraced Slaughter after the game and said, "That baldheaded son-of-a-gun can still run — did you see that fade-away slide?" I got in on the act, too. I interrupted Burkhart's stint on the mound by complaining to the ump that Ken was throwing a spitter, whereupon Burkhart feigned great anger. The whole thing was filmed for Garagiola's pre-game show, *Joe Garagiola's Baseball World,* and it was shown prior to a Monday night baseball game on NBC. It really was a lot of fun.

Another fun thing for me in that time was working with kids at baseball camps. I really enjoyed coaching youngsters on how to pay the game, and these camps gave me a great opportunity to teach. Bob Brasher's Show Me Baseball Camp was one of the outfits I worked most frequently with. It was a well run operation out of Branson, Missouri, with summer sessions right there in Missouri and winter sessions down in Sarasota, Florida. Plus I got to work with other ex-big leaguers like Chuck Stobbs, Wally Moon, Jerry Lumpe, and Steve Boros, to name a few.

One event that stands out in my mind as a great moment was when I traveled up to Cooperstown, New York, for Al Lopez's Hall of Fame induction in 1977. Al went in as a manager and was elected by the Veteran's Committee. Ray Berres was there, too, and we couldn't help but feel great pride in having been with Al for the bulk of his managerial career. There was some great Hall alumni there, too, guys like Roy Campanella, Red Ruffing, Rube Marquard, Cal Hubbard, Charley Gehringer, Bill Terry, Joe Cronin, Bob Feller, Luke Appling, Burleigh Grimes, Lloyd Waner, Stan Coveleski, Stan Musial, Buck Leonard, Monte Irvin, George Kelly, Cool Papa Bell, Whitey Ford, Earl Averill, Billy Herman, Judy Johnson, Freddy Lindstrom, Robin Roberts, and Jocko Conlan. It was quite an assemblage, and Al was obviously feeling awed to be included in such great company — but he deserved it. He looked wonderful, the picture of health after enjoying nearly seven years of stress-free retirement down in Tampa. Al did a great job in his speech, thanking everybody from the sportswriters to his family. Then he choked up a bit when he looked down at me and Ray and acknowledged our presence. "They didn't work for me," Al said, "We worked together, and they should be sharing this honor with me." Needless to say, Ray and I choked up a bit at that comment, too.

With my retirement from baseball in 1992 came a life of relaxation that I'd never known before. I played a lot of golf — but I didn't say how well I played. You noticed that, didn't you? Well, I didn't play very good, but I had fun playing. I played with a lot of my friends, and it was a great way to pass the time away.

While I've always loved golf, I didn't get to play as much as I would have liked while I was an active ballplayer. One of the benefits of my retirement, however, was that I got to play a lot of golf. In this picture, Whiz Kid hero Dick Sisler and I posed for the photographers in a golf course promotion we did together down in Florida.

My retirement also saw the continuing procession of reunions with my old Cardinals, Browns, Red Sox, and White Sox teams. It was always fun to attend those events and see all my old friends, as well as meet many of the fans. Of course, they're getting a little older just like the players whose exploits they used to follow. Many of the fans that I didn't get a chance to meet in person, however, now write to me. In fact, I get a lot of mail these day — more than I ever got when I was playing. I probably receive five or six letters a week. Most of it is requests for autographs or questions about the games that I played in. Many of them are young sports fans, but they want to know about the baseball that was being played back in 1930's, 40's, 50's, and 60's. I played, coached, or managed in five decades — the 1930's through the 1970's — so I guess they figure I ought to know something. It's funny, but I seem to get more accolades for one thing or another the longer I'm removed from my playing days. After my retirement I was voted into the Missouri Sports Hall of Fame and it was really a great honor. They said my ten years in St. Louis with the Browns and Cardinals warranted my admission into their Hall of Fame. Then my hometown of Pittsburg, Kansas, built a wonderful sports complex and named it after me — The Don Gutteridge Sports Complex. It's twelve or thirteen ball diamonds that they play softball and Little League baseball on. That's a legacy that really makes me proud.

Helen and I posed in front of the sign for the "Don Gutteridge Sports Complex" when it opened in my hometown of Pittsburg, Kansas. I was very honored that they named the facility for me, and it makes me very happy to know that kids will be playing ball there for years to come.

Life as a big league ballplayer was quite a bit different than anything I ever imagined as a kid growing up in Pittsburg. Pittsburg is a small town in southeastern Kansas, just a few miles across the Missouri-Kansas state line. Most of the people there worked in the mining industry or with Kansas City Southern (K.C.S.) Railroad. There was, of course, lots of farmers, too. I was born on the outskirts of Pittsburg on June 19, 1912. Our family was a typical working class family and we lived on about four or five acres of land. My father, Joseph Gutteridge, was a general car foreman for K.C.S. where he worked for fifty-some-odd years. He later became the mayor of Pittsburg. My mother, Mary Archer, was from Walker, Missouri, near Nevada. She, along with three sisters, came to Pittsburg to find work. All four of them found work — and husbands! They all married local Pittsburg fellows. In addition to me, my mom and dad had four other children — brothers Alfred, Earl, and Merle, and an older sister, Hazel.

I always wanted to play baseball from the time I was a little boy. As a matter of fact, I can't remember when I didn't want to play baseball. I would have my brothers play catch with me every chance I got. They weren't very athletically inclined, though, and they had other things to do — but I still got them to play ball with me whenever the opportunity arose. Sometimes I even had to bribe them to play! I'd throw a baseball, basketball, or football with them — any kind of ball I could get my hands on. When I was about eight years old we moved to 15th and Grand in town to be closer to school and work. I wasn't crazy about the change because I liked running wherever I wanted to run, whenever I wanted to run. It was kind of confined in town with so many houses around. But, as with a lot of negative things, there ends up being a positive side that you hadn't anticipated. That's where my wife Helen enters the picture. Her family lived literally right around the corner from our new home. If my family hadn't moved into town I might never have met her. Helen is the same age as me and she had a younger brother just like I did. We all played together and we just considered Helen one of the boys. Occasionally she wouldn't agree with us on something, but we always had a great time together — and still do.

Helen's dad had an auto repair garage nearby and there was an old fire station right there, too. We enjoyed playing baseball in the street because at that time there wasn't very much traffic to dodge. We played with something we used to call an "armory ball." They used the same type of ball in the local armory, so the term eventually worked its way into the local vernacular. Anyway, there was a fireman that used to come out and pitch to us. We'd put an old can down in the middle of street for home, and then we'd run to a tree on the right side of the street for first base. An old manhole cover in the middle of 15th Street served as second base, and another tree on the left side of the street was third base. You batted until you made an out and then you went to the outfield. You'd work your way around the positions as others made outs until you were back up to bat again. It was really fun and, believe it or not, that was where I started to develop the skills and the burning desire that would one day land me in the major leagues. We played there until we outgrew our little 15th Street diamond, and then it was on to bigger — but not necessarily better — fields of play. I've played everywhere from Yankee Stadium to Fenway Park, but there will always be something extra special to me about that makeshift diamond on 15th Street because that's where it all began for me. I still drive by that intersection from time to time. Amazingly, it still looks about the same as it did all those years ago. Helen's and my childhood homes are still there, as is the old firehouse. The old manhole, too! It really takes me back when I see those old icons of my youth.

My dream of playing big league ball was sealed into fate one summer day when I was about 12 years old. There used to be an evangelist that would come through town to spread the gospel to anybody who would listen. He'd pitch a tent, set up chairs, and then proceed to have a big revival meeting every night. Afterwards, he passed a hat around the crowd for contributions, and that's how he survived. Well, I had a notion that maybe he could help me, so I decided to go down there and see him. I told him all about my dream of playing in the major leagues. He told me that my dream was all well and good, but if I wanted to truly succeed in baseball I had to have God in my corner. The evangelist said I needed to talk to the Lord and He would help me. I liked the sound of that, so I decided to do it. I went down in front after the revival and said, "Lord, I really want to play baseball more than anything else. If You let me play in the major leagues — and play my whole life — I will do anything I can to help You and never embarrass You. You can use me any way you want to, Lord — just as long as I can play baseball." Well, He sure did fulfill His promise to me as over a half century in baseball proves! In return, I tried my best to be a good Christian, never drinking or smoking, and I always tried to be good to everybody.

As I reached my mid-teens I got interested in playing for the K.C.S. baseball team, or the Shop Team as they were called. My dad used his pull at K.C.S. to get them to bring me on as the team mascot — or batboy as they've come to be known these days. I did whatever they needed done, but most of what I did was lug the equipment around for them. I did get to shag balls while they took their batting practice, however, so I was developing my skills all along. I'd put all the bats, balls, and other equipment in a wagon and pull it all the way home. Then I'd pull it all the way back for the next practice. They didn't want to fool with all the equipment, so I took care of it for them because I'd have done anything to be out there with them. The Shop Team played in Pittsburg's Old City League. There were four teams made up of guys that worked at the railroad. They'd start the games after 5:00 P.M. when everybody got there from work. Eventually I graduated from scorekeeper/go-fer to player. My big break came when the fellow that played second base decided to step down because he felt he was getting a little old to play effectively anymore. I took over the position for them and I was just a junior in high school!

The K.C.S. team provided me with a place to develop my baseball skills, and it was my play with them that led me to be "discovered" and sent on to the minor

My hometown of Pittsburg in Kansas helped lay the foundation I would need to make it the big leagues. I was all-state in basketball for Pittsburg High School, but our school didn't have a baseball team, so I learned the game playing for the Kansas City Southern Shop Team in Pittsburg's Old City League. That's me on the left in the front row of the team photo below. Incidentally, that's my cousin Ray Mueller second from the left in the middle row. Ray also made it all the way to the major leagues.

leagues. I've focused on my major league career in this book, but that was not intended to be a slight to my minor league experience. The minors were very different than the majors for me, but it was still a wonderful time. I was attending Kansas State Teachers College in Pittsburg when I got word that I was being sent to Lincoln of the Nebraska State League. The college is still here, but it is now called Pittsburg State University — home of the Gorillas! It's a great school and it provides a lot of business for our town. But when given the choice of college or baseball — there was no question that I was going to choose BALL. Helen, who I'd eventually come to see as more than "just one of the boys," was now my sweetheart. She gave me her blessing and took me down to the train station where I headed off to Lincoln. It was really the first time I was out on my own.

I didn't know anything about Lincoln, so I had to ask someone at the train station where the ballpark was. They directed me across the tracks, so I walked on over. Sure enough, the ballclub was there practicing. Someone there asked who the hell I was, so I told them that scout Joe Becker had sent me. I guess those were the magic words because they tossed me a uniform and told me to get out there. So I had jumped on a train at about noon and by seven o'clock that night I was a professional ballplayer! It was Class D ball and the league wasn't affiliated with any major league teams, but it was professional baseball and I was proud to be there. I finished the 1932 season there and went back in '33. The Nebraska State League was unique in that they paid everybody the same wage regardless of whether you were a pitcher, catcher, or utility man — everybody got $75 a month in 1932. The Depression was very bad at that time and we had to take a pay cut down to $50 in 1933. I played 4-1/2 months, so I made maybe about $225 for the season — peanuts by today's standards! Of course, you could buy a loaf of bread for a nickel in 1933, but even then $255 wasn't exactly big money. It was really alright, though. The money simply wasn't the important thing to me. Sure, I needed to make money to survive, but just as long as I had a place to lay down I was happy because I was playing baseball.

Let me tell you, the traveling conditions in that league left a lot to be desired. The league, like everybody during the Great Depression, didn't have much money so we traveled in an old dilapidated bus. I use the term "bus" loosely because it actually wasn't a bus at all — it was a flat-bed Ford truck with seats across the back and a little false top on it. When it rained you got soaking wet. We'd play during the day and then travel to the next stop at night so they wouldn't have to pay for another night of hotel rooms. Everybody just slept on the bus. No bus driver, either — that would have cost a few more dollars. The players just took turns driving. Eventually I wised up a bit. On a day that I knew we were going to travel, I'd get dressed real quick and run out and sit down in the driver's seat so I'd get to drive. That way I was in front and out of the elements that hammered at the back of the truck. Nobody would dispute you driving until you had a close call on the road. If you almost had an accident or something like that, however, they would make you stop the motor and get out of the driver's seat —

then the next guy would get in there and drive.

I got to drive most of the time because I didn't have many close calls. We would get to the next town on the following morning and check into our hotel. The hotels we stayed in back then weren't exactly 5-star hotels, either. The rooms had wooden cots in them so five or six guys could sleep in one room. Usually two guys got in a bed and the other three or four had to sleep on the cots. The team gave us only a $1-a-day meal allowance, so we definitely learned to get by on very little. We all wanted to play ball so much that we were willing to suffer the hardships that went along with life in the minor leagues during the Depression. It was really fun, though, believe it or not, and it really was a great experience.

After my year-and-a-half in the Nebraska State League I was moved up to Houston of the Texas League for the 1934 season. There was one key difference in my personal status, however — I was no longer single. I caught Helen in a weak moment and she married me on the 16th of October, 1933. It was the beginning of a long and wonderful marriage, and we celebrated our 73rd

Helen and I on our wedding day — October 16th, 1933 — and we're still very happily married.

anniversary in 2006. Helen didn't go to Houston right away with me because we didn't have enough money for the both of us to go. She came down on the train by herself a little later on. That was our first summer together and it was the first time Helen had ever left home. We had a little apartment that started our years together. She was always very helpful to me. Whatever I wanted to do with baseball, she would help me. She'd started enjoying baseball back in the days when we played in the street, and it just grew from there. Helen's father and mother would take her and me to the semi-pro ball games that were played in Pittsburg on Sundays and we all really enjoyed watching those games.

Travel down in the Texas League was a lot better than it had been up in the Nebraska State League. We traveled mostly by train in the Texas League — and that was before they had air conditioning. The Texas League is legendary for the heat down there, and it was really hot riding on those trains. They used to have little fans about a foot square to keep the air moving, but most of the time they didn't work. Some people opened up the windows a little bit, but then all the cinders and dust from the coal-burning engine would blow in. You got filthy and the sheets had little cinders all over them. Traveling by train was as good as it got back then, but it was still was nothing like the comfort we know today when traveling by air.

I ended up having a pretty good season at Houston — but it was lucky. I say that because I had a little accident that could have been very serious. Three-quarters of the way through the season I was hitting well above .300, playing well in the field, and stealing bases. I was contributing very much to the ball club. Then I came home one day and discovered that the gas tank in our little apartment had gone out. I went to light it and it blew back in my face — singed all my hair and my eyelids. From that point on my hitting started to go down. Maybe I was just hitting a slump that coincidentally started the day after my gas tank accident, but I think it really did hurt my eyes. It could have been worse, though. Houston played clubs in Dallas, Oklahoma City, Fort Worth, Beaumont, Galveston — all over the state. All the ballparks in those cities had a resident big loudmouth that was a fixture in the stands. Some leather-lunged fan that's there hollering every day. It's a tradition, really. Well, there was a big old loudmouth guy sitting behind first base at a game in Oklahoma City when I uncorked a throw over the first baseman's head hitting someone sitting in the stands near him. I had a tendency to be wild with my throws from time to time back then. The next time the ball was hit to me the old loudmouth yelled, "Duck, he's got it again!" just as I was releasing the ball. The whole ballpark could hear him and everybody laughed — at my expense. I wish I'd have hit him, but no such luck. It really made me mad, I tell you. He'd be there every game torturing not only me, but every visiting player. I think that was his therapy or something, but it was also good for me because I had to learn to block out things like that so I could stay on top of my game. So thanks, loudmouth, wherever you are.

Every city had their own interesting group of unique individuals in the stands, but each city also had its own unique characteristics in regards to the surrounding landscape. Beaumont sticks out especially in my mind. It was kind of surrounded by lakes, and when we played there the wind would sometimes blow in from those lakes carrying in hordes mosquitoes. It seemed that those mosquitoes, if you didn't watch it, could pick you up and carry you away. They were sure big enough — an inch long — and they had the biggest teeth you'd ever seen. We often played at night and that made it even worse because the lights attracted them. They really would tear you up. We used to roll up newspapers and wear them underneath our socks so the mosquitoes couldn't bite us on the legs. The concession guys used Flit Guns to fight them off, and they would go through the stands selling three Flit Guns for a quarter.

My experience at Houston was made very enjoyable by our manager, Carey Selph. He was an infielder who had been up briefly with the Cardinals in 1929, then returning to the majors in 1932 to play in 116 games for the White Sox. He'd also been a star football and baseball player at Ouachita Baptist University in Arkansas. He really did a lot for me. He talked to me and guided me — he was a good minor league manager. Youngsters need guidance at that age, and Carey was perfect at that. I admired him because he was the manager — the authority figure — and whatever the manager said, as far as I was concerned, was what I was supposed to do. So with Carey's valuable guidance I was able to put together a nice year. Guiding youngsters was his true calling. In 1949 Carey opened up Ozark Boys Camp. It was a great facility that included camp buildings, cabins, a dining hall, a bathhouse, a gymnasium, an infirmary, and a small office. It was the perfect vehicle for Carey to continue to guide youngsters.

My 1935 and '36 seasons at Columbus of the American Association put the finishing touches on preparing me for entry into the big leagues with the Cardinals at the end of the 1936 campaign. This was Triple-A ball, the highest rung of the ladder until the majors, so everything was better — the travel, the hotels, and the competition. Helen and I had a little apartment there, and it was a wonderful city to live in. Columbus was a good team and a good group of guys. Ray Blades was our manager in 1935, and Burt Shotton took over for him in 1936 when Ray moved on to Rochester. Burt had been a good outfielder during his playing days in the teens and twenties. Now he was a good manager — a wonderful man and a good teacher of the game. Burt was the perfect fit for me at that time, and thanks to his help I was completely ready for the majors when I got called up at the end of '36. I have often looked back with fond memories of my big league career since my retirement in 1992, but none of those memories would have been possible without the solid foundation that was laid by my experience in the minors.

The number one benefit of my retirement has been, without question, being able to spend time with my family. While I was playing I didn't get to spend enough time with Helen and our only child, Don Jr. That's one of the drawbacks of being a professional ballplayer. You're always on the go, and the family usually stays home. My retirement allowed me to make up as much as possible for some of that lost family time. Sometimes it's hard for me to believe, but Don Jr. is now 64 years old. He was born on September 25th, 1942, and he was a great kid. Don, like me and Helen, attended Pittsburg High School — home of the Purple Dragons! He then attended the University of Kansas on a baseball scholarship, but upon his graduation he decided that he'd had his fill of baseball, so he stayed at Kansas and got his masters degree in law. He's been a practicing attorney in Oklahoma City for many years. Don Jr. married Sonja, a wonderful girl, in 1965, and they soon started a family of their own. They had three sons — Lance, Sean, and Joshua. They're all grown up now, too, with wives and children of their own. Lance and his wife Amy have three sons — Christian, Joseph (Don III), and Carder. Sean and his wife Rene have a son and a daughter — John Caleb and Cate. Joshua and his wife Cheri have four girls — Abigail, Ashley, Allison, and Audrey Ann. I enjoy each and every one of them. I've got pictures of all of them in my billfold, of course. I tell you, my billfold is fat — not with money, but with pictures! Rounding out my family is my brother Merle, the only brother I have left. He and his wife Maxine live just a few blocks from us. We see each other quite regularly in our retirement.

Baseball has allowed me to live an incredible life. It was a wonderful career, and I can honestly say that I loved every minute of it — EVERY minute. I didn't like losing ballgames, of course — I always wanted to win. But I loved playing baseball regardless of the outcome of the game. I enjoyed the camaraderie that I had with my teammates. I enjoyed the fine people that I met who were, and still are, some of my best friends. Baseball gave me a world of opportunities that most people, unfortunately, will never know. I am truly grateful for those opportunities. I owe a debt of gratitude to everyone who ever had anything to do with my baseball career, and while most of them have long since passed away, I still want to say thanks. And there's one more person I'd like to thank — YOU. Thank you for having an interest in my baseball career. I wrote this book to ensure that the wonderful characters that I played with and against, as well as the great on-field moments that I was involved in, would be around long after I am gone. It makes me happy to know that my experiences are now a part of you. By having read this book you will forever carry a part of me with you, and that makes me feel as good as I ever felt after getting a base it, making a great catch, or simply putting on a big league uniform.

MAJOR LEAGUE BATTING RECORD

	G	AB	H	2B	3B	HR	HR %	R	RBI	BB	SO	SB	BA	SA	Pinch Hit AB	Pinch Hit H	G by POS
1936 **STL N**	23	91	29	3	4	3	3.3	13	16	1	14	3	.319	.538	0	0	3B-23
1937	119	447	121	26	10	7	1.6	66	61	25	66	12	.271	.421	8	1	3B-105, SS-8
1938	142	552	141	21	15	9	1.6	61	64	29	49	14	.255	.397	2	0	3B-73, SS-68
1939	148	524	141	27	4	7	1.3	71	54	27	70	5	.269	.376	2	0	3B-143, SS-2
1940	69	108	29	5	0	3	2.8	19	14	5	15	3	.269	.398	20	2	3B-39
1942 **STL A**	147	616	157	27	11	1	0.2	90	50	59	54	16	.255	.339	1	1	2B-145, 3B-2
1943	132	538	147	35	6	1	0.2	77	36	50	46	10	.273	.366	1	0	2B-132
1944	148	603	148	27	11	3	0.5	89	36	51	63	20	.245	.342	1	0	2B-146
1945	143	543	129	24	3	2	0.4	72	49	43	46	9	.238	.304	1	0	2B-128, OF-14
1946 **BOS A**	22	47	11	3	0	1	2.1	8	6	2	7	0	.234	.362	1	0	2B-9, 3B-8
1947	54	131	22	2	0	2	1.5	20	5	17	13	3	.168	.229	5	1	2B-20, 3B-19
1948 **PIT N**	4	2	0	0	0	0	0.0	0	0	0	1	0	.000	.000	2	0	
12 yrs.	1151	4202	1075	200	64	39	0.9	586	391	309	444	95	.256	.362	44	5	2B-580, 3B-412, SS-78, OF-14
WORLD SERIES																	
1944 **STL A**	6	21	3	1	0	0	0.0	1	0	3	5	0	.143	.190	0	0	2B-6
1946 **BOS A**	3	5	2	0	0	0	0.0	1	1	0	0	0	.400	.400	0	0	2B-2
2 yrs.	9	26	5	1	0	0	0.0	2	1	3	5	0	.192	.231	0	0	2B-8

MAJOR LEAGUE MANAGERIAL RECORD

	G	W	L	PCT	Standing	
1969 **CHI A**	145	60	85	.414	4	5
1970	136	49	87	.360	6	6
2 yrs.	281	109	172	.388		

The left number indicates the position in the standings when Gutteridge took over as manager; the right number is the position in the standings at the end of the season with Gutteridge still managing.

The left number indicates the position in the standings when Gutteridge was fired as manager during the season; the right number indicates the position in the standings at the end of the season without Gutteridge as manager.

INDEX

Bold page numbers indicate person in photograph.

Index compiled by Sumner Hunnewell.